D0278678

The principalship:
FOUNDATIONS AND FUNCTIONS

JAMES M. LIPHAM
Professor of Educational Administration
University of Wisconsin–Madison

JAMES A. HOEH, JR.
Principal
Grosse Pointe South High School
Grosse Pointe, Michigan

HARPER & ROW, PUBLISHERS
New York, Evanston, San Francisco, London

To Charlotte, Beth, and Bill,
and
Faye, Ryan, and Angie

Sponsoring Editor: Michael E. Brown
Project Editor: Elizabeth Dilernia
Designer: Jared Pratt
Production Supervisor: Stefania J. Taflinska

The principalship: foundations and functions

Copyright © 1974 by James M. Lipham and James A. Hoeh, Jr.

All rights reserved. Printed in the United States of America. No part of this book may be used or reproduced in any manner whatsoever without written permission except in the case of brief quotations embodied in critical articles and reviews. For information address Harper & Row, Publishers, Inc., 10 East 53rd Street, New York, N.Y. 10022.

Library of Congress Cataloging in Publication Data
Lipham, James M.
    The principalship: foundations and functions.
    Includes bibliographies.
    1. School superintendents and principals. 2. School management and organization. I. Hoeh, James A., joint author. II. Title.
LB2831.9.L56   371.2'012   73–20865
ISBN 0–06–044032–5

Contents

List of figures

Preface

The motivation for writing this book grew out of the basic conviction that the principalship now represents—and will increasingly represent in the future—a potentially powerful position for effecting change in the schools. Hopefully, this reference will contribute toward improving the technical, human, and conceptual competencies of the school principal.

Although schools differ by size, level, location, and a host of other variables, we believe that the principalship holds much that is in common with other administrative roles—particularly insofar as the basic theoretical and conceptual foundations are concerned. The principalship also requires a unique set of competencies—particularly insofar as the basic functions or tasks of the principalship position are concerned. Therefore we have attempted to utilize administrative theory as a basis for developing a competency-based approach to the principal's role. This approach should provide prospective and practicing principals with specific processes, procedures, and products whereby effectiveness and efficiency in role performance may be evaluated and enhanced.

We are indebted to many of our colleagues for assistance in the various stages of preparing this book. First, we wish to acknowledge the contributions of Emmett James Duffy and John M. Sheehy, who initially suggested from the perspective of scholar-practitioners the broad domains of content that should be included. For their critical review of early drafts and for assistance with preparing and polishing the manuscript, we are indebted to the following colleagues who studied with us at the University of Wisconsin: Nancy J. Arold, Buel N. Bowlan, David M. Flannery, Charles G. Goodridge, Albert M. Holmquist, Louis Paul Lansing, John J. Lane, Daniel K. McGuire, Douglas A. Paul, Terrance J. Sheridan, Kenneth W. Wright, and Dennis C. Zuelke. To our colleagues in the Department of Educational Administration at the University of Wisconsin, especially Professors Russell T. Gregg, Donald N. McIsaac, Richard A. Rossmiller, and Dennis W. Spuck, we are also indebted for specific content and editorial suggestions concerning certain of the chapters. Finally, to students in our courses and seminars in the principalship and in organizational theory and behavior, we are appreciative of their critical reactions and helpful insights.

This book draws extensively upon the creative contributions of scholars, researchers, and practitioners from many fields. We acknowledge with gratitude the permissions granted and helpful assistance from the following individuals and organizations: Max G. Abbott; the *Administrator's Notebook;* Allyn & Bacon, Inc.; Mrs. E. Wight Bakke; Robert R. Blake; Dale L. Bolton; the *Canadian Administrator;* Roald F. Campbell; Francis S. Chase; Luvern L. Cunningham; the Center for the Advanced Study of Educational Administration, University of Oregon; Jacob W. Getzels; Jerald Hage; Andrew W. Halpin; Harper & Row, Publishers; Holt, Rinehart and Winston; the Metropolitan Detroit Bureau of School Studies; the Midwest Administration Center, University of Chicago; the National Association of Elementary School Principals; the National Association of Secondary School Principals; the National Society for the Study of Education; the *School Review;* the University of Chicago Press; and the Board of Education and Rosemary Lucas, Superintendent, School District 127, Worth, Illinois.

We acknowledge with appreciation the initial stimulus to write this book provided by John Guy Fowlkes, Emeritus Professor of Educational Administration, University of Wisconsin-Madison, and Advisory Editor of the Exploration Series in Education. To Voras D. (Jeff) Meeks, retired Executive Editor at Harper & Row, we are particularly indebted for his insightful suggestions and patient assistance.

We wish finally to express appreciation to Carol Jean Roche whose speed and skill in typing greatly facilitated the preparation of the manuscript.

James M. Lipham
Madison, Wisconsin

James A. Hoeh, Jr.
Grosse Pointe, Michigan

PART I

Introduction to the principalship

PART I PRESENTS AN INTRODUCTORY OVERVIEW OF TWO COMPLEMENTARY APPROACHES TO ANALYSIS OF THE PRINCIPALSHIP. THESE ARE THE FOUNDATIONAL OR THEORETICAL VIEW AND THE FUNCTIONAL OR COMPETENCY-BASED VIEW OF THE PRINCIPALSHIP. THE ASSUMPTION IS MADE THAT THESE VIEWS ARE UNIVERSALLY APPLICABLE TO THE PRINCIPALSHIP OF A SCHOOL—WHETHER ELEMENTARY, MIDDLE, OR SENIOR HIGH, AND WHETHER URBAN, SUBURBAN, OR RURAL.

CHAPTER 1

The principalship: an overview

To perform effectively in the principalship at least two productive alternative stances may be taken. The first and most current view we have termed the foundations of the principalship. It draws heavily on recent theories, constructs, and models from the basic and applied social, behavioral, and administrative sciences to describe and delineate the antecedents, correlates, or predictors of the behavior of the principal and those with whom he works. The second and most typical view we have termed the functions of the principalship. It focuses on the tasks, jobs, and activities that occupy the bulk of the principal's time and analyzes them according to the major competencies that must be demonstrated by an effective school principal. In this introductory chapter we present a brief overview of both the foundations of the principalship, which constitute Part II of the book, and the functions of the principalship, which constitute Part III.

Foundations of the principalship

The theories, constructs, models, and to some extent the research findings of the behavioral and administrative sciences are very useful in that they provide the principal with *concepts*—with alternative ways of viewing, understanding, and ordering the multitude of variables and with predicting and influencing the outcomes of issues with which he daily must deal. In a sense, each theoretical or foundational view serves the principal as a pair of spectacles, bringing into focus a few selected aspects of the world around him which he, perhaps negligently, would not otherwise have singled out for attention.[1] We also believe that the foundational-functional or theoretical-practical relationship is not dichotomous but continuous and that the principal on the job inevitably moves back and forth between foundations and functions or between theory

[1] Roald F. Campbell, W. W. Charters, Jr., and William L. Gragg, "Improving Administrative Practice: Three Essential Roles," in Roald F. Campbell and James M. Lipham, eds., *Administrative Theory as a Guide to Action*, Chicago, Midwest Administration Center, University of Chicago, 1960, p. 179.

and practice in resolving issues and making decisions. Thus we concur with Dewey's classic comment that theory is in the end the most practical of all things.[2]

Since the foundational approach to the analysis of administration is quite recent, considerable disagreement exists concerning which of the many theoretical models are most useful to performance in the principalship. Current theories, moreover, differ widely in generality, complexity, clarity, vitality, and novelty, as well as utility.[3] Even so, we feel that the following bodies of theory are foundational and that they hold great potential for assisting an individual to understand and thereby improve behavior in the principalship role:

1. General systems theory
2. Social systems theory
3. Values theory
4. Organization theory
5. Role theory
6. Decision theory
7. Leadership theory

The foundational bodies of administrative and behavioral science just enumerated by no means exhaust the list of theories having value to the principal. For example, learning theory and curriculum theory, as well as the history and philosophy of education, might well be added as foundational areas in which the principal must be well informed. Typically, however, in preparation for teaching, and subsequently for the principalship, training is obtained in required or cognate courses concerning these topics. Unlike conventional textbooks on the elementary or secondary school principalship, which deal to some extent with learning and curriculum theory or history and philosophy of education, this book does not treat these topics in detail.

By way of brief overview, we examine some of the major parameters of the behavioral and administrative science theories deemed most relevant for the principal.

GENERAL SYSTEMS THEORY

Chapter 2 is concerned with the application of general systems theory to the administration of the school. The systems approach to administration

[2] John Dewey, *The Sources of a Science of Education*, New York, Liveright, 1929, p. 17.

[3] James M. Lipham, "Content Selection in Organizational Theory and Behavior in Education," in Jack A. Culbertson et al., eds., *Social Science Content for Preparing Educational Leaders*, Columbus, Ohio, Merrill, 1973, pp. 316–318.

is interdisciplinary and provides a means for viewing the school in terms of its general properties and its specific dynamics. It focuses on the interrelationships and linkages between and among the subunits of the school as well as on the relationship of the school to its larger environment. Systems thought—methodical, coherent, designed, and analytic—has produced several logical and quantifiable tools to assist the principal in assessing educational needs, analyzing school programs, making educational decisions, monitoring educational projects, and evaluating educational outcomes.

The major antecedents to the current systems approach to administration, which include scientific management, human relations, and behavioral science approaches, serve as the background for consideration of quantitative systems theory. The properties of general systems apply to the school and provide a model for examining the school as a dynamic institution. Illustrative examples of the tools and techniques derived from the systems approach that are useful to the principal include the following: management by objectives (MBO), planning-programming-budgeting systems (PPBS), flow charting, and program evaluation review technique/critical path method (PERT/CPM). General systems theory not only fosters the use of innovative techniques, it also provides a heuristic gestalt for planning and implementing programs for improving the school's instructional and personnel services.

SOCIAL SYSTEMS THEORY

Social systems theory represents a focus on particular aspects—the social aspects—of general systems. In terms of social systems theory, the school is viewed as a complex, interactive, and dynamic system that is examined both structurally and operationally.[4] Structurally, the school is a unique social system within the hierarchy of superordinate, parallel, and subordinate relationships in the larger social system, the school district. This hierarchy of relationships is the locus for allocating and integrating personnel and material to achieve the goals of the system. Operationally, however, the administration of the school always functions within a network of person-to-person interaction. Thus the nature of these interpersonal relationships or, more broadly, social relationships, becomes a central factor in the administration of the school.

In Chapter 3 the concept of social system is defined, and we present several models depicting the relationships among the major dimensions of social systems—the normative, personal, and cultural dimensions.

[4] J. W. Getzels, James M. Lipham, and Roald F. Campbell, *Educational Administration as a Social Process,* New York, Harper & Row, 1968, pp. 52–53.

This theory has demonstrated particular utility for understanding the conflicts between the school and the community and between and among roles and individuals within the school. Consideration is also given to the mechanisms for integrating the individual and the organization. Finally, the theory is useful in assessing organizational and individual behavior, including important concepts of effectiveness, efficiency, satisfaction, and morale.

VALUES THEORY

Since theories of values deal simultaneously with the general values held by a society and with the specific values held by an individual, and since values involve anthropological, historical, sociological, and philosophical analyses, work in this domain is perhaps less integrated than that related to other foundational areas. Of particular significance to the principal, however, are treatments of the core or sacred American values of democracy, individualism, equality, and human perfectability, as well as treatments of the changing secular and operational values that characterize the current American scene. A theoretical model that demonstrates the interrelationships of sacred values, secular values, and operational values in the American society introduces Chapter 4.

We can state several common and recurring themes in the school-society relationship that condition the expectations held for the school as an institution: that the schools belong to the people, that education is a function of the state, that education is of federal interest, that education is in terms of one's abilities and interests, and that education is equally available to all. Differences in educational expectations for both the elementary and the secondary school, moreover, have been shown to be meaningfully and systematically related to such subpublic differences as social class, occupation, education, region, religion, political party identification, and other variables. Research has revealed that the values within the society have a powerful and continuing impact on the educational expectations for the school as an institution.[5]

The value orientations held by individuals—principals, teachers, students, and parents—are powerful determinants of behavior. Again, research has shown that the values held by individuals and the degree of similarity in values condition the role and personality relationships

[5] Cf. Lawrence W. Downey, Roger C. Seager, and Allen T. Slagle, *The Task of Public Education,* Chicago, Midwest Administration Center, University of Chicago, 1960; Marvin J. Fruth, Dennis W. Spuck, and Howard E. Wakefield, *Opening the Door,* Madison, Cooperative Educational Research and Services, University of Wisconsin, 1972.

within the school.[6] Thus the principal must be aware of both his own and others' value orientations.

ORGANIZATION THEORY

Ironically, a great deal of time and energy is spent in coping with life in contemporary organizations, yet little effort is devoted to attempting to understand it. In fact, it is not uncommon to encounter a principal who feels that he already knows all that he needs to know about organizations because he has lived and worked in one—as in the case of the demagogue who poses as a pedagogue because he once went to school.

Organization theory constitutes a foundational area that is treated in detail in Chapter 5. The principal must be familiar with the following classical organizational concepts: bureaucratic structure, power relationships, and the mechanisms for achieving coordination, such as unity of command, span of control, and line-staff relationships.

The formal structure of the organization in terms of its complexity, centralization, formalization, and stratification has been shown to be related to such outcomes of the organization as adaptiveness, production, efficiency, and job satisfaction. Moreover, theories of organization make it possible to analyze the extent to which the school is a mechanistic or bureaucratic organization, as contrasted with an organic or professional organization. Knowledge of the formal organizational parameters and their interrelationships should enable the principal to lead the school in the direction of a professional organization.

Just as the school may be analyzed as a formal organization, it is possible to analyze it as an informal organization—in terms of its organizational climate. Organizational climate is concerned with the organizational "personality" of the school—whether the working environment is open, autonomous, controlled, familiar, paternal, or closed. "Openness" or authenticity of behavior of principal and teachers alike is essential if leadership is to be initiated in the school and if conjoint satisfaction is to be realized concerning the accomplishment of both organizational and individual goals.

Understanding of both the formal and the informal organizations enables the principal to provide leadership in changing the school. Organizational change may be analyzed according to the following descrip-

[6] Cf. Richard D. Prince, "A Study of the Relationships Between Individual Values and Administrative Effectiveness in the School Situation," doctoral dissertation, University of Chicago, 1957; Max G. Abbott, "Values and Value-Perceptions of School Superintendents and Board Members," doctoral dissertation, University of Chicago, 1960; Gale W. Rose, "Organizational Behavior and Its Concomitants in Schools," *Administrator's Notebook*, 15 (March 1957), 1–4.

tors: types of change, processes of change, agents of change, and variables that affect change. The role of the principal as a change agent is crucial, since few changes of any importance can occur in a school without his active support.

ROLE THEORY

What the principal's role is or should be is of paramount and perennial concern to theorists and practitioners alike. The principal's role is continuously defined and redefined in the daily interactions of the individuals and reference groups with whom he works; in addition, role descriptions are derived from historical-legal precedents, the professional literature, and school district policies.

Role theory, described in Chapter 6, includes several models that are useful for viewing, assessing, analyzing, and improving the principal's role performance. Derived from social systems theory, role theory permits assessment of the role expectations held by the principal himself and by his significant reference groups—central office personnel, other principals, teachers, noncertificated employees, parents, citizens, and students. It also permits assessment of the extent to which one is able to perceive accurately the role expectations held by others.

Knowledge of role theory will enable the principal better to understand, adapt, modify, and fulfill his significant social role. Some of the major types of role conflict that are endemic to the principalship include: conflicts in expectations for the many roles the principal fulfills (simultaneously "wearing many hats"), conflicts in role expectations for the principalship held between and among different reference groups ("the man in the middle"), conflicts in role expectations for the principalship within a reference group ("caught in group crossfire"), and conflicts between the principal's role and his needs as a person ("the man vs. the job"). Moreover, significant differences often exist between "actual" role behavior and "idealized" role behavior of the principal. Studies of the relationship of role expectations, perceptions, and behavior to such variables as effectiveness, efficiency, satisfaction, leadership, and morale contain numerous implications for improved performance in the principalship.[7]

DECISION THEORY

The view of the principal as a decision maker is an accurate conceptualization of the role. This is true whether he is making appellate de-

[7] Cf. James M. Lipham, "Dynamics of the Principalship," *National Elementary Principal,* 41 (January 1962), 23–30; James M. Lipham, "The Role of the Principal: Search and Research," *National Elementary Principal,* 44 (April 1965), 28–33.

cisions ("Johnny hit me." "No, I didn't."); intermediary decisions ("I'm sorry, Miss Jones, but the business manager says that our budget won't stand it."); or, on occasion, creative decisions (designing innovative organizational modes to improve instruction). In addition to considering the origin of decisions, decision theory deals with the stages of decision making, the content of decisions, the analysis of decision-making behavior, and involvement in the decision-making process.

The systems model of decision theory, presented in Chapter 7, includes consideration of the impact of values and information on decision making, the weighing of outcomes in decision making, and the implementation of decisions. The types of decisions made by the principal—routinized or programmed, heuristic or creative, and compromise or negotiated—call for different decision strategies. Since most administrative decisions in the field of education are shared, the nature and extent of involvement of staff, students, parents, and others in decision making is becoming increasingly important. As one principal commented recently, "Decision making is the heart of my job. I used to make my own decisions, but now everyone gets into the act. Moreover, we have to be right more than 50 percent of the time." An understanding of decision theory on the part of the principal should increase this percentage.

LEADERSHIP THEORY

Everyone agrees that the principal should be the leader of the school. But what does this mean? Leadership theory, described in Chapter 8, provides insights concerning approaches to the analysis of leadership, definitions of leadership, valuation of leadership, locus for leadership, scope of leadership, stages of leadership, frequency and potency of leadership, and correlates or outcomes of leadership.

Historically, the modes for analyzing leadership include the great man, traitist, situational, and behavioral approaches, which supply the necessary perspective for viewing the current leadership role of the principal. The definition problem serves to question the essence of leadership and leadership behavior. The valuation of leadership is concerned with the extent to which leadership is accorded a positive connotation in the American culture. The locus for leadership examines the nature and boundaries of the focal social system (the school) within which leadership occurs. The stages of leadership include analysis of the sequential steps that one takes as he exercises leadership over time. Frequency and potency of leadership involve the frequency with which the principal leads, as well as the magnitude of his leadership acts. The outcomes of leadership examine the relationship of the many dimensions of leadership to measures of effectiveness, morale, climate, and achievement within the school.

Attention also is given in Chapter 8 to the various leadership styles, and the variables within the school that are systematically and meaningfully related to the leadership style of the principal are analyzed. Emanating from the research are several suggestions for improving the analysis of leadership, as well as some guidelines for improving the principal's leadership.

The foundational or theoretical view of the principalship is basic to the development of the competencies required to perform effectively the tasks of the principalship—termed the functional view of the principal's role.

Functional view of the principalship

What are the basic functions that must be fulfilled in providing leadership for the improvement of the school? Hundreds of studies have been conducted regarding the tasks that principals *actually* perform, and thousands of articles have been written concerning the tasks that they ideally *should* perform. Perhaps because the literature on the principalship abounds with so many "absolutely musts," "positively shoulds," and "certainly oughts," it was at one time popular within the field of educational administration to disparage the functional view as being a "cookbook" or prescriptive approach to understanding and performing in the role. Such criticism notwithstanding, one must be familiar with what is expected to be done; otherwise even the best foundational knowledge cannot be utilized.

Even though the principalship is a well-established role in the field of education, there is still some disagreement concerning the nature and boundaries of the major functional categories of the principal's role. There also is disagreement over the relative importance of role categories. Without engaging in such controversies, we wish simply to note that several major categories of functions account not only for a majority of the on-the-job time spent by principals but also for a majority of the specialized preparation in the form of areas of advanced study in the field of educational administration in preparation for the principalship. Therefore, we choose to group the tasks of the principal according to these five categories:

1. Instructional program
2. Staff personnel
3. Student personnel
4. Financial and physical resources
5. School-community relationships

The following paragraphs review the competencies required of the principal in each of the major functional categories.

INSTRUCTIONAL PROGRAM

With emerging emphases on multiunit or interdepartmental structures, team teaching, individualized learning, and computer-assisted instruction, one need only observe today's classrooms to appreciate the magnitude of the substantive changes being made in the instructional program of the school. If the principal is to become an educational leader, what, indeed, does this mean for his role vis-à-vis teachers, team leaders, supervisors, consultants, and other specialists, as well as with respect to parents and students who have a major stake in the instructional program?

Studies have revealed that of all the functional tasks in educational administration, those relating to work with the instructional program are most likely to be widely shared with others in the organization.[8] Because such work is shared, a tendency exists for many principals inappropriately to abrogate or delegate their responsibilities for leadership in curriculum development and instructional change. A study of elementary principals, for example, revealed that the principals spend much less time working with instruction than they would like.[9] Even though work with the instructional program may be complex, shared, and time consuming, it represents a basic responsibility of the principal.

Activities of the principal relating to the instructional program include assessing the community context for education, determining educational needs, stating educational objectives, planning and implementing instructional change, and evaluating program outcomes. Each of these major tasks subsumes a multitude of activities that require specific understandings, skills, and competencies. These are delineated in Chapter 9.

In assessing the context for the educational program, the principal must give attention to both societal change and community demands as they impinge on the program of the schools. In determining educational needs, attention is given to the learners in general, as well as to the learners in a particular community. Activities involved in stating educational objectives are directed toward the reduction of broad goals and purposes into measurable behavioral outcomes. Planning and implement-

---

[8] Glen G. Eye et al., *Relationship Between Instructional Change and the Extent to Which School Administrators and Teachers Agree on the Location of Responsibilities for Administrative Decisions*, Madison, University of Wisconsin, 1966, p. 96.

[9] *The Elementary School Principalship in 1968*, Washington, D.C., Department of Elementary School Principals, National Education Association, 1968, p. 51.

ing instructional change includes attention to the human and material inputs and processes required to change and improve the educational program. In assessing outcomes of the educational program, one must utilize appropriate techniques for evaluating both the processes and the products of instruction.

STAFF PERSONNEL

With the advent of collective negotiations in education, it is evident that the traditional *modus operandi* of principals in performing staff personnel functions has changed dramatically and will continue to change in future years. Although some see this development as a threat to the traditional authority of the principal, others view it as an expanded opportunity for providing staff leadership.[10]

The functional category of staff personnel includes responsibilities of the principal in recruiting, selecting, assigning, orienting, supervising, improving, and evaluating the staff members of the school. These activities are synthesized in systems terms and discussed in detail in Chapter 10.

Staff recruitment, selection, and assignment should be designed to maximize the degree of role-personality compatibility in the employment process. Improvement of staff includes leadership of the principal in the supervisory activities that will foster increased role effectiveness and maximum personal satisfaction of each staff member. In evaluating staff performance, the principal's activities include building agreement on purpose, recognizing differential work styles, judging role effectiveness, and, if necessary, reassigning or dismissing staff members.

The current trend toward differentiated staffing also has altered the traditional role of the principal in the staff personnel function. No longer does the principal work simply with teachers; he now works with a host of general, specialized, and volunteer personnel. In some urban schools in ghetto neighborhoods, for example, it may be that the student is sometimes bombarded with more help than he can readily assimilate. As the principal of one such elementary school commented recently,

> This morning it is a little wilder around here than usual. In addition to our regular teachers, student teachers, and teacher aides, we have with us today some volunteer PTA playground supervisors, Teacher Corps trainees, high school student reading tutors, AAUW fine arts performers, and, of course, you people from the University. With a ratio in the building of

[10] Patrick W. Carlton and Harold I. Goodwin, eds., *The Collective Dilemma: Negotiations in Education,* Worthington, Ohio, Jones, 1969.

about one adult to four children, we've had about all the help that we can stand!

In addition to those involved in instruction, the nonprofessional personnel —secretaries, clerks, cooks, engineers, and custodians—also look to the principal for leadership.

The principal not only provides staff leadership within the school, he also is expected to contribute meaningfully to certain district-wide staff personnel functions. These typically include developing or up-dating personnel policies, identifying long-range staffing needs, and, in some school systems, serving as a member of the school board's negotiating team.

STUDENT PERSONNEL

A veteran principal recently commented, "Most educators mouth the platitude that they 'like working with kids.' That's not enough. You have to love it." To be able to lead in the area of student personnel, the principal must develop a deeper understanding of the values of students, as well as the extent to which student values may be at variance with those of the school as an institution. A model illustrative of these relationships introduces Chapter 11.

No longer are students passive recipients of educational programs; instead they are active partners in initiating instructional change. Student involvement in decision making may readily be increased in student government and cocurricular programs. Student participation in decision making should be extended to other programs in the school as well.

A program of adequate guidance services constitutes the core of the student personnel function. Included should be the inventory, information, counseling, placement, and research services, which all converge on the needs of the individual student. As a leader, the principal must initiate the appropriate structures within the school for orchestrating the contributions of teachers, guidance counselors, and other student personnel specialists, to allow each student to increase his feelings of satisfaction, belongingness, identification, and achievement in present and projected life situations.

Currently several new laws and court decisions are altering significantly the role of the principal vis-à-vis the students. To be effective, the principal must remain abreast of legal rulings concerning compulsory school attendance, discipline, freedom of expression, freedom from search and seizure, and due process, since each area has implications for altering the principal-student relationship.

FINANCIAL AND PHYSICAL RESOURCES

The much debated, sometimes lamented, age of accountability is upon us.[11] Whereas formerly the principal took a largely managerial role with respect to material resources, the leadership required in planning, programming, budgeting, monitoring, and evaluating financial and physical resources now represents a dynamic dimension of the principalship.

In addition to concerns with planning, programming, and budgeting, major competencies are required of the principal with regard to the supervision of financial and physical resources. These include the following: purchasing and requisitioning supplies and materials; accounting for school monies (both curricular and cocurricular); maintaining an inventory of school property; supervising plant construction, maintenance, and operation; and supervising school lunch and other auxiliary services. Approaches to meeting these administrative and supervisory responsibilities of the principal are discussed in Chapter 12.

Although school districts generally have been furnishing increased numbers of clerical, bookkeeping, custodial, and maintenance personnel, principals continue to report that activities in this functional area require much more of their time than they would ideally desire.[12] Even so, one must acknowledge that the supervision of the school's financial and physical resources immediately reflects on the quality of the leadership of the principal.

SCHOOL-COMMUNITY RELATIONSHIPS

Citizens everywhere are demanding and exercising a stronger voice in the administration and operation of their individual schools.[13] No longer is it possible for the principal to fulfill his responsibilities in school-community relations by attending monthly meetings of the parent-teacher organization, occasionally conferring with individual parents, and periodically publishing a school newsletter. These and similar activities may be useful, but they are an inadequate response to persistent and increasing demands being made by citizens for school district decentralization.[14] In fact, it may be anticipated that many school systems

[11] "Eight Articles on Accountability," *Phi Delta Kappan*, 52 (December 1970), 193–239.

[12] *The Elementary School Principalship in 1968*, op. cit., p. 51.

[13] Seymour Evans, "The Urban Principal: Man in Transition," in Frank W. Lutz, ed., *Toward Improved Urban Education*, Worthington, Ohio, Jones, 1970, pp. 133–144.

[14] Luvern L. Cunningham, "Organization of Education in Metropolitan Areas," *Metropolitanism: Its Challenge to Education*, Chicago, National Society for the Study of Education, 1968, pp. 118–122.

may eventually become so decentralized that in many respects the principalship of tomorrow will be similar to the superintendency of today. This undoubtedly will first occur in the functional area of school-community relationships.

Major competencies required of the principal in fostering a sound program of school-community relationships include the following: assessing community needs and aspirations; analyzing the composition, relationships, and demands of community subpublics; working with community leaders, organizations, and agencies; working with parents and parent-teacher organizations; and communicating with the community about the purposes, programs, progress, and plans for the improvement of the school. In Chapter 13 the "why," "who," "what," "when," and "how" of communications are discussed, and a model is presented for improving the two-way process of school-community interaction. Shared-time programs, continuing education programs, and the process of involving the community in instruction also are viewed as mechanisms for the improvement of school-community relations.

Summary

The purpose of this chapter was to introduce the reader immediately to our two complementary views of the school principalship: the foundational view and the functional view. In essence, the foundational view poses the issue of *why* one behaves as he does. It utilizes established and emerging theoretical frameworks for analyzing the antecedents, predictors, correlates, or outcomes of administrative behavior. The following behavioral and administrative science theories are posited as possessing particular relevance to the principalship: general systems theory, social systems theory, values theory, organization theory, role theory, decision theory, and leadership theory.

The functional view poses the issue of *what* one does, or should do, as a school principal. It focuses on the tasks and activities in which one must be competent if he is to be an effective principal. The following categories of administrative and supervisory functions are viewed as comprising the major functions of the principalship: the instructional program, staff personnel, student personnel, financial and physical resources, and school-community relationships.

The foundational view of the principalship is treated in detail in the chapters in Part II; the functional view, in Part III. In the final chapter, we summarize the conceptual, human, and technical competencies required of the principal now and in the future.

SUGGESTED ACTIVITIES

1. Analyze an administrative incident or case study in terms of any one of the foundational theories of administration.

2. Document and describe the major eras in the field of administration generally and in educational administration specifically prior to the current emphasis on theoretical foundations.

3. Conduct a content analysis of textbooks in educational administration according to the emphasis placed on the functional vs. the foundational view of the school administrator.

4. Interview a principal or observe a principal for a full day and analyze his interactions in terms of the time devoted to each of the functional categories. Compare the findings by size, type, or location of school.

5. Review school bulletins, administrative calendars, or faculty minutes in terms of the attention given by the principal to the functional categories. Contrast the actual findings with your idealized expectations for the principal's role.

SELECTED REFERENCES

CAMPBELL, ROALD F., et al., *Introduction to Educational Administration,* 4th ed., Boston, Allyn & Bacon, 1971, chaps. 4 and 5.

CARVER, FRED D., and THOMAS J. SERGIOVANNI, *Organizations and Human Behavior: Focus on Schools,* New York, McGraw-Hill, 1969, pt. II.

FABER, CHARLES F., and GILBERT F. SHEARRON, *Elementary School Administration: Theory and Practice,* New York, Holt, Rinehart and Winston, 1970, pt. I.

GETZELS, J. W., JAMES M. LIPHAM, and ROALD F. CAMPBELL, *Educational Administration as a Social Process,* New York, Harper & Row, 1968, chaps. 1 and 2.

GRIFFITHS, DANIEL E., "The Nature and Meaning of Theory," *Behavioral Science and Educational Administration,* Sixty-Third Yearbook, pt. II, National Society for the Study of Education, Chicago, University of Chicago Press, 1964, chap. 5.

HACK, WALTER G., et al., *Educational Administration: Selected Readings,* 2nd ed., Boston, Allyn & Bacon, 1971, chap. 3.

LANE, WILLARD R., RONALD G. CORWIN, and WILLIAM G. MONAHAN, *Foundations of Educational Administration,* New York, Macmillan, 1966, chap. 2.

MCLEARY, LLOYD E., and STEPHEN P. HENCLEY, *Secondary School Administration: Theoretical Bases of Professional Practice,* New York, Dodd, Mead, 1965, chaps. 1–4.

OWENS, ROBERT G., *Organizational Behavior in Schools,* Englewood Cliffs, N.J., Prentice-Hall, 1970, chaps. 1 and 2.

SERGIOVANNI, THOMAS J., and FRED D. CARVER, *The New School Executive: A Theory of Administration,* New York, Dodd, Mead, 1973.

SHUSTER, ALBERT H., and DON H. STEWART, *The Principal and the Autonomous Elementary School,* Columbus, Ohio, Merrill, 1973.

PART II

Foundations of the principalship

THE SEVEN CHAPTERS IN THIS SECTION EXPLORE THE CONCEPTUAL FOUN-
DATIONS OF THE PRINCIPALSHIP. THE FOLLOWING BODIES OF ADMIN-
ISTRATIVE AND BEHAVIORAL SCIENCE THEORY ARE EXAMINED: GENERAL
SYSTEMS THEORY, SOCIAL SYSTEMS THEORY, VALUES THEORY, ORGANI-
ZATION THEORY, ROLE THEORY, DECISION THEORY, AND LEADERSHIP THE-
ORY. IMPLICATIONS FROM RESEARCH BASED ON THE THEORIES ARE DRAWN
FOR THE PRINCIPAL'S ROLE.

CHAPTER 2
Systems theory

L ogical and quantifiable tools to assist the school principal in analyzing school programs, monitoring educational projects, evaluating educational outcomes, and making educational decisions represent current systems approaches to administration. Needs assessment, management by objectives (MBO), planning-programming-budgeting systems (PPBS), program evaluation review technique (PERT), and management information systems (MIS) are but a few of the many tools and techniques that already have changed and will continue to alter the role of the principal. As is typically the case in an expanding domain, however, the principal may be called on to adopt or adapt one or more of the tools and techniques without thoroughly understanding the theoretical foundations involved.

In this chapter we first present a short review of three major antecedents to the current systems approach to administration. Next the concept of general systems is introduced, and the properties of general systems are discussed. Then a synthesis of the systems approach to the administration of the school is attempted, including systems procedures that can facilitate the role of the principal. The chapter concludes with a brief discussion of some problems and prospects relating to the systems approach for the improvement of the schools.

Historical antecedents

The application of systems procedures in the field of educational administration is a relatively recent development, yet the historical antecedents of what may broadly be termed the systems approach date from near the dawn of recorded history.[1] Egyptian architects employed a system of measurement in the construction of the pyramids; Phoenician astronomers devised a system of navigation based on the stars. Philosophers throughout the ages have attempted to systematize thought concerning man—his nature and his environment. Even as early as the third century in China, principles synthesizing laws, methods, and au-

---

[1] Richard A. Rossmiller, "Systems Analysis," *The College of Education Record*, University of North Dakota, 53 (October–November 1967), 2.

thority were derived in an effort to systematize management.[2] Nor can we ignore the contributions of scholars and researchers from the basic and applied physical and biological sciences and, more recently, the social sciences. The scientific method utilized by all the sciences parallels, even though it is not synonymous with, the systems approach.[3]

In terms of recent historical emphases, we may categorize systematic approaches to the study of administration in terms of the following: (1) scientific management, (2) human relations, (3) behavioral science, and (4) quantitative systems approaches to administration.

THE SCIENTIFIC MANAGEMENT APPROACH

Although scientific management is by no means equivalent to management science, it is widely acknowledged that one of the early systematic approaches to administration was that of management studies in industry at the turn of the century. Sustained interest in the study of management in the early 1900s was due partly to change from individual to corporate ownership of most businesses; therefore, operation or management of organizations was no longer the domain of the owner. With the industrial revolution, there developed larger organizations in which persons other than the owner were hired to manage. One's continuation in an organization was dependent not on being the owner but on being competent as a manager. This separation of ownership from management created a need for much greater attention to the problems of managing.

One of the first to attempt a systematic study of management was Frederick W. Taylor.[4] As an engineer, Taylor was initially concerned with procedural job analysis and work rates. In 1903 he published *Shop Management*, which considered methods of organizational structure and worker motivation, as well as worker efficiency. To point out the great loss that the country was suffering through inefficiency, to convince others that the remedy for inefficiency lay in systematic management, and to prove that management was a true science based on clearly defined principles and laws, he published in 1911 *The Principles of Scientific Management*, in which the essential points were as follows:

1. TIME-STUDY PRINCIPLE. All productive effort should be measured by accurate time study and a standard time established for all work done in the shop.

[2] Donald V. Etz, "The First Management Consultant?" *Management Review*, 53 (September 1965), 55.

[3] Lanour F. Carter, *The Systems Approach to Education—The Mystique and the Reality*, Report SP-3291, Santa Monica, Calif., System Development Corporation, 1969.

[4] Frederick W. Taylor, *Scientific Management*, New York, Harper & Row, 1911.

2. PIECE-RATE PRINCIPLE. Wages should be proportional to output and their rates based on the standards determined by time study. As a corollary, a worker should be given the highest grade of work of which he is capable. ✓

3. SEPARATION-OF-PLANNING-FROM-PERFORMANCE PRINCIPLE. Management should take over from the workers the responsibility for planning the work and making the performance physically possible. Planning should be based on time studies and other data related to production, which are scientifically determined and systematically classified; it should be facilitated by standardization of tools, implements, and methods.

4. SCIENTIFIC-METHODS-OF-WORK PRINCIPLE. Management should take over from the workers the responsibility for their methods of work, determine scientifically the best methods, and train the workers accordingly.

5. MANAGERIAL-CONTROL PRINCIPLE. Managers should be trained and taught to apply scientific principles of management and control (such as management by exception and comparison with valid standards).

6. FUNCTIONAL-MANAGEMENT PRINCIPLE. The strict application of military principles should be reconsidered and the industrial organization should be so designed that it best serves the purpose of improving the co-ordination of activities among the various specialists.[5]

Even though we might take issue with certain of Taylor's management principles, the analytical methods by which they were derived are utilized today, especially in solving industrial engineering and production management problems. They include research, particularly observation, concerning the variables bearing on the production function; standardization or uniformity in applying the analyses made; selection of persons in terms of job or role requirements; and training, either pre-service or in-service, for performing the roles analyzed.

Taylor's scientific approach to management was advanced through the work of Frank and Lillian Gilbreth and H. L. Gantt, among others.[6] Gantt's work resulted in the Gantt chart, which shows in terms of a single time dimension both the amount of work scheduled and the amount of work accomplished. Methodologically, this represented a forerunner to the program evaluation review technique (PERT), which is gaining widespread usage today. ✓

Scientific management principles were applied to the field of education by a number of early students of educational administration. In 1913, for example, Bobbitt wrote:

At a time when so much discussion is being given to the possibilities of "scientific management" in the world of material production, it seems desir-

---

[5] Quoted in Raymond Villers, *Dynamic Management in Industry*, Englewood Cliffs, N.J., Prentice-Hall, 1960, p. 29.

[6] Frank B. Gilbreth, *Motion Study*, New York, Van Nostrand Reinhold, 1911; Henry L. Gantt, *Industrial Leadership*, New Haven, Conn., Yale University Press, 1916.

able that the principles of this more effective form of management may be examined in order to ascertain the possibility of applying them to the problems of educational management and supervision.[7]

Bobbitt went on to stress that educators would do well to apply scientific procedures for setting the desired standards of production, the specific methods of production, the qualifications of the producers (the teachers), and the training of the producers, as well as to supply the teachers with "detailed instructions as to the work to be done, the standards to be reached, the methods to be employed, and the material and appliances to be used."[8] As Callahan documented, between World War I and World War II the business-industry "efficiency" ideology came to pervade the field of educational administration and persisted for several decades, during which thousands of comprehensive surveys were conducted to enhance the efficiency of the schools.[9] Many of the influential texts on school administration written during this period abound with prescriptive approaches to administration in which efficiency was the overriding criterion in determining "what" should be done.[10]

A somewhat separate strand of the scientific management approach involved the administrative process. The administrative process approach was a genuine forerunner of current quantitative systems approaches to administration. The process approach to administration was less concerned with "what" should be done than with "how" the organization should be managed. That is, the focus was not on the operative level at the bottom of the administrative hierarchy but on the managerial level at the top of the hierarchy. In 1916 Henri Fayol published *Administration Industrielle et Générale,* which dealt with the "life functions of administration" or the "elements of management."[11] These elements were described as: planning, organizing, commanding, coordinating, and controlling (POCCC). Utilizing the work of Fayol, Gulick formulated POSDCoRB, which included: planning, organizing, staffing, directing, coordinating, reporting, and budgeting.[12] Attention

---

[7] Franklin Bobbitt, "Some General Principles of Management Applied to the Problems of City School Systems," in *The Supervision of City Schools,* Twelfth Yearbook of The National Society for the Study of Education, pt. I, Chicago, University of Chicago Press, 1913, p. 7.

[8] Ibid., p. 89.

[9] Raymond E. Callahan, *Education and the Cult of Efficiency,* Chicago, University of Chicago Press, 1962.

[10] Cf. Edward P. Cubberly, *Public School Administration,* Boston, Houghton Mifflin, 1916; Ward G. Reeder, *The Fundamentals of Public School Administration,* New York, Macmillan, 1931.

[11] Henri Fayol, *Administration Industrielle et Générale,* translated by Constance Storrs, *General and Industrial Management,* London, Pitman, 1949.

[12] Luther H. Gulick and Lyndall F. Urwick, eds., *Papers on the Science of Administration,* New York, Institute of Public Administration, 1937.

also was directed to such well-known organizational concepts as line and staff, unity of command, span of control, centralization and de-centralization, and functional groupings of activities in terms of purpose, process, clientele, and location or place. Certain of these organizational concepts are still central in utilizing some of the recent quantitative systems techniques in administration—for example, locational budgeting in PPBS.

Conceptualizations of the administrative process have been particularly useful in the field of educational administration. Sears, who initially applied the process formulation to education, included the following stages: planning, organizing, directing, coordinating, and controlling.[13] In 1955 the yearbook of the American Association of School Administrators included the following five stages in the process formulation:

> 1. PLANNING or the attempt to control the future in the direction of the desired goals through decisions made on the basis of careful estimates of the probable consequences of possible courses of action.
> 2. ALLOCATION or the procurement and allotment of human and material resources in accordance with the operating plan.
> 3. STIMULATION or motivation of behavior in terms of the desired outcomes.
> 4. CO-ORDINATION or the process of fitting together the various groups and operations into an integrated pattern of purpose-achieving work.
> 5. EVALUATION or the continuous examination of the effects produced by the ways in which the other functions listed here are performed.[14]

In a penetrating application of the administrative process formulation to the field of educational administration, Gregg utilized the following stages: decision making, planning, organizing, communicating, influencing, coordinating, and evaluating.[15] As may be noted by comparing these stages with the earlier process formulations, Gregg's major conceptual contributions were the separation of decision making from the planning function and the emphasis on the human element in administration. Recognition of the human element constitutes the second major antecedent strain of management thought.

THE HUMAN RELATIONS APPROACH

An early protagonist for building and maintaining dynamic yet harmonious human relations in any enterprise was Mary Parker Follett. She

---

[13] Jesse B. Sears, *The Nature of the Administrative Process*, New York, McGraw-Hill, 1950.

[14] American Association of School Administrators, *Staff Relations in School Administration*, Washington, D.C., AASA, 1955, p. 17.

[15] Russell T. Gregg, "The Administrative Process," in Roald F. Campbell and Russell T. Gregg, eds., *Administrative Behavior in Education*, New York, Harper & Row, 1957, pp. 263–317.

made coordination the underlying strategy for the effective organization, reducing her principles of organization to four, as follows:

1. CO-ORDINATION BY DIRECT CONTROL OF THE RESPONSIBLE PEOPLE CONCERNED. That is, control should be effected horizontally through cross-relations between departments instead of up and down in line through the chief executive.

2. CO-ORDINATION IN THE EARLY STAGES. That is, the direct contact must begin while policy is being formed, not *after* a policy has been laid down when all that remains is compliance.

3. CO-ORDINATION AS THE RECIPROCAL RELATING OF ALL THE FACTORS IN A SITUATION. That is, an individual does not only adjust to another individual, but also is influenced by him, and so on, among all individuals and units within the organization.

4. CO-ORDINATION AS A CONTINUING PROCESS. That is, attention must be given to *new* machinery, procedures, information, and knowledge as the basis for renewal of both the organization and the individual.[16]

Although Follett was the first great exponent of the human relations view in administration, the systematic and empirical data in support of this view came from a number of experiments in human engineering carried out by Mayo and Roethlisberger and Dickson at the Hawthorne Plant of the Western Electric Company.[17] These experiments tested the effects on worker output of certain physical conditions, such as illumination, rest periods, length of work day, and methods of payment. For example, in one experiment, illumination levels were systematically varied; it was found that worker output increased with increased illumination, but when the illumination was decreased, output continued to increase. At first perplexed, the researchers finally concluded that the productivity increases were due primarily to psychological factors—that the group members were consulted, that comments were listened to and discussed, and that the members could overrule a managerial suggestion. According to Mayo, a new milieu was established in which the workers' self-determination and social well-being ranked first and the work was incidental. Even though the work of Mayo and his associates has been criticized,[18] one cannot deny that the research had great impact on administrative thought and practice.

[16] Mary Parker Follett, *Dynamic Administration: The Collected Papers of Mary Parker Follett,* Henry C. Metcalf and Lyndall F. Urwick, eds., New York, Harper & Row, 1941.

[17] Elton Mayo, *The Human Problems of an Industrial Civilization,* New York, Macmillan, 1933; Fritz J. Roethlisberger and William J. Dickson, *Management and the Worker,* Cambridge, Mass., Harvard University Press, 1939.

[18] Cf. Delbert C. Miller and William H. Form, *Industrial Sociology,* New York, Harper & Row, 1951, pp. 78–83; Reinhard Bendix and Lloyd H. Fisher, "The Perspectives of Elton Mayo," in Amitai Etzioni, ed., *Complex Organization: A Sociological Reader,* New York, Holt, Rinehart and Winston, 1961, pp. 113–126.

The human relations approach spread rapidly and became vastly influential in the field of education. Based largely on psychological theories as enunciated by Lewin, the National Training Laboratories of the National Education Association were established in 1947, originally at Bethel, Maine, for creating, experimenting with, utilizing, and providing training in human relation techniques. Encouraged by the gradual refutation of Freud's interpretation of human behavior, the human relations movement turned to theories of personality by Murray, Rogers, Maslow, and others who considered the total behavioral patterns of individuals.[19] More recently, human relations efforts have been directed toward the development and utilization of new techniques, such as T-groups, encounter groups, and other modes of sensitivity training. Course, seminar, workshop, and other pre-service and in-service training experiences are now utilized in many colleges, universities, and school districts to improve the human relations skills of principals and other educational personnel.

A major result of the work mentioned was that the human relations approach attracted the attention, involvement, and research interests of a wide variety of behavioral scientists.

THE BEHAVIORAL SCIENCE APPROACH

Although initial investigations of human relations in administration paid scant attention to theoretical formulations, subsequent research developed and applied several theories to explain or predict administrative phenomena. Chester Barnard was among the first to relate administration to the behavioral sciences.[20] In *The Functions of the Executive,* originally published in 1938, he set forth a theory of cooperation and organization in formal organizations. He emphasized that the organization is a system of consciously coordinated personal activities or forces. Another major contribution was the distinction he made between the concepts of effectiveness and efficiency. Effectiveness was defined as system-oriented, having to do with the achievement of cooperative and organizational goals; efficiency was defined as person-oriented, having to do with the feelings of satisfaction an individual derives from membership in the organization. As Campbell and others have noted, "This conception did much to put the work of Taylor and Fayol, who had

[19] Henry A. Murray, *Explorations in Personality,* New York, Oxford University Press, 1938; Carl Rogers, *Client-Centered Therapy—Its Current Practice, Implications and Theory,* Boston, Houghton Mifflin, 1951; Abraham H. Maslow, *Motivation and Personality,* New York, Harper & Row, 1954.

[20] Chester I. Barnard, *The Functions of the Executive,* Cambridge, Mass., Harvard University Press, 1964.

concentrated on organization achievement, and Follett and Mayo, who had tended to emphasize individual satisfaction, in appropriate perspective.[21]

Another influential work utilizing the behavioral sciences in the analysis of administration was *Administrative Behavior* by Herbert A. Simon.[22] He argued for a science of administration and asserted that the most fruitful approach to understanding and improving administrative behavior is through a decision-making framework. Not only did Simon propose that administration is a science in a framework of decision making, he also brought mathematical decision theory into administrative thought through the use of such concepts as limits of decisions, utility of decisions, maximization of decisions, and rationality of decisions.

Following Barnard and Simon, hosts of studies of both formal and informal organization have been conducted utilizing behavioral science concepts.[23] Many of these works are based on the conceptual work of two sociologists: Max Weber, who was concerned with bureaucracy, and Talcott Parsons, who developed a general theory of social systems.[24] According to Weber, bureaucracy is the ideal type of structured management for accomplishing organizational purpose. American schools have been particularly receptive to bureaucratic ideology, which has the following essential characteristics:[25]

[21] Roald F. Campbell et al., *Introduction to Educational Administration*, 4th ed., Boston, Allyn & Bacon, 1971, p. 111.

[22] Herbert A. Simon, *Administrative Behavior*, New York, Macmillan, 1945.

[23] Cf. Philip B. Applewhite, *Organizational Behavior*, Englewood Cliffs, N.J., Prentice-Hall, 1965; Chris Argyris et al., *Social Science Approaches to Business Behavior*, Homewood, Ill., Irwin, 1962; Peter M. Blau, *Bureaucracy in Modern Society*, New York, Random House, 1956; Bertram M. Gross, *The Managing of Organizations*, New York, Free Press, 1964; Paul R. Lawrence et al., *Organizational Behavior and Administration*, Homewood, Ill., Irwin, 1965; James G. March, *Handbook of Organizations*, Skokie, Ill., Rand McNally, 1965; Robert Presthus, *The Organizational Society*, New York, Knopf, 1962; William G. Scott, *Organization Theory*, Homewood, Ill., Irwin, 1967; James D. Thompson, *Organizations in Action*, New York, McGraw-Hill, 1967.

[24] Cf. Hans H. Gerth and C. Wright Mills, from Max Weber, *Essays in Sociology*, New York, Oxford University Press, 1946. (Weber's conceptualization of bureaucracy is also treated in Chapter 5.) Talcott Parsons, *The Structure of Social Action*, New York, McGraw-Hill, 1937; Talcott Parsons and Edward A. Shils, *Toward a General Theory of Action*, Cambridge, Mass., Harvard University Press, 1951, and *The Social System*, New York, Free Press, 1951. Parsons' social systems theory is also treated in Chapter 3.

[25] Adapted from Max G. Abbott, "Hierarchical Impediments to Innovation in Educational Organizations," in Max G. Abbott and John T. Lovell, eds., *Change Perspectives in Educational Administration*, Auburn, Ala., School of Education, Auburn University, 1965, p. 40.

1. A division of labor based on functional specialization. Since the tasks of an organization are too complex to be performed by a single individual, efficiency is promoted by assigning tasks and activities to specific offices or positions. Division of labor makes possible a degree of specialization that promotes improved performance in two ways: the employment of personnel on the basis of their technical qualifications, and the improvement of employee skills in a relatively narrow range of activities.

2. A well-defined hierarchy of authority. By arranging positions on the principle of hierarchy, there is a firmly ordered system whereby the lower offices are supervised by the higher ones having higher authority as well as responsibility for coordination.

3. A system of rules covering the rights and duties of employees. Rules that are more or less stable, more or less exhaustive, and can be learned constitute standards that assure reasonable uniformity in task performance. Together with the hierarchical structure, rules provide for both coordination of activities and continuity of operations.

4. A system of procedures for dealing with work situations. Formalization of procedures increases efficiency and productivity in performance and action, tending to preclude directives or performance based upon whim or caprice.

5. Impersonality of relationships. Rationality is enhanced by eliminating from official business love, hatred, and other emotional elements. Impersonality enhances rational decision making and equitable treatment of subordinates.

6. Selection and promotion based upon technical competence that constitutes a career. Promotion determined by seniority or achievement, tenure, fixed compensation rates, and retirement benefits assures protection from arbitrary treatment based partly on personal grounds.[26]

By contrast to Weber, who wrote primarily about a limited range of phenomena related to bureaucracy, Parsons developed a general theory of social action encompassing a wide range of individual, group, institutional, and even societal behavior. The following is only a sampling of Parsons' assumptions and concepts that are of value to the administrator:

1. Social action is goal-directed, and simple stimulus-response theories are inadequate to account for the facts of such action.

2. As a symbol-using animal, man is able to generalize from experience and to stabilize patterns of behavior through time.

---

[26] Cf. Max Weber, *The Theory of Social and Economic Organization,* translated by Talcott Parsons, New York, Free Press, 1947; Richard H. Hall, "The Concept of Bureaucracy: An Empirical Assessment," *The American Journal of Sociology,* 69 (July 1963), 33; and Abbott, op. cit.

3. These patterns may be analyzed most fruitfully in terms of systems.

4. Social action itself may be seen as a system representing a "compromise" in the interactions of the cultural, organic, personal, and social subsystems.

5. Perfect integration within an action system is not found in the empirical world, as motivated actors contend with the exigencies of survival in a particular environment.

6. Although perfect integration is probably unattainable, no system of action can survive unless the component subsystems are mutually consistent within some degree of tolerance.

7. In view of the strain toward inconsistency among the interconnecting systems, there is need for coordination within an action system so that there may be "continual action in concert."

8. The need for close coordination is most clearly seen in an organization, which may be defined as a "system of cooperative relationships" capable of "continual action in concert" and having "primacy of orientation to the attainment of a specific goal."

9. It is not sufficient for members of action systems to share cognitive and cathectic standards; they must also share value standards.

10. Among the value problems faced as "dilemmas of choice" in all action systems are:

   a. Affectivity–affective neutrality. That is, to get immediate gratification or to exercise self-restraint in the light of longer-term considerations.
   b. Self-orientation–collective orientation. That is, to serve self-interest or to serve the interest of a group to which one belongs.
   c. Universalism–particularism. That is, to treat objects and persons in accordance with a general norm covering all objects or persons in that class or to treat them in accordance with their standing in some particular relationship to oneself.
   d. Ascription–achievement. That is, to treat an object or person in the light of "what it is" or to treat it in the light of "what it does" or may be expected to do.
   e. Diffuseness–specificity. That is, to respond to many aspects of an object or person or to respond to a selection of those aspects.[27]

As with Weber's theory of bureaucracy, there also has been controversy regarding the ultimate value of Parsons' social systems theory. Even so, social systems theory has generated considerable empirical research, has led to the development of testable hypotheses, and has provided a frame of reference for describing and ordering complex phenomena in settings ranging from small groups to organizations to societies.[28]

[27] As cited in J. W. Getzels, James M. Lipham, and Roald F. Campbell, *Educational Administration as a Social Process,* New York, Harper & Row, 1968, pp. 48–49.

[28] Cf. R. Jean Hills, *Toward a Science of Organization,* Eugene, Center for the Advanced Study of Educational Administration, University of Oregon, 1968, p. 17;

Behavioral scientists, particularly in the fields of economics, sociology, and psychology, have come more and more to utilize mathematical and statistical procedures within the context of a general systems approach to study administration. Let us now turn to the contributions of this most recent trend in management thought—the quantitative systems approach to administration.

THE QUANTITATIVE SYSTEMS APPROACH

The quantitative systems approach to administration represents the fourth trend in management thought to originate during this century. In the mid-1920s the statistical probability theories of Pearson and Fisher were initially applied to decision problems of quality control in industry. During World War II, however, the application of quantitative methods received its greatest impetus. Such problems as radar placement, bomber losses, and convoy and submarine deployment were studied, analyzed, and solved mathematically through techniques that became known as operations research.[29] Operations research techniques utilized quantitatively based analytical methods to shed insight and generate recommendations for action concerning a wide range of decision problems.

The use of operations research and other quantitative techniques was extended considerably after World War II. Many problems that had been subjected to prescriptive or intuitive analysis prior to 1940 came under mathematical probing and scrutiny. The postwar development and utilization of electronic digital computers greatly increased the ability to perform with ease the analysis of many variables related to the solution of complex administrative problems. Many quantitative tools and techniques are currently being utilized in solving management problems in school administration. For example, linear and nonlinear programming have been applied to problems of student accounting, scheduling, and grade reporting, and to professional salary negotiations. Flow charting and PERT/CPM have been applied to such problems as management of research projects, schoolhouse construction or remodeling, and monitoring of curriculum development programs. Queuing theory has been utilized in studies of cafeteria efficiency. PPBS has been initiated for immediate and long-range planning in terms of programs, rather than traditional objects of expenditure. Simulation has

Robin M. Williams, Jr., "The Sociological Theory of Talcott Parsons," in Max Black, ed., *The Social Theories of Talcott Parsons; A Critical Examination,* Englewood Cliffs, N.J., Prentice-Hall, 1961, p. 99.

[29] James G. Crowther and Richard Whiddington, *Science at War,* New York, Philosophical Library, 1948, pp. 91–92.

developed as a technique for pre-service and in-service training of school principals. These quantitative tools and techniques may be properly viewed within the content of general systems theory.

Currently, there exists no single, all-inclusive, universally accepted, and clearly enunciated theory of general systems. The essence of systems thought, however, has been described by Immegart in terms of the following characteristics: [30]

1. The systems approach is a cross-disciplinary or interdisciplinary mode of thought, rich in both perspective and conceptual apparatus, which provides a viable approach to asking and answering questions. In a sense, it offers a "perspective on uncertainty."

2. The systems approach involves contextual, holistic thought that focuses on both wholes and relevant parts within an environmental context.

3. Systems thought includes the conscious process of reflection; it is methodical, coherent, designed, and analytic; and it accounts for referents, connections, interconnections, and direction.

4. Systems thought is concerned with linkages and patterns in time-space. Phenomena in the systems perspective are not viewed as isolated events but are assessed in context in an unfolding, irreversible time sequence. Furthermore, the systems approach is futuristic, focusing on what will be.

5. Systems thought analyzes structures through empirical referents, real proximity and juxtaposition, relevant parameters, and pertinent interfaces, not in abstract or superimposed terms.

6. The systems approach is ultimately operational, providing a realistic departure for manipulating variables in a complex context. End results are assessed not through rose-colored glasses, but in terms of relevant conditions and ultimate payoffs.

To understand the systems approach it is necessary to examine the nature of systems and the properties of systems.

Nature and properties of systems

Although several definitions of systems exist, the following global definition by Hall and Fagen incorporates the basic elements: "A system is a set of objects together with relationships between the objects and

[30] Adapted from Glenn L. Immegart, "The Systems Movement and Educational Administration," in Gerald G. Mansergh, ed., *Systems Approaches to the Management of Public Education*, Detroit, Metropolitan Detroit Bureau of School Studies, 1969, pp. 2–4.

between their attributes."[31] Grinker has defined a system as "some whole form in structure or operation, concepts or function, composed of united and integrated parts."[32] According to Hearn, it is possible to represent all forms of animate or inanimate matter as systems governed by certain constant principles discovered by scientists working in many fields, whether biology, gestalt psychology, or systems analysis.[33] Thus systems may range from small to large, simple to complex, or concrete to abstract.[34]

It has been observed that all systems exhibit the following properties:

STANDARD SET OF PROPERTIES THAT SYSTEMS EXHIBIT

1. All systems exist in *time-space*.
2. All systems tend toward a state of randomness and disorder, the ultimate of which is *entropy*, or inertia.
3. All systems have *boundaries*, which are more or less arbitrary demarcations of that included within and that excluded from the system.
4. All systems have *environment*, which is everything external to (without the boundary of) the system.
5. All systems have *factors* that affect the structure and function of the system. Factors within the system are *variables;* factors in the system's environment are *parameters*.
6. All but the largest systems have *suprasystems*.
7. All but the smallest systems have *subsystems*.[35]

A system may be viewed as open or closed, depending on the extent to which it exchanges matter, energy, and information with its immediately adjacent environment. That is, open systems have *inputs* and *outputs*. In this regard, of course, the school is an open system. At first glance, this statement may seem to be a tautology. The school principal receives and transmits information, communications, and resources, among a host of other exchange variables. But one of the difficulties in the administration of a school is the tendency of many to mix or confuse inputs with outputs. Consider, for instance, the student. Is he an input, an output, or a unique combination of both? For such purposes as budgeting and teacher allocations to the school, students in

[31] A. D. Hall and R. E. Fagen, "Definition of Systems," in *General Systems,* Yearbook of the Society for General Systems Research, vol. 1, 1956, p. 18.

[32] Roy R. Grinker, *Toward a Unified Theory of Human Behavior,* New York, Basic Books, 1956, p. 370.

[33] Gordon Hearn, *Theory Building in Social Work,* Toronto, Ont., Canada, University of Toronto Press, 1958, p. 38.

[34] James G. Miller, "Living Systems: Basic Concepts," *Behavioral Science,* 10 (July 1965), 201–209.

[35] Glenn L. Immegart, "Systems Theory and Taxonomic Inquiry into Organizational Behavior in Education," in Daniel E. Griffiths, ed., *Developing Taxonomies of Organizational Behavior in Educational Administration,* Skokie, Ill., Rand McNally, 1969, p. 167.

average daily membership (ADM) or average daily attendance (ADA) may be viewed as inputs. Yet in terms of assessment of the primary function of the school, facilitation of learning, the student is viewed as the school's prime output. Moreover, there often is even greater confusion not about what the inputs and outputs *actually are* but about what they *should be*. For these and other reasons, the administrative role in education, an intensive technology, is more complex than the administrative role in such other systems as those in processing or manufacturing technologies. Viewing the school as an open system alerts the principal to the input-output relationship and may prevent misunderstandings that can result when identical terms are being utilized within entirely opposite input-output contexts.

Other properties of open systems include their tendency to maintain themselves in *steady states* or *equilibrium* through *self-regulating* mechanisms. These properties encompass phenomena ranging from laws of physical motion to models of change; yet the principal who would be a leader—thereby disrupting some of the steady states of others—immediately senses the relevance of this principle in predicting both direction and intensity of resistance to his attempts to provide leadership. It should be observed, however, that the tendency toward a steady state need not be static; it may be dynamic. In a condition of dynamic equilibrium, the system is responding to change in either external or internal modifications in goals, objectives, or procedures. To reiterate, a steady state does not imply a static state; it might imply a continuous state of growth and change.

Open systems also display *equifinality;* that is, identical results may be obtained from initial conditions and circumstances that are quite different. The principle of equifinality calls attention to alternatives in the administrative processes of planning, organizing, stimulating, coordinating, and evaluating, where any one or combination of these activities may lead toward equally desirable outcomes.

Among other properties, open systems display *progressive segregation* (by dividing into hierarchically ordered subsystems) and *progressive mechanization* (by ordering certain activities and procedures into fixed arrangements). The school, for example, is typically segregated and mechanized in terms of such subsystems as departments or units, which are further comprised of classroom subsystems. Between and among the subsystems some conflicts inevitably occur. Although a tendency exists to regulate, resolve, or ameliorate persistent conflicts within or among the subsystems comprising a total system, such as a school, certain difficulties inherent in school administration exist because the subsystems are overlapping and sometimes poorly defined. For example, the formal subsystem organization of the school, divided along such lines as departmental or classroom subsystems, may bear only token resemblance to the informal subsystem organization (e.g., that developed among teachers along such lines as proximity, friendship, and age). Other subsystem structures may develop along the lines of leadership, decision making, or communication. Since more interaction occurs within subsystems than across subsystems, and since greater energy is required to transmit exchanges across subsystem boundaries than within them, articulation among subsystems becomes crucial if the total system or school is to operate smoothly. In the articulation process, the principal is located at critical points of tangency between and among the overlapping subsystems, hence the importance of his role.

A final property of open systems useful to the school principal is that *feedback* processes are essential if the system is to function effectively. Feedback, in a sense, is one output of a system (or subsystem), consisting of either informational or evaluative data useful to the total system and to the units within it. Feedback may be external or internal; it affects future system performance, serving as a control over changes in system and subsystem processes. The principle of feedback relates to both control and communication processes—cybernetic functions roughly analogous to the relationship of a thermostat to a furnace. One of the principal's main problems is determining how to structure adequate feedback processes within the school. In fact, there is some evidence that principals often depend on limited, biased, inaccurate, or even inappropriate data sources and feedback mechanisms. Another major problem facing the principal is deciding how to process the subsystem feedback that he does receive to restructure or realign inputs from the suprasystem to the subsystem.

The conceptualization of general systems permits one to view the school not only in terms of properties but also in terms of processes within a system or subsystem. A model of the school as a general system is shown in Figure 2.1, where inputs to the school in the form of operands and operators (principals, teachers, students, and material and facilities from the larger environment) are transformed into output (productivity, affectivity, and feedback) which, in turn, alter future system activity. Presumably, the resulting output and feedback subsequently affect both the new inputs to and processes of the system.

The process view of general systems helps one understand the relationships between and among the units and subunits within the school and between the school and the larger environment, including the school district and community. Increasingly, it is recognized that a major responsibility of the principal is to coalign inputs to the organization with the organizational structures, processes, and tasks to produce viable outcomes. Through the systems perspective, a comprehensive and extensive number of attributes of a school can be examined, and the linkages and relationships among the attributes can be scrutinized, analyzed,

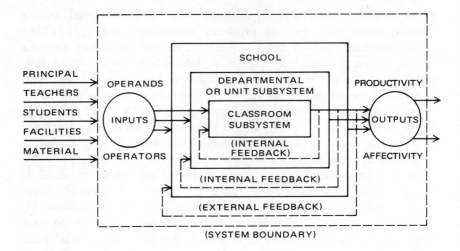

Figure 2.1
The school as a general system

and even costed. But how is this to be done? How may the principal utilize a systems approach in the administration of the school?

The principal and the systems approach

Although it may be too early yet to attempt a synthesis of the systems approach, we can draw on the work of others—particularly Kaufman, who has divided the systems approach to the administration of a school into two major categories: system analysis and system synthesis.[36] As Figure 2.2 indicates, system analysis includes the following steps: (1) identifying the problem, and (2) determining solution requirements and alternatives. System synthesis, on the other hand, involves three remaining steps: (3) choosing a solution strategy from alternatives, (4) implementing the solution strategy, and (5) determining performance effectiveness. System design or system modeling includes all five steps. In a systems approach we must consider each of the steps, including some tools and techniques useful to the school principal. Most principals already are familiar with the steps, since they approximate the stages in the scientific method.

[36] Roger A. Kaufman, "Systems Approaches to Education: Discussion and Attempted Integration," in Philip K. Piele, Terry L. Eidell, and Stuart C. Smith, eds., *Social and Technological Changes: Implications for Education,* Eugene, Center for the Advanced Study of Educational Administration, University of Oregon, 1970, pp. 162–163.

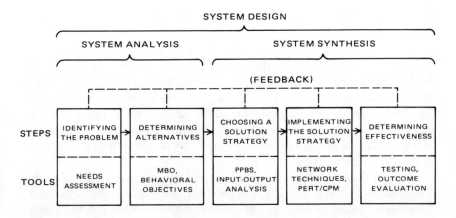

Figure 2.2
Administration in terms of system design, analysis, synthesis, stages, and tools for the improvement of education

SOURCE: Roger A. Kaufman, "System Approaches to Education: Discussion and Attempted Integration," in Philip K. Piele, Terry L. Eidell, and Stuart C. Smith, eds., *Social and Technological Change: Implications for Education,* Eugene, Oregon, Center for Advanced Study of Educational Administration, University of Oregon, 1970, pp. 143, 168.

IDENTIFYING THE PROBLEM

Whether through programmed situations or the assessment of unmet needs and emerging opportunities, becoming aware of the problem situation is the first stage in the systems approach to administration. Many of the decisions made by principals are programmed, routinized, or cyclical, and if roles are mutually understood and decision responsibilities clearly affixed, as stressed in the preceding section, such decisions present little difficulty to principals in terms of problem identification.

The assessment of unmet needs is another means for identifying the problem. In systems terms a need is a problem that exists because of a discrepancy that should be zero—a discrepancy that should not exist.[37] The discrepancy can be between two groups concerning a particular variable (e.g., Miss Jones' students on reading vs. Miss Smith's students on reading) or between the actual state ("what is") and the idealized state ("what should be"). For example, we may feel that no student in the school is being trained to be an "independent learner," which, of itself, may represent an educational need.[38] Once the educational needs have been expressed in terms of discrepancies, it is possible to generate

[37] John M. Gottman and Robert E. Clasen, *Evaluation in Education,* Itasca, Ill., Peacock, 1972, p. 46.
[38] Ibid.

measurable objectives by stating them as the reduction of needs over time.

Under prevailing conditions of scarce or limited resources, the principal must select the problem area that represents the greatest discrepancy or the most urgent need. While a needs assessment may start with symptoms or problems, it subsequently translates them into goals and objectives. Such objectives and goals should be stated in terms of performance or behavior rather than in terms of processes.[39] Thus a needs assessment will assist the principal in isolating significant problems and in designing appropriate alternative solutions.

The funding of federal projects, particularly those of Title III of the Elementary and Secondary Education Act, gave particular impetus to large-scale, statewide educational needs assessment. Although the studies done in some states were cursory, in other states the assessment of imperative educational needs was taken quite seriously. In Wisconsin, for example, individual interviews were conducted by trained survey researchers with representative random samples of school board members, educators, students, and citizens throughout the state.[40] The major thrust of the Wisconsin study was to determine educational needs and priorities in such areas as the following: subject fields, administrative services, teacher personnel, student personnel, educational programs, budget allocations, and instructional approaches.

The results were revealing. As might be expected, the respondent groups did not always agree regarding the priority that the educational needs should receive, yet several needs emerged as imperative. The following needs, in the order listed, were found to be most pressing in Wisconsin: reading, classroom facilities, individually guided instruction, education for teachers in motivating pupils, curricular development, and programs for students terminating formal education at the high school level. Results of needs assessment studies have proved to be particularly useful in making educational policy, program, and resource allocation decisions. Leading state departments, school districts, and schools throughout the nation have incorporated systematic and periodic needs assessment as an essential initial ingredient in their long-range planning.

DETERMINING ALTERNATIVES

The second stage of system analysis, formulating solution requirements and alternatives, involves the following:[41]

[39] Stephen Klein, Gary Fenstermacher, and Marvin C. Alkin, "The Center's Changing Evaluation Model," *Evaluation Comment*, Center for the Study of Evaluation, University of California, Los Angeles, 2 (January 1971), 9.

[40] James M. Lipham et al., *Wisconsin Educational Needs Assessment Study*, Madison, Wis., Department of Public Instruction, 1969.

[41] Adapted from Kaufman, op. cit., p. 148.

1. Conducting mission analysis. Mission analysis involves four stages:
   a. Identifying an overall mission objective: "Where are we going?"
   b. Determining constraints: "What are the things that will keep us from where we are going?"
   c. Removing constraints: "How do we eliminate those things that keep us from where we are going?"
   d. Preparing a mission profile: "What are the milestones along the way to where we are going?"
2. Performing function and task analysis: "What specifically must be done to get to each milestone?"
3. Performing methods-means analysis: "What are the possible alternatives for getting each function and task done?"
4. Formulating the criteria to be used in assessing alternatives.
5. Formulating the decision rules for selecting an alternative.

Techniques that are useful at this stage in system analysis include the utilization of management by objectives (MBO) at the administrative level and the specifying of behavioral objectives at the instructional level. Under MBO we find specifications of what is to be done, by whom, under what conditions, and in terms of which criteria. In the MBO approach the minimum, "average expected," and maximum results to be anticipated are also often specified. A major advantage of MBO is that it forces one to raise from an implicit to an explicit level the question, "Where are we going?" Principals who have utilized MBO also feel that the cooperative processes required in this approach increase the mutuality of understanding and empathy between organizational superiors and organizational subordinates.

CHOOSING A SOLUTION STRATEGY

The third stage in the systems approach is that of choosing a solution strategy from among the alternatives. It involves the following activities:[42]

1. Obtaining and assessing criterion information related to each decision alternative.
2. Applying the decision rules to the available criterion evidence. This may be straightforward and unambiguous or highly subjective and intuitive.
3. Choosing one alternative.
4. Reflecting on the efficacy of the indicated choice.
5. Confirming the indicated choice or rejecting it. The decision maker may seek more information, change the decision rules, formulate addi-

[42] Adapted from Phi Delta Kappa National Study Committee on Evaluation, *Educational Evaluation and Decision Making*, Itasca, Ill., Peacock, 1971, pp. 59–60.

tional alternatives, or retain the status quo, thereby choosing by default the alternative in use.

Three quantitative management tools—management information systems (MIS), planning-programming-budgeting systems (PPBS), and input-output (cost-effectiveness, cost-benefit, or cost-utility) analysis—are of particular significance at this stage, since each is designed to maximize the "wisdom" of the decision maker. Management information systems provide specific, instantaneous data along relevant dimensions concerning past and current system performance, thereby supplying the comparative information essential for an intelligent choice among alternatives. From MIS we acquire not only information but also procedures and techniques that are designed:

1. To measure progress being made toward specified objectives.
2. To modify or adjust objectives to reflect changes in the school.
3. To add, delete, or adjust programs to meet the modified objectives.
4. To provide multiyear forecasts of both objectives and programs.
5. To assist in choosing the most cost-effective set of programs to achieve either established or changing objectives.

Planning-programming-budgeting systems permit examination of the relative merits of alternatives by projecting programs into the future and by indicating the financial requirements of each program. The value of PPBS results from the systematic coordination of planning, programming, and budgeting. That is, PPBS do not and cannot apply only to a school's business operations. The major difference between a typical line-item budget of a school and a PPBS budget is that the conventional line-item budget is a statement of personnel, equipment, materials, and similar inputs to be bought, whereas PPBS is a statement of programs, objectives, or outputs to be accomplished. In PPBS the principal becomes intimately involved in initially designing, and subsequently costing, the program structure that is the heart of the process. In designing the program structure, attention may be given to subject matter (e.g., career education), grade level (e.g., third grade), target group (e.g., handicapped persons), object (e.g., textbooks), or specific activities (e.g., field trips) in instructional as well as supportive (e.g., guidance) services. Although the most desirable program structures have not yet been fully developed, PPBS hold great promise for formulating educational objectives more precisely and for coordinating curricular with fiscal planning. The principal is a key participant in developing, testing, or installing PPBS in all stages—planning or reducing goals to objectives, programming or devising program structures, and budgeting or assigning costs to the program structure.

Input-output (cost-effectiveness, cost-benefit, or cost-utility) analysis can be a means for examining alternatives by directly raising the questions, "What do I give?" and "What do I get?" Swanson explained the relationship of cost-benefit analysis to educational decision making as follows:

> Frequently a school system attempts to meet a set of objectives (normally unstated) through a variety of programs (normally undefined). For example, within a given system, at a given grade level, for a given subject, it is not unusual to find a variety of organizational patterns (i.e., self-contained classroom, team teaching, departmentalization, etc.). By systematically reviewing the resource requirements and the result of each alternative, the relative effectiveness of each becomes more apparent. If the alternative which most nearly meets the desired objectives also requires the least in inputs, the decision is obvious. However, if the most desirable output is also the most expensive in its input requirements, the decision makers must make value judgments concerning which will be to the system's advantage—high realization of objectives at high cost or a suboptimum realization of objectives at a lower cost. The decision makers' task is normally further complicated by the fact that the alternatives are not consistent in their superiority (or inferiority) in meeting specific objectives within the set of objectives. Once again value judgments must be brought to bear. Cost-utility analysis does not make decisions. It only makes available and arranges data in such a fashion as to sharpen the judgments of the decision makers.[43]

Figure 2.3 is a diagram of the relationship of input-output analysis to the decision processes in selecting solution strategies. As indicated, given the possibility of two alternative strategies for reaching an objective, estimations may be obtained of the output effect that is likely to be caused by altering controllable input variables, as well as by taking into account the noncontrollable environmental inputs. Such an analysis, if only an array of available information, may go a long way toward sharpening the judgment of the principal in selecting from alternatives a solution strategy to be implemented.

IMPLEMENTING THE SOLUTION STRATEGY

Even the decision thought to be best may founder at the decision-implementation stage. To monitor implementation of the solution strategy, two types of *process* evaluation—*implementation* evaluation and *progress* evaluation—are necessary. Implementation evaluation is designed to assess the extent to which the solution strategy is being carried out in the intended manner. Thus it involves investigating the degree to which the

---

[43] Austin D. Swanson, "Cost-Utility Analysis and Educational Decision Making," in Gerald G. Mansergh, ed., *Systems Approaches to the Management of Public Education,* Detroit, Michigan, Detroit Bureau of School Studies, 1969, p. 18.

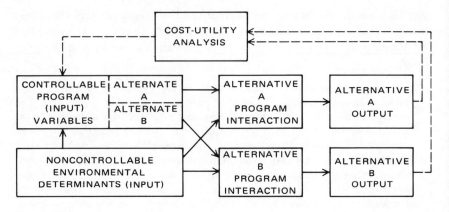

Figure 2.3

Use of input-output subsystem models in comparing the effectiveness of two allocation alternatives

SOURCE: Austin D. Swanson, "Cost-Utility Analysis and Educational Decision Making," in Gerald G. Mansergh, ed., *Systems Approaches to the Management of Public Education,* Metropolitan Detroit Bureau of School Studies, 1969, p. 19.

program plan or solution strategy is accurately and properly being carried out. Typical questions might be: "Did the supplies arrive on time?" "Are the students enrolled the ones for whom the program was intended?" or "Do the teachers have the qualifications needed to conduct the program?"[44] The information obtained is useful to the principal in deciding whether it is appropriate to allow the program to continue as it is presently operating or to make changes.

Progress evaluation, on the other hand, is aimed at determining whether the program is moving toward the achievement of its objectives.[45] A program may be implemented exactly as planned but still not reach its intended objectives. It would be clearly wasteful to install a program in the fall and wait until spring to learn that it had failed or that it might have been effective if corrective action had been taken earlier. Principals need information about progress at several junctures during the course of a program; this permits them to identify and quickly correct any problems that develop. Thus progress evaluation provides information on how a program is functioning relative to short-range objectives, as well as information about unforeseen or unanticipated outcomes that is also potentially valuable to the decision maker.[46] Implementation evaluation and progress evaluation are both forms of process

[44] Klein, Fenstermacher, and Alkin, op. cit., 9.

[45] Ibid.

[46] Ibid., 12.

evaluation and are discussed in greater detail in Chapter 9, which deals with the instructional program.

Several management tools are useful in both types of process evaluation, which are designed to monitor project implementation and progress. Although Gantt bar charts were initially conceived as one solution to the implementation monitoring dilemma, they did not fully integrate the parts of the system into a component whole as do more recent methods. To assist in planning the implementation of a solution strategy, procedures known as flow charting, flow graphing, or block-diagramming are often used. Flow chart methodology, which permits a synthesis of both the elements of the system and the operations that the system performs, is particularly useful in conceptualizing the relationship of functions to objectives. It highlights in interactive fashion both the major and the minor decisions that must be made.

In addition to use for monitoring particular projects or programs, the flow diagram can serve for conceptualizing the broad issues in administration. As an example, the entire systems approach originally shown as discrete stages in Figure 2.2 is depicted in flow chart terms in Figure 2.4. In this flow chart the decisions to be made by the principal are clearly highlighted in the diamond-shaped boxes.

Techniques more sophisticated than the simple flow chart have proved to be useful in monitoring program implementation. Network-based management techniques, such as program evaluation review technique (PERT) and critical path method (CPM), are particularly valuable in that they show not only what is happening in an overall effort but also how each activity affects all the other activities. According to Evarts, PERT/CPM usually requires as a first step the identification of program or project objectives.[47] Then the elements of the project are identified and placed in a hierarchical order, generally known as the workbreakdown structure, which may be composed of tasks, functions, or products. Based on the workbreakdown structure, a network consisting of activities or functions and events is developed in terms of workflow (usually read from left to right). The network integrates the constituent elements into their necessary sequence and dependency relationships, and it includes procedures for securing time estimates for the start and the completion of each of the activities or functions. Schedules are then developed for the accomplishment of the events or activities.

Cook summarized the entire process of PERT/CPM as follows:

> Once the project definition phase involving analysis has been completed, the workbreakdown structure prepared, the process of synthesis accom-

[47] Harry F. Evarts, *Introduction to PERT,* Boston, Allyn & Bacon, 1964, p. 11.

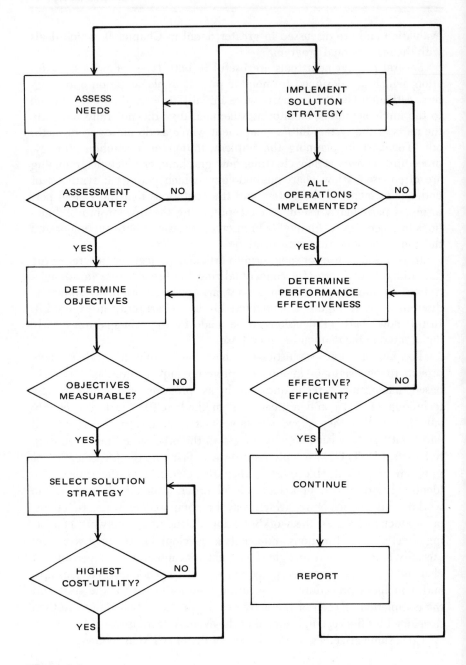

Figure 2.4
Flow diagram of the systems approach to administration

plished through the network or flow graph procedure, and the time esti-mates/schedule procedure completed, the essential steps of project planning have been accomplished. The result is a plan for the future—a graphical representation of the project tasks as they are to be accomplished in order to achieve the project objective.[48]

Although PERT and CPM are similar, the major difference between them should be noted. PERT is a probabilistic model that attempts to take into account the error in estimating the duration of each activity and consequently the project. The solution of a PERT network would lead to such statements as the following: There is a 95 percent chance that the project will be completed in between 50 and 60 days, or there is a 75 percent chance that the project will be completed before day 47.

The CPM model, on the other hand, is deterministic. Rather than focusing on errors of estimating activity duration, the CPM model as-sumes a linear relationship between time and cost, and time is expressed as a function of cost. We have two time estimates, normal time and crash time, and two cost estimates, normal cost and crash cost. The successive solutions to a time-cost CPM network may be many, since it is clear that duration of any activity can be shortened by incurring additional costs. As the duration estimates vary, so also will the critical path and activity slack leading to a number of solutions. The solution that best fits the budget or the time constraint, or, more frequently, that which best fits both, may be selected.

The difference between PERT and CPM rests in the identification of time associated with each activity. Activity durations based on proba-bilistic considerations reflect PERT, and durations based on cost func-tions reflect CPM. Computer programs are available to provide complete solutions to either PERT or CPM models.

An illustrative application of PERT/CPM to the conduct of a com-munity survey is presented in Chapter 13. Many other applications of PERT/CPM have been made in the field of education, including the establishment of new colleges and schools, the construction of schools, the staffing of programs, the scheduling of students, and the conduct of research projects. In one comprehensive high school with which we are familiar, the major activities that would need to be planned and orga-nized for the entire school year were identified through a review of memos, bulletins, calendars, and files.[49] Through PERT, the various ac-tivities were combined, responsibilities assigned, free and slack times

[48] Desmond L. Cook, *Better Project Planning and Control Through the Use of System Analysis and Management Techniques,* Columbus, Ohio State University, No-vember 1967, p. 12.

[49] Clinton R. Barter, *A PERT Network for James Madison Memorial High School,* Madison, Department of Educational Administration, University of Wiscon-sin, unpublished, 1970.

computed, and deadline dates established in chronological order for the principal, assistant principals, guidance counselors, department chairmen, teachers, secretaries, custodians, and students, as well as for committees, the central office, and feeder school personnel. The PERT diagram was widely distributed to all personnel. Not only did the principal attest to the viability of the procedure, the staff members, too, appreciated being able to plan in advance for their major responsibilities. They felt that they were able to develop a better understanding of their own and other peoples' contributions to the total administration and operation of the school. Communication throughout the school was greatly enhanced.

DETERMINING EFFECTIVENESS

The final stage in the systems approach to administration is the determination of the general worth of the implemented solution. Such judgments, typically called program certification, are based on *outcome* evaluations. These evaluations are concerned with examining the extent to which the objectives have been achieved, as well as with assessing the impact of the outcomes on subsequent decisions.[50] Outcome evaluation deals with questions such as, "Shall we extend the program to third graders as well as to second graders?" "Shall the program be tried in different subject fields?" and "Should we continue the program next year?" At this juncture, norm-referenced testing and criterion-referenced testing are the most obvious techniques for determining performance effectiveness, although a variety of other evaluative methods and instruments, such as interviews, observations, case studies, and rating scales, may be used.

Two types of tests, norm referenced and criterion referenced, are relevant to the making of decisions about performance effectiveness.[51] Norm-referenced measures, such as California, Iowa, STEP, SCAT, and other standardized tests, are used to assess an individual's performance in relationship to the performance of other individuals on the same measuring device. Criterion-referenced measures serve in assessing an individual's status with respect to some criterion, that is, a performance standard. The differential utility of these two kinds of information for various types of evaluation problems has led to using norm referenced measures for student evaluations and criterion-referenced tests for pro-

[50] Marvin C. Alkin, "Evaluation Theory Development," *Evaluation Comment,* Center for the Study of Evaluation, University of California, Los Angeles, 2 (October 1969), 5.

[51] Stephen Klein, "Evaluating Tests in Terms of the Information They Provide," *Evaluation Comment,* Center for the Study of Evaluation, University of California, Los Angeles, 2 (June 1970), 2.

gram as well as individual student evaluations. Although the two types of tests may require considerable effort in test construction, test taking, test scoring, and test analysis, both are necessary to provide the information needed for determining performance effectiveness. They are discussed in greater detail in the section of Chapter 9 that deals with the evaluation of the educational program.

Concerning the assessment of program effectiveness, several points should be emphasized. First, care should be taken to ensure that the assessment information does, in fact, bear a logical and direct relationship to identified needs and program objectives. Second, the assessment should be comprehensive, rather than based on a few, perhaps easily measurable, objectives. Finally, there exists a great need to develop and utilize a variety of assessment strategies, procedures, and measures. Excessive reliance on paper-and-pencil student achievement tests, for example, has been cited as only one of several limitations of the systems approach to school administration.

Problems and prospects of the systems approach

Utilization of the systems approach in school administration entails several pressing problems and reveals several promising prospects. Before looking to the systems approach as a panacea, one would be well advised to consider some of the problems involved in applying the systems approach in education. These include the following, some of which have been alluded to earlier:

1. PHILOSOPHICAL OBJECTIONS. In the systems approach, emphasis is on testing, efficiency, accountability, and orderliness, which can be antithetical to the essence of human life and freedom, as well as to organizational decentralization.[52]

2. CENTRALIZING TENDENCY. Since many of the systems procedures are more economically efficient if planned, installed, and operated at the central office level, there is a tendency for control to be centered at this level, instead of at the school building level.

3. CONFUSION OVER TERMINOLOGY. Dozens of acronyms exist for procedures that may be similar or even identical, and this may make for misunderstanding or misapplication of concepts.[53] PERT. SPED etc.

4. PREOCCUPATION WITH MATHEMATICAL MODELS. Because models are complex it does not follow that they are adequate.[54] Models should be

---

[52] Kaufman, op. cit., pp. 171–172.

[53] Harry J. Hartley, "Educational Planning, Programming, and Budgeting: A Systems Approach," in Mansergh, ed., op. cit., p. 27.

[54] Immegart, "The Systems Movement and Educational Administration," op. cit., p. 10.

carefully examined to see that they represent or fit into the specific operational context of a school.

5. GOAL DISTORTION. There may be a tendency to place greater emphasis on minimal goals that can be easily measured, to the neglect of more important goals that are difficult to measure quantitatively.[55] Moreover, weak measures may be substituted as evidence of important goals, thereby distorting the goals themselves.[56]

Although many other conceptual, operational, and even philosophical limitations might be noted, the power and utility of the systems approach, with its new generation of management tools and techniques, offer great potential for increasing the rationality of the principal in making educational decisions. As indicated earlier, the systems approach to planning is interdisciplinary, drawing its concepts from many formerly disparate fields. It involves the conscious process of reflection, it is methodical and analytical, it accounts for actual referents and operational relationships, and it includes a number of useful management tools. In a sense, it is a mode of thought that sets the proper stage for decision making in that the decisions made thereby become more rational, objective, and systematic. In the next chapter we treat the play mounted on that stage, the school as a social system.

Summary

In this chapter antecedents to the systems approach to the study of administration were discussed, including scientific management, administrative process, human relations, behavioral science, and quantitative approaches to management. Next the concept of general systems was introduced in terms of system properties and system processes. A synthesis of the systems approach was presented in the following five stages: identifying the problem, determining alternatives, choosing a solution strategy, implementing the solution strategy, and determining effectiveness. The utility to the principal of several management tools in the systems approach was discussed, including management by objectives (MBO), planning-programming-budgeting systems (PPBS), input-output analysis, flow charting, program evaluation review technique/critical path method (PERT/CPM), and norm-referenced and criterion-referenced testing. Finally, some limitations and some advantages of the systems approach to school administration were briefly considered.

[55] Hartley, op. cit., p. 29.

[56] Thorne Hacker, "Management by Objectives for Schools," *Administrator's Notebook*, 20 (November 1971), 1–4.

SUGGESTED ACTIVITIES

1. Compare and contrast the historical antecedents in educational administration with the historical antecedents in business or public administration.

2. Conduct a systematic educational needs assessment and contrast the results by type of school or community.

3. Utilizing an MBO approach, have a principal meet with either his superintendent or his teachers to derive a set of educational objectives. Critique the objectives in terms of the evidence necessary to measure them.

4. In terms of PPBS, devise a program structure for given subjects, grades, target groups, objects, or activities, and assign costs to the program structure. Compare the PPBS budget with the traditional line-item budget.

5. Develop a flow chart or PERT/CPM network for an administrative task. Compare charts and/or networks in terms of tasks and personnel involved in various types of schools.

SELECTED REFERENCES

ALIOTO, ROBERT F., and J. A. JUNGHERR, *Operational PPBS for Education,* New York, Harper & Row, 1971.

BANGHART, FRANK W., *Educational Systems Analysis,* New York, Macmillan, 1969.

BLOOM, BENJAMIN S., J. THOMAS HASTINGS, and GEORGE F. MADAUS, *Handbook on Formative and Summative Evaluation of Student Learning,* New York, McGraw-Hill, 1971.

GOTTMAN, JOHN M., and ROBERT E. CLASSEN, *Evaluation in Education, A Practitioner's Guide,* Itasca, Ill., Peacock, 1972.

GRIFFITHS, DANIEL E., ed., *Developing Taxonomies of Organizational Behavior in Educational Administration,* Skokie, Ill., Rand McNally, 1969.

IMMEGART, GLENN L., and FRANCIS J. PILECKI, *An Introduction to Systems for the Educational Administrator,* Reading, Mass., Addison-Wesley, 1973.

KNEZEVICH, STEPHEN J., *Administration of Public Education,* 2nd ed., New York, Harper & Row, 1969, chap. 29.

MANSERGH, GERALD G., ed., *Systems Approaches to the Management of Public Education,* Detroit, Metropolitan Detroit Bureau of School Studies, 1969.

PIELE, PHILIP K., TERRY L. EIDELL, and STUART C. SMITH, *Social and Technological Change, Implications for Education,* Eugene, The Center for the Advanced Study of Educational Administration, University of Oregon, 1970.

THOMAS, J. ALAN, *The Productive School, A Systems Analysis Approach to Educational Administration,* New York, Wiley, 1971.

VAN DUSSELDORP, RALPH A., DUANE E. RICHARDSON, and WALTER J. FOLEY, *Educational Decision-Making Through Operations Research,* Boston, Allyn & Bacon, 1971.

CHAPTER 3

Social systems theory

The school is a social system whose administration is above all a social process. Understanding of social systems theory, therefore, is basic for effective performance in the principalship.

After a basic definition of social system has been presented, we examine the institutional, personal, cultural, and other dimensions of social systems with particular emphasis on the school.[1] Next the utility of social systems theory for achieving organizational-individual integration is demonstrated. In the final section we trace the relevance of social systems theory for the understanding of satisfaction, effectiveness, efficiency, and morale within the school.

Definition of social system

The basic concept of social systems theory was derived by Parsons;[2] the basic application of social systems theory to administration was delineated by Getzels and others.[3] Parsons defined a social system as follows:

> . . . a plurality of individual actors interacting with each other in a situation which has at least a physical or environmental aspect, actors who are motivated in terms of a tendency to the "optimization of gratification" and whose relation to their situations, including each other, is defined and mediated in terms of a system of culturally structured and shared symbols.[4]

---

[1] Portions of this chapter are drawn from J. W. Getzels, James M. Lipham, and Roald F. Campbell, *Educational Administration as a Social Process*, New York, Harper & Row, 1968.

[2] Talcott Parsons, *The Social System*, New York, Free Press, 1951.

[3] J. W. Getzels and Egon G. Guba, "Social Behavior and the Administrative Process," *School Review*, 65 (1957), 423–441; J. W. Getzels and Herbert A. Thelen, "The Classroom as a Unique Social System," in Nelson B. Henry, ed., *The Dynamics of Instructional Groups*, Chicago, National Society for the Study of Education, University of Chicago Press, 1960, pp. 53–62.

[4] Parsons, op. cit., pp. 5–6.

Carr has likewise defined a social system as an "aggregation of individuals and institutional organizations located in an identifiable geographical locality and functioning in various degrees of interdependence as a permanent organized unit of the social order."[5] Thus social systems are concerned with the behavioral aspects of systems.

Some fundamental explanatory characteristics of social systems noted in the definition are the presence of individuals in purposive interaction, the interdependence of the interaction, and the structure of interaction into institutions or organizations having a physical or geographic referent. In addition to being viewed purposively, structurally, and functionally, social systems may also be viewed geographically, historically, economically, and politically. The emphasis herein, however, is on the anthropological, sociological, and psychological aspects of social systems.

In general usage, the concept of a social system has referred to large aggregates of human interaction, such as a neighborhood community, a city, a region, a state, or "total society." But the concept need not be restricted by the size of the interactions under consideration. As Homans has observed:

> The activities, interactions, and sentiments of the group members, together with the mutual relations of these elements with one another during the time the group is active, constitute what we shall call the *social system*. . . . Everything that is not part of the social system is **part** of the environment in which the system exists.[6]

Understanding of the concept of social systems will be useful to the principal regardless of the level or magnitude of the system under consideration—whether a classroom, a department or team unit, a school, a school district, or an entire community. Our major focus, however, is on the school as a social system and the role of the principal, the leader of the school.

The school as a social system

The school may be conceived as a social system involving two classes of phenomena that are independent and at the same time interactive. These are, first, the institutions, having certain roles and expectations, that will fulfill the goals of the system; and second, the individuals, having certain personalities and need-dispositions, who inhabit the system. The social

[5] Lowell J. Carr, *Analytical Sociology, Social Situations and Social Problems,* New York, Harper & Row, 1955, p. 167.

[6] George C. Homans, *The Human Group,* New York, Harcourt Brace Jovanovich, 1950, p. 87.

behavior of those inhabiting the system may be understood as a function of these major elements: institution, role, and expectation, which together constitute the *normative* or *nomothetic* dimension; and the individual, personality, and need-disposition, which together constitute the *personal* or *idiographic* dimension of activity in a social system. To understand, predict, or control observed behavior in a social system, one must understand the nature and interaction of the elements.

THE NORMATIVE DIMENSION

In a sense, the normative dimension may be thought of as the sociological level of analysis of social behavior. The component conceptual elements of the normative dimension are institution, role, and expectations.

All societies have certain imperative functions that through time come to be accomplished in routinized patterns (e.g., governing, policing, healing, or educating), and these functions become "institutionalized." Thus the school has become the *institution* devoted to educating. Like all institutions, the school is purposive, peopled, and normatively structured.

An important unit of the institution is the role. *Roles* represent dynamic aspects of positions, offices, or statuses within the institution. Thus the school may be viewed in terms of such established roles as principal, teacher, and student. Roles are defined in terms of role *expectations,* which are the normative rights and duties of a role incumbent. When the role incumbent puts these rights and duties into effect, he is performing his role.

Roles are complementary in that each role derives its meaning from other interlocking roles within an institution. A role, in a sense, is a prescription not only for a role incumbent but also for the interlocking role; thus the rights of the one may be the obligations of the other, or the expectations of the one may constitute the sanctions for the other. For example, the role of the principal cannot be defined fully except in relation to the role of the teacher, and the converse is true. This characteristic of complementarity fuses the roles into a coherent, interactive unit and makes it possible to conceive of an institution as having a characteristic structure.

As Coladarci and Getzels have noted, roles may vary greatly in scope, ranging from functionally diffuse to functionally specific.[7] In a functionally diffuse relationship the role incumbents are bound in such a way that the mutual rights and obligations are taken for granted and are in a sense limitless. In such a relationship it is necessary to prove that a par-

[7] Arthur P. Coladarci and J. W. Getzels, *The Use of Theory in Educational Administration,* Stanford, Calif., School of Education, Stanford University, 1955, pp. 19–23.

ticular expectation is *not* within the province of the relationship—for example, the family relationship wherein "blood is thicker than water." In a functionally specific relationship the rights and obligations are restricted to the elements in the relationship defined by the institutional status or technical competence of the participants. In such a relationship it is necessary to prove that a particular expectation *is* within the province of the relationship—for example, the principal-teacher relationship. Although administrative relationships are typically set up in functionally specific terms, through extended formal and informal contact over time, functionally specific relationships may drift toward functional diffuseness. This circumstance is neither a vice nor a virtue, but it can pose problems for the principal.

Although roles are institutional "givens" in that they are ordinarily formulated before the actors who will fulfill particular roles are known, roles are to some extent flexible. The behaviors expected of a role may be thought of as lying along a continuum from "required" or "absolutely must" to "prohibited" or "absolutely must not." That is, behaviors crucial to the role are held as mandatory; other behaviors are forbidden. Between the two extremes lie other behaviors; some may be encouraged and others discouraged, but all might be permissible. Their exact nature is a function not only of the role expectations but also of the particular role incumbent, and we now turn to a consideration of the individual, personality, and need-disposition.

THE PERSONAL DIMENSION

Thus far behavior in social systems has been seen as deriving from the normative dimension, as if all role incumbents were actors and would implement a role in a given way. But roles are filled by individuals, and no two are exactly alike. Each individual stamps the roles he occupies with the unique style of his own pattern of behavior. Despite adherence to district-wide role descriptions for the principalship, for example, no principal administers a school, even in the same district, in exactly the same way as another principal. To understand, predict, or control behavior in a specific social system, therefore, it is also necessary to know what kinds of individuals inhabit the roles and their modes of perceiving and reacting to the expectations. That is, the psychological aspects as well as the sociological aspects of behavior, or the personal dimension as well as the normative dimension, must be considered.

Just as it was possible to analyze the institution in terms of role and expectation, we can also analyze the individual in terms of personality and need-disposition. Although, like "role," the term has had a wide variety of meanings in popular usage, *personality* is defined as the dynamic organization within the individual of the need-dispositions and capacities that determine his unique interaction with the environment. The dynamic aspect implies that personality is motivational, constantly evolving and self-regulating.

Need-dispositions, a conjoined term, refers on the one hand to the tendency to fulfill some requirements or to accomplish some end states of the organism; on the other hand, it refers to a disposition to do something with an object designed to accomplish this end state. Need-dispositions are goal-oriented, referring to the motivating forces in personality that coordinate activity of an individual in the direction of definable, short-term aims as well as long-term goals. Need-dispositions influence not only the goals an individual will try to attain but also the way an individual will perceive and cognize the environment itself. In a study of teaching teams, for example, Gilberts found that some teachers preferred a team teaching arrangement to a traditional school structure for the opportunities the former provided to fulfill a need for inclusion and interaction with others.[8] Still others preferred team teaching because it offered opportunities to fulfill a need for control and dominance over others. Thus the influence of need-dispositions on perception and cognition is of great importance, for it suggests that an individual not only will seek a given role in accordance with his personality but also will tend, consciously or unconsciously, to perceive, cognize, and structure the role in accordance with his need-dispositions.

Like role expectations, which may vary in functional specificity or diffuseness, need-dispositions may vary in the specificity or generality of objects, roles, or goals through which they find expression. In the one case, termed the "universalistic alternative," the significance of an object, role, or goal depends on its membership in a general class; in the other case, termed the "particularistic alternative," only a particular object, role, or goal will serve to satisfy the need-disposition. Just as an organizational role is ordinarily flexible enough to permit effective performance by a variety of personalities, the individual personality is ordinarily flexible enough to perform satisfactorily in a variety of roles.

Finally, need-dispositions are patterned and interrelated. As Maslow has indicated, needs are organized hierarchically (as well as patterned horizontally) to give personality a structure not explicable by a mere listing of separate need attributes.[9] He has categorized the arrangement of needs in a hierarchy of greater or less priority or potency and has indicated that the satisfaction of one need has an effect on the activation of

[8] Robert D. Gilberts, "The Interpersonal Characteristics of Teaching Teams," doctoral dissertation, University of Wisconsin, 1961.

[9] Abraham H. Maslow, *Motivation and Personality,* New York, Harper & Row, 1954.

other needs. Thus the personality and its relation to a role is not static, but dynamic. We next consider the dynamic role-personality relationship.

THE BASIC MODEL

Review 53 & 54

How do the dimensions of behavior, the normative and the personal, come together to produce observed behavior? In the basic model (Figure 3.1), the normative dimension of behavior appears at the top of the diagram, consisting of institution, role, and expectation, and each term is the analytic unit for the term preceding it. Similarly, the personal dimension of behavior (bottom of diagram) consists of individual, personality, and need-disposition, each term again serving as the analytic unit for the term preceding it. An act of social behavior derives simultaneously from the normative and the personal dimensions. Behavior in a social system is a function of the interaction between a given institutional role, defined by the expectations attaching to it, and the personality of a particular role incumbent, defined by his need-dispositions. That is, social behavior may be understood as resulting from an individual's attempts to cope, in ways consistent with his own patterns of needs and dispositions, with an environment composed of patterns of expectations for his behavior.

The proportion of role and personality factors varies with the specific system, the specific role, and the specific personality involved. The interaction of factors entering into a given segment of social behavior is depicted in Figure 3.2. Behavior may be regarded as a balance between normative and personalistic variables represented by a broken vertical line cutting through the role and personality possibilities represented by the rectangle. At the left (line A), the proportion of behavior dictated by considerations of role expectations is relatively large (as in the military,

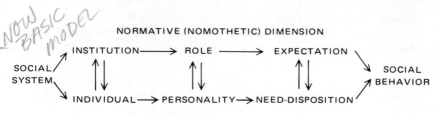

KNOW BASIC MODEL

Figure 3.1
Normative and personal dimensions of social behavior

SOURCE: Adapted from J. W. Getzels and E. G. Guba, "Social Behavior and the Administrative Process," *School Review*, 65 (1957), 429. Copyright © 1957 by the University of Chicago.

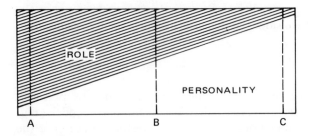

Figure 3.2

Varying proportions of role and personality components in social behavior

SOURCE: Adapted from J. W. Getzels and E. G. Guba, "Social Behavior and the Administrative Process," *School Review*, 65 (1957), 430. Copyright © 1957 by the University of
Chicago.

where much behavior is prescribed). At the right (line C), the proportions are reversed; behavior is dictated largely by considerations of personality (as in an artists' colony, where much is left to individual choice).
It might be hypothesized that in schools the proportions of role and personality considerations would be balanced somewhere between the two
extremes (line B). Interestingly, however, even in informal discussions
principals may utilize a military analogy—"We run a 'loose ship' around
here."

Recognizing that sociological and psychological considerations were
essential, but not sufficient, to account for the manifold variation in observed behavior in social systems, Getzels and Thelen extended the basic
model to include additional dimensions.[10]

THE CULTURAL DIMENSION

Expectations for behavior in a given institution derive from the requirements of the social system of which the institution is a part and from the
values of the culture that is the context for a particular social system.
These value differences impinge directly not only on the institution but
also on specific roles and individuals within the institution and are related to variations between total cultures, as well as within cultures. In
a sense, the cultural dimension may be considered to be the anthropological level of analysis. Thus the role of headmaster in a British secondary
school may differ considerably from that of principal in an American
secondary school, or the role of principal in an inner-city school may
differ substantially from that of principal in a rural consolidated school.
An older principal of an urban ghetto school, perhaps unconsciously,

[10] Getzels and Thelen, op. cit., pp. 53–82.

was observing such cultural impingement when he lamented somewhat as follows:

> This job is not what it used to be. I'll bet that 90 percent of my time is spent with compensatory programs, the police, community meetings, black or brown berets, teacher aides, student disruptions, and extended day programs. Now we even serve breakfast. I'm ready to requisition a couch.

Just as it was possible to analyze the normative dimension in terms of role expectations, and just as it was possible to analyze the personal dimension in terms of need-dispositions, it is possible to analyze the cultural dimension in terms of *value orientations*. The term *value*, like role or personality, has been variously defined. Kluckhohn called value "a conception, explicit or implicit, distinctive of an individual or charac- teristic of a group, of the desirable which influences the selection from available modes, means, and ends of action."[11] Spindler similarly defined values as objects of possession, conditions of existence, personality or categorical features, and states of mind that are conceived as desirable and act as motivating determinants of behavior.[12] One should observe that in these definitions cultural values relate both to the normative and to the personal dimensions.

In examining the American culture, Getzels drew a distinction be- tween *sacred* values and *secular* values.[13] He defined sacred values as those constituting the basic and undivorceable beliefs—democracy, indi- vidualism, equality, and human perfectibility. Conflict concerning these values is minimal, since most people subscribe to them, at least in the ideal sense. Secular values, on the other hand, are characterized by nu- merous conflicts and cleavages based on regional, rural-urban, social class, and other differences. Noting that secular values are transformed through social change from *traditional* to *emergent*, Getzels conceptual- ized this shift in values and Prince developed an instrument to measure value orientations according to the following major changes: (1) from the work success ethic to an ethic of sociability, (2) from future-time orientation to present-time orientation, (3) from personal independence to group conformity, and (4) from moral commitment to moral rela- tivism.[14] The *emergent* secular values now appear to be changing, if not

[11] Clyde Kluckhohn et al., "Values and Value Orientations in the Theory of Action," in Talcott Parsons and Edward A. Shils, eds., *Toward a General Theory of Action*, Cambridge, Mass., Harvard University Press, 1951, p. 395.

[12] George Spindler, "Education in a Transforming American Culture," *Harvard Educational Review*, 25 (Summer 1955), 156.

[13] J. W. Getzels, "Changing Values Challenge the Schools," *School Review*, 65 (1957), 92–102.

[14] Ibid.; Richard Prince, "Individual Values and Administrative Effectiveness," *Administrator's Notebook*, 6 (December 1957), 1–4.

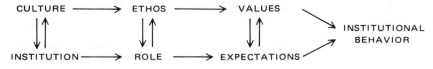

Figure 3.3

Relationship of the cultural and institutional dimensions of behavior

SOURCE: Adapted from J. W. Getzels and H. A. Thelen, "The Classroom as a Unique Social System," in N. B. Henry, ed., *The Dynamics of Instructional Groups,* Fifty-Ninth Yearbook of the National Society for the Study of Education, Chicago, University of Chicago Press, 1960, p. 72.

recycling, in the direction of *postemergent* values: (1) from an ethic of sociability to one of social responsibility, (2) from present-time orientation to an ethic of relevance, (3) from group conformity to personal authenticity, and (4) from moral relativism to moral commitment.[15]

The relationship between the anthropological and sociological dimensions is represented in Figure 3.3. The diagram indicates that institutional behavior may be understood as a function not only of the institution, with its structural roles and expectations, but also of the cultural ethos, with its predominant values.

Thus far we have examined the relationship between cultural values and institutional expectations as if the cultural values were "out there"—an extraorganizational force. For certain purposes, of course, this conceptualization is correct. As an example, we need only reflect on the plight of an elementary principal faced with a rabidly traditional community group that not only expects but demands that he throw out the existing reading program and adopt the McGuffy readers. Similar values-expectations conflicts could be documented many times over regarding such issues as career education, ethnic history, and sex and family life education. In fact, most of the attempts to legislate the curriculum at the state level and many of the cabals to change local curricula highlight the nature and extent of the cultural values–insitutional expectations relationship.

As the definitions by Kluckhohn and Spindler indicate, however, values not only define a culture, they also describe the individual. The personality of the individual is fundamentally and integrally related to the values of the culture in which the organism grows up. Certainly the individual is not born with a ready-made set of cultural values; rather, he acquires a set of adaptive attitudes, beliefs, and values through the processes of identification and socialization. For school personnel who are explicitly or implicitly charged with responsibility for "transmission

[15] J. W. Getzels, "On the Transformation of Values: A Decade after Port Huron," *School Review,* 80 (August 1972), 505–519.

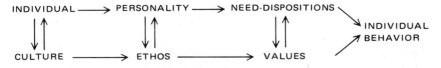

Figure 3.4
Relationship of the personal and cultural dimensions of behavior

of the cultural heritage" or "inculcation of values," this relationship needs no amplification. Suffice it to observe, therefore, that just as institutional role expectations are related to a context of value, individual personality dispositions are related to a context of value.

Figure 3.4 depicts the relationship between the anthropological and the psychological dimensions. The diagram suggests that individual behavior may be understood as a function of both the need-dispositions and the values of the individual.

OTHER DIMENSIONS

Behavior in social systems, of course, derives from many considerations other than the normative, personal, and cultural dimensions. Among these patterned considerations are, at least, the biological, economic, and political dimensions, which are treated only briefly, since no formulation can deal equally with all the complex determinants of behavior.

In the biological dimension, as Getzels and Thelen have observed, the inherent capacities, impulses to action, mental and physical abilities, and predispositions of the organism are powerful behavioral determinants.[16] Although concern with these matters often falls within the domains of biological and medical science, their relevance, particularly to the personal dimension of social behavior, must not be overlooked. In this regard, for example, one need only reflect about the short-term and long-range effects on the total social system of a school when the principal suffers a heart attack. A limited number of studies, particularly those concerned with leadership of social systems, have included measurement of such biological variables as height, weight, size, and metabolism, and a few investigations associated with manned space flight have examined the effects of temperature, weightlessness, and confinement on decision making and social interaction; but additional collaboration between social and biological scientists is needed to expand our frontiers of knowledge in this domain.

Regarding the economic dimension, the resources brought to bear on the institution and the individual are powerful determinants of social be-

[16] Getzels and Thelen, op. cit., p. 72.

havior.[17] In terms of the normative dimension, for example, many compensatory educational programs and federal title programs are tangible expressions of the complex interrelationships of economic resources, cultural values, and expectations for the school as an institution. In terms of the personal dimension, we need only observe that matters of salary, fringe benefits, and working conditions, most of which involve economic considerations, are also of great concern to the individual and have direct effect on the school as a social system. This was observed recently by a principal who stated: "During the first semester when you go in the teachers' lounge they are all talking kids; during the second semester, they are all talking money."

Regarding the political dimension, it is increasingly obvious that organized power relationships external to the social system of the school and internal to the school are altering significantly our notions concerning the political insularity of the school. Indeed, the school has become the arena wherein some of the most bitterly fought political issues, formerly settled at other levels, are being decided. Again, only a few isolated case studies of the political dimension of behavior in the school as a social system have been conducted utilizing such concepts as power relations, distributions, and linkages; power processes; and power exercise and utilization. In fact, it is still not uncommon to encounter naïve principals who mourn their "loss of power" yet have little understanding of the relationship of the political to the other dimensions of the school as a social system.

THE OPERATIONAL MODEL

In terms of the basic social systems model (Figure 3.1), it was proposed that the primary determinants of social behavior consisted of two major dimensions, the normative and the personal. Other dimensions—cultural, biological, economic, and political—were also considered. But the cultural dimension is particularly relevant. Since to some extent the institutional role expectations and the individual need-dispositions have their source in and are related to the culture in which the system operates, the operational model in the analysis of the administrative relationships of the school principal is viewed as composed of these salient elements: the interaction of *role* and *personality* in the context of *value*. The relationships among these dimensions are represented graphically in the operational model shown in Figure 3.5.

In the foundational chapters that follow, this operational model serves to explicate the complex relationships and conflicts with which the principal must deal, as well as to clarify the leadership role of the principal. However, the model also illuminates both the nature of the individual-

---

[17] Getzels, Lipham, and Campbell, op. cit., p. 103.

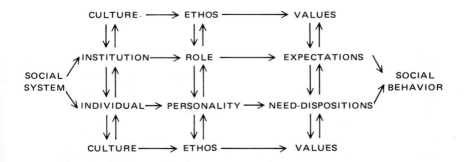

Figure 3.5
Operational model of major dimensions of social behavior
SOURCE: J. W. Getzels, "Conflict and Role Behavior in the Educational Setting," in W. W. Charters, Jr., and N. L. Gage, eds., *Readings in the Social Psychology of Education,* Boston, Allyn & Bacon, 1963, p. 312.

institutional relationship and the criteria for assessing behavior in organizations, and we now discuss these conceptual derivations from the model.

Organizational-individual integration

The social systems model demonstrates power and parsimony in dealing with the relationship of the individual to the organization. The relevance of the model for the school principal becomes apparent when it is observed that the administration of a school inevitably entails the fulfillment of both normative (institutional) role expectations and personal (individual) need-dispositions while the goals of the school and the goals of the individual are being achieved. It is a unique function of the principal to integrate the expectations of the organization and the dispositions of the individual in a way that is simultaneously fruitful for the organization and satisfying for the individual.

When an individual performs in accordance with expectations, he is *adapting to the role*. The adaptive person seeks criteria for behavior outside himself; he adjusts his behavior in terms of the expectations of those above, below, and even parallel to him in the organization. He typically makes his way in the system through conformity rather than creativity, becoming an "organization man" or, in the case of the pupil, a "model student." He does not so much act as react, and as Abbott has noted, the actions he does take may be "status charades" of the bureaucratic type.[18] In short, in Halpin's terms the person becomes "inauthen-

---

[18] Max G. Abbott, "Hierarchical Impediments to Innovation in Educational Organizations," in Max G. Abbott and John T. Lovell, eds., *Change Perspectives in Educational Administration*, Auburn, Ala., School of Education, Auburn University, 1965, pp. 40–53.

tic"—playing rather than living a role; agreeing when his impulse is to disagree; smiling when his impulse is to cry.[19] At the extreme, he may become withdrawn and altogether fearful of taking any actions or making any significant decisions.

Conversely, when an individual performs in accordance with his needs he is actualizing himself. The self-actualizing person seeks criteria for behavior within himself; he stresses his own rather than organizational goals, feeling free to disregard even mandatory role expectations when they are contrary to his need-dispositions. His orientation is not to the organization but to self. The sanctions that can be applied in a school, including assignment to undesirable duties, personal ostracism, and isolation, are invoked against the "maverick"—typically to the great discomfort of all involved. The consequence for the person is loss of a sense of belongingness, resulting in alienation.

The principal must cope with the indicated dysfunctional modes of behavior so that ideally a given behavioral act will facilitate both role adaptation and self-actualization—so that the relationship between the individual and the organization is integrated. Two forces that may be brought to bear on the problem are *personalization* of the role and *socialization* of the personality. Together, these forces constitute what Bakke has called the *fusion* process (see Figure 3.6).[20] Within this view, the interaction between position and function of the organization and

---

[19] Andrew W. Halpin and Don B. Croft, *The Organizational Climate of Schools,* Chicago, Midwest Administration Center, 1963, pp. 77–116.

[20] E. Wight Bakke, *The Fusion Process,* New Haven, Conn., Labor and Management Center, Yale University, 1953.

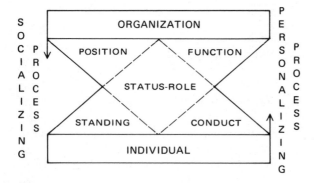

Figure 3.6

The fusion process

SOURCE: Adapted from E. Wight Bakke, *The Fusion Process,* New Haven, Conn., Labor and Management Center, Yale University, 1953, p. 20.

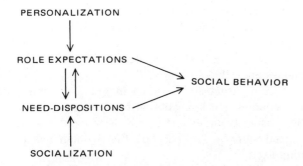

Figure 3.7
Personalization and socialization forces on normative and personal axes of behavior
SOURCE: J. W. Getzels, James M. Lipham, and Roald F. Campbell, *Educational Adminis-
tration as a Social Process*, New York, Harper & Row, 1968, p. 123.

standing and conduct of the individual is seen as simultaneously recon-
structing both the individual and the organization. The fusion or integration process is illustrated in social system terms in Figure 3.7, where
personalization appears as a force acting on role expectations, whereas
socialization appears as a force acting on need-dispositions, each tending
to push the normative and personal axes toward congruence.

It might seem that the school is so structured that little can be done
with personalization of roles. But as we shall indicate (particularly in
Chapter 9, which deals with the instructional program), the emerging
practices of differentiated staffing, team teaching, and individualized instruction seem to hold promise for altering the traditional role structures
of the school to take into account the idiosyncratic needs and capacities
of teachers, paraprofessionals, students, and other organizational role
incumbents. Regarding the socialization of personality, we shall also discuss (particularly in Chapter 10, which deals with staff personnel)
emerging practices concerning preinduction, selection, orientation, supervision, in-service training, promotion, and evaluation—all activities that
are directed toward socialization of the individual, thereby enhancing individual-institutional integration.

Effectiveness, efficiency, satisfaction, and morale

Like any other administrator, the principal is greatly concerned with fostering social behavior that is institutionally productive and effective and,
at the same time, individually efficient and rewarding. Few distinctions
about organizational behavior have been made more frequently than that
between institutional effectiveness and individual efficiency. In 1938, for

example, Barnard stated: "The persistence of cooperation depends upon two conditions: (a) its effectiveness; and (b) its efficiency. Effectiveness relates to the accomplishment of the cooperative purpose, which is social and non-personal in character. Efficiency relates to the satisfaction of individual motives, and is personal in character."[21]

Generalizing on the basis of extensive research in group dynamics, Cartwright and Zander concluded: "It appears that most, or perhaps all, group objectives can be subsumed under one or two headings: (a) the achievement of some specific group goal, or (b) the maintenance or strengthening of the group itself."[22]

The series of investigations of leadership of social systems conducted at Ohio State University likewise isolated two important factors: (1) *initiating structure,* which refers to a leader's behavior in delineating the relationship between himself and the members of the work group and in endeavoring to establish well-defined patterns of organization, channels of communication, and methods of procedure; and (2) *consideration,* which refers to behavior indicative of friendship, mutual trust, respect, and warmth in the relationship between a leader and the members of a work group.[23]

Other bipolar conceptualizations of organizational-individual relationships include those of McGregor, Argyris, and Blake and Mouton. McGregor described Theory X, which views behavior in terms of organization, control, and direction, and Theory Y, which views behavior in terms of human growth, self-expression, self-direction, and self-fulfillment.[24] Argyris has made the point that the demands of the organization may be inimical to the development of the individual.[25] Blake and Mouton have similarly posited two dimensions, concern for production and concern for people, and have developed measures that permit plotting, on a grid, the behavior of a manager.[26]

Although the foregoing formulations are not precisely equivalent, they are phenotypically similar and have stimulated further investigation

---

[21] Chester I. Barnard, *The Functions of The Executive,* Cambridge, Mass., Harvard University Press, 1964, p. 60. (Originally published in 1938.)

[22] Dorwin Cartwright and Alvin Zander, eds., *Group Dynamics, Research and Theory,* 3rd ed., New York, Harper & Row, 1968, p. 541.

[23] Andrew W. Halpin, *The Leadership Behavior of School Superintendents,* Columbus, College of Education, Ohio State University, 1956.

[24] Douglas McGregor, *The Human Side of Enterprise,* New York, McGraw-Hill, 1960, pp. 33–57.

[25] Chris Argyris, *Integrating the Individual and the Organization,* New York, Wiley, 1964.

[26] Robert R. Blake and Jane S. Mouton, *The Managerial Grid,* Houston, Gulf, 1964.

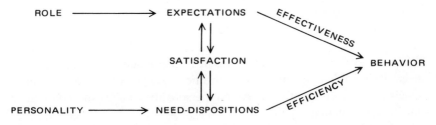

Figure 3.8

Relation of role expectations and need-dispositions to effectiveness, efficiency, and satisfaction

SOURCE: Adapted from J. W. Getzels and E. G. Guba, "Social Behavior and the Administrative Process," *School Review,* 65 (1957), 433. Copyright © 1957 by the University of Chicago.

of the organizational-individual relationship. In terms of the social systems model, the two classes of phenomena are schematized in Figure 3.8, where the significant distinctions among effectiveness, efficiency, and satisfaction and their relationship to the basic elements of the model are represented.

Effectiveness, in terms of the model, is the extent to which the observed social behavior is congruent with expectations held for the role. In assessing effectiveness, the measurement of behavior alone is insufficient; the criterion must be behavior *relative* to the expectations held by the rater. Consequently, the *same* behavior may be labeled "effective" and "ineffective" at the *same* time as a result of different expectations held by different persons. For example, the same principal's behavior may be rated highly effective by the school superintendent and highly ineffective by the teachers at the same time. Moreover, the *same* behavior may be rated effective at one point in time and ineffective at another point in time by the same person, depending on his expectations for the behavior. To reiterate, effectiveness is relative to the expectations held for the role.

Efficiency, in terms of the model, is the extent to which the observed social behavior is congruent with the need-dispositions of the individual. When behavior conforms to needs, it is pleasurable and forthcoming with a minimum of strain or expenditure of psychic energy. The converse, inefficiency, is popularly referred to as the "ulcer index." It is possible, therefore, for behavior to be inefficient and effective at the same time, as in the case of a teacher who performs as his principal expects him to but does so grudgingly or unwillingly. Efficiency, then, is relative to the need-dispositions of the individual fulfilling a role.

Satisfaction, in terms of the model, is the extent to which the institutional role expectations are congruent with personal need-dispositions. In this sense, satisfaction is a measure of the extent to which the role "suits" or "fits" the individual, and conversely. At the high extreme, such "contentment" conceivably could result in homeostasis; in practice, however, it is seldom possible for institutional expectations and personal needs to coincide exactly, hence role-personality conflict and consequent low satisfaction may result.

Although satisfaction has sometimes been confused with morale, Chase drew a clear distinction between the terms in his conceptualization of the work cycle (Figure 3.9), as follows:

> The dynamics of work, that is, of purpose-achieving behavior, in an organization may be summed up as follows: motivation releases energy for work directed toward organization objectives; work under appropriate conditions leads to achievement; a sense of achievement, when accompanied by recognition and other rewards, tends to produce satisfaction; the experience of satisfaction predisposes toward further achievements in the belief that they also will prove rewarding and thus, is transformed into morale, or the disposition to productive work; this disposition is vitalized and the stored energy released by motivation; work follows, leading to satisfaction, and so the cycle continues . . . the figure, represents a gross oversimplification of a complex behavior cycle affected simultaneously by cultural pat-

Figure 3.9

The work cycle

SOURCE: Adapted from Francis S. Chase, "The Administrator as Implementor of the Goals of Education for Our Time," in Roald F. Campbell and James M. Lipham, eds., *Administrative Theory as a Guide to Action*, Chicago, Midwest Administration Center, University of Chicago, 1960, p. 192.

terns, social structure, and personality syndromes—behavior that is influenced by reason and emotion mixed in indeterminate proportions.[27]

Clarification of the complex behavior cycle involving morale may be obtained by referring to Figure 3.10. The familiar relationship between role expectations and need-dispositions is presented with the addition of one important consideration—the goals of the system.

In terms of this model it is posited that *morale* is a function of three variables: belongingness, rationality, and identification. *Belongingness* refers to the role incumbent's feeling that he will be able to achieve satisfaction in the role, since institutional expectations appear to be in accord with his personal needs—in a sense, it is "all for one and one for all." *Rationality* represents the extent to which the expectations of a role are felt to be appropriate to achievement of the professional goals of the system—in a sense, it is "obviously the thing to do." *Identification* refers to the extent to which the goals of the system are integrated with the needs and values of the individual—in a sense, it is "kick my school, kick me."

[27] Francis S. Chase, "The Administrator as Implementor of the Goals of Education for Our Time," in Roald F. Campbell and James M. Lipham, eds., *Administrative Theory as a Guide to Action*, Chicago, Midwest Administration Center, University of Chicago, 1960, pp. 192–194.

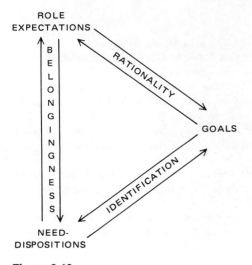

Figure 3.10
The dimensions of morale

SOURCE: Adapted from J. W. Getzels and E. G. Guba, "Social Behavior and the Administrative Process," *School Review*, 65 (1957), 439. Copyright © 1957 by the University of Chicago.

Morale is a function of all three variables—belongingness, rationality, and identification—and cannot be sustained at a high level if any of the variables is at a minimum. In this sense the efforts the principal directs toward developing and maintaining a high level of morale within the school should focus on the establishment of reasonable levels of congruence among the expectations of roles, the needs of the role incumbents, and the goals of the school. Satisfaction, effectiveness, and efficiency should result.

Summary

In this foundational chapter the school and the principalship were viewed in terms of social systems theory. The concept of social system was defined, and several models depicting the relationships among the normative, personal, cultural, and other dimensions of social systems were presented. Within this formulation the administrative relationships of the principal were considered to be composed of the interaction of normative role expectations and personal need-dispositions in the context of cultural value orientations. The theory was shown to possess utility for understanding the process of individual-organizational integration and for assessing behavioral outcomes in terms of effectiveness, efficiency, satisfaction, and morale.

SUGGESTED ACTIVITIES

1. Analyze case studies or simulation materials, such as the University Council for Educational Administration "Monroe City" school district, in terms of the major dimensions of the social systems model.
2. Identify similarities and differences between the social systems model by Getzels and the models by Argyris, Bakke, Halpin, McGregor, and Blake and Mouton.
3. Analyze different institutions (military, business, hospital, custodial, and educational) in terms of personalization of role and socialization of personality.
4. Identify in the current periodical educational literature different actual and intended usages of the terms *effectiveness, efficiency, satisfaction,* and *morale.*
5. Obtain and administer current instruments utilized to measure faculty or student morale; compare and contrast the results by location or type of school of respondents.

SELECTED REFERENCES

ARGYRIS, CHRIS, *Integrating the Individual and the Organization,* New York, Wiley, 1964.

BAKKE, E. WIGHT, *The Fusion Process,* New Haven, Conn., Yale University Press, 1953.

CARTWRIGHT, DORWIN, and ALVIN ZANDER, *Group Dynamics: Research and Theory,* 3rd ed., New York, Harper & Row, 1968.

CAMPBELL, ROALD F., et al., *Introduction to Educational Administration,* 4th ed., Boston, Allyn & Bacon, 1971, chap. 8.

FABER, CHARLES F., and GILBERT F. SHEARRON, *Elementary School Administration Theory and Practice,* New York, Holt, Rinehart and Winston, 1970, chap. 10.

GETZELS, J. W., JAMES M. LIPHAM, and ROALD F. CAMPBELL, *Educational Administration as a Social Process,* New York, Harper & Row, 1968, chaps. 3–5.

GETZELS, J. W., and HERBERT A. THELEN, in N. B. Henry, ed., *The Dynamics of Instructional Groups,* National Society for the Study of Education Yearbook, pt. II, Chicago, University of Chicago Press, 1960, chap. 4.

GUBA, E. G., "Research in Internal Administration—What Do We Know?" in Roald F. Campbell and James M. Lipham, eds., *Administrative Theory as a Guide to Action,* Chicago, Midwest Administration Center, University of Chicago, 1960, chap. 7.

HALPIN, ANDREW W., *Theory and Research in Administration,* New York, Macmillan, 1966.

HILLS, R. JEAN, *Toward a Science of Organization,* Eugene, Center for Advanced Study of Educational Administration, University of Oregon, 1968.

PARSONS, TALCOTT, and EDWARD SHILS, *Toward a General Theory of Action,* Cambridge, Mass., Harvard University Press, 1951.

CHAPTER 4
Values theory

F or the principal to function effectively as the leader of the school, he must understand both the cultural-institutional relationship and the cultural-individual relationship. Because of current crises in our changing culture, he needs to gain perspective regarding not only the sacred, secular, and operational values of society, but also the major mechanisms whereby these values receive expression in the form of legal, structural, and operational guidelines for the school as a social system. Since individual values condition the making of all educational decisions, the principal also must become aware of his own value system and its interface with the value systems of others with whom he works.

We first present a model for the analysis of values, next reviewing briefly some dominant themes in the school-society relationship and citing some of the research studies that relate differences in cultural values to expectations for the school as an institution. Then the relationship between individual values and expectations for the principal's role is explored. Finally we cite some operational guidelines for the role of the principal that have grown out of the research on cultural and individual values.

Model for the analysis of values

"In one way or another value conflicts at all levels, metaphysical, societal, personal, within value domains and among them, sooner or later come to roost on the shoulders of the school," Broudy observed.[1] He continued, "And because the highest responsibility rests with the administrator, he must inevitably divide his attention between coping with value conflicts on an institutional basis and acting out his own role as a value witness."[2] In shouldering his responsibilities, how may the principal interpret conceptually the analysis of his own and others' values?

Several conceptual approaches to the analysis of values have been

[1] Harry S. Broudy, "Conflicts in Values," in R. E. Ohm and William G. Monahan, eds., *Educational Administration—Philosophy in Action,* Norman, Okla., College of Education, 1965, p. 49.

[2] Ibid.

made at differing levels of abstraction. For example, Allport and Vernon identified and studied the following value types: theoretic, economic, aesthetic, social, political, and religious.[3] Glaser and Maller investigated what they called interest values, utilizing four value types found by Thurstone: theoretic, esthetic, social, and economic.[4] Woodruff identified the following values: wealth, social position, political power, social service, home life, comfort, religion, security, personal attractiveness, excitement, friends, and intellectual activity.[5] Battle, and subsequently Goldman, represented values in terms of the following ten dimensions: religious, economic, political, aesthetic, altruistic, social, hedonistic, physical, ethical, and theoretical.[6] More recently, Harman described and compared belief value positions in terms of U.S. middle-class, new humanistic, behavioral science, and American origin value systems.[7] Reich has described changes in values in terms of three types of consciousness: the American dream, the corporate state, and the new generation.[8] Within all these views, a value may be defined as a conception, implicit or explicit, of that which is held to be desirable, and it is to this definition of values that we subscribe.

Just as Maslow concluded that personality needs are structured hierarchically in terms of greater or less primacy or potency, so may we propose that values are structured hierarchically in terms of endurability or, conversely, in terms of their propensity to change.[9] Within this view, a model for ordering and understanding value orientations, at least within the American culture, has been constructed (see Figure 4.1). At the core of our society, Level I in the center of the diagram, are those *sacred* values that constitute our relatively stable and basic ideals and beliefs. In the American culture, as Getzels has observed, these include

[3] Gordon W. Allport and P. E. Vernon, *Study of Values,* Boston, Houghton Mifflin, 1951.

[4] Edward M. Glaser and Julius B. Maller, "The Measurement of Interest Values," *Character and Personality,* 9 (September 1940), 69.

[5] Asahel D. Woodruff, "A Study of Directive Factors in Individual Behavior," doctoral dissertation, University of Chicago, 1941, pp. 21–25.

[6] Haron J. Battle, "Application of an Invested Analysis in a Study of the Relation Between Values and Achievement of High School Pupils," doctoral dissertation, University of Chicago, 1954; Samuel Goldman, "Sub-Public Perceptions of the High School Graduate and Roles of Institutions in His Development," doctoral dissertation, University of Chicago, 1961.

[7] Willis W. Harman, "Beliefs and Values in Transition," in Philip K. Piele and Terry L. Eidell, eds., *Social and Technological Change, Implications for Education,* Eugene, Ore., Center for the Advanced Study of Educational Administration, 1970, pp. 21–26.

[8] Charles A. Reich, *The Greening of America,* New York, Random House, 1970.

[9] Abraham H. Maslow, *Motivation and Personality,* New York, Harper & Row, 1954.

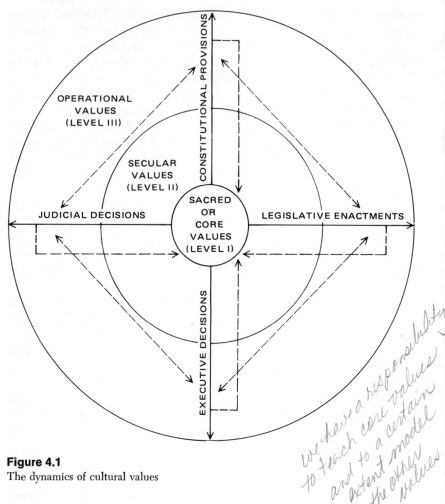

Figure 4.1
The dynamics of cultural values

democracy, the belief that the experience of the many is more inclusive than the experience of the few, that what people want is what they need, and that the people are the best judges of their needs; *individualism,* the belief that the individual is the source of energy, initiative, and responsibility in society and that he has a right to self-expression; *equality,* the belief that all should have the same opportunity to develop their talents, with rewards acquired by achievement, not by ascription; and *human perfectability,* the belief in the progressive movement of the person and his society toward the ideal of democracy, individualism, and equality.[10] These values, sometimes referred to as "Sunday" values, are the ones

---

[10] J. W. Getzels, "Changing Values Challenge the Schools," *School Review,* 65 (1957), 92–102.

cited when it is urged that the schools teach the "American way of life," and it is to these values that we appeal when we wish to legitimize significant social action.[11]

The sacred or core values serve as a source for the legal and political structure of our society and receive expression in: (1) the constitutional and charter provisions of national, state, and local governments; (2) laws and ordinances; (3) judicial decisions and interpretations by the courts; and (4) executive decisions in the form of orders, and board and administrative regulations. In addition to serving as a source, the sacred values serve as a screen or "ultimate validity check" for these manifestations, which at the same time perform "intermediate validity checks," one upon the other.

Emanating from the sacred values are the beliefs, constituting our *secular* (Level II) values, that are subject to wide interpretation and differential implementation of the sacred or core values. Traditionally, the secular, "Monday through Saturday" values have included a work-success ethic, a future-time orientation, independence or the autonomous self, and moral commitment.[12] But the secular values have been and continue to be in transition as conditions in the society change. Examples of changes through time in each of the secular values have been reported recently by Getzels.[13] Although the traditional, hard-work achievement ethic gave way to an antimaterialistic ethic of sociability, a central concern in the 1970s is with social responsibility—relevant careers, occupations, and work. Regarding time, the traditional orientation of self-denial and delayed gratification subsequently gave way to a present-time ethic of self-indulgence. Now, with the environment and similar concerns with "spaceship earth" emerging as paramount, we have powerful manifestations on the American scene of a renewed emphasis on relevance and future planning. Similar shifts may be observed regarding independence —from the independent and autonomous self to organizational and group conformity to renewed stress on personal authenticity. Likewise, shifts in moral orientation—from Puritan morality to a relativistic "God is dead" philosophy to a renewed idealism of moral commitment—all could be observed within the span of two decades. Since the current rush of societal change brings a kind of instant antiquity,[14] shifts in secular values that formerly required decades may now occur within years or even months. *another example: marriage in the 70's & 80s*

[11] J. W. Getzels, James M. Lipham, and Roald F. Campbell, *Educational Administration as a Social Process*, New York, Harper & Row, 1968, pp. 96–97.

[12] Ibid., pp. 97–98.

[13] J. W. Getzels, "On the Transformation of Values: A Decade After Port Huron," *School Review*, 80 (August 1972), 505–519.

[14] John W. Gardner, "Toward a Self-Renewing Society," *Time* (April 1969), 40.

The earlier secular values of work success, future-time orientation, independence, and moral commitment have been termed *traditional* values. These gave way to the secular values of sociability, present-time orientation, group conformity, and moral relativism—termed *emergent* values. Although in one sense current secular values seem to represent a return to traditional values, such a position would be a naïve over-simplification, denying the reality of the intervening political, social, and technological forces. Whether termed a "reawakening" a "new conscious-ness," or a "new humanitarianism," the socially responsible, relevant, authentic, and morally committed orientation that is extant might, for clarity in analysis, be termed *postemergent* secular values.

Just as the core or sacred values are subject to differential orientation in terms of the secular values, the secular values are subject to even greater differences in behavioral manifestations as one implements the sacred and secular values from which behavior derives. As indicated in Figure 4.1, these constitute the third level of analysis, one's *operational* values.

Let us consider an example to illustrate the utility of the values model for understanding value-institutional-individual relationships in the case of the school. As indicated, one of the sacred values in our society is the core value of individualism. Thus at level I of analysis all would agree that each student is of paramount importance. But in terms of level II, the secular values, traditional teachers undoubtedly will view this sacred value differently from emergent teachers or from postemergent teachers, thereby posing the possibility of major cleavages within a faculty. But at level III of analysis, even the teachers who similarly possess emergent values, for example, may choose drastically different means to "individualize instruction," thereby introducing additional value cleavages. Although the value differences may not be so starkly apparent, the principal must be able to understand the relationship of cultural value orientations to institutional expectations, individual needs, and social behavior if he is to function effectively as the leader of the school. Knowing one's values permits the prediction of much social behavior. To start developing such knowledge, let us review some of the dominant themes in the relationship of the school to the American culture.

Themes in the school-society relationship

Detailed historical or philosophical analysis of the school-society rela-tionship is beyond the scope of treatment here. However, there exist cer-tain dominant cultural themes that are of such recurring and paramount concern to the school principal that they might be cited as basic princi-ples of American education. These derive largely from the sacred values of the society, and they tend to permeate the entire structure and operation of the school. Five of these principles are reviewed.

1. THE SCHOOLS BELONG TO THE PEOPLE. This principle, which relates to the sacred value of democracy, implies that the individual citizen has a right not only to an education but to influence education for what he believes to be the individual or common good. Thus ultimate decision-making power and control of the schools rest with the lay citizens who own them. Ideally, these powers are exercised through elected or appointed boards of education or school trustees, who are expected to set goals and policies attuned to the values and expectations of the people in a local school district. However, since there typically exist within a district multimodal values and expectations (no one set of which is "right"), school personnel face a perennial challenge. As any principal will readily attest, various individuals and groups often directly exercise, even with impropriety, their proprietary interest in the schools.

2. EDUCATION IS A FUNCTION OF THE STATES. The Tenth Amendment to the Constitution says: "The powers not delegated to the United States by the Constitution, nor prohibited by it to the States, are reserved to the States respectively, or to the people." The states have recognized and assumed their responsibility for education through their constitutional provisions and through mandatory or permissive laws controlling the number, size, operation, function, and partial financing of local educational districts to which many powers are delegated.

Two concerns relative to the state control of education have recently been expressed: first, that within certain industrialized megalopolitan areas the educational problems may transcend state political boundaries and might better be attacked on an interstate, regional, or compact basis. Already the courts have been petitioned to decide whether urban school districts and their outlying suburban school districts should be merged. The second issue relative to state control brings out the following point: If the state is not responsive to needs, the final words in the Tenth Amendment "to the people" imply direct "power to the people." As has been noted, however, the courts have held generally and consistently to the principle that education is a function of the state.[15] Recent decisions concerning equality of financing of education at the district level tend strongly to reinforce the tenet that education is a state rather than a local function.[16]

3. EDUCATION IS OF FEDERAL INTEREST. Since the days of the early federal land grants for support of schools and colleges, the federal government has maintained an interest in education, primarily through financial

[15] LeRoy J. Peterson, Richard A. Rossmiller, and Marlin M. Volz, *The Law and Public School Operation,* New York, Harper & Row, 1969, p. 11.

[16] *Serrano v. Priest,* 487 P. 2d, 1241.

categorical aids for specialized programs—veterans' education, Indian education, military schools, vocational education, special education, education for the disadvantaged, and early childhood education, to mention only a few. Many of these programs have been operated by the federal government directly, some through federal-state partnership, others through federal-local partnership, and still others through various combinations of partnerships.

Thus far, some have feared direct federal involvement in education as a threat to the local control of education, but this fear appears to be unwarranted.[17] Some educators who feel constrained by the legislative and administrative requirements of categorical aids have argued cogently for unrestricted or "block grant" federal funds under the general welfare provisions of the Constitution. Such funding for schools may increase in the future in the form of revenue sharing.

4. EDUCATION IS IN TERMS OF THE INDIVIDUAL. This principle, derived from the sacred value of individualism, states that education should be provided in accordance with one's abilities and interests. In providing the maximum education for each student, the program of the schools must be flexible and adjustable enough to accommodate individual abilities and interests ranging from the physically or mentally handicapped to the academically talented or gifted. Moreover, at least to a certain age, compulsory school attendance is mandated, since education for each individual is viewed as the foundation of democratic government.

This principle also implies that the schools are organized and operated democratically, respecting the rights of the individual to participate in the making of decisions that affect him, rather than giving blind obedience to authority. Thus when a student asserts, even defiantly, to a principal, "I've got my rights," he is exactly correct, as the courts and recent legislation protecting the rights of human subjects continue to affirm.

5. EDUCATION IS EQUALLY AVAILABLE TO ALL. This principle, which derives primarily from the sacred value of equality, expresses the ideal that all should have the same opportunity to develop their talents, regardless of economic condition, religion, or race. Although much progress has been made toward the achievement of this ideal, wide differences exist in the financial support and resultant quality of the schools among the states, within a state, and even within a school district. The economic status of the individual student, moreover, continues to be a major determining factor in his ability to pursue education, particularly at the post-high school level.

Wide differences among states also persist regarding such issues as regulation of private and parochial schools, religious practices in the

<hr>

[17] Roald F. Campbell et al., *The Organization and Control of American Schools*, 2nd ed., Columbus, Ohio, Merrill, 1970.

public schools, sectarian objections to public education, and financial support of religious schools—whether in terms of shared programs and facilities, such specialized "child benefit" aids as textbooks or transportation, or such generalized "social benefit" aids as voucher payments to parents. Regarding race, although the Supreme Court concluded in 1954 that the doctrine of "separate but equal" educational facilities has no place in American life because separate is inherently unequal, marked racial segregation of the schools persists in all sections of the nation. Boards of education and administrators faced with the task of desegregating the schools as one remedy for the social ills besetting our society face enormous problems, for it is this domain that the articulations among the sacred (Level I), secular (Level II), and operational (Level III) values of our society appear to be most divergent, as may be illustrated by examination of some of the current trends in education.

Current educational trends

In the dynamic interface between the values of society and the values of the schools, certain contemporary trends are of compelling and continuing concern to educators and citizens alike. If one accepts or subscribes to the somewhat sacred principles of American education, and if one also assumes a current, postemergent secular values stance, several trends relating to such categories as educational involvement, instructional change, staff and student personnel, educational finance, and educational control may be discerned. The following trends, which are viewed as exemplary rather than exhaustive, impinge directly on the principal's leadership role.[18]

Regarding future education in the United States, it is predicted that there will be an *increase* in:

1. The proportion of the population involved in education—perhaps as much as a third of the nation.

2. The extension of education to include industry-based, community-based, and home-based models.

3. The extension of education both downward through early childhood and upward through adult and continuing education programs.

4. The use of flexible modes of instruction, including multigrouping and individualized instruction.

5. The range and choice of instructional media, including audiovisual aids, programmed materials, and computer-based devices, as well as conventional materials.

[18] Many of the trends were originally cited in Harman, op. cit., pp. 58–59.

6. The development of basic academic, social, and personal skills with a corresponding reduction in emphasis on subject content mastery.

7. The establishment of cooperative working relationships, since the current stress on competition may operate to lower both self-respect and self-expectations.

8. The involvement of staff and students in making educational decisions—perhaps in response to a concomitant increase in staff and student militancy.

9. The involvement of "external" citizen advisory groups in making policies, setting goals, and resolving issues.

10. The utilization of alternative organizational structures for the sharing of power among organizational participants, including lower participants.

11. The decentralization of school districts, particularly in large urban areas.

12. The differentiation in teaching and learning roles, to include learning specialists, consultant services, and teacher aides.

13. The equalization of educational costs, programs, and opportunities within school districts, within states, and within the nation.

14. The proportion of educational costs to be borne at the national level.

Certain of the trends may be at variance with one another, since even a given set of values, such as the postemergent values on which they are based, may on certain points receive contradictory expression at level III, the operational level of educational values. The trends may be at still greater variance with certain of the traditional or emergent secular values, which continue to be held by many. Moreover, it can be predicted that drastic changes in the prevailing secular cultural values will alter significantly both the intensity and the direction of any or all of the trends. Thus the principal must understand the relationship between the cultural values and the expectations for the school as an institution. The following research illuminates this relationship.

Cultural values and institutional expectations

In what ways do the values of society receive expression in terms of the expectations for the school as an institution? This relationship was depicted earlier in the model of the school as a social system in Figure 3.3. This model suggests first that the values held in the society are systematically related to expectations for the school as an institution. Second, it suggests that differences in both the values and the expectations held are meaningfully related to the various subcultural groupings in our society.

EXPECTATIONS FOR THE SCHOOL

"What should the schools be doing?" is a perennial question raised by educators and citizens alike. In 1918 the Commission on the Reorganization of Secondary Education enumerated its now famous Cardinal Principles, including: (1) health, (2) command of fundamental processes, (3) worthy home membership, (4) vocational preparation, (5) civic education, (6) worthy use of leisure, and (7) ethical character.[19] These principles, which represented a considerable liberalization of education, were widely accepted for many years.

In 1938 the Educational Policies Commission restated the goals of American education in terms of the following general sets of objectives:[20]

1. The Objectives of Self-Realization
2. The Objectives of Human Relationship
3. The Objectives of Economic Efficiency
4. The Objectives of Civic Responsibility

The National Association of Secondary Schools presented a statement of the goals of secondary schools in terms of Ten Imperative Needs of Youth. In essence, these restated earlier goals, but with two differing emphases: increased attention to the individual student and increased stress on vocational education.[21] Shortly thereafter, a two-day conference on vocational education, sponsored by the U.S. Office of Education,[22] adopted the Prosser Resolution calling for "life adjustment" education; this resolution set in motion the appointment of several national and state commissions designed to foster education for life adjustment.[23] Life adjustment was defined as education designed to equip "all American youth to live democratically with satisfaction to themselves and profit to society as home members, workers, and citizens,"[24] but with special concern for those who were less well served in the schools than the college-bound or vocational groups. Perhaps because of a failure of educators to identify

[19] Commission on Reorganization of Secondary Education, *Cardinal Principles of Secondary Education,* Washington, D.C., Bureau of Education, 1918.

[20] Educational Policies Commission, *Education for all American Youth in American Democracy,* Washington, D.C., The Commission, 1938.

[21] National Association of Secondary School Principals, *Planning for American Youth,* Washington, D.C., The Association, 1951.

[22] Edward A. Krug, *Salient Dates in American Education,* New York, Harper & Row, 1966, pp. 131–132.

[23] Commission on Life Adjustment Education, *Vitalizing Secondary Education,* Washington, D.C., U.S. Office of Education Bulletin No. 3, 1951.

[24] Second Commission on Life Adjustment Education and Youth, *A Look Ahead in Secondary Education,* Washington, D.C., U.S. Office of Education Bulletin No. 4, 1954.

life adjustment education with specific goals and programs, many citizens reacted critically to life adjustment education, regarding it as trivial and antiintellectual.[25] As is often the case, the movement toward life adjustment education was only partially effective because of differences between citizens and educators in the educational expectations held for the school.

In 1955 another restatement of the expectations for the schools was made by the White House Conference on Education. The Conference agreed that the schools should continue to foster development of the following:

1. The fundamental skills of communication—reading, writing, spelling, as well as other elements of effective oral and written expression; the arithmetical and mathematical skills, including problem solving.

2. Appreciation for our democratic heritage.

3. Civic rights and responsibilities and knowledge of American institutions.

4. Respect and appreciation for human values and the beliefs of others.

5. Ability to think and evaluate constructively and creatively.

6. Effective work habits and self-discipline.

7. Social competency as a contributing member of his family and community.

8. Ethical behavior based on a sense of moral and spiritual values.

9. Intellectual curiosity and eagerness for life-long learning.

10. Aesthetic appreciation and self-expression in the arts.

11. Physical and mental health.

12. Wise use of time, including constructive leisure pursuits.

13. Understanding of the physical world and man's relation to it as represented through basic knowledge of the sciences.

14. An awareness of our relationships with the world community.[26]

Downey, Seager, and Slagle reviewed, synthesized, and ordered all the pronouncements and statements on American education into four dimensions, each with four representative expectations for the task of public education, as follows:

A. Intellectual dimensions
   1. Possession of knowledge: A fund of information, concepts
   2. Communication of knowledge: Skill to acquire and transmit
   3. Creation of knowledge: Discrimination and imagination
   4. Desire for knowledge: A love for learning
B. Social dimensions
   5. Man to man: Cooperation in day-to-day relations
   6. Man to "state": Civic rights and duties

25 Krug, op. cit., p. 134.

26 Committee for the White House Conference on Education, *A Report to the President*, Washington, D.C., U.S. Government Printing Office, 1956, p. 90.

7. Man to country: Loyalty to one's own country
8. Man to world: Interrelationships of peoples
C. Personal dimensions
9. Physical: Bodily health and development
10. Emotional: Mental health and stability
11. Ethical: Moral integrity
12. Aesthetic: Cultural and leisure pursuits
D. Productive dimensions
13. Vocational guidance: Information and selection
14. Vocational preparation: Training and placement
15. Home and family: Housekeeping and family
16. Consumer: Personal buying, budgeting, and investment.[27]

Based on this framework, an instrument was developed that permitted respondents to assign priorities by sorting the 16 expectations from "most important" to "least important." In studies of the task of public education, the expectations were sorted by more than 1000 educators and more than 2000 citizens, first for the secondary school and next for the elementary school. Respondents were drawn from the Far West, the Midwest, the South, New England, and Canada. In addition to being analyzed for educator-noneducator, elementary-secondary, and regional differences, the data were examined for differences in expectations held by various subpublic groupings.

The results of the studies were quite revealing. A high similarity was found between the expectations held for the task of the elementary school and those held for the task of the secondary school. In terms of the overall job to be done, therefore, one might assume that the principalships of the elementary school and the secondary school are more similar than dissimilar. In terms of specific tasks, three of the four intellectual items were among the first four priorities for both elementary and secondary schools. First priority was given to the three Rs—the basic skills for acquiring and transmitting knowledge. Second priority was given to the desire for knowledge—the cultivation of an inquiring mind and "love of learning." Recent research studies have revealed that citizens' and educators' expectations for the schools are remarkably stable. Although the original studies by Downey, Seager, and Slagle were conducted in 1958, similar results were obtained in 1972.[28]

But what of the differences between educators and noneducators? Because so many critics of the schools have branded educators as "anti-

[27] Lawrence W. Downey, Roger C. Seager, and Allen T. Slagle, *The Task of Public Education*, Chicago, Midwest Administration Center, University of Chicago, 1960, p. 24.

[28] Marvin J. Fruth, Dennis W. Spuck, and Howard E. Wakefield, *Opening the Door*, Madison, Cooperative Educational Research and Services, University of Wisconsin, 1972.

intellectual," great differences might be presumed to exist between the citizens representative of the larger culture and the educators representative of the school. Such was not the case in either the 1958 or the 1972 study of the task of public education. Educators and noneducators were generally in high agreement on their expectations for the school. Among the differences that appeared, educators in fact accorded a slightly greater emphasis to desire for knowledge than did noneducators.

Some of the differences in educational expectations might, of course, be attributable to differences in amount of schooling. As amount of schooling of all respondents increased, greater emphasis was placed on possession of knowledge, desire to learn, creativity, aesthetics, and emotional stability, and less on man-to-man cooperation, patriotism, physical education, vocational education, and consumer education. Somewhat similar findings resulted when the expectations were analyzed in terms of occupational groups ranging from professionals to unskilled laborers.

Utilizing a two-factor index of social class position, occupational status, and educational level, Hills studied in depth the relationship of social class to expectations held for the school.[29] He found that upper-, upper-middle, and middle-class respondents expressed a strong preference for an intellectually oriented curriculum, giving secondary emphasis to a socially oriented curriculum. The vocational aspects of curriculum were minimized. For the lower-class and lower-middle-class respondents, in contrast, the social aspects of education were paramount, followed very closely by vocational and intellectual expectations for the schools; but the upper classes tended to show disregard for vocational education expectations for the schools. He concluded that vocational expectations may be the greatest source of potential conflict concerning education between the social class groups. Such a conclusion would be valid for both the highest and the lowest strata in society. In many poverty areas citizens voice strong opposition to vocational programs, viewing them as second-rate offerings that deter upward social mobility. Likewise, one observes strong opposition to programs in career education by upper-class citizens—particularly those who erroneously equate career education with vocational training.

Through individual interviews, Hills also found that parents held expectations not only for the school as an institution but also for specific roles within the school. In some schools the parents did not hesitate to tell the teacher what to teach and even how to teach. Moreover, principals now attest that parents wish also to dictate who will teach.

The task of public education studies also revealed that significant differences exist by geographic region. Respondents in New England

[29] R. J. Hills, "Social Class and Educational Views," *Administrator's Notebook,* 10 (October 1961), 1–4.

placed a high valuation on moral training and less emphasis on education for social skills and physical development. In the South, great emphasis was given to physical education and less to the intellectual and aesthetic aspects. Respondents in the West assigned high priority to education for social skills and low priority to moral training and consumer education. Canadians held high expectations for intellectual and aesthetic development but minimized the physical and patriotic aspects of schooling. Midwestern respondents assumed a middle position; their priorities assumed a position comparable to the average of the sample as a whole. Although these regional differences may not be as compelling in a specific school as the social class differences would be, they do indicate that in terms of the cultural values in which the school is imbedded, the role of principal in a school in New England may be quite different from that of a principal in the South, for example, and that such differences may stem in part from differing regional preferences in educational ideology. In any case, the principal would do well to study, analyze, and understand the values of the community with which the goal-directed behaviors in his school must interface.

The studies of the task of public education also showed that subpublic differences in educational expectations were related to age. Older respondents tended to stress the importance of physical education, moral training, patriotism, and aesthetic appreciation more than did the younger respondents. Conversely, younger respondents generally emphasized strongly the intellectual and world citizenship aspects more than did the older respondents.

Catholics tended to stress education for morality more than did Protestants, who tended to stress desire for knowledge and physical education more than did Catholics. In a subsequent study of the relationship of religion to expectations for the school, Meggers identified several specific differences in expectations between parochial-school-oriented and public-school-oriented parents concerning such perennial issues as shared-time programs, summer school programs, level of teacher salaries, and school transportation.[30]

In a separate study of the relationship of political party identification to expectations for local schools, Streich noted strong relationships between the political party to which citizens belong and their expectations for the schools.[31] Democrats and independents, to a greater degree than Republicans, favored granting academic freedom in the schools, pro-

[30] John F. Meggers, "Expectations for the Role of the Board of Education Held by Parochial- and Public-School Oriented Parents," doctoral dissertation, University of Wisconsin, 1966.

[31] William H. Streich, "Political Party Identification and Expectations for Local Schools," doctoral dissertation, University of Wisconsin, 1966.

viding a wide number and range of social services in the schools, and increasing levels of local financial support and federal aid to the schools.

There is evidence from a recent Oklahoma study that other variables, such as size of a school district and mobility of the population in a district, also relate to the kinds of expectations held for the schools.[32] This study also revealed that the expectations of those within the schools may not be in harmony with the expectations held by citizens and community leaders outside the schools.

THE PRINCIPAL AND EDUCATIONAL EXPECTATIONS

From the findings of the studies of cultural values and institutional expectations, we may draw several guidelines that have implications for the behavior of the principal. Many principals have been conditioned through training and experience to think of the cultural environment of the school in terms of "the public." In fact, many so-called public relations programs undoubtedly fail exactly because they apparently are aimed at everyone in general and no one in particular. As a first guideline, the studies suggest that a more appropriate view would reflect awareness of the many contrasting subpublics of the school.

Second, it would be unwise to presume that the subpublic differences reflected by the averages apply to the individual—of course, they do not. Related to this is the often observed tendency, even on the part of principals who are aware of subpublic cleavages, to categorize or ascribe inappropriate or erroneous expectations based simply on one indicator concerning an individual (e.g., educational level or religion), without knowing the nature or interaction of the other indicators. Thus one should not be merely acquainted with but should know those with whom he interacts.

A third guideline relates to the extent of conflict in expectations for the schools. Much of the early literature in school administration implied —sometimes demanded—that the principal ameliorate and mediate the conflicting viewpoints and expectations—that he operate the school on a "consensus mode," as it were. Data from the research suggest, however, that a "conflict mode" may be more typical, since the expectations for the schools are related to if not derived from such basic factors as socioeconomic class, region, age, religion, and political affiliation.

A fourth guideline concerns the cultural values–institutional expectations relationship; namely, that the principal should take time to formulate and reflect on his own expectations for the school as an in-

[32] Max D. Skelton, "Reference Group Expectations for the Superintendency," doctoral dissertation, University of Oklahoma, 1969.

stitution. Although it is a principle of American education that the schools belong to the people, it may be that the schools are responding to and accommodating pressures for programs, services, and functions which they are ill equipped to provide, thereby jeopardizing if not neglecting their primary agreed-on functions. It is imperative, therefore, that the principal who would act, rather than merely react, clearly define, openly state, and be prepared to defend his own set of educational priorities.

Fifth, the methodology of the studies on educational expectations is of immediate practical use to the principal in assessing educational values. In the planning of an in-service educational program for teachers in a comprehensive high school with which we are familiar, teachers were asked to rank their educational expectations—not for secondary schools in general, but in terms of their own school. Grouped by subject-matter departments, the teachers then compiled the results and reached consensus concerning which expectations were most important. Next they compared these expectations with their habitual classroom behavior. The results were quite revealing. Whereas they had ranked the fostering of creativity as very important, they found that they were giving far more attention to the possession of a fund of knowledge. Similar discrepancies were found for many of the items. As a result, a meaningful in-service educational program was developed to increase the degree of congruence between espoused values and operational values. At least in this school, the faculty attested to the utility of theory and research on educational expectations and values for improving educational practice. In a different educational setting the methodology was also found useful in reaching agreement, not only on tasks and functions but on goals, purposes, and long-range plans for the total institution.[33]

Finally, there are powerful indicators of a renewed emphasis on developing a better understanding of the cultural values–institutional expectations relationship in pre-service collegiate programs for all educators. For example, several states now require applicants for all educational certificates to have completed training in human relations components planned to develop the ability of educators to:[34]

1. Understand the contributions and life styles of the various racial, cultural, and economic groups in our society.

2. Recognize and deal with dehumanizing biases, discrimination, and prejudices.

[33] Joseph M. Braysich, "The Functions of the Western Australia Institute of Technology," doctoral dissertation, University of Wisconsin, 1971.

[34] Cf. State of Minnesota, School Code, chap. 27, EDU 521, par. (b), sec. (2), 1971; State of Wisconsin, Administrative Code, Wisconsin Department of Public Instruction, PL 3.03 (1), 1972.

3. Create learning environments that contribute to the self-esteem of all persons and to positive interpersonal relations.

4. Respect human diversity and personal rights.

We now consider diversity in individual values and the relationship of such diversity to role expectations and relationships within the school.

Individual values and role relationships

Thus far we have focused on the relationship of cultural values to expectations for the school as a social institution. In terms of the general social systems model (Figure 2.6), however, we recall that values not only define a culture, they also describe the individual. Viewed organizationally, values are not only in subpublics "out there," they also are in people "in here." Thus it may be hypothesized that the nature and extent of differences in values between and among complementary role incumbents will have systematic effects on their working relationships.

INDIVIDUAL VALUES AND BEHAVIOR

Several studies of the relationship of individual values to role relations have been conducted within the educational setting. At the classroom level, Battle demonstrated that similarity in values was related to student success; he found that teachers awarded higher grades to students who held values like their own.[35] Prince, and subsequently Stone, discovered that students with a value pattern that includes the work-success ethic and future-time orientation achieved higher grades than did those with a value pattern that includes the ethic of sociability and present-time orientation.[36]

Rose conducted a penetrating analysis of the relationship of individual values of teachers to both the behavioral style of the school and pupil response to the school.[37] Figure 4.2 represents the interrelationships involved. It was hypothesized that the traditionalism of the teachers' values would be reflected in the formality in a school—assessed in terms of the emphasis on status differences, freedom for faculty to interact,

---

[35] Battle, op. cit.

[36] Richard D. Prince, "A Study of the Relationships Between Individual Values and Administrative Effectiveness in the School Situation," doctoral dissertation, University of Chicago, 1957; Shelley C. Stone, "A Study of the Relationships Among Values, Family Characteristics, and Personality Characteristics of Adolescents," doctoral dissertation, University of Chicago, 1960.

[37] Gale W. Rose, "Organizational Behavior and Its Concomitants in Schools," *Administrator's Notebook*, 15 (March 1967), 1–4.

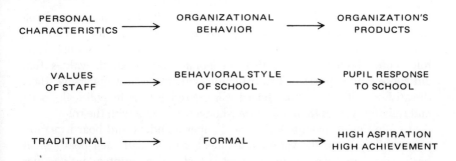

Figure 4.2
Individual values and organizational dynamics
SOURCE: Gale W. Rose, "Organizational Behavior and Its Concomitants in Schools," *Administrator's Notebook,* 15 (March 1967), 2.

openness of faculty meetings, and freedom of student movement in the halls. The criteria for measuring student response included measurement of student aspirations for further education and their academic achievement on tests. The findings supported both the generalized and the specific hypotheses: The more traditional the teachers, the more formal was the organizational behavior in the school and the higher were the aspiration and achievement levels of the students, the product of the school.

Just as the role relations between teacher and student may be affected by individual value orientations, so is the relation between teacher and principal similarly affected. Prince also investigated the relationship of teacher-principal agreement on values by administering to principals and their teachers a values inventory and by having teachers rate the effectiveness and confidence in the leadership of their principals.[38] He found that teachers with emergent values tended to perceive as highly effective and to have high confidence in the leadership of a principal who also had emergent values. Likewise, teachers with traditional values tended to perceive as highly effective and to have high confidence in the leadership of a principal who also had traditional values.

At the school district level, Abbott observed that similarity in values between school superintendents and their school board members was systematically, directly, and positively related to the confidence expressed by board members in the leadership of their superintendent of schools.[39] Within boards of education, Larson discovered that when the members of a school board were highly congruent in their values,

[38] Prince, op. cit., pp. 95–97.

[39] Max G. Abbott, "Values and Value-Perceptions of School Superintendents and Board Members," doctoral dissertation, University of Chicago, 1960.

they expressed significantly more satisfaction with the school board role than when a board lacked congruence in values.[40] He also found that school board members who expressed satisfaction with the school board role scored higher in theoretical, economic, and aesthetic values than did those who expressed dissatisfaction with the role. Conversely, those dissatisfied with the school board role scored higher in political, social, and religious values than did those who were satisfied with the role.

In addition to having each school superintendent and board member respond directly to the values instrument, Abbott had each board member respond in terms of his perceptions of his superintendent's values. When actual values of perceiver and perceived were dissimilar, there was a marked and significant tendency for one to presume a greater similarity with his own values than was actually the case. Thus individuals having traditional values tend to project that others are more traditional than they really are. Likewise, individuals having emergent values tend to project that others are more emergent than they are.

A study to determine the relationship of individual value orientations to leadership behavior of the school principal was conducted by Stromberg.[41] From data obtained from principals and teachers in Pennsylvania and New York schools, he discovered that principals having an emergent value orientation [as measured by the Differential Values Inventory (DVI)], were perceived by their teachers as being higher on the leadership dimensions of initiating structure and consideration [as measured by the Leadership Behavior Description Questionnaire (LBDQ)] than were principals having a traditional value orientation. Moreover, he found the leadership behavior of the principal to be more strongly related to his value orientation than to such variables as type of school (elementary or secondary), school size, community type (rural or urban), or the principal's age.

Hefty likewise found the individual value orientations of principals to be associated with their leadership styles.[42] In a random sample of Wisconsin secondary schools, principals and teachers responded to the DVI and the LBDQ. It was learned that principals with traditional value orientations were perceived by teachers as maintaining less cordial relations with superiors, being less able to influence superiors, being less able to tolerate uncertainty and postponement without anxiety or upset, and being less inclined to strive for positions of higher status than were

[40] Raymond O. Larson, "School Board Members' Values, Belief Systems, and Satisfaction with the School Board Role," doctoral dissertation, University of Wisconsin, 1966.

[41] Robert P. Stromberg, "Value Orientation and Leadership Behavior of School Principals," doctoral dissertation, Pennsylvania State University, 1966.

[42] John C. Hefty, "The Relationships Between the Value Orientations, Leader Behavior, and Effectiveness of Secondary School Principals in Selected Middle Sized School Systems," doctoral dissertation, University of Wisconsin, 1971.

principals having emergent value orientations. Additional study is needed concerning the impact of values on leadership and decision-making behavior.

Additional research is also needed concerning the role of the school in inculcating or changing values. Much of the work strongly indicates that the ability of the school as an agency for shaping the values of students may not be nearly as pervasive as is commonly supposed—particularly when the variable of selective school attendance is taken into account.[43] Instead, variables within the total milieu of home, church, and peer groups appear to be more powerful influences than those of the school. Additional study is also needed concerning the extent to which either the principal or the teacher is able to serve as a model for influencing the various types of student values—sacred, secular, and operational. And conversely, in an era of postemergent secular values, one may only surmise from a glimpse at the length of the principal's sideburns or the teachers' skirts the extent to which the student influences the values of his organizational superiors.

THE PRINCIPAL AND INDIVIDUAL VALUES

Some obvious guidelines for improving the principal's organizational role relations derive from the research on individual values. First, although individual values are typically viewed as a private matter, their understanding and analysis may go far toward explaining and predicting both interpersonal and role behaviors. In effect, having a clue to an individual's values permits prediction of the stand he will take on a given issue, and perhaps on a host of seemingly unrelated issues. Thus the principal should become sensitive to the individual value orientations of those with whom he frequently interacts.

A second guideline derived from the research suggests that the principal assess both his own values and the strength of his tendency to ascribe or project these values to others. Being conscious of one's own role as a consistent and accurate value witness is a significant dimension of ethical professional behavior.

Third, from the research on values it would appear that the extent of agreement on individual values emerges as equally powerful as the kind of values held in explaining such output variables as confidence in leadership, satisfaction, effectiveness, efficiency, and morale. This is not to suggest that in matters of staff selection, for example, one strives to create a homogeneous staff; at least, however, the limits of

[43] Cf. Andrew M. Greeley and Peter H. Rossi, *The Education of Catholic Americans*, Chicago, Aldine, 1966; Donald A. Erickson, "Do Schools Affect Student Values?" *Administrator's Notebook*, 11 (December 1962), 1–4; J. Thomas Finucan, "The Values and Attitudes of Catholic Parochial School Teachers," doctoral dissertation, University of Wisconsin, 1970.

tolerance for value differences might be explored at the time of employment.

Finally, the principal should recognize that in the decision-making aspects of his role, individual values held by the decision maker play a continuing and significant part. In a sense, values serve as a screen through which decision alternatives are filtered, since decisions ultimately are based on one's conceptions of the desirable. Administrative relationships often might be improved if the principal made explicit the values on which his decisions were based.

Summary

This chapter presented a theoretical model of values, including three levels of analysis—sacred, secular, and operational values. Shifts in secular values from traditional to emergent to postemergent were described. Derived from the sacred values were certain principles of American education: The schools belong to the people, education is a function of the states, education is of federal interest, education is in terms of one's abilities and interests, and education is equally available to all. Derived from the postemergent secular values were certain trends in contemporary education related to involvement, instructional change, personnel, educational finance, and educational control. Authoritative recommendations regarding society's expectations for the schools were synthesized next, and research regarding the relationship of cultural values to expectations for the school as an institution was presented, revealing the extent of educator-noneducator, elementary-secondary, and regional differences. Expectations for the school also were found to vary systematically in terms of schooling, occupation, social class, age, religion, and political party affiliation of various subpublics.

Research into the relationship of individual values to role relations within the institution revealed that both the nature of individual values and the extent of agreement on individual values were related to such outcomes as achievement, effectiveness, satisfaction, confidence in leadership, and morale. Some guidelines for the behavior of the principal were drawn concerning the cultural values–institutional expectations relationship and the individual values–role expectations relationship.

SUGGESTED ACTIVITIES

1. Using an instrument such as the Task of Public Education (TPE) Opinionnaire, obtain and assess the expectations held by different subpublics within a community. Compare the results across communities.

2. Utilizing a sociometric-type diagram, plot the interrelationships of agencies, councils, committees, and organizations in a community. Compare by type or location of school their number and interface with the school.

3. Interview community leaders or position holders regarding their value orientations or expectations for the schools. Predict the stances they will take regarding current educational trends and issues.

4. Assess either the individual values (using the DVI) or the educational expectations (using the TPE Opinionnaire) held by the teachers or students within a school. Compare the results by age, sex, grade level, or other meaningful variables.

5. Project alternative educational trends or futures utilizing the three different sets of secular values—traditional, emergent, and postemergent.

SELECTED REFERENCES

ALLPORT, GORDON W., and P. E. VERNON, *Study of Values,* Boston, Houghton Mifflin, 1951.

CAMPBELL, ROALD F., et al., *Introduction to Educational Administration,* 4th ed., Boston, Allyn & Bacon, 1971, chaps. 2 and 3.

DOWNEY, LAWRENCE W., *The Task of Public Education,* Chicago, Midwest Administration Center, 1960.

DRUCKER, PETER, *The Age of Discontinuity,* New York, Harper & Row, 1968.

FABER, CHARLES F., and GILBERT F. SHEARRON, *Elementary School Administration, Theory and Practice,* New York, Holt, Rinehart and Winston, 1970, chaps. 1, 5–8.

FROMM, ERICH, *The Revolution of Hope: Toward a Humanized Technology,* New York: Bantam, 1958.

GETZELS, J. W., JAMES M. LIPHAM, and ROALD F. CAMPBELL, *Educational Administration as a Social Process,* New York: Harper & Row, 1968, chaps. 6 and 10.

HACK, WALTER G., et al., eds., *Educational Administration, Selected Readings,* 2nd ed., Boston, Allyn & Bacon, 1971, chap. 2.

HARMAN, WILLIS W., "Nature of Our Changing Society: Implications for Schools," in *Social and Technological Change: Implications For Education,* Eugene, Center for Advanced Study of Educational Administration, University of Oregon, 1970, chaps. 1–8.

MCLEARY, LLOYD E., and STEPHEN P. HENCLEY, *Secondary School Administration, Theoretical Bases of Professional Practice,* New York, Dodd, Mead, 1965, chaps. 1–3.

OHM, ROBERT E., and WILLIAM G. MONAHAN, eds., *Educational Administration —Philosophy in Action,* Norman, College of Education, University of Oklahoma, 1965.

OSTRANDER, RAYMOND H., and RAY C. DETHY, *A Values Approach to Educational Administration,* New York, American Book, 1968, chaps. 1–2.

REICH, CHARLES A., *The Greening of America,* New York, Random House, 1970.

THOMPSON, JAMES D., *Organizations in Action,* New York, McGraw-Hill, 1967.

CHAPTER 5
Organization theory

ince the school is a complex organization, the analytic characteristics that distinguish it as such possess great utility for examining
its structural and operational dynamics. The necessity for concern
with organizational theory arises because the programs of the school
require a high degree of coordinated effort. Attention must be given,
therefore, to hierarchical power relationships, organizational structure,
and interpersonal interaction in the school. Knowledge of organizational
theory is essential if the principal is to give leadership in effecting organizational change.

To serve as a background for recent and emerging organizational
theories, the school is first described according to some classical concepts
of organizational structure—hierarchy, power, and mechanisms for achieving coordination. Next the school is examined in terms of formal organizational theory focusing on organizational means and ends. The informal organization is then considered, specifically with respect to the
organizational climate of the school. The following concepts concerning
organizational change are next addressed: types of change, processes
of change, agents of change, and variables that affect change. The
chapter concludes with a delineation of some implications of organizational theory and research for the principal's role.

Classical organization theory

For many years organizational theorists have been concerned with the
institutional dimension of social systems. Although there has been some
dispute over the exact definition of a formal organization, scholars generally agree that formal organizations have certain common characteristic elements including the following: *have these 4*

fits in with Guba's theory

1. GOAL ORIENTATION. Organizations have goals that typically have
been legitimized by the larger culture of which they are a part, and
these goals provide unity of purpose for the organization.

2. HIERARCHICAL STRUCTURE. In organizations, power is distributed
through formally defined superordinate-subordinate relationships.

3. ORGANIZATIONAL STRUCTURE. In organizations, the functions and
processes are distributed into defined role relationships and procedures
for the regulation and evaluation of activities.

4. INTERPERSONAL INTERACTION. In organizations, the coordinated activities take effect in situations involving person-to-person interaction.

Concepts from classical organizational theory that are useful in analyzing or structuring the school include consideration of the hierarchical nature of organizations, power relationships and compliance within organizations, and the coordination of effort within organizations.

HIERARCHICAL STRUCTURE OF THE SCHOOL

As Weber indicated, the principle of hierarchy is the most commonly utilized means for channeling authority and responsibility in an organized manner.[1] The scalar concept of hierarchy includes a delineation of the scope of authority of superiors over subordinates; it typically takes the shape of a pyramid consisting of the various organizational levels—"top" management, "middle" management, and the "bottom" or technical level.

Early analyses of the hierarchical structure of the school organization tended to view the board of education and the school superintendent as "top management," the school principal as "middle management," and the classroom teacher at the technical or operational level. Indeed, for certain functions this simplistic view may be appropriate. As Parsons pointed out, however, in his analysis of the hierarchical structure of the school, there are critical points at which one finds qualitative breaks in the simple continuity of "line" authority in the school organization.[2] Those at the top levels do not tell those at the lower levels "what to do," because the functions at each level in the organization are qualitatively different.

In Parsons' view, the hierarchy of the school may be more appropriately viewed as consisting of three system levels—the institutional level, the managerial level, and the technical level. The institutional level comprises the community and the larger social system which is the source of "meaning," legitimation, and support for the school. As principals will attest, there are many direct points of articulation between the community and the school or even the individual classroom. To insist or even suggest that parents channel all their concerns through the hierarchical structure of the school system is folly. Instead, parents usually relate not to school systems but to schools. In many facets of its operation, therefore, the school consistently violates strict adherence to the scalar principle of hierarchy.

[1] Max Weber, "Bureaucracy," in Joseph A. Litterer, ed., *Organizations*, New York, Wiley, 1959, p. 173.

[2] Talcott Parsons, "Some Ingredients of a General Theory of Formal Organization," in Andrew W. Halpin, ed., *Administrative Theory in Education*, Chicago, Midwest Administration Center, University of Chicago, 1958, pp. 41–47.

The managerial level, including the superintendent, supervisors, and principals, *controls* or administers the technical suborganization in terms of the tasks to be performed, personnel to be employed, purchasing policy, and so on, in the traditional hierarchical sense of organizational form. But as both Parsons and Hills have observed, the managerial level also *services* the suborganization by mediating between the suborganization and those who use its pupils as products and by procuring the resources necessary for carrying out the technical (e.g., teaching) functions.[3] Thus it may readily be seen that in many decisions the technical expert (the teachers, in the case of the school) must participate in decision making and must assume some responsibility for the consequences of decisions made, the manager (the principal, in the case of the school) being powerless to implement or plan implementation without the competence of the expert. Therefore, when someone indicates that he has "served" as a principal, in a sense he has done just that. Both the technical and the managerial levels are important, since either can interfere seriously with the functioning of the other by withholding its important contribution.

Within the school organization several mechanisms have been established for better articulation among the three system levels—the institutional level, the managerial level, and the technical level. Serving as interstitial bridges between the community or institutional level and the managerial level of the schools are the boards of education and lay advisory committees. Similarly, parent-teacher organizations have long bridged the community or institutional level and both the managerial and technical levels of the school. Recently professional negotiations committees have begun to act primarily as a bridge between the technical and the institutional levels of the school.

The concept of the hierarchical structure of the school in terms of the three system levels is particularly useful to the school principal. It permits examination of the articulations among the system levels, generating questions such as the following: "Are the bridging mechanisms adequate in terms of number and scope?" "Are the mechanisms truly representative of the system levels?" "Are the mechanisms serving their intended purposes?"

POWER RELATIONSHIPS IN THE SCHOOL

When the hierarchical structure of the school is conceived in terms of the three system levels, it is apparent that each possesses a certain degree of power vis-à-vis another. The institutional level possesses the power

---

[3] R. Jean Hills, *Toward a Science of Organization*, Eugene, Center for the Advanced Study of Educational Administration, University of Oregon, 1968.

to sustain or withhold financial support for the schools, the managerial level possesses power to control and to service the schools, and the technical level possesses power to control the amount and quality of teaching.

Etzioni, who has examined the types or ways of exercising power in organizations insofar as control over the lower participants is concerned, names three types: coercive power, or the ability to force one to comply through the application of punishment; remunerative power, or the control over such material rewards as salaries, wages, and commissions; and normative power, which is based on the allocation and manipulation of symbolic rewards, such as esteem, prestige, and peer group mores and values.[4] Reactions of organizational subordinates to these three types of power are as follows: Coercive power results in alienative involvement, remunerative power results in calculative involvement, and normative power results in moral involvement.

As a rule, a school is viewed in terms of the relationship between normative power and moral involvement. That is, it is the general norm that schools exist to fulfill laudable tasks of education, and the students, as lower organizational participants, should have moral commitment to this norm. Yet through compulsory attendance laws, the schools also possess coercive power. Moreover, the typical student has few alternative schooling options available to him, other than perhaps private, parochial, or more recently "alternate" schools. Therefore, it should not be surprising to find among many students a high degree of alienation. Because of graduation requirements, course credits, and grading practices, the school also exercises considerable remunerative power. In some recent experimental learning programs recognition of this power has been extended to rewarding the student with candy or money. Student reaction to remunerative power may be expected to be calculative.

Many of the recent issues in education—compulsory attendance, alternate schools, and pay or reward for learning—may be viewed as mechanisms for using different types of power in the school vis-à-vis the student. Additional research is needed to determine whether and for what reasons the different expressions of power relationships might be quite effective with certain types of students. An open-minded attitude toward such research is preferable to that of flatly declaring that the school should exercise only normative power, then expecting moral compliance from the students.

Just as the student reaction to the three types of power may be analyzed, a similar analysis of teacher reaction to the three types of power relationships may be instructive. Concerning coercive power, there are few things indeed that a principal can force a teacher to do. Regarding

---

[4] Amitai Etzioni, *A Comparative Analysis of Complex Organizations*, New York, Free Press, 1961, pp. 12–21.

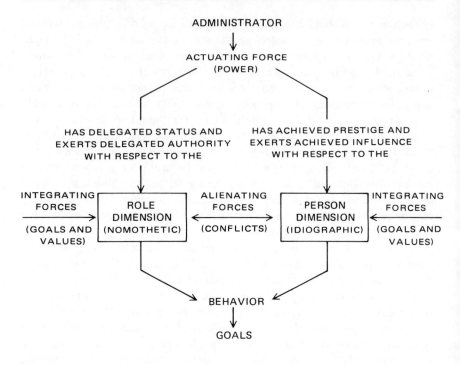

Figure 5.1

Model of administrative power relationships

SOURCE: E. G. Guba, "Research in Internal Administration—What Do We Know?" in Roald F. Campbell and James M. Lipham, eds., *Administrative Theory as a Guide to Action,* Chicago, Midwest Administration Center, University of Chicago, 1960, p. 124.

remunerative power, the single salary schedule practically precludes differentiation in pay based on meritorious performance. Hence the remaining type of power left in the principal-teacher relationship is that of appealing to the norms of the educational profession, the goals of the organization, and the values of the individual.

To depict the normative power relationships in the educational organization, Guba designed the model shown in Figure 5.1. Within this framework it may be observed that the major function of the principal (the administrator at the top of the diagram) is to elicit human behavior consistent with and tending to fulfill certain goals.[5] As we indicated in our discussion of social systems theory in Chapter 3, both the role and the personality dimensions must be taken into account if behavior is to

[5] Egon G. Guba, "Research in Internal Administration—What Do We Know?" in Roald F. Campbell and James M. Lipham, eds., *Administrative Theory as a Guide to Action,* Chicago, Midwest Administration Center, University of Chicago, 1960, p. 123.

be structured in given ways; thus the arrows from the administrator to the goals admit of two routes—via each of these dimensions.

The force or drive implied by the arrows flowing downward from the principal consists of two kinds of power, which Guba described as follows:

> In terms of the role dimension, the administrator is the officially constituted authority to carry out such functions as defining roles, applying rewards or punishments, and making decisions. His status in this connection is intimately tied to his office, and the power he wields is ascribed to his office. We may summarize these facts by describing the administrator's power along the role dimension as *delegated*. In terms of the person dimension, however, the administrator has no "official" power; instead, he must develop his prestige and influence on the basis of merit. We may say that whatever prestige and influence the administrator has he personally has *achieved*.[6]

As Guba's model shows, all principals have some degree of delegated power—that is, authority; but not all have achieved power—that is, influence. Half-powerless is the principal who lacks the esteem of the individuals with whom he works; half-powerless also is the principal who chooses to abdicate his delegated authority (sometimes in the mistaken notion that to do so is to be "democratic") and who tries to operate his school via the personalistic dimension only.[7] As we discuss in greater detail in the subsequent chapter on leadership, the exercise of both forms of power is essential to achieve coordination within the organization.

COORDINATION IN THE SCHOOL

A number of classical organizational concepts have utility for achieving coordination within the school, including unity of command, span of control, and line-staff relationships. Each of these should be considered briefly, if only to indicate instances in which they consistently seem to be violated in the school.

UNITY OF COMMAND. The principle of unity of command—that an individual should report directly to, or be supervised directly by, no more than one individual—is usually viewed as the desirable norm on which school district organizational charts and tables are based. Qualitative breaks in the behavioral structure of the schools notwithstanding, such organizational charts typically specify that the principal is in an intermediate position between the superintendent and the teachers and that he serves as the head of the school. Even so, in some school systems

---

[6] Ibid., pp. 123–125.
[7] Ibid.

the principal must report directly to several superordinates, depending on the problem to be resolved or the function to be performed. Moreover, considerable variance may exist in school districts between the duties or decision-making responsibilities as described on paper and those as defined in day-to-day operations. In such situations it is not unusual to hear principals comment: "I'm supposed to report to the Assistant Superintendent for Instruction, but actually I report to the Superintendent and anyone else down there who will listen."

It is our observation that the principle of unity of command frequently is violated in large urban school systems that are moving toward regional or other decentralized administrative arrangements. Principals of schools in large urban districts undergoing such change often find it necessary to report to more than one line officer, since many of the current plans for decentralization are somewhat a charade—they make public claims that the school system is decentralized when in fact everything that really matters still must be decided "downtown."

Violations of the principle of unity of command typically occur in the area of building maintenance, as well. Although it is generally recognized (and we subsequently recommend) that the principal should supervise the custodial and maintenance personnel in the school, in some school systems maintenance supervisors have primary responsibility for this function. In any event, agreements must be reached to avoid subjecting the custodian simultaneously to conflicting expectations for his role performance.

SPAN OF CONTROL. The concept of span of control dictates that only a reasonable number of persons should report directly to any one position. Early authorities in administration have recommended that 8 to 12 subordinates reporting directly to one position is reasonable; and when such range is exceeded, the number of interactions required to manage the organization increases in geometric proportions.[8]

Campbell has examined the concept of span of control in the educational organization, however, and has shown that the number of persons supervised may be increased substantially without inviting dysfunction if (1) the subordinates display a relatively high degree of training and expertise (as in the case of teachers), (2) the tasks to be performed are relatively routinized (as in the case of the tightly scheduled school with standardized curricula), and (3) there is provided adequate supportive staff (specialists) to assist with unique problems.[9]

[8] V. A. Graicunas, "Relationship in Organization," in Luther Gulick and Lyndall F. Urwick, eds., *Papers on the Science of Administration*, New York, Institute of Public Administration, 1937, pp. 181–187.

[9] Roald F. Campbell, "What Peculiarities in Educational Administration Make It a Special Case?" in Andrew W. Halpin, ed., *Administrative Theory in Education*, Chicago, Midwest Administration Center, University of Chicago, 1958, pp. 166–185.

We have observed that a reasonable span of control is increasingly violated in the case of the school principal. Concerning the instructional leadership function, for example, programs of individualized instruction call for increasing diversification of curricula. That is, programs of study are becoming less routinized—in class schedules, course content, and use of space and facilities, for example. These changes frequently require attention and adjudication by the principal.

Regarding staff personnel, it is indeed rare that the principal has only 8 to 12 teachers to supervise, since schools continue to increase in size. And even though multiunit or departmental arrangements may be utilized, the heads of these subunits typically do not assume full line authority—rather, they perform a staff function. For example, team leaders and department heads typically continue to belong to the bargaining unit of the teachers' organization and are often prohibited from conducting formal evaluation activities that might lead to teacher transfer or dismissal. Thus the principal may be required to visit each teacher formally and personally to conduct staff evaluations, regardless of the size of the school. Moreover, many staff personnel activities, such as orientation of new teachers, cannot be effectively delegated *in toto* to subordinates.

Concerning span of control in the student personnel function, the principal, of course, does not directly supervise the students. Yet it is the established norm that the principal should have as much direct contact with students as possible—not only when there are negative problems, such as the most difficult discipline and truancy cases, but also when there are positive programs, such as assemblies, cocurricular athletic games and performances, and informal conferences with students.

Concerning relationships with citizens and parents, it also is evident that in a sense the principal has a span of control that is as wide as the attendance area is large. Although each person in the school has responsibilities for relating appropriately with the community, individuals and groups of parents often seek out the principal directly for leadership or assistance with their problems. In short, parental demands to talk to "the man" must be honored.

In summary, the concept of a reasonable span of control for the principal seems to be violated consistently in the day-to-day operation of the school. This places the principal in direct proximity to many individuals, reference groups, and subpublics, but it also tends to reduce the amount of time that he can give to dealing with each person or treating each problem "in the round." Our observations of the on-the-job behavior of principals in large urban schools, for example, reveal that the nature of the problem and the persons with whom the principal interacts change on the average of every 3.8 minutes during a "normal" day. Little wonder that the principal goes home tired. In addition, however, he is typically plagued with guilt feelings over a failure to engage in systematic planning, even though the demands of the role render contemplative thought almost impossible. Reducing the span of control of the principal should ameliorate this difficulty.

LINE AND STAFF. Although school systems may be officially structured in terms of line and staff relationships, it is our view that the traditional division of responsibilities—line for administration and staff for supporting services, as in the military—is of limited utility in operating a school. In fact, this notion may have served to hinder rather than foster leadership.

Research has revealed that instead of a monocratic form of bureaucracy, at least at the level of the individual building, the school is typically duocratic—if not multicratic.[10] For example, consider the organization from the viewpoint of a teacher who has requested assistance with a problem in teaching and learning. He not only may receive assistance from the principal, the line officer, but typically he will seek assistance from subject supervisors, general supervisors, learning specialists, or even outside consultants. In fact, our informal observations in schools lead us to believe that principals spend more time with parents, secretaries, custodians, and cooks than they do with teachers. Teachers, on the other hand, tend to interact more often with other teachers, department heads, and other generalized and specialized "staff" personnel than with principals—particularly in large urban schools. Thus in the workflow of the schools the administrative and supervisory responsibilities typically are not divided in terms of line and staff but in terms of functions to be performed.[11] These functions, such as supervision, obviously cut across line-staff roles.

Although workable alternatives to the bureaucratic line-staff form of organization have not been found, several approaches have been tried in attempting to integrate, rather than separate, essential organizational functions. These include development of the management team concept, utilization of councils and committees, and formation of task forces for specific problems and issues. Each of these alternatives may help to improve the administration of the school.

Formal organization of the school

The principal is the head of a formal organization that has some characteristics similar to other organizations as well as some that are unique.

---

[10] B. Bordon Funk, "Two Roles in the Administration and Supervision of Instruction," doctoral dissertation, Claremont Graduate School, Claremont, Calif., 1964.

[11] W. W. Charters, Jr., "An Approach to the Formal Organization of the School," in Daniel E. Griffiths, ed., *Behavioral Science and Educational Administration*, Chicago, National Society for the Study of Education, 1964, pp. 243–261.

It likewise follows that in some ways the principal's role is less complex, yet in others it is more difficult. For example, the principal seldom needs to be greatly concerned with marketing and merchandising, variable supply and demand, detailed inventory control, and similar complex parameters. On the other hand, he works in an institution faced with conflicting external demands and controls; this institution utilizes an underdeveloped intensive technology (teaching) and is subject to considerable stress and conflict. Despite these differences, it is useful to examine the school in terms of general theories of complex organizations.

To order the structural and functional relationships within organizations, Jerald Hage, of the University of Wisconsin, conceived and proposed a general axiomatic theory of organizations that has generated considerable research regarding the formal organization of the school.[12] Based on the earlier work of Weber, Barnard, and Thompson, propositions were derived relating four organizational means to four organizational ends or outcomes.[13] The four organizational *means* variables are as follows:

1. COMPLEXITY (SPECIALIZATION)—the number of occupational specialties and the level of training required.

2. CENTRALIZATION (HIERARCHY OF AUTHORITY)—the proportion of jobs that participate in decision making and the number of areas in which decisions are made by the decision makers.

3. FORMALIZATION (STANDARDIZATION)—the proportion of jobs that are codified and the range of variation allowed within jobs.

4. STRATIFICATION (STATUS SYSTEM)—the differences in income and prestige among jobs and the rate of mobility between low- and high-ranking jobs or status levels.

The four organizational *ends* variables are as follows:

1. ADAPTIVENESS (FLEXIBILITY)—the number of new programs in a year and the number of new techniques in a year.

2. PRODUCTION (EFFECTIVENESS)—the number of units produced per year and the rate of increase in units per year.

3. EFFICIENCY (COST)—the cost per unit of output per year and the amount of idle resources per year.

4. JOB SATISFACTION (MORALE)—satisfaction with working conditions and rate of turnover in job occupants per year.

---

[12] Jerald Hage, "An Axiomatic Theory of Organizations," *Administrative Science Quarterly,* 10 (December 1965), 289–320.

[13] Max Weber, *Theory of Social and Economic Organization,* translated by A. M. Henderson and Talcott Parsons, New York, Oxford University Press, 1947, pp. 333–336; Chester I. Barnard, "Functions and Pathology of Status Systems in Formal Organizations," quoted in William Foote Whyte, ed., *Industry and Society,* New York, McGraw-Hill, 1946; Victor A. Thompson, *Modern Organization,* New York, Knopf, 1961.

The major theme of the axiomatic theory is the concept of functional strains, as discussed by Parsons, Bales, and Shils, or the concept of organizational dilemma, as discussed by Blau and Scott.[14] These concepts mean that an increase in one variable results in a corresponding decrease in another variable, or that the maximization of one social means results in the minimization of another. The variables behave as if they are inversely proportional. Although the idea of this type of interaction of two variables is an old one, the real problem is to specify which variables are in opposition to one another and, even more important, why they are in opposition.

Seven propositions in the axiomatic theory are as follows:

    I. The higher the centralization, the higher the production.
   II. The higher the formalization, the higher the efficiency.
  III. The higher the centralization, the higher the formalization.
  IV. The higher the stratification, the lower the job satisfaction.
   V. The higher the stratification, the higher the production.
  VI. The higher the stratification, the lower the adaptiveness.
 VII. The higher the complexity, the lower the centralization.[15]

Although it may be useful to examine each of the propositions, it is even more instructive to consider two extreme types of organizations suggested by the variables—the organic organization with an emphasis on adaptiveness and the mechanistic organization with an emphasis on production. Each is the converse of the other, as indicated below:[16]

ORGANIC ORGANIZATION	MECHANISTIC ORGANIZATION
High complexity	Low complexity
Low centralization	High centralization
Low formalization	High formalization
Low stratification	High stratification
High adaptiveness	Low adaptiveness
Low production	High production
Low efficiency	High efficiency
High job satisfaction	Low job satisfaction

When one variable in the mechanistic constellation is increased, each of the other variables in the same constellation also increases while variables in the organic constellation decrease. Conversely, a decrease in any one of the mechanistic variables leads to similar decreases in

[14] Talcott Parsons, Robert Bales, and Edward Shils, *The Working Papers in the Theory of Action,* New York, Free Press, 1958; Peter Blau and W. Richard Scott, *Formal Organizations,* San Francisco, Chandler, 1962.

[15] Hage, op. cit., 297–299.

[16] Ibid., 305.

the others, but variables in the organic constellation increase. The theory proposes similar relationships for changes in the organic constellation. The mechanistic constellation may be said to describe the bureaucratically oriented school, and the organic constellation may be said to describe the professionally oriented school.

Sergiovanni and Starratt have observed that schools that approach the mechanistic model in structure and orientation tend to be precise in defining roles, obligations, duties, rights, and relations (high formalization and high stratification); are detailed in prescribing rules and regulations as they seek to program decision making for teachers and clients (high formalization); seek to funnel decision making that is varied and unpredictable to the top while standardizing decision making at lower levels (high centralization); and are concerned with processing the largest number of students at the least cost in terms of personnel, money, equipment, space, and the like (high production and high efficiency).[17]

Hetzel was among the first researchers to apply axiomatic organizational theory to the schools.[18] He examined departments of curriculum and instruction in a sample of medium-sized midwestern school districts and found a definite relationship between the organizational structure (means) variables and adaptiveness of the school systems, defined as the number of new programs and new services implemented. Recently Walter has discovered that the four structural variables are meaningfully related to adaptiveness and innovation in the elementary school.[19] Similarly, a recent study by Herrick revealed that the multiunit elementary school that stresses individually guided education (IGE-MUS/E) is a more dynamic organization—particularly on the variables of centralization and stratification—than is the nonmultiunit school.[20] Moreover, he found that teacher motivation—particularly concerning social relations and involvement in decision making—is significantly higher in multiunit than in nonmultiunit elementary schools.

With regard to organizational structure, all schools appear to be moving in the direction of an organic organization. Concerning complexity, an increasing number of specialized roles are being utilized—team leaders, teacher aides, and subject specialists, for example. No

[17] Thomas J. Sergiovanni and Robert J. Starratt, *Emerging Patterns of Supervision: Human Perspectives*, New York, McGraw-Hill, 1971, pp. 64–65.

[18] Robert W. Hetzel, "The Relationship Between Organizational Structure and Organizational Adaptability in Departments of Curriculum and Instruction," doctoral dissertation, University of Wisconsin, 1971.

[19] James E. Walter, "Relationship of Organizational Structure to Adaptiveness in Elementary Schools," doctoral dissertation, University of Wisconsin, 1973.

[20] H. Scott Herrick, "Organizational Structure and Teacher Motivation in Multiunit and Nonmultiunit Elementary Schools," doctoral dissertation, University of Wisconsin, 1974.

longer is the school a simplistically structured organization. Regarding centralization, there is considerable evidence that collective bargaining has increased substantially the involvement of teachers in decision making and that student activism has gained for students the right to meaningful participation in making decisions. Although a formalization trend is less discernible, it is generally viewed as desirable practice to reduce the degree of standardization in teaching through emphasizing individualized instruction. Similarly, concerning stratification, there is some evidence that the differences between salary and status levels of principals and teachers are becoming less pronounced.

Trends regarding the organizational ends or outcomes of the school, however, are less clear. Considerable attention has been directed for several years toward increasing both the innovativeness of the school and the morale of the organization. Recent demands for accountability, however, have stressed that the schools should increase both productivity and efficiency. Axiomatic organizational theory gives the principal a framework not only for assessing the conflicting trends but also for weighing the "tradeoffs" he must make in moving the school in the direction of a dynamic, professional organization.

Informal organization of the school

Few distinctions have greater utility for the principal than that made between the formal and the informal structure of the school. Whereas the formal organization consists of a set of structured roles, the informal one is characterized by interpersonal interactions. Whereas the principal may exert formal authority, he is half-powerless without having achieved prestige. Whereas the formal structure prescribes decision responsibility, the informal one regulates degree and quality of decision involvement. Whereas the formal organization has well-defined lines of communication, the informal one has grapevines that are perhaps equally effective. Whereas the formal organization may invoke positive or negative sanctions, pay, and promotions, the informal one may give or withhold favors and rewards. Such instructive comparisons are endless.

As Iannaccone has aptly demonstrated, the formal and informal organizations are inextricably entwined in the complex power structure of the school—particularly at the school building level.[21] Functioning within the school are many informal primary groups of people who tend to see things somewhat similarly, who may meet over a cup of coffee at

[21] Laurence Iannaccone, "An Approach to the Informal Organization of the School," in Daniel E. Griffiths, ed., *Behavioral Science and Educational Administration*, Chicago, National Society for the Study of Education, 1964, pp. 223–242.

work, and who may socialize together after school. Moreover, the primary groups may be linked by overlapping memberships and activities. This is a highly personal form of interaction and operates continually to modify the goals, purposes, procedures, and outcomes of the formal organization. Because of changes in membership and leadership, the informal groups may not be entirely stable, yet they can be intensely active at any given time. Obviously the principal, as head of the formal organization, wishes the informal organization to develop and operate in modes that if not compatible at least are not inimical to the attainment of organizational goals.

It is evident that individuals relate in different ways to both the formal and the informal structure of the school. Presthus, in his analysis of personnel in complex organizations, has divided people into three types: (1) the "upward mobiles," whose views typically are congruent with organizational goals and who usually exert great effort on the job; (2) the "indifferents," who have little concern with organizational goals and who "just work here"; and (3) the "ambivalents," who would like to succeed but are either unwilling to put forth the effort or unsure how to go about it.[22] The ambivalents are often those who are most influenced by the goals set within the informal structure of the organization.

Another useful description of how personnel relate to the organization was defined by Merton and refined by Gouldner to include (1) "cosmopolitans," who are low on loyalty to the employing organization, high on commitment to specialized role skills, and likely to use an outer reference group orientation; and (2) "locals," who are high on loyalty to the employing organization, low on commitment to specialized role skills, and likely to use an inner-reference-group orientation.[23] In short, the local confines his interests to his own community; the cosmopolitan relates to the outside world as well as to the local community. Typically it is the local who relies more heavily on the informal network of personal relationships within the school.

Although the classifications by Gouldner and Presthus are generally descriptive, they are not situationally analytic. To analyze informal structures within the school, sociometric and observational studies of individual member preferences have long been utilized—at least to identify primary groupings. A refreshing empirical approach to analysis of informal relationships within the school, however, was originally con-

[22] Robert Presthus, *The Organizational Society,* New York, Vintage, 1962.

[23] Robert Merton, *Social Theory and Social Structure,* New York, Free Press, 1957; Alvin W. Gouldner, "Cosmopolitans and Locals: Toward an Analysis of Latent Social Roles," *Administrative Science Quarterly,* 2 (December 1957; March 1958), 281–306; 444–480.

ceived by Halpin, who started from the observation that organizational climate can be construed as the organizational "personality" of a school (figuratively, "personality" being to the individual what "climate" is to the organization).[24] Accordingly, an instrument was developed based on intuitive observations within schools. Concerning these observations, Halpin and Croft commented: "In gathering material for OCDQ items, one struck us forcibly: that an essential determinant of a school's 'effectiveness' as an organization is the principal's ability—or his lack of ability—to create a 'climate' in which he, and other group members, can initiate and consummate acts of leadership."[25]

From a large number of initial items, the Organizational Climate Description Questionnaire (OCDQ) was constructed and pilot tested. The following items represent the flavor of the instrument:

1. There is considerable laughter when teachers gather informally.
2. Teachers ramble when they talk in faculty meetings.
3. The principal sets an example by working hard himself.
4. Faculty meetings are organized according to a tight agenda.
5. The teachers accomplish their work with great vim, vigor, and pleasure.[26]

Four factors descriptive of the behavior of the teachers and four descriptive of the behavior of the principal, subsequently identified as the basic determinants of a school's climate, are as follows:

TEACHERS' BEHAVIOR

1. DISENGAGEMENT indicates that the teachers do not work well together. They pull in different directions with respect to the task; they gripe and bicker among themselves.

2. HINDRANCE refers to the teachers' feeling that the principal burdens them with routine duties, committee demands, and other requirements which the teachers construe as unnecessary busy-work.

3. ESPRIT refers to "morale." The teachers feel that their social needs are being satisfied, and that they are, *at the same time,* enjoying a sense of accomplishment in their job.

4. INTIMACY refers to the teachers' enjoyment of friendly social relations with each other.

PRINCIPAL'S BEHAVIOR

5. ALOOFNESS refers to behavior by the principal which is characterized as formal and impersonal. He "goes by the book" and prefers to be guided by rules and policies rather than to deal with the teachers in an informal, face-to-face situation.

---

[24] Andrew W. Halpin and Don B. Croft, *The Organizational Climate of Schools,* Chicago, Midwest Administration Center, University of Chicago, 1963.

[25] Ibid., pp. 7–8.

[26] Ibid., pp. 30–31.

6. PRODUCTION EMPHASIS refers to behavior by the principal which is characterized by close supervision of the staff. He is highly directive and task-oriented.

7. THRUST refers to behavior marked not by close supervision of the teacher, but by the principal's attempt to motivate the teachers through the example which he personally sets. He does not ask the teachers to give of themselves anything more than he willingly gives of himself; his behavior, though starkly task-oriented, is nonetheless viewed favorably by the teachers.

8. CONSIDERATION refers to behavior by the principal which is characterized by an inclination to treat the teachers "humanly," to try to do a little something extra for them in human terms.[27]

A subsequent factor analysis yielded the following six profiles:

1. THE OPEN CLIMATE describes an energetic, lively organization which is moving toward its goals, and which provides satisfaction for the group members' social needs. Leadership acts emerge easily and appropriately from both the group and the leader. The members are preoccupied disproportionately with neither task achievement nor social-needs satisfaction; satisfaction on both counts seems to be obtained easily and almost effortlessly. The main characteristic of this climate is the "authenticity" of the behavior that occurs among all the members.

2. THE AUTONOMOUS CLIMATE is described as one in which leadership acts emerge primarily from the group. The leader exerts little control over the group members; high *esprit* results primarily from social-needs satisfaction. Satisfaction from task achievement is also present, but to a lesser degree.

3. THE CONTROLLED CLIMATE is characterized best as impersonal and highly task-oriented. The group's behavior is directed primarily toward task accomplishment, while relatively little attention is given to behavior oriented to social-needs satisfaction. *Esprit* is fairly high, but it reflects achievement at some expense to social-needs satisfaction. This climate lacks openness, or "authenticity" of behavior, because the group is disproportionately preoccupied with task achievement.

4. THE FAMILIAR CLIMATE is highly personal, but undercontrolled. The members of this organization satisfy their social needs, but pay relatively little attention to social control in respect to task accomplishment. Accordingly, *esprit* is not extremely high simply because the group members secure little satisfaction from task achievement. Hence, much of the behavior within this climate can be construed as "inauthentic."

5. THE PATERNAL CLIMATE is characterized best as one in which the principal constrains the emergence of leadership acts from the group and attempts to initiate most of these acts himself. The leadership skills within the group are not used to supplement the principal's own ability to initiate leadership acts. Accordingly, some leadership acts are not even attempted.

---

[27] Andrew W. Halpin and Don B. Croft, "The Organizational Climate of Schools," *Administrator's Notebook,* 11 (March 1963), 1–2.

In short, little satisfaction is obtained in respect to either achievement or social needs; hence *esprit* among the members is low.

6. THE CLOSED CLIMATE is characterized by a high degree of apathy on the part of all members of the organization. The organization is not "moving"; *esprit* is low because the group members secure neither social-needs satisfaction nor the satisfaction that comes from task achievement. The members' behavior can be construed as "inauthentic"; indeed, the organization seems to be stagnant.[28]

A further analysis of the school climate profiles yielded yet another set of factors:

1. AUTHENTICITY: The "authenticity" or "openness" of the leader's and the group members' behavior.

2. SATISFACTION: The group members' attainment of conjoint satisfaction in respect to task accomplishment *and* social needs.

3. LEADERSHIP INITIATION: The latitude within which the group members, as well as the leader, can initiate leadership acts.[29]

To indicate that the OCDQ has been useful for stimulating inquiry about the informal organizational structure of organizations is a classic understatement. By 1972 the OCDQ had been utilized in more than 200 empirical studies, and the results had been correlated with almost every situational, organizational, or personalistic parameter imaginable. In our view, the results of the specific studies are perhaps less important than the concepts. Halpin's conceptualization of the informal organization, like Hage's theory of the formal organization, provides the principal with a useful perspective for analysis of the organization, including factors related to organizational change.

Organizational change

Having developed an understanding of both the formal and the informal relationships in the school, the principal is in a better position to initiate organizational change. As Counts indicated back in the 1930s, schools may change in response to external forces and pressures or schools may lead, not only in changing themselves but in altering their large environment.[30] Regardless of the source, the fact is that schools do change and the principal has a key role in the process—if not as the initiator of change, then certainly as the facilitator.

Probably as much analysis of change has occurred in education as in any other field; even so, we still have no general and overarching

[28] Ibid., 2–3.

[29] Ibid., 4.

[30] George S. Counts, *Dare the School Build a New Social Order?* New York, Day, 1932.

theory of change, just as there is no comprehensive theory of administration—and probably never will be. The closest thing to a general theory of change is in terms of the physical science laws of equilibrium—pressures and counterpressures, forces and counterforces—yet these may not be entirely appropriate in social systems.[31]

Many change theorists have directed attention to the factors that may be important in developing coherent theories of change. Guba, for example, felt that one must understand the process of innovation, the nature of the adapting system, and the nature of the agency carrying out the innovation before a change can be successfully institutionalized.[32] Chin likewise stated that there are different strategies for effecting change—empirical-rational, normative-reeducative, and power-compliance—and the selection of a procedural strategy ought to depend on the problem, the nature of the change itself, the biases and values concerning the change, and the process of changing.[33]

Most theorists and researchers concerned with change have analyzed certain specific elements or descriptors of change. These may be grouped according to the following elements: (1) the types of change, (2) the change process, (3) the agents of change, and (4) the intervening variables that affect change.

TYPES OF CHANGE

Typologies of change that usually include three or four categories have been proposed by various theorists. In industry, Leavitt typified change according to three basic categories: structural change, technological change, and behavioral change.[34] In education, Glatthorn and Bowman described three general types of change: one of structure, one of program, and one of people; as did Miller: change of organization, change of program, and change of methodology.[35] Saville described four cate-

---

[31] J. W. Getzels, James M. Lipham, and Roald F. Campbell, *Educational Administration as a Social Process,* New York, Harper & Row, 1968, p. 398.

[32] Egon G. Guba, "Diffusion of Innovation," *Educational Leadership,* 25 (January 1968), 292–295.

[33] Robert Chin, "Basic Strategies and Procedures in Effecting Change," in Edgar L. Morphet and Charles O. Ryan, eds., *Planning and Effecting Needed Changes in Education,* Denver, Colo., Designing Education for the Future, 1967, pp. 39–57.

[34] Harold J. Leavitt, "Applied Organizational Change in Industry: Structural, Technological, and Humanistic Approaches," in James G. March, ed., *Handbook of Organization,* Skokie, Ill., Rand McNally, 1965, pp. 1144–1168.

[35] Allan A. Glatthorn and Thomas R. Bowman, "Into Each Innovation Some Grief Must Fall," *The Abington Conference: Strategies for Change,* Abington, Pa., Abington Learning Association, 1969; Richard I. Miller, "Some Observations and Suggestions," in Richard I. Miller, ed., *Perspectives on Educational Change,* New York, Appleton, 1967, p. 369.

gories of change in education: new technical advances, new processes, new goals, and new curriculum advances.[36]

Several researchers have examined the relationship between the type or kind of change and its rate of diffusion or adoption. Rogers and Shoemaker concluded that a change would be diffused and adopted more readily if it were perceived as (1) more advantageous to the user than what was being used at the moment, (2) less complex, (3) more compatible to the user's value system, (4) more open for trial, and (5) more able to produce observable results.[37] Lippitt found that innovations in education were successfully institutionalized when they (1) were perceived as being relevant to the needs of the students, (2) were able to be undertaken gradually, (3) had built in evaluative techniques, and (4) could be duplicated easily.[38] Zander suggested that resistance to change might be minimized if careful attention is given beforehand to the following matters: what the change should be like, how it should be implemented, and who should participate in making decisions about the change.[39] Moore and Mizuba felt that if a change program were credible, had a visible advantage over the present program, had a simplistic and divisible design, and had measurable objectives, then it could be more readily accepted.[40] Each of these variables provides the principal with cues for assessing the innovation itself, as well as for selecting processes appropriate to a particular change.

THE CHANGE PROCESS

In general, the process of change may be analyzed according to the following conceptualizations: (1) a problem-solving model; (2) a research, development, and diffusion (RD&D) model; (3) an organizational development (OD) model; and (4) a linkage process model that includes elements of the other three.

The traditional model of changing, expounded by Jung and Lippitt, is essentially a problem-solving or decision-making model, since it is concerned with the process of rational thought that goes on inside the

[36] Anthony Saville, "Topography of Change," *Clearing House,* 42 (January 1968), 271–273.

[37] Everett M. Rogers and F. Floyd Shoemaker, *Communication of Innovations: A Cross-Cultural Approach,* 2nd ed., New York, Free Press, 1971, pp. 22–23.

[38] Ronald Lippitt, "The Teacher as Innovator, Seeker, and Sharer of New Practices," in Miller, ed., op. cit., p. 310.

[39] Alvin Zander, "Resistance to Change—Its Analysis and Prevention," *Advanced Management Journal,* 15 (January 1950), 9–11.

[40] Samuel Moore and Kiyoto Mizuba, "Innovation Diffusion: A Study in Credibility," *Educational Forum,* 33 (January 1969), 181–185.

head of the user.[41] As such, this model of the change process is particularly useful when applied to the problems of the school principal or the individual classroom teacher. Jung and Lippitt identified the six basic elements of this model, as follows: (1) identifying the problem, (2) diagnosing the problem, (3) retrieving related knowledge and discussing its implications for overcoming the problem, (4) forming alternatives to action, (5) testing the feasibility of the alternatives, and (6) adopting and implementing the selected alternative. Henrie and Bailey identified the following six phases of this model: (1) clarifying the goals, (2) defining the objectives, (3) defining the mission, (4) analyzing the tasks, (5) establishing the management system, and (6) setting up the evaluative mechanisms.[42] This model, in effect, is the application to change in the school of the general systems concepts described in detail in Chapter 2.

The second process model of change, the RD&D model, gained wide currency in the field of education because many theorists and practitioners began to see that schools and school districts had common problems. This is a formal model that includes identifiable phases in the approach to change. At first this model consisted of three phases—research, development, and diffusion. Thelen described these phases from the vantage point of the user as consisting of enthusiasm, vulgarization, and spread of an innovation.[43] In the latter part of the 1960s, however, when it had become apparent that the diffused changes were not being institutionalized, theorists added a new phase to the RD&D model. Hencley defined the new process model as one of the research, development, diffusion, and adoption of change.[44] In time, other proponents of this process model have added a few refinements to each of the phases. Havelock, for example, feels that: (1) there should be a rational sequence in the evaluation and application of an innovation; (2) research, development, and packaging of a program change should occur before dissemination of the program change; (3) there should be planning on a massive scale; (4) there should be a rational division of labor and coordination of jobs; and (5) the proponents of the innovation should be willing to accept high initial development costs prior to any dis-

[41] Charles Jung and Ronald Lippitt, "The Study of Change as a Concept in Research Utilization," *Theory into Practice*, 5 (February 1966), 25–29.

[42] Samuel N. Henrie, Jr., and Higgins D. Bailey, "Planning Carefully or Muddling Through: An Educator's Choice," *Journal of Secondary Education*, 43 (December 1968), 349–352.

[43] Herbert A. Thelen, "New Practices on the Firing Line," *Administrator's Notebook*, 12 (January 1964), 1–4.

[44] Stephen P. Hencley, "Supplementary Statement to Basic Strategies and Procedures in Effecting Change," in Morphet and Ryan, eds., op. cit., p. 57.

semination acivity.[45] In addition, he feels that a passive but rational consumer population will accept and adopt a proposed innovation if it is offered in the right place, in the right form, and at the right time. Research and development centers, demonstration centers, regional educational laboratories, and experimental schools are examples of the kinds of strategies and programs that have evolved from this model of change.

Because of some feeling that the RD&D model focused excessively on formal organizational rather than informal personalistic variables, a third model, the organizational development (OD) model, was developed. The OD model stresses social interaction and disagrees with some of the assumptions of rationality in social systems underlying both the problem-solving and the RD&D models. Such proponents of the OD model as House, Kerins, and Steele and Schmuck and Miles feel that the user population is not passive and cannot be shaped solely by the process of dissemination itself.[46] Instead, they argue that innovations are institutionalized in a school because of the workings of the social interaction network within the school. In the OD approach to change, intraorganizational groups are viewed as the media, the targets, and the agents of change. The most important variables in this process of changing, as described by Chin, are variables describing the informal as well as the formal structural arrangements of a school.[47] Therefore, considerable attention is given to describing the kinds of action that must be undertaken by the change agent to improve and shape teachers' attitudes and feelings about change. Management training programs, resident change agents, school district in-service programs, and university feedback and systems planning programs are some of the strategies that have evolved from this process model of change.

The final model of change, defined by Havelock in 1970, is the linkage process model.[48] It incorporates some of the phases and strategies of the other three models and has four important phases. The first phase incorporates the stages of the problem-solving process. As such, new knowledge relevant to the problem to be considered is searched for and retrieved. The second phase incorporates the stages of the research process. As such, educational researchers (as in the RD&D model) carry on the process of research, development, and diffusion of research findings to the school. The third phase incorporates the OD model. Here

[45] Ronald G. Havelock, "Experimental School Networks, Theory and Reality," *Journal of Secondary Education,* 46 (April 1971), 179.

[46] Ernest R. House, Thomas Kerins, and Joe M. Steele, "A Test of the Research and Development Model of Change," *Educational Administration Quarterly,* 8 (Winter 1972), 1–14; Richard A. Schmuck and Matthew B. Miles, *Organization Development in Schools,* Palo Alto, Calif., National, 1971.

[47] Chin, op. cit., pp. 48–50.

[48] Havelock, op. cit., 183–184.

attention is focused on the relationships and communication systems between and among the researcher, developer, practitioner, and consumer. The fourth and final phase is that of the linkage process model itself. In this phase each separate role incumbent is helped to see what the other role incumbents are doing in their respective parts of the process of changing. Because this model attempts to synthesize and utilize strategies of the other three models, it has considerable potential for use in the schools.

AGENTS OF CHANGE

Another important consideration of change is the kind of role assumed by the agent of change. In general, change theorists see three types of roles of change agents—the technical consultant, the educational researcher, and the school administrator.

If the agent of change is seen as a technical consultant, his role is taken to be similar to that of a project manager. His role in this case, as described by Blanchard and Cook, is one of planning and controlling the process of change.[49] The techniques and skills involved are those of managing the time, cost, and performance of the client system. Delbecq and Van De Ven feel that the project manager in nonprofit organizations is a technical administrator, concerned with problem solving, project implementation, and project control.[50]

If the agent of change is seen as an educational researcher, his role is viewed as similar to that of a project scientist. Some have felt that the educational researcher should be involved not only in securing relevant information on the characteristics of the schools but also in determining the effects of changes deliberately introduced into the school.[51] For example, Stake stated that the role of educational research is to seek generalizations about educational practices and to make judgments about educational programs.[52] In the research approach to change, data concerning behavioral objectives are systematically gathered and then utilized to make program alterations and change.

When the educational administrator is the agent of change, his role is viewed in terms of leadership initiation. Bennis saw the administrator's

[49] Gary F. Blanchard and Desmond L. Cook, "Project Management and Educational Change," *Educational Technology,* 11 (October 1971), 51–53.

[50] André Delbecq and Andrew Van De Ven, "Organizational Roles in Program Management," Madison, University of Wisconsin, 1972, unpublished paper, pp. 20–24.

[51] John Hayman, *A Plan for Reorganization of the Research and Evaluation Operations Within the School District,* Philadelphia Public Schools, 1967, unpublished paper, pp. 3–8.

[52] Robert E. Stake, "The Countenance of Educational Evaluation," *Teachers' College Record,* 68 (April 1967), 523–540.

role as that of providing consultative and psychological support for the client system during the transactional phases of change, and encouraging the clients to test out their competencies, cooperate with one another, and experiment with the change.[53] Davis said that the role of the administrator as change agent is to help provide prestige for the experimentation of the client system and to help develop a feeling of belonging and commitment to the overall process of change.[54] Cunningham stated that the role of the administrator as a change agent is to understand the concepts of social system, change agent, diagnosis, and intervention.[55]

Considerable research has focused on the attributes of the agents of change. In his classic studies of school superintendents, Carlson found that superintendents who were from outside the system, opinion leaders among superintendents, and superintendents who were persuasive, communicative, and involved in many educational activities tended to adopt innovations earlier than superintendents without these characteristics.[56] He also discovered that the more innovative superintendents tend to have more formal education, participate in more professional meetings, be better known and more often asked for advice, hold more prestigious superintendencies, perceive more support for change among school board members, and rely more on outside sources of information and advice than the less innovative superintendents.[57] Kimbrough found that the superintendent who would effect change had to be familiar with and able to manipulate the power structure within the community.[58]

VARIABLES THAT AFFECT CHANGE

Many variables have been found to relate to organizational change. Those which the principal will need to take into account involve both the community and the school.

Only recently has research been directed to the community variables that may affect educational change. Barnes learned that communities

[53] Warren G. Bennis, *Changing Organizations,* New York, McGraw-Hill, 1966, p. 176.

[54] J. Clark Davis, "Supplementary Statement to Planning for Changes in Education," in Morphet and Ryan, eds., op. cit., p. 35.

[55] Luvern L. Cunningham, "Viewing Change in School Organizations," *Administrator's Notebook,* 11 (September 1962), 3.

[56] Richard O. Carlson, *Executive Succession and Organizational Change,* Chicago, Midwest Administration Center, University of Chicago, 1962.

[57] Richard O. Carlson, *Adoption of Educational Innovations,* Eugene, Center for the Advanced Study of Educational Administration, University of Oregon, 1965.

[58] Ralph B. Kimbrough, *Political Power and Educational Decision-Making,* Skokie, Ill., Rand McNally, 1964.

characterized by discrepant value systems, heterogeneous populations, public apathy, regional isolationism, and uncoordinated local governments were less likely to foster programs of change.[59] Brickell found that communities unwilling to pay for quality programs or attract professional teachers and administrators would be less likely to accept change.[60] He also felt, however, that a community probably would not hinder a new program if it were not aroused against change.[61]

Several variables at the building level seem to be related to change. Lippitt et al. found that schools holding regular staff meetings, establishing team links, and defining horizontal links between teams were more likely to be successful in the institutionalization of change.[62] Brickell discovered that if communication links are close and well utilized within a school unit, the institutionalization of change is facilitated.[63] Several studies have found organizational climate to be related to successful institutionalization of change. As Hughes indicated, an open organizational climate is most important because it provides for the development of a spirit of inquiry and choice.[64]

The role of the principal as a change agent is a crucial factor in initiating change. Howsam stressed that teachers are more likely to accept educational change programs if the principal is perceived as actively supportive of the teacher's role in implementing the change.[65] Abbott and Eidell felt that a change program is more likely to succeed if the administrator works to (1) understand the organization as a total system, (2) support teachers in their experimentation with the change program, (3) develop the skills and tools for using information sources more adequately, and (4) clarify the division of labor in the school.[66] In summary, it is unlikely that any major change can come about in the school without the active support of the principal.

[59] Melvin Barnes, "Planning and Effecting Needed Changes in Urban and Metropolitan Areas," in Morphet and Ryan, eds., op. cit., pp. 204–221.

[60] Henry M. Brickell, "Organizing for Educational Change," in Glen F. Ovard, ed., Change and Secondary School Administration, New York, Macmillan, 1968, p. 138.

[61] Henry M. Brickell, Organizing New York State for Educational Change, Albany, New York (State) University and the Commissioner of Education, 1967, pp. 20–21.

[62] Lippitt, op. cit., pp. 321–334.

[63] Brickell, op. cit., p. 26.

[64] Larry W. Hughes, "Organizational Climate—Another Dimension to the Process of Innovation?" Educational Administration Quarterly, 4 (Autumn 1968), 16–28.

[65] Robert B. Howsam, "Effecting Needed Changes in Education," in Morphet and Ryan, eds., op. cit., p. 76.

[66] Max G. Abbott and Terry L. Eidell, "Administrative Implications of Curriculum Reform," Educational Technology, 10 (May 1970), 62–64.

The principal and organization theory

Although specific applications of organization theory appear in subsequent chapters dealing with program, personnel, resources, and the community, several points emerge that are worthy of consideration.

First, the principal should recognize that the traditional, hierarchical scalar view of the school is an inaccurate oversimplification. Because of qualitative differences among the three system levels—institutional, managerial, and technical—each level possesses not "power over" but "power with" the other. Viewed in this light, for example, teachers' professional negotiations become not a battle to be fought but a force to be utilized. The principal, along with the board of education and the superintendent, is in a management position. His leadership of the staff must be based on factors other than the claim of expertise in all teaching fields.

Second, it is clear that other classical organizational concepts—unity of command, span of control, and the line-staff relationship—have limited utility when applied to the school. Principals, as well as other personnel, should reexamine the extent to which they utilize such shibboleths for avoiding responsible behavior. Instead, they should be willing to experiment with new organizational structures and mechanisms for channeling group endeavor.

Third, in the exercise of power within the school, the principal should examine the extent to which he makes appeals either to authority and status or to prestige and influence. Ideally, both should be utilized. Indeed, several definitions of authority place it at the control of subordinates—only when the subordinates accept it may one say that authority has been exercised. Cognizance of this view may, indeed, liberate the principal, allowing him to behave authentically. As the studies of the informal organization reveal, trust, openness, and authenticity are essential in working with others to achieve both organizational and individual goals.

Fourth, from the axiomatic theory of formal organizations, the perceptive principal is able to realize that the administration of the school involves complex organizational factors that require a series of ordered "tradeoffs." It is clearly impossible for anyone to maximize simultaneously incompatible organizational means and ends. Yet it is the job of the principal to move the school in the direction of a dynamic rather than a mechanistic organization.

Finally, from the studies of organizational change the principal must realize that it is not enough to be a proponent of change. Since he occupies a key role in influencing community, organizational, and personalistic variables related to successful institutionalization of change within the school, he must analyze the change itself and must utilize processes appropriate to that change.

Summary

In this chapter, the school was first viewed in terms of some classical organizational concepts. Concerning the hierarchical nature of the school, it was shown that the various levels in the organization perform functions that are qualitatively different, yet interdependent. A model of power relationships was presented suggesting that the principal exercise both authority and influence in the administration of the school. Concepts of coordination, including unity of command, span of control, and the line-staff relationship, were utilized to analyze the school.

Analysis of the formal organization of the school included attention to the relationship of the structural means (complexity, centralization, formalization, and stratification) to the organizational ends (adaptiveness, production, efficiency, and job satisfaction). It was suggested that the school should approximate the organic, as contrasted with the mechanistic, organization.

Regarding the informal organization of the school, it was shown that the variables of disengagement, hindrance, esprit, and intimacy (for teachers) and aloofness, production emphasis, thrust, and consideration (for the principal) are basic to the school's organizational climate, which may range from open to closed. Authenticity, satisfaction, and leadership initiation were viewed as crucial determinants of the success of the school.

Types of organizational change—structural, technological, and behavioral—were considered, and the following four models of the change process were described: a problem-solving model, an RD&D model, an OD model, and a linkage process model. The principal's role as an agent of change was seen as a central one—particularly insofar as he is able to alter community, organizational, and personalistic variables that serve as impediments to change.

The chapter concluded with the application of organizational theory to several parameters of the principal's role.

SUGGESTED ACTIVITIES

1. Observe a principal or analyze a principal's calendar for a full day and determine the extent to which the concepts of scalar principle of hierarchy, unity of command, span of control, and line-staff relationships are violated. Devise a table of organization descriptive of the actual relationships.

2. Obtain or devise measures of the organizational means and ends variables and analyze different types and sizes of schools in terms of the extent to which they are mechanistic or organic.

3. Administer the OCDQ in a school, provide feedback to the principal and the staff, and subsequently test for systematic changes in the organizational climate of the school.

4. Analyze three or four major changes that have recently occurred within a school in terms of type of change, change processes, and agents utilized to effect change.

5. Utilizing the linkage process model, devise a systematic plan for organizational change taking into account the major variables that are likely to affect the change. Specify procedures for dealing with the variables.

SELECTED REFERENCES

APPLEWHITE, PHILIP B., *Organizational Behavior*, Englewood Cliffs, N.J., Prentice-Hall, 1965.

BELL, GERALD D., ed., *Organizations and Human Behavior*, Englewood Cliffs, N.J., Prentice-Hall, 1967.

CARVER, FRED D., and THOMAS J. SERGIOVANNI, eds., *Organizations and Human Behavior: Focus on Schools*, New York, McGraw-Hill, 1969.

ETZIONI, AMITAI, *A Comparative Analysis of Complex Organizations*, New York, Fress Press, 1961.

GOODLAD, JOHN I., and HAROLD G. SHANE, eds., *The Elementary School in the United States*, Chicago, National Society for the Study of Education, 1973.

GRIFFITHS, DANIEL E., ed., *Behaviorial Science and Educational Administration*, Chicago, National Society for the Study of Education, 1964, pp. 223–302.

HAGE, JERALD, and MICHAEL AIKEN, *Social Change in Complex Organizations*, New York, Random House, 1970.

HALPIN, ANDREW W., and DON B. CROFT, *The Organizational Climate of Schools*, Chicago, Midwest Administration Center, University of Chicago, 1963.

MARCH, JAMES G., *Handbook of Organizations*, Skokie, Ill., Rand McNally, 1965.

MORPHET, EDGAR L., and CHARLES O. RYAN, eds., *Planning and Effecting Needed Changes in Education*, Denver, Colo., Designing Education for the Future, 1967.

SCHMUCK, RICHARD A., and MATTHEW B. MILES, *Organization Development in Schools*, Palo Alto, Calif., National, 1971.

SCOTT, WILLIAM G., *Organization Theory*, Homewood, Ill., Irwin, 1967.

THOMPSON, JAMES D., *Organizations in Action*, New York, McGraw-Hill, 1967.

CHAPTER 6
Role theory

y far the largest body of literature on the principalship relates to the question, "What is, or should be, the principal's role?" The principal who possesses an understanding of role relations in the educational organization has taken a significant step toward effective performance in the principalship.

In this chapter the major sources of expectations for the school principal's role are first delineated according to historical-legal precedents, the professional literature, and school district policies.[1] Next we present models for the examination of role relations within the educational organization. In terms of the models, theory and research on the role of the principal are cited to include: conflicts in expectations for the various roles the principal fulfills, conflicts in expectations for the role of the principal held between and among different reference groups, and conflicts in expectations for the role of the principal within the same reference group. The relationship of the principal's role to personality variables of the role incumbent are then explored. The chapter concludes with a critique of research on the role of the school principal and some suggestions for improving the principal's role performance.

Sources of the principal's role

The major sources from which the stereotypic occupational syndrome of the principal's role derives are historical-legal antecedents, the professional literature, and school district policies.

HISTORICAL-LEGAL SOURCES

In terms of historical-legal precedents, it is generally observed that the role of the principal gradually evolved operationally as graded schools became larger and the need appeared for someone at the building level

---

[1] Portions of this chapter are drawn from James M. Lipham, "Dynamics of the Principalship," *National Elementary Principal*, 41 (January 1962), 23–30; and James M. Lipham, "The Role of the Principal: Search and Research," *National Elementary Principal*, 44 (April 1965), 28–33.

to coordinate such functions as grade reporting, record keeping, building maintenance, and similar management functions that now are largely considered to be supportive services. Typically, a head or principal teacher was designated to fulfill such duties while continuing to teach either full or part time. More often than not, the choice of the principal teacher was dependent on length of service in the school or other personal considerations. In many communities the principal teacher was chosen from among those who taught the higher grade levels—particularly in elementary schools.

At the junior and senior high school levels, the task of maintaining student discipline was quickly added to the emerging role as a major responsibility of the principal. Thus the evolution of the principalship began primarily in response to internal system needs during an era of efficiency management and centralized control, when the responsibility for leadership in the major administrative, policy, and curricular decisions lay at the district office level. It is not surprising, therefore, that the role of the principal is scarcely mentioned in the school codes or the administrative regulations of the education departments of the various states, in terms of either mandatory or permissive duties or role expectations, except indirectly in the specification of licensing requirements to serve as principal.

THE PROFESSIONAL LITERATURE

The second major source of generalized expectations for the principal's role is the professional literature in educational administration. Many books on the principalship not only describe what the principal should and should not do but also prescribe how or when he should or should not do it. Typically, such references examine the presumed unique features of the elementary or the secondary school principalship rather than synthesizing the elements of the role that are common to all levels or types of schools. In addition, we may note the professional journals concerned with education generally, and the national, state, and school district publications sponsored by associations of elementary and secondary school principals; these have been a powerful force, since the bulk of their content has been directed to molding and upgrading the professional role of the principal. In recent years, particular emphasis has been placed on the leadership aspects of the principal's role—particularly in the functional area of instruction and curriculum development.

The research contributions of major departments of educational administration in colleges and universities throughout the nation also have contributed greatly toward the development and enlargement of the principal's role. For example, the Southern States Cooperative Program in Educational Administration, one of the programs sponsored by the W. K. Kellogg Foundation, identified the following as critical task areas in school administration:[2]

CRITICAL TASK AREA: INSTRUCTION AND CURRICULUM DEVELOPMENT

1. Providing for the formulation of curriculum objectives.
2. Providing for the determination of curriculum content and organization.
3. Relating the desired curriculum to available time, physical facilities, and personnel.
4. Providing materials, resources, and equipment for the instructional program.
5. Providing for the supervision of instruction.
6. Providing for in-service education of instructional personnel.

CRITICAL TASK AREA: PUPIL PERSONNEL

1. Initiating and maintaining a system of child accounting and attendance.
2. Instituting measures for the orientation of pupils.
3. Providing counseling services.
4. Providing health services.
5. Providing for individual inventory services.
6. Arranging systematic procedures for the continual assessment and interpretation of pupil growth.
7. Establishing means of dealing with pupil irregularities.

CRITICAL TASK AREA: STAFF PERSONNEL

1. Providing for the recruitment of staff personnel.
2. Selecting and assigning staff personnel.
3. Developing a system of staff personnel records.
4. Stimulating and providing opportunities for professional growth of staff personnel.

CRITICAL TASK AREA: COMMUNITY-SCHOOL LEADERSHIP

1. Determining the educational services the school renders and how such services are conditioned by community forces.
2. Helping to develop and implement plans for the improvement of community life.

[2] Adapted from Southern States Cooperative Program in Educational Administration, *Better Teaching in School Administration*, Nashville, Tenn., George Peabody College for Teachers, 1965, as cited in Charles F. Faber and Gilbert F. Shearron, *Elementary School Administration, Theory and Practice*, New York, Holt, Rinehart and Winston, 1970, pp. 225–227.

CRITICAL TASK AREAS: SCHOOL PLANT AND SCHOOL TRANSPORTATION

1. Developing an efficient program of operation and maintenance of the physical plant.
2. Providing for the safety of pupils, personnel, and equipment.

CRITICAL TASK AREA: ORGANIZATION AND STRUCTURE

1. Developing a staff organization as a means of implementing the educational objectives of the school program.
2. Organizing lay and professional groups for participation in educational planning and other educational activities.

CRITICAL TASK AREA: SCHOOL FINANCE AND BUSINESS MANAGEMENT

1. Preparing the school budget.
2. Accounting for school monies.
3. Accounting for school property.

Since its inception the University Council for Educational Administration (UCEA) has been very influential in shaping and upgrading college preparatory programs for school principals at all levels. Outstanding among these efforts has been the conceptualization, development, and widespread distribution of realistically based simulation materials for use in pre-service and in-service programs of preparation for elementary, junior high, and senior high school principals. Earlier versions of these materials included the Whitman School and the Madison School District simulations. More recently, they include in-basket exercises, role play situations, and filmed cases for the Abraham Lincoln Elementary School, the Janus Junior High School, and the Wilson High School in the simulation of a large urban school district, Monroe City.

In addition to supplying the thrust in instructional materials concerned with the principal's role, the UCEA has been instrumental in removing the parochial and insular barriers surrounding the preparation of principals—particularly through an emphasis on the utilization of social and behavioral science concepts in preparation for performance in the principalship.[3] Moreover, efforts are currently being made to formulate, develop, and test in practice theoretical knowledge and concepts utilizing a competency-based approach to analysis of the principalship. Within the UCEA principalship project, areas in which the principal should develop competence have been identified as follows:[4]

1. Responding to social change
2. Evaluating school processes and products

[3] Jack A. Culbertson et al., eds., *Social Science Content for Preparing Educational Leaders*, Columbus, Ohio, Merrill, 1973.

[4] Adapted from Jack A. Culbertson, Curtis Henson, and Ruel Morrison, eds., *Performance Objectives for School Principals*, Berkeley, Calif., McCutchan, 1974.

3. Administering and improving the instructional program
4. Making effective decisions
5. Preparing the organization for effective response to change
6. Achieving effective human relations and morale

The domains just listed do not describe the totality of the principal's role; neither are they unique to building-level administration. As with any taxonomy of role behavior, moreover, there may be considerable interaction among the domains. Even so, they do provide a means for analyzing specific administrative behavior within the school organization and for examining the fundamental competencies required in the principalship.

In addition to historical-legal and professional sources of expectations for the principal's role, the third major source for describing the principalship is that of school district policies.

SCHOOL DISTRICT POLICY SOURCES

Most of the current descriptions of the principalship are embodied in descriptions of either the administrative structure or the personnel regulations of school district policies. Analyses of the principalship have revealed that it is not the mere existence of such position descriptions but the extent to which such position descriptions are mutually developed, understood, and utilized that makes a difference in the administration of the schools. Many examples of this approach to clarifying the major expectations of the principalship could be cited. An illustrative example is that of the Worth, Illinois, School District, which has adopted policies that describe the principal's role in terms of certain major responsibilities. In the policies of the Worth Board of Education it is stated that all principals shall be:

1. Responsible to the superintendent of schools for the organization, administration, and supervision of the schools to which they have been assigned, and for keeping the superintendent informed as to the operation of the schools and the activities therein.

2. Responsible for providing leadership for the students, teachers and parents of the school district in accord with the philosophy of the board of education that every child in the district is to receive equal opportunity to quality education.

3. Responsible for providing professional leadership to the teachers of the schools to which they have been assigned. They shall schedule and take charge of faculty meetings. They shall inform teachers of their duties and responsibilities, and insist that teachers fulfill such duties and responsibilities. They shall work cooperatively with the teaching staff for the best interests of the students and strive for the betterment of the educational program of the entire district.

4. Responsible for assisting in the development of the several curriculums and in planning and adopting the courses of study which will fulfill the needs and interests of the students.

5. Responsible for constant appraisal and evaluation of the instructional program.

6. Responsible for making recommendations concerning the selection, assignment, and evaluation of building teachers to the superintendent of schools.

7. Responsible for the assignment of duties of the teaching staff and ascertaining that each staff member has an equitable amount of class and extra-class assignments.

8. Responsible for maintaining a comprehensive program of in-service training for teachers and for conducting meetings during the first month of school to orient teachers to evaluation procedures.

9. Responsible for employing substitute teachers for teachers who are absent.

10. Responsible for the classification, promotion, or retention of students within their buildings.

11. Responsible for promoting an effective system of student guidance, developing reasonable rules for student conduct in cooperation with the building faculty, and for maintaining high standards of student courtesy. Upon approval of the superintendent of schools they may suspend students from school for a maximum period of seven days for serious violation of school regulations.

12. Responsible for overseeing the attendance, conduct, and health of the students, including responsibilities for:

    a. Fire, air raid, and tornado drills.

    b. School enterprises and activities.

    c. School exhibits.

    d. Noon lunch organization.

    e. Collection of money by the building clerk when necessary.

13. Responsible for maintaining good public relations with the community and for utilizing fully the community resources to enrich the learning process.

14. Responsible for supervision of the keeping of all records for the school building and making all reports that are required for their school by law or requested by the superintendent of schools.

15. Responsible for the care of the school buildings, grounds, furniture, and other property of the school, and for requiring high standards of custodial services and building sanitation in cooperation with the assistant superintendent of the school district.

16. Responsible for insuring the proper requisitioning of supplies, equipment, and teaching aids for the educational program.[5]

In assisting principals in the Worth School District to meet the foregoing responsibilities, specific procedures have been spelled out for such

---

[5] Policies of the Worth School District No. 127, Worth, Ill., 1972, Section 2400b.

duties as visits to classrooms, evaluation of teachers, and other major functions. In the original school board policies the duties also are cross-referenced to other relevant policies, thus becoming a useful guide to the on-the-job behavior of principals. As operational problems arise that may be in conflict with the major role responsibilities, the code is cooperatively reviewed by the administrative staff and, if necessary, amended annually by the board of education. Such review is basic if a school district is to move toward the use of more definitive and systematic procedures of management by objectives (MBO) or planning-programming-budgeting systems (PPBS).

Historical-legal, professional, and school policy sources embody the more generalized and formal descriptions of expectations for the principal's role. Operationally, however, these generalized expectations receive daily expression in the face-to-face interactions of the principal with his significant reference groups. In the model that follows, these role relationships are examined.

A model of role relationships

In Chapter 3, which depicted the school as a social system, we indicated that a role is a dynamic aspect of a position, office, or status within an institution. We also noted, after Getzels, that roles are defined in terms of role expectations—the normative rights and duties that define within limits what a person should or should not do under various circumstances while he is the incumbent of a particular role within an institution.[6] The following characteristics of roles also were delineated: (1) They are complementary and interlocking (e.g., principal-teacher); (2) they are institutional givens and not "made to order"; (3) they are somewhat flexible, having behaviors ranging along a continuum from "required" to "prohibited"; and (4) they vary in scope from functionally specific to functionally diffuse. Finally, a role incumbent's effectiveness can be measured by the extent to which his on-the-job behavior meets with the expectations held for the role.

Since role effectiveness is of universal concern, how may role expectations be depicted or described? As we observed in our consideration of the sources of expectations for the principal's role, there are many alternative methods for describing the major dimensions of a significant social role. The first, and most common, is termed the *task approach;* here the role is described, perhaps by categories, in terms of the tasks to be per-

[6] J. W. Getzels, "Administration as a Social Process," in *Administrative Theory in Education,* Andrew W. Halpin, ed., Chicago, Midwest Administration Center, University of Chicago, 1958, reprinted, New York, Macmillan, 1967, p. 153.

formed, activities to be conducted, or, as in the example of the Worth School District policies, the major role responsibilities to be fulfilled. Although the principalship is a relatively well-established role, to date there is no universally agreed-on listing of either the categories or the specific tasks within the categories; hence descriptions of the principalship range from quite global to very specific. In some districts where the principals have negotiated a uniform contract with the board of education or where management consultants have analyzed the work structure, lists of the principal's duties may include more than 100 specific tasks or duties. In still other districts, no specific duties have been spelled out. As the superintendent in one such district commented recently, "I just hire good principals and tell them to get out there and principalize." Nor did he specify the criteria he uses for hiring good principals.

An approach somewhat different from task analysis in describing the principalship involves defining the role in terms of the major decisions that rest with the position. This decision-making approach is gaining widespread usage, and, as we shall see in Chapter 7, it possesses certain advantages over the task approach. For example, it is possible not only to indicate which decisions fall within the province of the role but also to specify both the type and nature of the involvement required in making the major decisions.

Whether specified as tasks to be done or decisions to be made, the process of role analysis obtains expectations for a role incumbent's behavior along relevant continua from required to prohibited, such as: the incumbent "absolutely must (5)," "probably should (4)," "may or may not (3)," "probably should not (2)," or "absolutely must not (1)" display the behavior described on the several task or decision items. Other continua, such as: "always (5)," "often (4)," "sometimes (3)," "seldom (2)," or "never (1)" may be utilized. Another useful methodology in analyzing role expectations is that of requiring respondents to rank or Q-sort the role items, one against the other, in terms of their importance. Still another methodology that is sometimes used calls for assessment of the amounts of time allotted to the various role items, such as analyzing a principal's calendar or observing the on-the-job behavior of principals.

Regardless of the methodologies utilized, two types of useful role analysis data may be obtained—"real" or actual role of the principal, and "idealized" or preferred role of the principal. Difference scores or discrepancy comparisons between the real and the ideal role descriptions are often quite revealing. In the case of the role incumbent, the principal himself, the difference between his actual role behavior and the idealized role behavior that he posits for his position is considered to be a derived measure of role adequacy. In the case of others—teachers or students, for example—the difference between the role behavior that the principal actually exhibits as contrasted with the behavior that they ideally would like to see him exhibit is considered to be a derived measure of their perception of the principal's effectiveness.

We may take the complementary principal-teacher role relationship as an example to depict three types of role expectations and the interactions between and among them. These three types of expectations are self-role expectations, alters' role expectations, and perceived alters' role expectations.

SELF-ROLE EXPECTATIONS

As may be observed in Figure 6.1, which deals with actual but not with ideal role expectations, point A relates to one's own role expectations. In obtaining this set of expectations a list of role items is presented to the respondent, in this case the principal, in terms of the prompt, "As principal, I . . ." or "As principal, I am expected to . . . ." By way of an illustration only, we may utilize the role item or task ". . . serve as a member of the board team in teacher negotiations." If the principal feels that

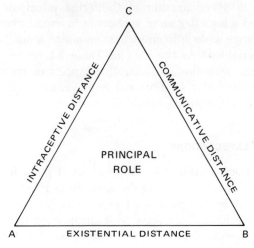

PRINCIPAL'S PERCEPTIONS OF TEACHERS'
EXPECTATIONS FOR THE PRINCIPAL'S ROLE
("I believe that my teachers expect me to . . .")

C

INTRACEPTIVE DISTANCE

COMMUNICATIVE DISTANCE

PRINCIPAL
ROLE

A   EXISTENTIAL DISTANCE   B

PRINCIPAL'S SELF-EXPECTATIONS
FOR THE PRINCIPAL'S ROLE
("As principal, I am expected to . . .")

TEACHERS' EXPECTATIONS FOR
THE PRINCIPAL'S ROLE
("I expect my principal to . . .")

Figure 6.1
Role expectation and role perception relationships

he is in fact expected to serve as a member of the board team, he would respond affirmatively, either "absolutely must (5)" or "always (5)." Across a whole series of items, therefore, his role as he sees it can be described and quantified.

Utilizing a similar procedure, one also can obtain a measure of the principal's ideal role expectations. To do this, the prompt utilized is, "Ideally, as principal, I should . . . ." Many principals feel that introspective self-role analysis alone—that is, comparing their actual with their idealized role expectations—is a particularly valuable and worthwhile experience that pinpoints areas of discrepancy to which they may direct greater attention. Typical survey studies of the principal's role, especially those conducted by the school principals' associations, are of this nature, for they compare the amount of time actually devoted to certain role tasks with the amount of time principals ideally would like to devote to them.

Several revealing analyses have been made of the difference between the actual role and the ideal role of the principal. In a sample of elementary school principals in Idaho, Foster examined and compared what the principals did with what they would like to do.[7] He found that they would like to devote more time to supervision of instruction and student personnel activities and less time to public relations and clerical duties. Melton compared the results of two studies, one of Michigan principals conducted in 1958 and another of California principals conducted in 1968, and noted a high degree of agreement in expectations for the principal's role, despite wide differences in community, school, and individual background variables.[8] As the data in Table 6.1 reveal, the principals spent more time with the administrative aspects of their role and less time with the curricular, professional improvement, and evaluation responsibilities than they ideally would like to do.

ALTERS' ROLE EXPECTATIONS

Alters' expectations—in this case, the teachers at point B in Figure 6.1— may be obtained by administering the same list of role items to the teachers but preceded by the prompt, "I expect my principal to . . . ." On the same sample item, ". . . serve as a member of the board team in teacher salary negotiations," let us assume that the teachers respond

[7] Zeph H. Foster, "A Comparative Study of the Ideal Role and the Actual Role of the Elementary School Principal in Idaho," doctoral dissertation, University of Idaho, 1964.

[8] Joseph Melton, "Role Perceptions of the Elementary School Principalship," *National Elementary Principal*, 50 (February 1971), 40–43.

Table 6.1
REAL AND IDEAL ROLE EXPECTATIONS HELD
BY ELEMENTARY SCHOOL PRINCIPALS

ROLE CATEGORY	ACTUAL ROLE Percent of time		IDEAL ROLE Percent of time	
	1956	1968	1958	1968
1. CURRICULUM AND INSTRUCTIONAL LEADERSHIP (includes philosophical and psychological theories, program supervision, curriculum improvement)	19	18	28	31
2. PERSONAL GUIDANCE (includes professional personnel, service personnel, pupil personnel)	16	19	17	18
3. SCHOOL-COMMUNITY RELATIONS (includes communications, community-school development, curriculum interpretation)	16	11	15	12
4. ADMINISTRATIVE RESPONSIBILITY (includes relationship with central staff, physical school plant, routine operational procedure)	29	33	14	14
5. EVALUATION RESPONSIBILITY (includes evaluation of objectives, teacher and pupil progress, and self-evaluating)	12	11	15	14
6. PROFESSIONAL IMPROVEMENT (includes in-service education, research, recruitment, participation in professional organizations)	8	8	11	11
Total	100	100	100	100

SOURCE: Joseph Melton, "Role Perceptions of the Elementary School Principalship," *National Elementary Principal*, 50 (February 1971), 41.

"may or may not (3)" or "sometimes (3)." Thus the difference in our example between the principal's self-role expectations and the role expectations held for the principal by the teachers on the 5-point scale is 2 points. From analyzing an entire series of role items, a measure of role agreement or consensus or, conversely, role disagreement or conflict potential, may be obtained in both direction and magnitude.

Utilizing the same procedure with the prompt to teachers, "Ideally, my principal should . . . ," provides a measure of alters' idealized role expectations. As indicated, the discrepancy between what teachers see the principal as actually doing and what they would ideally like him to be doing is a derived measure of the extent to which the principal is effective, at least in the eyes of the teachers. Again, feedback or knowledge of such data, the discrepancy scores, is of great benefit to a role incumbent in modifying either his role behavior or the expectations held by others.

A signal study of the effect of feedback on the principal's behavior of how the teachers feel about the principal's role was reported by Daw and Gage.[9] In 455 schools in California, teachers described their actual principal and their ideal principal on the following 12 items selected on the basis of their importance, improvability, and noticeability:

1. Encourages teachers with a friendly remark or smile.
2. Gives enough credit to teachers for their contributions.
3. Does not force opinions on teachers.
4. Enforces rules consistently.
5. Criticizes without disparaging the efforts of teachers.
6. Informs teachers of decisions or actions which affect their work.
7. Gives concrete suggestions for improving classroom instruction.
8. Enlists sufficient participation by teachers in making decisions.
9. Demonstrates interest in pupil progress.
10. Interrupts the classroom infrequently.
11. Displays much interest in teachers' ideas.
12. Acts promptly in fulfilling teacher requests.[10]

In experimental schools, as contrasted with control schools, the actual and ideal responses of the teachers were reported to the principal in tabular and graphic form for each of the role items. The principal could thereby see the extent of any discrepancy between his actual behavior and the ideal behavior posited by his teachers. Subsequently the measures were readministered. The results were straightforward and confirmed the major hypothesis. Feedback influenced the principal to change his behavior on all 12 items in the direction that his teachers had posited as ideal. Thus it was concluded that in the eyes of the teachers, at least, feedback of role expectations did improve the behavior of their principals. A subsequent study by Burns corroborated this finding.[11] Feedback to principals of the idealized expectations of teachers for the principal's role was found to be a very effective means for producing positive behavioral change in principals.

The line between point A in Figure 6.1, the principal's own expectations, and point B, the teachers' expectations, represents basic philosophical differences that may be caused by differences between principals and teachers on such variables as training, group membership, hierarchical organizational position, role empathy, and previous experiences. The length of line AB represents the role distance between the principal and the teachers; it may range from complete agreement to complete dis-

[9] Robert W. Daw and N. L. Gage, "Effect of Feedback from Teachers to Principals," *Journal of Educational Psychology*, 58 (June 1967), 181–188.

[10] Ibid., 184.

[11] Mildred L. Burns, "The Effects of Feedback and Commitment to Change on the Behavior of Elementary School Principals," doctoral dissertation, Stanford University, 1969.

agreement. In the diagram, therefore, line AB has been labeled *existential distance*.

PERCEPTIONS OF ALTERS' EXPECTATIONS

In addition to the direct differences in role expectations held by the principal himself (point A) and those held by the teachers for the principal (point B), disagreements and misunderstanding also can derive from another source—point C in Figure 6.1. These differences in expectations are not existential but *perceptual*. That is, the principal may believe that he and his teachers hold significant differences in their expectations when in fact they are the same; or conversely, he may believe they are the same when in fact they are different. To obtain the measure of one's perceptions of alters' role expectations, such prompts as the following are used: "I feel (think, believe, or perceive) that my teachers expect me to . . . ." Again, the same list of role items may be used to obtain comparable data.

Since we live and act in terms of the world as we see it, perceptions of alters' expectations become exceedingly important. Hencley,[12] among others,[13] has investigated the nature of such perceptions, including the extent of perceptual error, among school administrators and has identified the following typology of conflict in perception of role expectations:

1. TROUBLE SEEKING. This type of administrator perceives a reference group's expectations to be significantly different from his own when in fact they are not. In effect, he is looking for trouble or for conflicts that do not exist.

2. INNOCENT. This is the reverse of trouble seeking. The administrator perceives no differences between his own and others' expectations, when in fact significant differences do exist. In effect, he is innocent and may encounter conflict from many unexpected sources.

3. KEEN. This type of administrator perceives accurately the expectations of his reference groups, even though a significant difference may exist between his own expectations and those of the reference group. In effect, he is keen and accurate in his perceptions.

Depending on the magnitude of the differences and the placement of the three scores—self, alter, and perceived alter—Hencley further refined the typology to include the following: (1) "Cautious Semikeen," in

[12] Stephen P. Hencley, "The Conflict Patterns of School Superintendents," *Administrator's Notebook,* 8 (May 1960), 1–4.

[13] Max G. Abbott, "Values and Value-Perceptions in Superintendent-School Board Relationships," *Administrator's Notebook,* 9 (December 1960), 1–4.

which the administrator perceives an existing conflict but underestimates its magnitude; (2) "Bold Semikeen," in which the administrator perceives an existing conflict but overestimates its magnitude; (3) "Overlooked Support," in which the administrator and his reference group are in essential agreement but the former fails to recognize his strong reference group support; and (4) "Reversed Polar," in which the reference group expectations are the exact opposite of what the administrator perceives them to be.

In terms of our example for the role item ". . . serve as a member of the board team in teacher salary negotiations," we may readily sense the potency and utility of Hencley's typology. The keen principal would perceive accurately the teachers' expectations; in this example the principal would perceive accurately that the teachers' expectations were that he "may or may not (3)" so serve. However, if the principal perceived erroneously that the teachers' expectations were in agreement with his own response, "absolutely must (5)," when in fact they were not, this would be an innocent response. If the principal also perceived erroneously that the teachers' expectations were of the order "absolutely must not (1)" when in fact they had responded "may or may not (3)," he may be trouble seeking—braced for more difficulties than he is likely to encounter. Obviously, other possible combinations among the three responses are possible.

These phenomena largely are concerned with line AC in Figure 6.1, which we have termed *intraceptive distance*. Two points should be emphasized here, since knowledge of them may improve a principal's performance. First, research on perception has revealed that more often than not there exists a systematic tendency to perceive the expectations of others to be closer to one's own than in fact they are. This tendency toward projection seems to be true whether it is role, value, or even personality variables that are being perceived.[14] Thus principals would do well to try to determine the extent to which they commit such projective error (i.e., assuming line AC to be shorter than it is) in their relations with others.

A second major finding concerning intraceptive distance is that intraception is a variable that can be altered and improved. The variable of intraception is composed of both need and ability components. The need for intraception has been defined by Edwards as follows:

> To analyze one's motives and feelings, to observe others, to understand how others feel about problems, to put one's self in another's place, to judge

---

[14] Cf. Kenneth C. DeGood, "Can Superintendents Perceive Community Viewpoints?" *Administrator's Notebook*, 8 (November 1959), 1–4; Max G. Abbott, "Values and Value Perceptions of School Superintendents and Board Members," doctoral dissertation, University of Chicago, 1960.

people by why they do things rather than by what they do, to analyze the behavior of others, to analyze the motives of others, and to predict how others will act.[15]

Research in group interaction reveals that it is possible to improve and develop one's intraceptive skills. These skills appear to be composed of at least two factors: perceptual discrimination, that is, the ability to observe categories of phenomena and to separate the categories into different or discrete factors; and perceptual integration, that is, the ability to organize and interrelate one's judgments on the discrete factors into a meaningful gestalt. Undoubtedly, the principal should try to improve his ability to assess accurately the expectations and the behavior of those with whom he daily interacts. Many university programs for preparing principals are now utilizing simulation or in-basket exercises to assist in the development of intraceptive skills, since such exercises permit the standardization of stimuli to which the participant principalship trainee responds.

Some brief observations also should be made concerning the difference or distance between what the teachers actually expect and what the principal thinks they expect. This difference (line BC in Figure 6.1) has been labeled *communicative distance*. In the school situation cited, for example, if the principal meets and communicates often with his teachers, whether formally or informally, one might predict that the distance between points B and C would indeed be small. That is, opening and increasing the communication channels, reducing the communicative distance between the principal and the teachers, would tend to harmonize points B and C in that the principal would know and assess accurately the teachers' expectations. Most studies of organizational roles have revealed that ineffectiveness and inefficiency are due less to the differences in expectations that are out in the open and understood than to those that are underground and misunderstood. Thus the principal would do well to discuss with teachers freely and openly their mutual expectations for each other's roles—in effect, reducing the communicative distance between complementary organizational role incumbents.

Concerning the mutuality of complementary organizational roles, we have thus far examined only expectations and perceptions for one-half of the interaction, the principal's role. Similar expectation and perception dynamics are operative for the teacher's role for which the following data would be obtained: A′, teacher expectations for his own role ("As teacher, I am expected to . . ."); B′, principal expectations for the teacher role ("I expect my teachers to . . ."); and C′, teacher perceptions of the new principal's expectations for the teacher role ("I believe that my

[15] Allen L. Edwards, *Manual for the Edwards Personal Preference Schedule,* New York, The Psychological Corporation, 1959, p. 11.

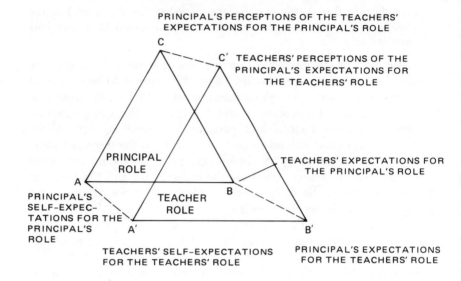

PRINCIPAL'S PERCEPTIONS OF THE TEACHERS' EXPECTATIONS FOR THE PRINCIPAL'S ROLE

C' TEACHERS' PERCEPTIONS OF THE PRINCIPAL'S EXPECTATIONS FOR THE TEACHERS' ROLE

PRINCIPAL ROLE

TEACHERS' EXPECTATIONS FOR THE PRINCIPAL'S ROLE

TEACHER ROLE

PRINCIPAL'S SELF-EXPEC-TATIONS FOR THE PRINCIPAL'S ROLE

TEACHERS' SELF-EXPECTATIONS FOR THE TEACHERS' ROLE

PRINCIPAL'S EXPECTATIONS FOR THE TEACHERS' ROLE

Figure 6.2

Complementarity in role expectations and perceptions between interlocking organizational roles

principal expects me to . . ."). Figure 6.2 is a schematic depicting the complementarity between the interlocking principal-teacher roles. Role complementarity in this model is represented by the relationship between triangles ABC and A'B'C', or lines AA', BB', and CC'. To increase role complementarity, it has been found desirable to consider the major role expectations (tasks or decision items) in terms of the extent to which the sanctions of the one become the benefits of the other or the rights of the one the privileges of the other. This is precisely the advantage cited in current MBO approaches to the administration of the school wherein several types of complementarity—for example, superintendent-principal, principal-teacher, principal-parents, and principal-student role relationships—are considered.

The role theory models presented are particularly useful for examining the major types of role disagreement or conflict with which the principal must deal.

Role conflict in the principalship

All institutional roles, particularly those in public institutions, are subject to numerous sources and types of disagreement or conflict. But few

seem so fraught with conflict potential as that of the public school principal. The major types of role conflict in the principalship are as follows:
(1) interrole conflict or disagreement between two or more roles simultaneously fulfilled by the principal—from the principal "wearing many
hats"; (2) inter-reference-group conflict or disagreement in two or more
reference groups in their expectations for the role of principal—"the man
in the middle"; (3) intra-reference-group conflict or disagreement within
a reference group in their expectations for the role of the principal—
"caught in group crossfire"; and (4) role-personality conflict or disagreement between the expectations for the role of the principal and his personality need-dispositions—"the man vs. the job." A substantial body of
literature has developed concerning each of these types of role conflict.

INTERROLE CONFLICT

Because of the complexity of the principalship, one may often experience considerable interrole conflict from simultaneously fulfilling two or
more incompatible roles—in effect, from wearing many hats. Having but
one head, the principal often finds that this is one of the most stressful
types of conflict with which he must deal.

A conspicuous example of interrole conflict can be found in school
districts, particularly the smaller ones in some states, wherein one individual must serve not only as a building principal, but also as the chief
executive officer responsible directly to a board of education—he is something of a hybrid, namely, principal-superintendent. As those who fulfill
such positions will readily testify, all too frequently they are torn from
an urgent operational problem within the building and forced to attack
a policy question relating to the district as a whole. Although some rare
individuals have acquired facility in "doffing the hat of the principal to
don that of the superintendent," we could legitimately ask why the superintendent's role often seems to take precedence.

Similar instances of conflict between incompatible roles will immediately be recognized by those who serve as supervising principals of more
than one building and who find on many occasions that they should be in
at least two places at the same time. One afflicted principal lamented
somewhat as follows: "I'm always at the wrong building. Just as soon as
I get to one place all hell breaks loose at the other."

Another prime example of interrole conflict exists in the case of the
part-time or teaching principal, who undoubtedly has thought to himself
hundreds of times while conducting his classes, "If there's just one more
knock on that door. . . ." In an examination of the role behavior of part-
time principals, Schreiner learned that their leadership behavior was significantly different from that of full-time principals with respect to several

leadership variables.[16] Part-time principals were higher than full-time principals in actively assuming the role, in reconciling conflicting demands from various individuals and groups, and in tolerating ambiguity and uncertainty. Conversely, full-time principals placed greater emphasis on productive output than did part-time principals.

In addition to the foregoing ambivalent organizational arrangements that have been historically or expediently foisted on far too many potential school leaders, substantial conflict seems to be built into all principalships. As incumbent of a status position, the principal is often looked to for leadership, or at least participation, in many community groups—religious, fraternal, patriotic, political, and social. Since examples of inter-role conflict in the principalship are too numerous to belabor, only a few are cited. What does the principal do when his church or synagogue wishes to use the school gym but the time overlaps slightly with basketball practice; his lodge or veterans' group wishes to sponsor yet another essay contest; his political party wishes to provide "nonpartisan" curricular materials for social studies; his golfing partner wants to have his youngster placed in a different teacher's class; or the principal's own children beg to go fishing or to a ball game when the school budget is due? In addition, it is usually expected that the principal will have more than a passive interest in numerous professional groups that may demand much of his time during working hours. Even if the principal is able to minimize conflicting demands between and among these many reference groups, he still may find that his roles in these organizations conflict substantially with his role as head of a school. And even for the single role as principal there are substantial inter-reference-group conflicts.

INTER-REFERENCE-GROUP CONFLICT

A second source of role conflict stems from the requirements that the principal work with many groups, each of them likely to hold different and often conflicting expectations for his role *as principal.*

Consider, for example, the principal's position with regard to the procurement-disposal function—only one of a multitude of functional problems he faces daily. From the viewpoint of teachers, the principal may legitimately be expected to maximize, or at least endorse, requests for supplies, materials, repairs, or facilities which they deem essential for their instructional needs. On the other hand, the superintendent of schools, the business manager, or perhaps some frugal board member may view the appropriate role of the principal as one of reducing, or at

---

[16] Jerry O. Schreiner, "An Exploratory Investigation of Leader Behavior of Full-time and Part-time Elementary School Principals," doctoral dissertation, Oklahoma State University, 1968.

least minimizing, educational expenditures. In effect, any final decision by the principal, even one of compromise, may be viewed by either reference group as largely unsatisfactory. A list of dilemmas, of which the foregoing is typical, might be expanded indefinitely, since the complexity of decisions concerning the educational enterprise is increasing.

Several studies have highlighted the nature and extent of inter-reference-group conflict. Using a list of 53 role expectations of the principal, Frazier conducted 150 individual interviews in Oregon school districts with superintendents, principals, and teachers who indicated their expectations for the principal.[17] Twenty-seven major differences were noted among the respondent groups, the bulk of the differences being between superintendents and teachers. These differences, moreover, were dispersed across a variety of role functions. Similarly, Falzetta used a list of 47 role items to obtain the expectations for the role of the principal held by 250 superintendents, 250 principals, and 250 teachers in New Jersey. On 20 of the 47 items there were significant conflicts in expectations for the principal's role.[18] From a study in Texas of the decision-making role of the principal, Newberry also concluded that there are significant differences in the perceptions of the principal's domain of decision making in several task areas as perceived by superintendents, teachers, and principals themselves.[19] Similarly, intergroup differences were found in other studies, not only for the actual role expectations but also for the idealized role expectations of the principal.[20]

In addition to differences in expectations for the principal's role, there are differences in the perceptions of his actual role behavior. Utilizing 26 behavioral categories, McNeil observed the on-the-job behavior of a sample of Texas principals and obtained parallel measures of each principal's behavior from the subjects themselves and from their superintendents, teachers, and school secretaries.[21] Although the principals' and the teachers' observations agreed more closely with researcher's observations than did either the superintendents' or, surprisingly enough, the school

[17] Calvin M. Frazier, "Role Expectations of the Elementary Principal as Perceived by Superintendents, Principals, and Teachers," doctoral dissertation, University of Oregon, 1964.

[18] John N. Falzetta, "Role Expectations Held for the Elementary Principal by Teachers, Principals, and Superintendents in New Jersey," doctoral dissertation, Temple University, 1967.

[19] William C. Newberry, "The Elementary Principal's Influence and Decision-Making Role," doctoral dissertation, University of Texas, 1966.

[20] Duane W. Smith, "Descriptions of an Ideal Secondary School Principal by Four Sampled Populations," doctoral dissertation, University of Nebraska, 1965; and Thomas L. Strick, "An Investigation into the Status of the Role of the Elementary Principal Within a Decentralization Program," doctoral dissertation, University of Wisconsin, 1971.

[21] Charles A. McNeil, "Perceptions of the Administrative Behavior of Selected Elementary School Principals," doctoral dissertation, University of Texas, 1967.

secretaries' observations, none of the reference groups were in high agreement, either among themselves or with the observer, in their perceptions of the principal's actual role behavior. Lark similarly found substantial disagreement in perceptions of the actual role behavior of assistant principals.[22]

Some of the intergroup differences, of course, might be expected because of such existential factors as age, training, hierarchical organization position, and the like, as well as the perceptual factors of intraceptive and communicative distance. But it is of value to the principal to know whether the intergroup differences are systematic. Several studies have examined this issue. Utilizing the nomothetic-transactional-idiographic framework for assessing the role expectations of principals, Moser discovered that the principal's teachers and his superintendent subject him to markedly different sets of leadership expectations and that the principal's behavior varies according to whether he is with superiors or subordinates.[23] The principal was found to emphasize *nomothetic* behavior (stressing goal achievement, institutional regulations, and centralized authority) in his relations with the superintendent and *idiographic* behavior (stressing individual needs and wants, minimum rules, and decentralized authority) in his interactions with teachers.

In a more recent study, Muse utilized the same social systems framework to examine not only the responsibilities but also the leadership orientation desired by the principal and his alter groups.[24] A number of significant differences were found to exist between principals and their reference groups in their expectations for the principalship. As in Moser's study, moreover, there were distinct preferences for certain leadership styles. Whereas the principals preferred a nomothetic leadership style, their organizational subordinates expressed a greater desire for the principal to display an idiographic leadership style.

Just as there may be conflict between reference groups in their expectations for the principal's role, systematic differences may exist within a group.

INTRA-REFERENCE-GROUP CONFLICT

Intra-reference-group conflict, wherein one is caught in group crossfire, constitutes a third type of conflict in the principal's role. Although many examples could be cited, we are reminded of the plight of the principal

[22] Larry L. Lark, "The Effectiveness of the Assistant Principal's Role as a Function of Expectations and Behavior," doctoral dissertation, University of Wisconsin, 1971.

[23] Robert P. Moser, "The Leadership Patterns of School Superintendents and School Principals," *Administrator's Notebook*, 6 (September 1957), 1–4.

[24] Ivan D. Muse, "The Public School Principalship: Role Expectations by Alter Groups," doctoral dissertation, University of Utah, 1966.

in an urban school district in which we worked. Half the man's faculty was out on strike while he and the other half were attempting to keep school. As he looked out the window at the striking teachers huddled against the bitter cold and snow, he observed, "It's awfully hard to smile and say 'Good morning!' when you cross a picket line. But I know that when this thing is over we must find ways to work together again."

Cleavages within the teacher group in expectations for the principal's role are probably more typical than unusual—old timers–newcomers, music boosters–athletic boosters, discipline-oriented–child-centered, traditional–innovative, academic–vocational, lower grades–upper grades, are but a few examples. Neville found, for example, that male-female differences were apparent in teachers' real and ideal expectations for the supervisory role of the principal.[25]

In a study we conducted in 31 Wisconsin school systems, teachers were asked to express their expectations for administrative decision making concerning 25 functions, such as providing for a program of in-service training, orienting new staff members, selecting textbooks, evaluating the curriculum, regulating pupil conduct, and preparing the school budget.[26] Sharp differences appeared in what teachers expected the principal's role to be. Faculties in some schools were almost equally divided about whether the principal "positively should" or "absolutely must not" exhibit the behavior described—not simply on a few but on many items.

Obviously, intra-reference-group conflict in expectations is endemic to groups other than the faculty. As we indicated in Chapter 4, it is probably more accurate to conceive of the public in terms of several systematic subpublic cleavages. And even within a subpublic or group, such as the PTA, there are often widely varying and conflicting expectations for the principal's role.[27]

Like inter-reference-group conflict, intra-reference-group conflict is not simply related to operational or functional tasks. In a study of the type of leadership teachers want, Moyer had teachers react to 80 statements dealing with "leader-centered" and "group-centered" behavior on the part of the principal.[28] At the same time, they were asked to rate their

[25] Richard F. Neville, "The Supervisory Function of the Elementary School Principal as Perceived by Teachers," doctoral dissertation, University of Connecticut, 1963.

[26] Glen G. Eye et al., *Relationship Between Instructional Change and the Extent to Which Administrators and Teachers Agree on the Location of Responsibilities for Administrative Decisions,* Cooperative Research Project No. 5-0443, Madison, University of Wisconsin, 1966.

[27] Howard R. Sleight, "Expectations of the Elementary School Principalship Regarding School-Community Relations with Specific Focus on the Parent-Teacher Association," doctoral dissertation, Columbia University, 1969.

[28] Donald C. Moyer, "Leadership That Teachers Want," *Administrator's Notebook,* 3 (March 1955), 1–4.

personal and professional satisfaction derived from their working situation. One of Moyer's major findings was that a generalized preference appeared for group-centered behavior by the principal. A more recent study by Eberhart revealed that teachers having a strong professional role orientation, as compared with those having a strong bureaucratic-employee orientation, likewise expressed a preference for the principal to behave in a "democratic" fashion.[29]

Another major finding of Moyer's study was:

> The greater the unity within a group in attitudes toward leadership, the higher the satisfaction in the group. When faculties were compared on the basis of their solidarity or homogeneity of attitudes toward leadership, those school faculties high in homogeneity were also high in over-all satisfaction derived from the work situation.[30]

Evidently, congruence in expectations among the members of a group is a factor fully as significant as the actual leadership style of the principal.

The fourth and final type of conflict to be considered is that of role-personality conflict, also called self-role conflict.

ROLE-PERSONALITY CONFLICT

The extent to which "the man makes the job or the job makes the man" may be a relative matter. Neverthless, a major source of conflict derives from discrepancies between the basic need-dispositions of an individual and the demands placed on him as principal of a school. No doubt every practicing principal could cite numerous instances of this type of conflict. For example, he as a person may immensely dislike speaking before groups, yet as a principal he seems constantly to be mounting some podium. Or at a somewhat deeper level, he may be an intense and introspective person, yet on the job each train of thought seems to be abruptly shattered.

There are at least two major approaches to assessing the extent of role-personality conflict. The first, the sociological approach, asks the role incumbent to state the expectations for his role on the several task or decision items utilizing the familiar prompt, "As principal, I am expected to . . . ." This is point A, actual role expectations, in the model of role-personality relations shown in Figure 6.3. Utilizing the same list of task or decision items but preceding them with the prompt, "As a person, I like (need, want, or enjoy) . . ." provides, in a sense, a measure of personal needs. Thus line AC, the distance or discrepancy between the role

---

[29] John A. Eberhart, "An Investigation of Secondary Teachers' and Principals' Role Orientations and Their Expectations for the Principal's Role Behavior," doctoral dissertation, University of North Carolina at Chapel Hill, 1970.

[30] Moyer, op. cit., 3.

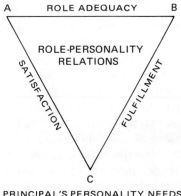

PRINCIPAL'S ACTUAL
ROLE EXPECTATIONS
("As principal, I am expected
to . . .")

PRINCIPAL'S IDEAL
ROLE EXPECTATIONS
("Ideally, as principal
I should . . .")

A   ROLE ADEQUACY   B

ROLE-PERSONALITY
RELATIONS

SATISFACTION

FULFILLMENT

C

PRINCIPAL'S PERSONALITY NEEDS
("I need, like, want, or
enjoy . . .")

Figure 6.3
Actual and ideal role-personality relations

and the personality, is a measure of role satisfaction. As indicated in the
social systems model in Chapter 3, role *satisfaction* is a measure of the
compatibility of the role and the personality.

In addition to actual role expectations, however, it is often desirable
to obtain a measure of idealized role expectations utilizing such prompts
as, "Ideally, as principal, I should . . ." or "The ideal principal is expected to . . . ." Again, it is useful to examine the discrepancy scores. The
difference between the actual role and idealized role (line AB in Figure 6.3) is a measure of the *adequacy* of the principal's present role.
The difference between idealized role expectations and personality dispositions (line BC in Figure 6.3) may be considered to be a measure of
role *fulfillment*. The sociological approach has been particularly useful in
studies of the teacher role,[31] and is equally applicable to analysis of the
principal's role.

The second method used to assess the role-personality relationship is
the psychological approach. This is the more common method utilized
in personnel testing and selection procedures wherein the focal role, in
this case the principalship, is conceived in terms of a stereotypic personalistic syndrome of personality variables required for effective performance in the role. For example, the principalship may be conceived

[31] Merton V. Campbell, "Teacher-Principal Agreement on the Teacher Role,"
Administrator's Notebook, 7 (February 1959), 1–4.

as requiring such behaviors as social interaction, achievement orientation, or feelings of security. Then personality tests or measures are administered to assess the extent to which an individual's personality is
compatible with the role.

Lipham utilized the psychological approach to examine the relationship of personal variables to on-the-job effectiveness of public school
principals.[32] From an analysis of the administrative role, it was argued
that the principal normatively could be expected to engage in purposeful
activity, to strive for positions of higher status, to relate well to others,
and to feel secure in the fact of highly affective stimuli. It was hypothesized, therefore, that principals having a personality structure tending to
produce the aforementioned behaviors would suffer less strain in fulfilling
their roles; they would be rated more effective than those whose personal
needs were incongruent with the role expectations. Interviews, observations, and personality instruments administered to 84 principals in a midwestern city school system provided data substantiating the hypothesis.
The principals rated more effective by the superintendent of schools and
members of the central office staff scored significantly higher than the
principals who were rated less effective in activity drive, achievement
drive, social ability, and feelings of security.

An interesting ancillary analysis also was made of Lipham's interview
and observation data, not in terms of the verbal responses but in terms of
the nonverbal behaviors of the effective and the ineffective school principals.[33] Noting after Halpin[34] that the muted language of nonverbal
communication is a rich source of cues in determining the course of interpersonal relations, the investigator used the interview situation to
observe certain behavioral patterns, which he subsequently categorized
for quantitative analysis. At the time the observations were made, he had
no knowledge of the effectiveness rankings or of the scores on the personality measures of the individuals being observed. Significant differences were observed between the effective and the ineffective principals
in each of the following behavior patterns, the former tending to manifest
the indicated behavior, the latter not:

1. Meeting the interviewer at the door of the office.
2. Offering to take the interviewer on a tour of the building or to
observe classroom teachers.
3. Hanging up the coat and hat of the interviewer or arranging for a
secretary to do so.

---

[32] James M. Lipham, "Personal Variables of Effective Administrators," *Administrator's Notebook,* 9 (September 1960), 1–4.

[33] James M. Lipham and Donald C. Francke, "Non-Verbal Behavior of Administrators," *Educational Administration Quarterly,* 2 (Spring 1966), 100–109.

[34] Andrew W. Halpin, "Muted Language," *School Review,* 68 (Spring 1960),
85–104.

4. Having in the office some item of interest, such as a paperweight of unusual design, a drawing, a citation, or some other objects not obtainable in an office supply store.

5. Arranging a private place for the conference—instead of talking in the presence of secretaries, teachers, or pupils.

6. Seating the interviewer at the side of the desk instead of directly across the desk.

7. Having few interruptions, either directly or by telephone.

8. After the conference, walking with the interviewer either to the door of the office or to the outside door of the school—instead of remaining behind his desk.

By itself, each item seems innocent enough and hardly noticeable until pointed out. But consider the cumulative image projected by a person who meets a visitor at the door, as against one who lets the caller walk across the room to greet him; arranges a private room or office for the conference, as against one who does not take the trouble to make any such arrangement and is forced to use whatever space happens to be available; courteously escorts the visitor to the door, as against one who remains behind his desk and lets the visitor make his way out alone. We do not want to suggest that any administrator who imitates this behavior will automatically become more effective, yet we would argue that the extent of the conflict between an individual and his role may become apparent also through his habitual interpersonal acts, to which he pays no attention. Indeed, the "muted language" of unpremeditated behavior may be louder than carefully measured speech, not only in reflecting the congruence or conflict between any institutional role and the role incumbent's personality, but in determining the effectiveness or lack of effectiveness of the administrator in fulfilling the institutional and individual goals for which he is responsible in the social system.

Numerous recent studies have examined the nature and relationship of personality variables to performance in the principal's role. Olson found, as did Lipham, that school principals classified as having effective leadership patterns differed substantially from principals classified as ineffective with respect to their personality needs as measured by an activities index.[35] In a study of Minnesota secondary school principals, Sargent observed that certain personality characteristics of principals, as measured by Cattell's *Sixteen Personality Factor Questionnaire*, were related to the degree of openness of organizational climate within the schools.[36] Similarly, Berends noted a systematic relationship between

[35] Gary F. Olson, "Congruence and Dissonance in the Ecology of Educational Administrators as a Basis for Discriminating Between Patterns of Leadership Behavior," doctoral dissertation, Illinois State University, 1967.

[36] James C. Sargent, "An Analysis of Principal and Staff Perceptions of High School Organizational Climate," doctoral dissertation, University of Minnesota, 1966.

teacher perceptions of the principal's personality and organizational climate in elementary schools in Michigan.[37]

In addition to personality characteristics, such other variables as graduate training and professional experience appear to be related to the degree of role-personality conflict. In a study by Wagoner, principals reported that although they gain most of their abilities to perform their roles after they become principals, they felt that graduate preparation in administration was a significant factor in their effective role performance.[38] They also felt that teaching experience is not a particularly important source of skill development in the successful execution of the principal's role. Concerning professional experience as a principal, in a study of New York principals, Kaplan found that those with less experience in a particular school differed substantially from those with more experience in certain leadership behaviors.[39] For example, those with less experience showed greater concern for initiating structure than did those with more administrative experience.

The foregoing studies are representative of the growing body of fruitful research that is adding substantially to our knowledge of the role of the principal. These investigations have not presented "what ought to be." They have, however, described more adequately the relationships among significant, crucial variables. On the basis of these relationships, numerous implications may be drawn both for further research and for practice in the principalship.

Implications of the role studies

Before turning to the implications of role theory for improving the principal's performance, we should critique and examine certain aspects of the role studies conducted to date.

TOWARD A DEEPER UNDERSTANDING

First, increased attention in future studies of the principal's role should be given to the validity and reliability of many of the role assessment

[37] Eugene H. Berends, "Perceptions of the Principal's Personality: A Study of the Relationships to Organizational Climate," doctoral dissertation, Michigan State University, 1969.

[38] Jack L. Wagoner, "The Validity of Teaching Experience as a Prerequisite for the Principalship," doctoral dissertation, University of Northern Colorado, 1969.

[39] Bert K. Kaplan, "An Analysis of Changes in the Adaptive Behavior of Elementary School Principals as Related to Their Lengths of Experience in One Building," doctoral dissertation, New York University, 1969.

instruments. Some of the role instruments contain an implicit bias in the descriptive items—the "good-bad" syndrome. Investigators utilizing leadership taxonomies tend to commit this error more frequently than others. For example, in one study the item, "Ideally, the principal should cut people short when they are speaking," undoubtedly was coded as leader-centered behavior. It was not surprising, therefore, to discover that most people (and here there was substantial agreement) preferred the principal to be group-centered. "Rudeness" is not an idealized expectation for the principalship or for any other social role.

Aside from the good-bad syndrome, another shortcoming of the role or decision items on some of the instruments is their tendency to be quite generally, even esoterically, worded. Like statements pertaining to God, motherhood, and the objectives of education, the usefulness of such inexplicit items as guides for behavior is limited. The item, "Ideally, the principal should provide instructional leadership," may serve as an example. This descriptive item alone subsumes enough task or decision items for several studies of diverse expectations.

A second suggestion for improving studies of the principal's role relates not to the instrumentation but to the respondents sampled. In some of the studies, for example, size of the respondent group is ignored even though it should be obvious that as the number of respondents is increased, the likelihood of discovering agreement diminishes. In studies of one's perceptions of alters' expectations, moreover, the attribution of expectations from one person to another is difficult enough; they mount even further when a person is asked to estimate the expectations for a whole group, such as teachers or citizens. Also, respondents are sometimes forced to state their expectations when they really are unfamiliar with the focal role being studied. In our studies of the school board role, for example, we found that whereas citizens do hold expectations for the school as an institution, they are not familiar enough with the inner workings of the school organization to allocate these expectations differentially to specific roles.[40] "Don't know" may be a legitimate response.

The third major suggestion for improving future analyses of the principal's role relates to the meaning of role conflict. In terms of Pondy's classification schema, most of the present role studies do not measure manifest, open-warfare-type conflict; they simply measure disagreement or potential for conflict.[41] In this regard, several studies of expectations

[40] James M. Lipham, Russell T. Gregg, and Richard A. Rossmiller, *The School Board as an Agency for Resolving Conflict*, Cooperative Research Project No. 5-0338-2-12-1, Madison, Wis., 1967.

[41] Louis R. Pondy, "Organizational Conflict: Concepts and Models," *Administrative Science Quarterly*, 12 (September 1967), 296–320.

for the principal's role seem to end precisely where they should begin. They merely identify the extent of potential conflict in expectations within and between individuals and groups. But what are the sources of such potential conflict? How often does latent or potential conflict become manifest? How might such conflicts be resolved? Answers to these questions undoubtedly demand studies of schools through time rather than the typical snapshot-type investigations of the present.

Fourth, investigations are needed that focus less on a single organization role than on the complementarity of organizational roles. Most functions within the educational organization are shared, perhaps because the roles are professional. In dealing with the problem of pupil discipline, for example, teachers, guidance counselors, psychologists, principals, the superintendent, and the school board may all have parts. It is conceivable in this regard that any one of these roles studied in isolation might be quite clearly understood, yet overlap in points of tangency among the discrete roles might be minimal. Increasingly, attention must be given to the complementarity of roles and to the relationship of subunits within a social system to the larger social system—for example, the relationship of the classroom to the school, the school to the school district, and the school district to the community.

Finally, it apparently is assumed in many role studies that a conflict in expectations for the principal's role is somehow "bad"—but such is not necessarily the case. Moreover, it often has been assumed that a linear relationship exists between extent of conflict and degree of effectiveness—that when conflict goes up, effectiveness goes down. Instead, studies are needed to determine the extent to which the conflict-effectiveness relationship is not linear but curvilinear. An extremely low level of conflict might characterize a school that is in a state of homeostasis; conversely, an extremely high level of conflict might characterize a school that is in a state of chaos. Surely, for example, many principals have had the experience of working with a disgruntled teacher whose expressed expectations are at variance with those of others, only to find later that such variant expectations made a significant contribution toward the achievement of organizational goals. Clearly, additional study is needed regarding the minimal-maximal acceptable range of role conflict within the school.

The findings of the role studies conducted to date possess several implications for improved practice in the principalship.

TOWARD IMPROVED ROLE PERFORMANCE

Implications for improving the principal's role performance may be drawn from studies related to each of the types of role conflict.

WEARING MANY HATS. Because of the need to strengthen the ultimate symbiotic relationship that must obtain between the school and its larger community, it is frequently urged that the principal not only hold leadership roles in many groups but also motivate teachers to do so. This, no doubt, remains a need in many communities, but there is some evidence to indicate that the principals who are least effective are the ones who are at the extremes of the participatory continuum—either underextended or overextended, as it were.[42] Some participation may be good, but it does not follow that more is better. It may well be that many principals should examine and perhaps even reduce their range of leadership and membership roles in an effort to determine the extent to which professional matters, such as reading and research, are ignored—not to mention personal matters, such as recreation and responsibilities to one's self and family.

Aside from the number of roles, the degree of conflict among multiple roles represents an area in which the principal may make immediate contributions. In his work with teachers, he can assist them in more thoroughly examining conflicts between such roles as teacher and parent; in his contacts with the community he can be alert to incompatible roles demanded both of him and of his teachers. Such conflicts usually can be lessened somewhat by interpreting their nature and extent to the community. That situations may vary widely does not absolve the principal of this responsibility.

MAN IN THE MIDDLE. Recognition that the principalship is an intermediate position between the superintendent and the teachers should provide the principal with a more realistic framework for decision making. The goal to be "right" is a powerful force, and it influences all decisions that a leader makes. Yet from the standpoint of the principal's conflictful, hierarchical position, there may be many situations for which there exists no "right" solution. Hence the principal should not feel guilty or incompetent over the decisions he makes if, on many occasions, he finds substantial elements of one or more clienteles displeased with his actions.

Consider, however, the untenable position of the principal whose decisions displease others. The absence of a suitable measure of excellence in education almost precludes evaluation of the extent to which a school is achieving its goals—much less evaluation of the principal's leadership contribution. Thus evaluation tends to focus not on how well the school is doing its job but on how smoothly it operates—the extent to which "the ship is well oiled."

Even so, respective roles must complement each other if the organi-

---

[42] James M. Lipham, "Personal Variables Related to Administrative Effectiveness," doctoral dissertation, University of Chicago, 1960.

zation is to achieve its goals. We may, therefore, conclude that principals would be investing their hours wisely if they took time to discuss frankly and openly with their superintendents, teachers, students, and other reference groups mutual expectations held for each other's roles.

CAUGHT IN GROUP CROSSFIRE. The results of research concerning conflict within groups suggest immediately to the perceptive principal that he must become increasingly alert to individual, subgroup, and collective differences in expectations held by a group for his leadership. In this regard, there has probably been limited opportunity for a type of upward communication, particularly concerning expectations held by teachers for the principal. Although some might tend to disparage such interchange, they will be quick to admit that the typical teacher's viewpoint of the principal's role seems indeed restricted, if not naïve. The principal is being somewhat less than facetious when he says, "If Miss X could be principal for only one day. . . ."

But this shoe also fits the principal who needs to be equally alert to conflicting demands he may make on others. Principals caught in the morass of operational problems often neglect to communicate clearly the expectations they hold for others. Consider, for example, the use of that familiar administrative device, the committee. Often endless hours have been wasted and the work of a committee has foundered because the principal has failed to define at the outset the expectations he holds for the committee in terms of policies, participation, processes, or products. Increasingly, mutual expectations must be raised from an implicit to an explicit level.

THE MAN VS. THE JOB. The findings of investigations in this area—role-personality conflict—imply that principals should give increased attention to the bases they use in the assignment of curricular and extracurricular responsibilities to present members of the staff. Studies of role-personality conflict also contain important implications for the initial selection of staff members. The principal should reexamine carefully his criteria for rendering judgments about candidates. Rather than focusing entirely on the job as he defines it, or instead of concentrating entirely on the qualifications of the candidate, the principal may need to lean more heavily on a visualization of the person in the role.

A similar visualization should be made concerning the selection of principals, since all good teachers do not necessarily make good principals. Moreover, there is evidence to indicate that the principals who are effective were not self-selected but were, as teachers, encouraged by their principals to receive requisite training for administrative responsibilities.[43] Therefore, principals are derelict in a major responsibility to

[43] Ibid.

their profession if they do not provide such encouragement to individuals they perceive as potentially effective administrators.

In conclusion, it should be noted that the research that has been cited and the implications that have been drawn supply the practicing principal with numerous ways of viewing the dynamic aspects of his role. The foregoing investigations are only representative of the expanding body of theory and research on the principal's role, but they serve to sharpen the focus on relevant sources of conflict and ambivalence with which all principals are inevitably faced.

School principals devote their entire lives to the ideal of maximizing the attainment of both institutional and personal goals. This leadership ideal is indeed stimulating, although quite complex. Those who would increase their understanding of the complex leadership role may do so through at least two approaches: through analyzing and studying the theory and the research that yield useful guides for action, or through continuously attempting to work their way out of one role conflict after another. The former is eminently more desirable than the latter. As Andrews discovered, principals who utilize a higher theoretical orientation to problem solving than their colleagues also fulfill their role expectations more satisfactorily.[44]

Summary

In this chapter the principalship was viewed in terms of role theory. Major sources of expectations for the principal's role, including historical-legal, professional, and school district policies were delineated. Models of role expectations and role perceptions, role complementarity, and the role-personality relationship were presented as a basis for examining the major types of role conflict in the principalship. Salient findings of research on the principal's role were cited concerning the following types of role conflict: (1) interrole conflict, or disparity between and among two or more roles the principal is simultaneously fulfilling; (2) inter-reference-group conflict, or disagreement between and among the principal and his reference groups regarding the expectations held for his role as principal; (3) intra-reference-group conflict, or disagreement within a reference group regarding the expectations held for the role of the principal; and (4) role-personality conflict, or divergence between the role expectations and the personality needs of the principal. The chapter concluded with suggestions for enhancing future studies of the principal's role and with guidelines for improving performance in the principalship.

[44] Richard L. Andrews, "Theory Orientation of School Principals as Related to Attainment of Selected Behavioral Goals of the Organization," doctoral dissertation, Purdue University, 1968.

SUGGESTED ACTIVITIES

1. Analyze descriptions of the principal's role in school district policies in terms of the functional categories, major responsibilities, or leadership styles expected of the principal. Compare the results by type of district or by school level—elementary, middle, or secondary.

2. Observe principals or analyze their daily calendars and compare the actual amounts of time they spend on various activities with the data in Table 6.1.

3. Interview citizens, board members, superintendents, principals, teachers, and/or students concerning the major expectations they hold for the principal's actual or idealized role. Compare and contrast the expectations.

4. Devise or utilize a prepared instrument listing expectations for the principal's role and administer it to a class or seminar in the principalship. Compare and discuss the reasons for differences within the group in the expectations they hold.

5. Utilizing student dyads in a principalship class or seminar, have each person respond to a role instrument for self and perceived alter's expectations for the principalship. Calculate intraceptive and communicative distance both for the dyads and for the total group. Readminister the instruments to test the effects of the feedback procedure.

SELECTED REFERENCES

CARVER, FRED D., and THOMAS J. SERGIOVANNI, eds., *Organizations and Human Behavior: Focus on Schools,* New York, McGraw-Hill, 1969, pt. III.

CULBERTSON, JACK A., et al., eds., *Social Science Content for Preparing Educational Leaders,* Columbus, Ohio, Merrill, 1973.

CULBERTSON, JACK A., CURTIS HENSON, and RUEL MORRISON, eds., *Performance Objectives for School Principals,* Berkeley, Calif., McCutchan, 1974.

FABER, CHARLES F., and GILBERT F. SHEARRON, *Elementary School Administration, Theory and Practice,* New York, Holt, Rinehart and Winston, 1970, chap. 9.

GETZELS, J. W., JAMES M. LIPHAM, and ROALD F. CAMPBELL, *Educational Administration as a Social Process,* New York, Harper & Row, 1968, chaps. 7, 8, and 10.

GROSS, NEAL, and ROBERT A. HERRIOTT, *Staff Leadership in Public Schools: A Sociological Inquiry,* New York, Wiley, 1965.

HACK, WALTER G., et al., *Educational Administration, Selected Readings,* 2nd ed., Boston, Allyn & Bacon, 1971, pt. VI.

MCCLEARY, LLOYD E., and STEPHEN P. HENCLEY, *Secondary School Administration, Theoretical Bases of Professional Practice,* New York, Dodd, Mead, 1965, chap. 4.

TRACY, NEAL H., "Profile of the Principal," in *Encyclopedia of Education,* vol. 7, New York, Macmillan and Free Press, 1971, pp. 211–216.

CHAPTER 7
Decision theory

ecision making is a central responsibility of the principal. Knowledge of decision theory should enable the principal to sharpen and improve his decision-making skills.

In this chapter decision theory is first viewed in terms of two global approaches to the analysis of decision making—the administrative process approach and the general systems approach.[1] Next a definition and a model of decision making are presented that define and depict key concepts and dimensions of the decision process. The dimension of decision content is then explored both in terms of the tasks or functions of the principal and in terms of the types of decisions made by the principal —routine, heuristic, and compromise decisions. The final parts of the chapter include consideration of the organizational-structural dimension; attention is focused on actual and ideal involvement in decision making, as well as the nature of such involvement on the part of the principal. In presenting recent research on decision theory, applications are made to the principal's role in terms of five basic competencies required for effective decision making.

Approaches to decision making

Although decision making is currently approached in a general systems context, earlier conceptualizations of the administrative process continue to be of great utility.

THE ADMINISTRATIVE PROCESS

As Gregg indicated, "decision making is at the very heart of the administrative process."[2] Similarly, McCamy stated: "The reaching of a decision is the core of administration, all other attributes of the administrative process being dependent on, interwoven with, and existent for the mak-

---

[1] Portions of this chapter are drawn from James M. Lipham, "Making Effective Decisions," in Jack A. Culbertson, Curtis Henson, and Ruel Morrison, eds., *Performance Objectives for School Principals*, Berkeley, Calif., McCutchan, 1974.

[2] Russell T. Gregg, "The Administrative Process," in Roald F. Campbell and Russell T. Gregg, eds., *Administrative Behavior in Education*, New York, Harper & Row, 1957, p. 275.

ing of decisions."[3] Simon took the view that decision making is synonymous with managing.[4] Earlier, Barnard wrote: "The essential process of adaptation in organizations is decision, whereby the physical, biological, personal, and social factors of the situation are selected for specific combination by volitional action."[5] Thus decision making pervades the entire administrative process, since it includes not only a decision but also the acts necessary to put the decision into operation and so affect the course of action of an organization.[6]

Although several different formulations of the administrative process have been proposed, the process stages of planning, organizing, stimulating, and evaluating have particular relevance for the decision-making role of the principal.

PLANNING. Some have described the principal as a person who really enjoys planning but who never gets the chance. Observations of on-the-job administrative behavior, however, reveal this caricature to be inaccurate.[7] Throughout a typical school year the principal finds need to spend considerable time in making planning-type decisions.

Despite sustained attention of authorities in administration to planning, there is widespread disagreement over operational definitions of the term. Some view planning as a highly personalistic process, tending to equate planning with the "mental effort" from which a plan evolves.[8] In the same vein, others dating as far back as Fayol, tend to define planning in an almost clairvoyant way as "forecasting the future."[9] Still other authorities take a much broader view, making planning almost synonymous with the total administrative process and including such stages as determining goals, specifying objectives, developing strategies, and making long-range decisions.[10] We concur with the broad definition and con-

[3] James L. McCamy, "An Analysis of the Process of Decision Making," *Public Administration Review,* 7 (Winter 1947), 41.

[4] Herbert A. Simon, *The New Science of Management Decision,* New York, Harper & Row, 1960.

[5] Chester I. Barnard, *The Functions of the Executive,* Cambridge, Mass., Harvard University Press, 1938, p. 286.

[6] Daniel E. Griffiths, *Administrative Theory,* New York, Appleton, 1959, p. 76.

[7] Staff Associates, *Observation of Administrator Behavior,* Chicago, Midwest Administration Center, University of Chicago, 1959, p. 134.

[8] George A. Steiner, *Top Management Planning,* London, Collier-Macmillan, 1969, p. 8.

[9] Henri Fayol, *General and Industrial Management,* translated by Constance Storrs, London, Pitman, 1949, pp. 43–52.

[10] Cf. E. Kirby Johnson, *Long Range Planning: The Executive Viewpoint,* Englewood Cliffs, N.J., Prentice-Hall, 1966, p. 21; George C. F. Bereday and Joseph Lauwerys, *Educational Planning,* New York, Harcourt Brace Jovanovich, 1967.

ceive of planning as those activities of the school principal related to defining and clarifying goals, purposes, and objectives; investigating conditions and operations related to purposes and objectives; considering possible alternatives; and recommending changes to be made. Thus planning may precede a major decision.[11] However, it may also follow a decision and be concerned with the implementation of it.[12]

Principals have long been accustomed to working with intraorganizational groups in curricular planning and, to a lesser extent, in financial and educational facility planning. With the addition, particularly in large urban school districts, of divisions of long-range planning and development, the planning process is likely to be extended to all functional, task, or content dimensions of the principal's role. An accompanying trend toward improving the planning process in extraorganizational agencies (e.g., in municipal, regional, and state governments, and in numerous specialized federal agencies concerned with health, housing, and welfare) indicates that the principal of the future will either plan or perish.

ORGANIZING. As with the concept of planning, different viewpoints exist concerning the concept of organizing. Again, there are those who view this stage of the administrative process in highly personalistic terms, in the sense of an ability to organize.[13] These views have great popular appeal, since there exists a strong cultural bias in favor of such ability. We recently observed an example of this bias when analyzing the performance of principals in a certain school district. Concerning the ability of one of his principals, the superintendent remarked, "Confidentially, I can't think of one thing Principal X does with which I can agree strongly. But I will say this, whatever he does is very well organized."

In some definitions, organizing is viewed in terms of the entire structural-hierarchical view of formal and informal organization.[14] Other conceptualizations utilize the terms "programming," "coordinating," and "implementing," and the combination of these closely approximates our definition. In our view, organizing includes the processes utilized by an administrator in making a plan operational. This stage includes decisions concerning the following: selecting specific rational processes to implement a plan, assigning primary role responsibilities or relating people and events, assessing the time frame for each responsibility and event,

[11] Herbert A. Simon, "Decision Making and Administrative Organization," *Public Administration Review,* 4 (1944), 26.

[12] Gregg, op. cit., p. 282.

[13] Ernest Dale, *The Great Organizers,* New York, McGraw-Hill, 1960.

[14] Gregg, op. cit., pp. 286–294.

and providing the necessary personnel, facilities, or equipment to accomplish each responsibility.

STIMULATING. In the process stage of stimulating, one recognizes that administration primarily and inevitably involves working with people to achieve organizational and individual goals. Because of the complexity of the human personality, it is not possible to deal prescriptively with this domain. Even so, concepts of personality structure, power and influence, value orientations, and individual and group relationships provide great insight to the principal as he continually tries to stimulate others to internalize and implement an organized plan. The process of stimulating involves the decisions that are directed toward increasing the identification of individuals with the objectives and activities of a plan; increasing the rationality of a plan; enhancing on-the-job satisfaction of individuals; communicating plans, problems, and progress; providing supportive relationships; and influencing individuals to change.

The human relations view of administration is derived largely from analyses of administration by Mayo, Follett, and others.[15] Undoubtedly the principal must be or become increasingly skilled in both formal and informal interpersonal relationships if he is to stimulate others, not only toward maximum organizational achievement but also toward maximum individual fulfillment—simultaneously, it is hoped.

EVALUATING. The final administrative process stage of evaluating includes decisions concerning the extent to which plans are being effected or have been achieved. Although some use the term "appraising" to describe this stage of the process, we prefer the more commonly utilized term of evaluating, since most principals already are familiar with evaluation in their work with teachers and students. Decisions relating to evaluation include: reviewing plans and objectives; obtaining data regarding inputs, processes, and outputs; interpreting the data obtained; drawing implications for future planning; and reporting results. Evaluation has recently been defined as the process of delineating, obtaining, and providing useful information for judging decision alternatives.[16] Thus evaluation is central to the making of decisions.

[15] Elton Mayo, *The Human Problems of an Industrial Civilization*, New York, Macmillan, 1933; Henry C. Metcalf and Lyndall F. Urwick, *Dynamic Administration: The Collected Papers of Mary Parker Follett*, New York, Harper & Row, 1940; cf. F. J. Roethlisberger and W. J. Dickson, *Management and the Worker*, Cambridge, Mass., Harvard University Press, 1939; Chris Argyris, *Integrating the Individual and the Organization*, New York, Wiley, 1964; Douglas McGregor, *The Human Side of Enterprise*, New York, McGraw-Hill, 1960.

[16] Phi Delta Kappa National Study Committee on Evaluation, *Educational Evaluation and Decision Making*, Itasca, Ill., Peacock, 1971, p. 40.

Because school personnel tend to slight evaluative processes in their decision making, greater attention to systematic evaluation is now mandated for participation in many educational programs financed at federal and state levels. If principals are to improve the quality of decisions that are made, it is obvious that they must either develop skills in the evaluative process or draw again and again on the evaluation specialist.

As we conceive the administrative process, the principalship is considered in terms of four interrelated stages of behavior—planning, organizing, stimulating, and evaluating. Decision making is seen as a central aspect of each stage in the administrative process. It is likewise a central concern in the systems approach to administration.

THE SYSTEMS APPROACH

The systems approach to administration is particularly relevant for the analysis of decision making, in terms of both describing the process of decision making and assessing the principal's decision behavior.

As indicated in Chapter 2, the systems approach to the analysis of decision making includes the following five steps or stages:

1. Identifying the nature of the problem
2. Determining solution requirements and alternatives
3. Choosing a solution strategy from alternatives
4. Implementing the solution strategy
5. Determining performance effectiveness[17]

We also noted in Chapter 2 that the systems approach has fostered the use of several viable management tools and techniques—needs assessment, management by objectives (MBO), planning-programming-budgeting systems (PPBS), input-output analysis, program evaluation and review technique/critical path method (PERT/CPM). All these can serve to sharpen considerably the decision-making skills of the principal. A contribution even greater than specific tools and techniques, however, is the focus in the systems approach on the question, "What are the types of behaviors exhibited at each stage in the decision process?"

To answer this question, a promising procedure known as decision behavior analysis (DBA) is being widely explored. In many ways it is analogous to the procedure utilized in the assessment of leader behavior. Based on the stages in the systems approach, items such as those shown in Figure 7.1 are developed. Rather than being specific to a school district

[17] Roger A. Kaufman, "Systems Approaches to Education: Discussion and Attempted Integration," in Philip K. Piele, Terry L. Eidell, and Stuart C. Smith, eds., *Social and Technological Changes: Implications for Education*, Eugene, Center for the Advanced Study of Educational Administration, University of Oregon, 1970, p. 160.

DECISION BEHAVIOR ANALYSIS (DBA) SCALE

In making decisions, my principal . . .
(Sample items only)

	ALWAYS	OFTEN	SOME-TIMES	SELDOM	NEVER
	5	4	3	2	1
1. Identifies the emotional elements of a problem.					
	5	4	3	2	1
2. Seeks alternative solutions from others.					
	5	4	3	2	1
3. Determines who will be affected by each alternative.					
	5	4	3	2	1
4. Gains support for his decisions.					
	5	4	3	2	1
5. Allows others to implement decisions.					
	5	4	3	2	1
6. Seeks unique alternative solutions.					
	5	4	3	2	1
7. Computes the costs of various alternatives.					
	5	4	3	2	1
8. Maintains feedback mechanisms.					
	5	4	3	2	1
. . . n.					
	5	4	3	2	1

Figure 7.1
Sample instrument for assessing the principal's decision process behavior

or a school, the items used to measure decision-process behavior may be quite amenable to generalization.

As in studies of roles or leadership styles, one may utilize the items to obtain a measure of actual self-perceptions of decision behavior ("In making decisions, I . . ."), as well as to obtain a measure of alters' actual expectations of decision behavior ("In making decisions, my principal . . ."). Through changing the prompts, it also is possible to obtain measures of idealized self-perceptions of decision behavior ("Ideally, in making decisions I should . . .") and of alters' idealized expectations of decision behavior ("Ideally, in making decisions my principal should . . ."). Finally, through changing both the prompt and the response set, it is possible to utilize the decision process behavioral items to obtain ratings of the perceived effectiveness of one's decision behavior. To reiterate, the systems approach provides not only tools that are useful to the decision maker but also concepts that can serve in the analysis of the decision-making process.

A model of the decision-making process

Decision making is a process wherein an awareness of a problematic state of a system, influenced by information and values, is reduced to competing alternatives among which a choice is made based on perceived outcome states of the system. This definition contains a number of key concepts, and the first of these is that of process, itself.

Process implies action—a particular set of continuing activities, steps, stages, or operations. Process is always inferred, usually sequential, and sometimes cyclical. Since process is inferred, it is only an abstraction for the analysis of decision-making behavior. As Halpin cautioned, "An outside observer can never observe 'process' qua 'process'; he can observe only a sequence of behavior or behavior-products from which he may infer process."[18] Thus in analyzing the decision-making process it is necessary to obtain data from the decision maker himself, as well as from observers of the behavior.

In terms of their sequential nature, process formulations are usually such that one step serves logically as the basis for the next step. In decision making, however, since the limits of a problem define the decision to be made, the process may be entered at any stage. In fact, some on-the-job interactions of administrators appear to satisfy multiple process stages simultaneously.[19] In analyzing decision-making behavior, such multiple category analyses should be neither ignored nor denied.

The cyclical nature of process implies that the iterative steps are recycled in a continual test of system states and attainments at any point in the process.[20] In decision making, incremental judgments are made

[18] Andrew W. Halpin, "A Paradigm for Research on Administrative Behavior," in Roald F. Campbell and Russell T. Gregg, eds., *Administrative Behavior in Education,* New York, Harper & Row, 1957, p. 195.

[19] Staff Associates, op. cit., 1959, pp. 138–140.

[20] Phi Delta Kappa National Study Committee on Evaluation, op. cit., p. 83.

concerning whether to continue, terminate, or change the major or minor decisions made. Contrary to typical views, recycling may and often does occur at any time or many times in the decision process.

AWARENESS OF A PROBLEMATIC STATE

Awareness of a problematic state of a system constitutes the first stage or step in the decision-making process. At this juncture, such awareness may range from evident to intuitive, objective to subjective, cognitive to affective, ordered to random, or specific to diffuse.

Barnard was among the first to observe that the nature of a problem —its origin and urgency—is an important consideration in deciding whether one should or should not attempt to solve it. He stated succinctly: "The fine art of executive decision consists in not deciding questions that are not now pertinent, in not deciding prematurely, in not making decisions that cannot be made effective, and in not making decisions that others should make."[21]

Barnard indicated that there are three occasions when one should make decisions: (1) authoritative communication from superiors, (2) cases referred by subordinates, and (3) cases originating on the initiative of the individual concerned.[22] From these occasion situations, the following typology of decisions evolved: (1) intermediary decisions, (2) appellate decisions, and (3) creative decisions.[23] Both intermediary and appellate decisions are a function of the organizational role structure and, since they originate outside the person of the decision maker, they seldom cause difficulty in terms of problem awareness.

Creative decisions, which originate with the decision maker, may represent a change in goals, policies, procedures, or relationships. More likely than not, they reflect a discrepancy between a "real" and an "idealized" state—at least as perceived by the decision maker. Thus it is in the making of creative decisions that such personalistic variables as mental ability, intraception, training, and experience of the decision maker, and such situational variables as power, resources, and role relations of the organization come into play most vividly.

As indicated in Figure 7.2, awareness of the problematic state is the initial concept to be considered in making decisions.

INFORMATION

To say that information serves as the basis for decision making seems like belaboring the obvious, yet three points are worthy of consideration:

[21] Barnard, op. cit., p. 194.

[22] Ibid., p. 190.

[23] Griffiths, op. cit., pp. 98–102.

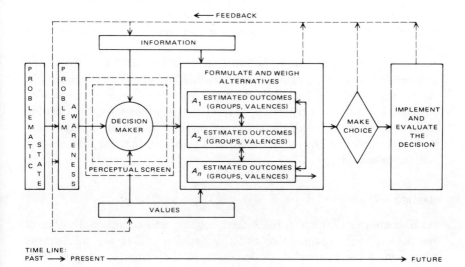

Figure 7.2

Model of the decision-making process

SOURCE: James M. Lipham, "Making Effective Decisions," in Jack A. Culbertson, Curtis Henson, and Ruel Morrison, eds., *Performance Objectives for School Principals*, Berkeley, Calif., McCutchan, 1974.

amount, form, and flow of information. Regarding amount of information, research on administrative simulation has revealed that the search for additional information—whether by communicating with others in writing, by telephone, or face-to-face—logically constitutes a significant first step in the preparation for making a decision. Analysis of a decision maker's perceived information needs and search patterns provides initial tangible evidence of his decision-making skills. Some decision makers, for example, tend erroneously to view themselves as the "gatekeepers of information"; others tend to utilize limited data sources or information-gathering procedures; still others engage in "information overload" by obtaining reams of data that may be only tangentially related to the problem at hand. These and related tendencies may easily be assessed and subsequently changed.

Concerning form, information must be more than a mere collection of random data; it must be organized if it is to be useful. Thus organizations must be fully aware of the importance of obtaining information relevant for decision making. Research has revealed that the form in which information is presented influences directly and systematically the behavior of the decision maker.[24] Recently powerful management infor-

[24] Glen A. Easterday, "Information, Decision-Making, and Role Behavior in a Simulated Educational Environment," doctoral dissertation, University of Iowa, 1969.

mation tools and evaluation procedures have been developed which present data that are organized according to parameters relevant to each decision situation.

Finally, concerning flow, information must be made available when it is needed, since all decisions are ultimately bound within a time frame. As shown in Figure 7.2, problem awareness may range from past to present, but information bears a present-time relevance for the decision maker. There is the need, therefore, for responsive communication channels that foster the flow of information downward, parallel, and upward within organizations.

VALUES

As indicated in Chapter 4, the sacred, secular, and operational values of the society, the organization, and the decision maker are inextricably entwined in the making of all decisions. In the first place, values serve as a perceptual screen for the decision maker, affecting both his awareness of the problematic state of a system and his screening of information relative to the problem. Second, values condition the screening of possible alternatives, which involves estimations of the extent to which the possible alternatives will be congruent with the value systems of those who will be affected by a decision. Finally, values serve as the criteria against which higher-order goals are assessed and projected, since the decision maker serves simultaneously as a value analyst and as a value witness in the process of making decisions.

Although we lack systematic knowledge about the relationship of value orientations to decision behavior, it is both possible and desirable to examine further this relationship. For example, how do program cost decisions made by a principal who holds a traditional value orientation compare with those of a principal who holds an emergent value orientation? Or, how do decisions made by a principal who subscribes to the value assumptions of McGregor's Theory Y compare with those made by a principal who subscribes to Theory X? How important to the principal's decision-making behavior is similarity or dissimilarity of values between him and, say, the teachers? Further study is needed not only concerning how values may be related to decision behavior, but also concerning how values may *affect* decision behavior.

An additional note should be added regarding the interaction of values with rationality in decision making. Heretofore, some have presumed that nonrational decision making is a function of either inaccurate conceptions of goals or incomplete and untimely information. Yet from the model it can be observed that a decision believed to be rational by a decision maker in terms of his value orientations may be judged to be nonrational, irrational, or even indefensible by others who hold different value orientations. Thus rationality also is a function of dissimilarities of values.

PERCEPTUAL SCREEN

Many factors in addition to values constitute the perceptual screen of the decision maker, including such personalistic variables as intelligence, creativity, need-dispositions, abilities, and even biological states of the organism. Not to be overlooked are training and previous experiences that influence greatly the ways in which one cognizes, structures, and perceives the environment—in this instance, the decision situation. Moreover, situational or organizational variables, such as who in the formal or informal structure has the "ear" of the decision maker, reputations of others for supplying reliable input, mutual respect for divergent points of view, and the exercise of political or power relationships serve to impinge directly on the perceptual screen of the decision maker.

As shown in Figure 7.2, the perceptual screen surrounds the decision maker, in a sense, and affects all elements of the decision process, including problem awareness, information processing, value estimates, formulating and weighing alternatives, and making the decision choice. Since one lives and acts in terms of the world as he sees it, the perceptual screen of the decision maker is of great significance.

COMPETING ALTERNATIVES

Competing alternatives represent actions that might be taken or things that might be done to solve the problematic state of a system. Early in the decision process the competing alternatives are typically viewed as substantive matters, dealing with alternative needs, problems, or opportunities; subsequently, the competing alternatives are typically procedural, dealing with structuring, providing, and assessing possible courses of action to reduce the problematic state of a system. The formulation of competing alternatives includes consideration of the criteria against which possible outcomes will be assessed, such as validity, reliability, objectivity, relevance, scope, credibility, efficiency, and effectiveness.

To say that alternatives are in competition suggests that in most situations the decision maker is faced with conflict—potential or actual, latent or manifest. Since such conflict may concern goals, roles, or individuals, it is endemic to the decision-making process and is particularly evident at the stage of formulating and weighing alternatives. Hence it is often useful to conceive of decision making as a conflict-resolution process.

At the juncture of resolving conflict over competing alternatives, it frequently is deemed necessary to collect additional data. However, the collection of additional data does not of itself make the decision. Contrary to popular notions, additional data often complicate rather than facilitate the decision-making process.

CHOICE

The act of selecting a solution strategy from among the decision alternatives is termed the *decision choice*. It involves judging the outcomes or consequences of each decision alternative and selecting the solution deemed most likely to reduce the problematic state of the system. Often this stage in the process is an individualistic or personalistic matter, although through formal organizational or informal group processes, agreement on the choice may cause the choice to be termed an organizational or a collaborative decision.

Some have tended to equate the "moment of choice" with the entire decision-making process; however, it is only one stage, albeit a crucial one, at which the decision maker is poised at the decision point—that of considering the maximum input-probable outcome relationship. At the decision point, the decision maker continues to weigh each decision alternative, estimating the probable outcome states of each, until a decision is made.

Regarding the timing of the decision choice, undoubtedly there are decision skills that can be practiced and learned. Some decision makers apparently are able to evaluate alternatives more quickly and accurately than others; they can make decisions of great potency, even in rapid-fire order. Others take considerable time to make a choice—even engaging in decision-avoidance behavior, perhaps hoping that the necessity of making a choice will go away, perhaps seeking additional information, perhaps attempting to formulate additional alternatives, or perhaps returning to reformulate the problem. Since the decision-making process is time bound, however, it must be realized that even the decision not to decide is also an alternative.

ESTIMATED OUTCOME STATES

Estimation of the outcome state of a system involves posing the question, "If this, then what?"

As Bross stressed, for each decision alternative the consequences can be predicted only in terms of a probable, rather than a certain, chain of events.[25] In social systems, factors to be estimated include the nature and number of individuals or referent groups to which the decision is relevant, the intensity of identification of each individual or group with the decision, and the presumed rationality of the decision to each individual

[25] Irwin D. J. Bross, *Design for Decision*, New York, Macmillan, 1953, pp. 25–26.

or group. Again, communication of information and perceptions of the value orientations of others are crucial considerations for school principals, since it is the nature of the principal's role that most of the decisions deal with people rather than things.

The principal's decision-making role

In obtaining a better understanding of the principal's decision-making role, attention must first be directed to the substantive content of the role and next to the types of decisions made by the principal.

DECISION CONTENT

Although it is possible, as in the preceding sections of this chapter, to conceive of decision making in the abstract, decisions always relate to the major substantive content of a focal role. In the case of the school principal, such substantive content typically has been termed the tasks of the principal, which we categorize in the forthcoming functional chapters as follows:

1. Instructional program
2. Staff personnel
3. Pupil personnel
4. Financial and physical resources
5. School-community relations

Other categorizations have also been utilized to analyze the principalship.[26]

As indicated in Chapter 6, which was concerned with role theory, the typical analysis of the principal's role focuses on the tasks or functions performed. A somewhat different approach, called decision role analysis (DRA), is that of defining the role in terms of the decisions that rest with the position. The process of decision role analysis obtains expectations for a role incumbent's behavior along relevant continua from required to prohibited, such as the incumbent "absolutely must (5)," "probably should (4)," "may or may not (3)," "probably should not (2)," or "absolutely must not (1)" make the decisions described. As in the case of role studies, utilization of this procedure permits one to obtain measures of self-decision expectations, alters' decision expectations, and perceived alters' decision expectations, both for the principal's

---

[26] Cf. Robert E. Greene, *Administrative Appraisal: A Step to Improved Leadership,* Washington, D.C., National Association of Secondary School Principals, 1972, pp. 30–32.

actual decision role and for the idealized decision role—as well as to assess existential, intraceptive, and communicative distances. Other useful methodologies for DRA include requiring respondents to rank the decision content items in terms of their importance or assessing the amounts of time allotted to the various decision items, such as observing the decision-making behavior of principals on the job.

Several recent studies of the principal's decision-making role have been conducted utilizing such procedures.[27] From these studies it can be concluded that there is a high degree of commonality in the substantive content of the decision issues with which elementary, middle or junior high, and senior high school principals deal; the differences in types of communities in terms of such variables as socioeconomic status directly influence the content of the decisions with which principals are faced; that size of school system is related to the content of the decisions made by the principal; and that in large urban districts efforts at school district decentralization have not yet substantially affected the content of decisions made by the principal. Certain of these personal and situational variables are likewise related to the types of decisions made by the principal.

TYPES OF DECISIONS

In addition to analyzing the content of the decisions made by the principal in terms of major functions or tasks, it also is very useful to analyze the content in terms of decision types. Earlier analyses conceived of administration in terms of three types of problems about which principals make decisions: technical, human, and conceptual.[28] For some kinds of analyses this tripartite concept is particularly useful, even though there is substantial interaction among the types, particularly with the human element.

As we noted in the preceding section dealing with problem identification, another useful tripartite schema for analyzing decision content was based on the origin of the decision: intermediary decisions, deriving from above the principal in the administrative hierarchy; ap-

[27] Thomas L. Strick, "The Role of the Elementary Principal," doctoral dissertation, University of Wisconsin, 1971; Roger M. Giroux, "Changes in Decision-Making Processes in a Sub-District Reorganization of an Urban School System," doctoral dissertation, University of Wisconsin, 1970; and Glen G. Eye et al., *Relationship Between Instructional Change and the Extent to Which School Administrators and Teachers Agree on the Location of Responsibilities for Administrative Decisions,* U.S. Office of Education, Cooperative Research Project 1913 (5-0433), Madison, University of Wisconsin, Department of Educational Administration, 1966.

[28] Robert L. Katz, "Skills of an Effective Administrator," *Harvard Business Review,* 33 (February 1955), 33–42.

pellate decisions, deriving from below; and creative decisions, deriving from the decision maker himself.[29] Studies utilizing this typology have produced interesting and helpful findings. For example, Blaine discovered that junior high school principals encounter more appellate decision problems than do elementary school principals, and the latter encounter more intermediary and creative decision problems.[30] He also discovered that principals in high-socioeconomic-level school communities encounter a proportionately large number of creative problems, compared with their counterparts in low-socioeconomic-level communities, where the principals face many intermediary and appellate problems.

Recent theories suggest yet a different typology for the analysis of decision making, particularly in group situations. Within this framework there is concern for the structure of the relationship between individuals, the behavior required to facilitate decision making, the processes or manner of proceeding in decision making, and the social-emotional tone of the interpersonal relationships. This typology includes *routine* decision making, *heuristic* decision making, and *compromise* decision making.

ROUTINE DECISION MAKING. Perhaps most of the decisions that the principal makes are routine—whether they are intermediary or appellate, deriving from above or below him in the organizational hierarchy. In Simon's terms, this is the "programmed" type of decision.[31] That a decision may be routine or programmed does not at all imply that it is unimportant, simply that the organization has established the requisite goals, roles, procedures, and technologies for dealing with the decision. In routine decision making the situation is usually structured hierarchically (e.g., the principal and the teachers), role behavior is characterized by specialized yet coordinated effort, the processes utilized are largely formal, and the relationships themselves are likely to be somewhat stressful. Many examples in the principalship come readily to mind, such as the principal's transmitting changes made by the school board, his approving teachers' requisitions, or his enforcing student attendance regulations.

HEURISTIC DECISION MAKING. In heuristic or creative decision making, there is a lack of emphasis on hierarchical structure; role behavior is

[29] Cf. Barnard, op. cit., p. 194; and Griffiths, op. cit., pp. 98–102.

[30] Robert G. Blaine, "Problem Situations Encountered by Principals in Junior High Schools Located in High and Low Socioeconomic Communities," doctoral dissertation, University of Minnesota, 1969.

[31] Herbert A. Simon, *The New Science of Management Decisions*, New York, Harper & Row, 1960, pp. 5–20.

characterized by freedom for each individual to explore all ideas bearing on the problematic state; the processes utilized are characterized by free, full, and open problem definition and alternative generation; and the emotional-social tone is relatively relaxed, giving evidence of openness, originality, and the seeking of consensus. Working with students or teachers in solving a curricular issue may be an example of heuristic decision making, particularly if there is no agreed-upon method for dealing with the issue.

Some principals immediately experience difficulty in deciding whether a particular problem should be treated in a routinized or heuristic fashion. Others—particularly energetic, decisive, or action-oriented principals —are hard put to utilize the heuristic mode, even when it is called for. Still others attempt to resolve an issue by vacillating between the modes, as in the case of the principal who calls his staff together and says, "We have a very serious matter here about which I need your help. Now here's how I think we should handle this. . . ."

COMPROMISE DECISION MAKING. In compromise decision making, also called negotiated decision making,[32] the principal is concerned with a strategy for dealing with conflict that may occur because of differences in cultural values, role expectations, or vested interests of individuals. In such situations, one individual or group may stand in opposition to another individual or group concerning means or ends or both (e.g., in teacher negotiations). In such situations the group is composed of proportional representation with a presumably impartial chairman; each person represents his faction; group processes usually involve orderly communication, formalized voting procedures, and analytical approaches; and emotional tone may vary from hostility to candor to mediation to conciliation, evoked by the desire to reach agreement or acceptable compromise.

Increasingly, the principal is being called on to engage in decision making of the compromise type—whether because of inter-reference-group conflict (teachers vs. board, parents vs. teachers), or because of intra-reference-group conflict (one community group vs. another, one teacher group vs. another, or one student group vs. another). Again, our observations lead us to suggest that many principals resist unduly and delay unnecessarily the utilization of the compromise decision-making technique. Instead, they continue to depend inappropriately on routinized or heuristic decision making. By its very nature, the principalship demands not only that the principal establish a compromise decision struc-

---

[32] Andre L. Delbecq, "The Management of Decision-Making Within the Firm; Three Strategies for Three Types of Decision Making," *Academy of Management Journal*, 10 (December 1967), 329–339.

ture but also that he serve as the impartial mediator in the decision-making process.

Obviously, the different types of decisions—routine or programmed, heuristic or creative, and compromise or negotiated—call for differential involvement in the decision-making process.

Involvement in decision making

Recently considerable attention has been focused on involvement in decision making. Questions of concern to the principal are: "How may such involvement be assessed?" and "What are the outcomes of decision involvement?"

DECISION INVOLVEMENT ANALYSIS

One of the major complications in the analysis of decision making in complex organizations is that decisions are shared; that is, more than one role incumbent is typically involved in the decision process. Moreover, such involvement may be differential. Concerning the sharing of decisions, a procedure known as decision involvement analysis has proved to be fruitful.[33] In analyzing decision involvement, the major decision items are usually derived in terms of local needs, as in the decision role analysis (DRA), although a standard list of decisions dealing with such functions as curriculum, staff personnel, student personnel, finance, and school-community relations can be utilized. Next the school system's specific position titles, ranging from the board of education to students, are identified, and respondents are asked to indicate who is primarily responsible for making each decision. When data are obtained from respondents at all organizational levels, it becomes possible to compare perceptions of the decision-making structure of the organization. [A sample format for decision involvement analysis (DIA) appears in Figure 7.3.] It also is possible to obtain respondents' ideal perceptions —"Who should make each decision?"—thereby comparing the actual with the ideal decision structures.

One's own involvement in the decision-making process may range from high to low, as follows:

5. Make the decision
4. Recommend an alternative
3. Develop possible alternatives

---

[33] Gordon E. Wendlandt, "Faculty Involvement in the Decision-Making Process and Experience in Collective Negotiations," doctoral dissertation, University of Wisconsin, 1970.

DECISION INVOLVEMENT ANALYSIS (DIA) SCALE

QUESTIONS

Please answer these four questions in terms of your school or school system by placing the appropriate number of the response in the boxes provided for each decision item. Place only one answer in each box.

1. Which person (or persons) is (are) primarily responsible at the present time for making this decision?

2. Which person (or persons) do you believe *should be primarily responsible* for making this decision?

3. What is the *present nature* of your involvement in making this decision?

4. What do you believe *should be the nature of* your involvement in making this decision?

Sample Item: The decision on the selection of teachers	
1.	3
2.	4
3.	4
4.	5

RESPONSES FOR QUESTIONS 1 AND 2

The person (or persons) primarily responsible for making the decision:

1 – Board of Education

2 – Superintendent of Schools

3 – Assistant Superintendent, Business Manager, or Director of Instruction

4 – Principal

5 – Department or Grade Level Chairman

6 – Teacher

7 – Student

RESPONSES FOR QUESTIONS 3 AND 4

Nature of your involvement in the decision-making process:

5 – Make the decision

4 – Recommend an alternative

3 – Develop possible alternatives

2 – Provide information

1 – No involvement

Figure 7.3
Sample instrument for assessing involvement in decision making

2. Provide information only
1. No involvement

Utilizing the DIA, each respondent is able to describe specifically his own involvement in each decision. Again, it is possible to obtain expressions of the idealized (desired) nature of one's involvement and to make actual and ideal comparisons. The findings from such studies are quite useful. They have revealed, for example, that principals may be quite involved in making some decisions that they do not care to make, yet they may be only minimally involved in making some decisions that they do wish to make.

In analyzing decision involvement it is possible, and perhaps desirable, to expand the response format of the DIA to include consideration of frequency or "how often" a person is involved in decision making, as well as to obtain a measure of the type of one's involvement. In addition, it is possible to obtain data and to analyze the mechanisms utilized for involvement in decision making—the ubiquitous cabinets, councils, and committees in schools and school systems. Studies featuring decision involvement methodologies have produced several useful findings.

DECISION INVOLVEMENT OUTCOMES

A study of involvement in decision making conducted in 31 Wisconsin school systems revealed that both within school systems and within schools individuals differ greatly in their involvement in the making of decisions that affect them.[34] In a study of 546 Connecticut elementary schools, based on an inventory and interviews with principals and teachers, Godfrey found teacher participation in decision making to be quite widespread.[35] More than 90 percent of the teachers were involved in decision making to a medium or high degree. The author discovered, however, that such participation was limited largely to such routinized decisions as scheduling of activities, grouping of students, school lunch, and discipline problems. There was little evidence of planned faculty involvement in major policy determinations (i.e., philosophy or curriculum) or in the areas identified by the staff as most in need of change.

Several studies have found the extent of involvement in decision making to be systematically and directly related to curricular change and innovation. In a study conducted in 15 Eastern high schools, Minin-

[34] Eye et al., op. cit.

[35] Margaret P. Godfrey, "Staff Participation in Decision-Making Procedures in Elementary Schools," doctoral dissertation, University of Connecticut, 1968.

berg learned that the closer to himself in the administrative hierarchy the teacher perceives the locus of responsibility for making decisions, the more likely he will be to perceive himself as involved in innovative activity.[36] He also found, as did McLimans,[37] that the more a teacher perceives himself to be a participant in decision making, the more likely he will be to perceive himself as involved in innovative activity. Similarly, Johansen found that teacher participation in curriculum development activities increased the likelihood of curriculum implementation.[38] Moreover, the perception by teachers that they were influential in the curriculum development process further increased the likelihood of curriculum implementation.

Several investigators have sought to determine whether the personal characteristics of principals may serve as predictors of their own or their teachers' involvement in decision making. Shaffer found the principal's attitudes toward the teaching staff's professional status to be significantly related to teacher participation in decision making.[39] In a study of New York secondary schools, it was discovered that teacher participation in decision making was significantly related to nonauthoritarian personality, consideration, and initiating structure characteristics of principals.[40] Finally, Weiss reported a significant and positive relationship between the job satisfaction of elementary school principals and their perceived participation in decision making.[41]

In summary, the results of the studies of decision involvement conducted to date have been especially useful in clarifying the nature of decision making in the schools, in relating decision involvement to cur-

[36] Elliot I. Mininberg, "The Relationship Between Decision-Making and Innovative Activity: A Study of the Relationship Among Teacher Perceptions of the Locus of Decision Making, Their Own Participation in Decision Making and Their Own Involvement in Innovative Activity in Selected Suburban Senior High Schools," doctoral dissertation, New York University, 1970.

[37] Dorothy F. McLimans, "Teacher Innovativeness," doctoral dissertation, University of Wisconsin, 1967.

[38] John H. Johansen, "An Investigation of the Relationships Between Teachers' Perceptions of Authoritative Influences in Local Curriculum Decision Making and Curriculum Implementation," doctoral dissertation, Northwestern University, 1965.

[39] George E. Shaffer, "The Principal's Orientation Toward Teacher Participation in Decision Making," doctoral dissertation, University of Illinois, Urbana-Champaign, 1971.

[40] Frank Ambrosie and Robert W. Heller, "The Secondary School Administrator and Perceived Teacher Participation in the Decision-Making Process," *Journal of Experimental Education,* 40 (Summer 1972), 6–13.

[41] Donald J. Weiss, "A Study of the Relationship of Participation in Decision Making, Selected Personality Variables, and Job Satisfaction of the Educational Research and Development Council, Elementary School Principals," doctoral dissertation, University of Minnesota, 1968.

ricular outcomes, and in predicting which personalistic variables of the principal are related to decision involvement. Of perhaps even greater significance is the finding from an experimental study conducted in Wisconsin that feedback of data concerning the decision structure and involvement in a school is particularly useful in altering or changing the decision-making process.[42] Moreover, in the experimental schools where the decision-making process was changed and clarified, there subsequently was a higher degree of curricular planning, as well as implementation of the curricular plans.

Decision-making competencies of the principal

In a synthesis of the competency-based approach to the analysis of the principalship, Abbott identified five decision-making skills that contribute to the effectiveness of the school principal.[43] These include: (1) skill in differentiating among types of decisions, (2) skill in determining the amount and type of information needed to reach a decision, (3) skill in determining the appropriate involvement of other people in reaching decisions, (4) skill in establishing priorities for action, and (5) skill in anticipating both intended and unintended consequences of decisions.

DIFFERENTIATING AMONG TYPES OF DECISIONS

Decisions differ by type, and recognition of this difference constitutes a basic decision-making skill. Our discussion of decision content included a decision typology based on the administrative functions—instruction, personnel, finance, and the like. Another typology that was presented concerned the origin of the decision—intermediate, appellate, and creative. Still another decision typology included routine, heuristic, and compromise decision situations.

Differences among types of decisions have significant implications for the amount and type of information needed, the relationship and involvement of individuals in decision making, and the processes or manner of proceeding in making, implementing, and evaluating the decision.[44]

As Darling discovered from observing the on-the-job behavior of principals, intermediary decisions are handled differently from appellate

[42] Eye et al., op. cit.

[43] Max G. Abbott, "Administrative Performance in the School Principalship: A Synthesis," in Culbertson, Henson, and Morrison, eds., op. cit.

[44] David A. Sands, "The Content of Decisions Made at Different Hierarchical Levels in the Administration of Public Elementary and Secondary Schools in Texas," doctoral dissertation, University of Texas, 1964.

decisions, appellate decisions are handled differently from creative decisions, and creative decisions are handled differently from intermediary decisions.[45] The principal, therefore, cannot take appropriate action unless he has knowledge of decision typologies and skill in discriminating among types of decision issues.

DETERMINING THE INFORMATION NEEDED FOR DECISION MAKING

We pointed out that the search for information constitutes a significant first step when preparing to make a decision. The principal who consistently makes decisions without adequate information frequently finds himself enmeshed in problems of his own making. This may occur when he initiates action to solve a problem that does not exist, when he fails to recognize a problem that clamors for attention, or when his perception of a problem is so inaccurate that any action taken is destined to be inappropriate.[46]

We indicated that it is possible to err by taking action without adequate information or by delaying action unduly while a search for further information is undertaken. Those who postpone decision making until *all* the information is in need again to be reminded that *all* the information can never be assembled. Since the decision-making process is time bound, problem situations do not remain static; they change with the passage of time. It is never possible to know whether one has reached the best decision; it is possible only to determine whether one has reached a satisfactory decision. As March and Simon have pointed out, decision making, whether individual or organizational, is concerned with the discovery and selection of satisfactory alternatives; only in exceptional cases is it concerned with the discovery and selection of optimal alternatives.[47]

The effective principal, then, is one who can sense the point at which he has sufficient information to justify action. This may call for a certain amount of judgment, but it also involves skill, and this skill may be increased through training.

DETERMINING THE APPROPRIATE INVOLVEMENT OF OTHERS

Teachers, students, parents, and others should participate in decision making for many obvious reasons, and such participation is essential on many occasions. For example, a decision that depends on the under-

[45] David W. Darling, "The Development of a Decision-Making Model and the Empirical Testing of the Model Using Selected Elementary School Principals in Decision-Making Situations," doctoral dissertation, University of Texas, 1964.

[46] Abbott, op. cit.

[47] James G. March and Herbert A. Simon, *Organizations*, New York, Wiley, 1958, pp. 140–141.

standing and support of a school faculty for its successful implementation requires the faculty's participation. Furthermore, employee participation frequently is advantageous for the total organization because such participation tends to decrease the visibility of power relations in the organization, thus enhancing employee morale.

On many occasions, however, decisions must be made unilaterally without the direct involvement of organizational subordinates. Sometimes this need arises because of the urgency for action. At other times, the decision to be made is of little direct interest to employees. On still other occasions the decisions are of such overriding importance to the organization that they must be made from a managerial perspective, even at the risk of lowering the morale of organization subordinates.[48]

An effective principal must be able to make defensible judgments concerning the nature and degree of involvement of others. He needs to be skillful in recognizing when involvement is needed and when it is unnecessary, and in judging what degree of participation is essential for decision implementation. Although it is unreasonable to expect any principal to maintain a perfect score in this regard, we can expect that serious errors will seldom occur. It also is possible to improve the principal's skill in assessing the appropriate involvement of others in decision making.

ESTABLISHING PRIORITIES FOR ACTION

A new principal soon discovers that many more problems and issues will be brought to his attention than he can possibly deal with effectively. Some will be crucial, some will be trivial; some will require immediate attention, others can or should be deferred; and some will require the personal attention of the principal, while others can be delegated. A principal is constantly confronted with the necessity to establish priorities. He can do so deliberately and with forethought, or he can allow priorities to be set fortuitously. Regardless, priorities are established.

The skillful setting of priorities, however, involves much more than merely reviewing a series of items and establishing a time schedule for action. Priority setting requires the judicious use of information, and some of it may be readily available, whereas some will need to be assembled. It also involves skill in anticipating the consequences of acting immediately or of deferring action, of taking action personally or of delegating action. The sounding of a fire alarm provides a cue for action that can be ignored or deferred only with extreme risks. On the other hand, a conflict between two teachers occasionally will benefit from a period of benign neglect.[49]

[48] Abbott, op. cit.
[49] Ibid.

As with the other skills related to decision making, skill in setting priorities can be increased with experience. Also like those other skills, however, this skill can be enhanced appreciably through the use of appropriately designed training activities.

ANTICIPATING CONSEQUENCES

As we have pointed out, decision making consists essentially of estimating the outcome state of a system. That is, reaching a decision involves making choices based on predictions of the probable consequences of alternative courses of action. However, no decision produces only one effect or set of effects. Nor are the consequences of a decision ever limited to those intended. A decision to initiate a course of action to solve one problem may create other problems, or it also may generate a response entirely different from that intended.

As an example of such a response, we might cite the case of a principal who attempted to deal with the problem of late arrival among a few teachers in the school. When the teachers involved failed to respond to informal reminders that they should be in their classrooms a reasonable period of time prior to the opening of school, the principal announced a new policy: All teachers were required to report at least one-half hour before classes opened and to remain at least one-half hour after classes were dismissed. Although the new policy accomplished the intended purpose, at least temporarily, it generated an unintended—and undesirable—response. Some teachers who had arrived on time consistently and had remained after school as long as was necessary to prepare for the following day were offended by the arbitrariness of the new policy. Under the new rules, therefore, they remained only the required period at the end of the day, then left the school.[50]

Lortie relates another case, this one involving a high school principal who was puzzled at the resistance he encountered when he attempted to initiate a new school schedule. The new plan was popular with the faculty, and the principal could detect no obvious weaknesses in the new schedule, yet opposition persisted. On closer examination, it was discovered that the new schedule had the unintended effect of disrupting the informal interaction patterns of a group of respected and influential senior teachers. When steps were taken to eliminate that feature of the schedule, the plan was willingly accepted.[51]

These examples support literature on decision making in which heavy emphasis is placed on the consideration of alternatives. Input-

[50] Ibid.

[51] Dan C. Lortie, "Change and Exchange: Reducing Resistance to Innovation," *Administrator's Notebook,* 12 (February 1964), 1–4.

output analysis was cited as one means of weighing and comparing alternative courses of action. In using input-output analysis, however, one must not overlook some of the most significant costs in human endeavors. Although many costs associated with any set of activities can be translated into dollars (e.g., personnel, materials, facilities, and equipment), other costs cannot readily be equated with money. Such factors as lower staff morale, conflict, student unrest, and a high turnover rate cannot be easily converted to dollars. At times, they can be disruptive enough virtually to nullify other organizational effects; they almost always occur as concomitant consequences of decisions intended to produce beneficial effects.[52]

In some decision situations an assessment will reveal unintended consequences that have potential for serious disruption. With advance information, the organization is prepared to take steps to minimize or to counteract those disruptive effects. In other instances, the harmful aspects of unintended consequences of a proposed decision will be judged to be so seriously inimical to the organization that the decision is rendered untenable. Such judgments cannot be made in time to prevent disaster unless the unintended consequences are anticipated. A crucially important decision-making skill, therefore, is the ability to elaborate and to make explicit the possible consequences, both intended and unintended, of each decision proposed, thus reducing to a minimum the unanticipated consequences of each decision reached.[53]

Summary

In this chapter decision making was viewed as central to all stages of the administrative process. Within the context of a systems approach, decision making was defined as a process wherein an awareness of a problematic state of a system, influenced by information and values, is reduced to competing alternatives among which a choice is made, based on estimated outcome states of the system. Three analytical dimensions—decision behavior (DBA), decision role (DRA), and decision involvement (DIA)—were posited as useful and necessary for assessing or improving the school principal's decision-making role and skills. Relationships among the three dimensions are depicted in Figure 7.4.

Although the dimensions are conceptually independent, in practice they are usually examined in viable combinations—decision role with decision behavior, decision role with decision involvement, or decision behavior with decision involvement. Moreover, it is possible and often

[52] Abbott, op. cit.
[53] Ibid.

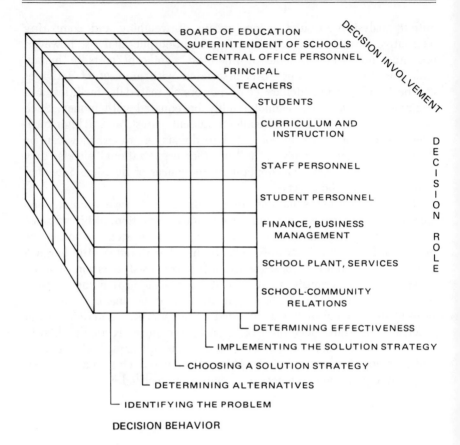

Figure 7.4
Dimensions of decision making

desirable to focus on only some of the factors rather than all the factors within the dimensions. Several recent research studies were cited that examined one, some, or several of the factors within the dimensions or the cells in Figure 7.4, as they related to other important organizational characteristics of the school and personal variables of the principal.

The chapter concluded by stressing the following basic competencies required for effective decision making on the part of the principal: skill in differentiating among types of decisions, skill in determining the amount and kind of information needed, skill in determining the appropriate involvement of others, skill in establishing priorities for action, and skill in anticipating both intended and unintended outcomes of decisions. Each of these skills can be increased through experience and training in decision making.

SUGGESTED ACTIVITIES

1. Observe a school principal for a full day and analyze his on-the-job behavior in terms of decision content, decision behavior, and decision involvement. Compare the results by size of school, type of community, and level of school (elementary or secondary).

2. Observe a number of school faculty meetings and compare and contrast the decision-making content, behavior, and involvement of the principal and faculty.

3. Prepare a list of major decisions made in a school and assess the degree of actual and ideal involvement of the principal, teachers, and students. Report the results in the school and subsequently check to determine changes in decision involvement.

4. Interview practicing principals to ascertain the nature and relative frequency of heuristic decisions made in the principalship. Compare and contrast the responses.

5. Administer an in-basket simulation exercise or administrative problem and critique the decisions made in terms of the five decision-making competencies required of the principal.

SELECTED REFERENCES

ABBOTT, MAX G., "Administrative Performance in the School Principalship; A Synthesis," in Jack A. Culbertson, Curtis Henson, and Ruel Morrison, eds., *Performance Objectives for School Principals*, Berkeley, Calif., McCutchan, 1974.

BARNARD, CHESTER I., *The Functions of the Executive*, Cambridge, Mass., Harvard University Press, 1966.

BROSS, IRWIN D. J., *Design for Decision*, New York, Macmillan, 1953.

DILL, WILLIAM R., "Decision Making," *Behavioral Science and Educational Administration*, Sixty-Third Yearbook, National Society for the Study of Education, Chicago, University of Chicago Press, 1964, pp. 199–222.

GORTON, RICHARD A., *Conflict, Controversy, and Crisis in School Administration and Supervision: Issues, Cases, and Concepts for the '70's*, Dubuque, Iowa, Brown, 1972, chap. 8.

GRIFFITHS, DANIEL, *Administrative Theory*, New York, Appleton, 1960.

LIPHAM, JAMES M., "Making Effective Decisions," in Jack A. Culbertson, Curtis Henson, and Ruel Morrison, eds., *Performance Objectives for School Principals*, Berkeley, Calif., McCutchan, 1974.

MARCH, JAMES G., and HERBERT A. SIMON, *Organizations*, New York, Wiley, 1958.

OWENS, ROBERT G., *Organizational Behavior in Schools*, Englewood Cliffs, N.J., Prentice-Hall, 1970, chap. 5.

PHI DELTA KAPPA NATIONAL STUDY COMMITTEE ON EVALUATION, *Educational Evaluation and Decision Making*, Itasca, Ill., Peacock, 1971.

SIMON, HERBERT A., *The New Science of Management Decision*, New York, Harper & Row, 1960.

CHAPTER 8
Leadership theory

he leadership of the principal is a critical factor in the success of any program in the school. Knowledge about leadership, therefore, is a prime prerequisite if an individual is to fulfill effectively the principalship role.

In this chapter, three antecedent approaches to the study of leadership are delineated—the psychological. approach, the situational approach, and the behavioral approach.[1] Next leadership is defined, and some issues in the analysis of leadership are raised concerning the locus for leadership, the stages of leadership, the frequency and potency of leadership, and the scope of leadership. Theoretical models of leadership and some empirical studies of leadership styles that may be of use to the school principal are then examined. Some guidelines for improving the leadership of the principal conclude the chapter.

Approaches to the study of leadership

The concept of leadership has been a perennial topic of concern and investigation in many fields. Scholars and practitioners in such basic and applied social science disciplines as administration, anthropology, business, economics, education, history, psychology, philosophy, political science, and sociology, and in numerous subdisciplinary, interdisciplinary, and multidisciplinary fields all view leadership as a phenomenon of primary concern. Although diverse fields are represented, the major themes in the study of leadership may be grouped according to psychological, sociological, and, more recently, behavioral approaches to the analysis of leadership.

[1] Portions of this chapter are drawn from James M. Lipham, "Leadership and Administration," in Daniel E. Griffiths, ed., *Behavioral Science and Educational Administration,* Sixty-Third Yearbook, National Society for the Study of Education, Chicago, University of Chicago Press, 1964, pp. 119–141; James M. Lipham, "Administration, Educational: Leadership Behavior," *The Encyclopedia of Education,* New York, Macmillan and Free Press, 1971, pp. 77–81; James M. Lipham, "Leadership: General Theory and Research," in Luvern L. Cunningham and William J. Gephart, eds., *Leadership: The Science and the Art Today,* Itasca, Ill., Peacock, 1973, pp. 1–15.

THE PSYCHOLOGICAL APPROACH

The psychological approach to the study of leadership is based largely on the common recognition that an individual's behavior is determined in part by his unique personality structure. That is, what a person "is" may be fully as significant a determinant of his leadership behavior as what he "is expected to do."

One theme in the psychological approach to the study of leadership, the "great man" view, holds to the notion that leaders basically are different from others. Thus there is the search for what makes the difference in terms of the lives of great men. Much of the early literature on leadership contained analyses of great men, particularly political and business leaders. Many biographical analyses and autobiographical memoirs dealt extensively with leadership phenomena, although few of the authors made explicit the criteria constituting the bases on which the so-called great men were selected for study. The philosophy underlying many of these works was heavily oriented toward the viewpoint that leaders were born and not made, that nature was more important than nurture, and that instinct was more important than training. Without resurrecting such controversies, we may simply observe that some learning of leadership by example was assumed; otherwise the effort to document, analyze, and critique the lives of the exemplars could not have been justified in terms of investigating leadership.

In the field of education, as contrasted with other disciplines, limited scholarly effort has been directed toward analysis of leadership by utilizing the great man approach. Existing studies tend more to enshrine leaders than to explain leadership. Even so, it is currently popular (and not necessarily erroneous) to view leadership in terms of the great man approach. It is everywhere obvious that school principals can and do "turn schools around," making a substantial difference in the policies, programs, and operations of a school. Plaques, portraits, and even the names of many schools attest to the magnitude of the achievements of principals who have demonstrated leadership skills through time. Commenting on a full-length portrait of his predecessor hanging in the school, a neophyte principal recently said, "This man was a great inspiration to all of us. It may be that some day I'll get hung in these halls."

A second theme in the psychological approach to the study of leadership focused less on the lives of great men than on the isolation and measurement of leadership traits—even among lesser men. Regarding the necessary traits for effective leadership in the educational organization, some investigation and much speculation was reported in the literature. From self-report tests of personality and from descriptions of leaders by superiors and subordinates, long lists of desirable personality traits were derived. Over a period of time, these lengthy lists became not unlike descriptions of the model Boy Scout. Furthermore, in the absence of suitable psychological taxonomies, such lists frequently included mutually contradictory traits—steady yet flexible, forceful yet cooperative. It still is not uncommon to encounter descriptions of the leadership of the principal expressed entirely in personalistic terms. And many principals will attest that they are called on almost daily to rate the leadership or leadership potential of teachers, students, and others—either in global terms or with respect to specific leadership traits.

Historically, the search for desirable personal qualities turned from a listing of traits to the use of "scientific" measures of personality. Believing that the failure to discover significant personality characteristics of leaders was due primarily to the naïve use of research procedures, many investigators adapted or developed a variety of ingenious devices to measure leadership traits. Thurstone, for example, administered a figure test of perception and a card-sorting test to a number of federal executives.[2] Using the relationship of salary to age as the criterion of successful leadership, he discovered that successful executives scored higher than unsuccessful ones both in accuracy of perception and in ability to differentiate among categories in sorting cards. Chapple and Donald constructed a machine called an interaction chronograph, which measured certain verbal and nonverbal behaviors of an individual during a structured interview.[3] From use of the chronograph in interviews held with supervisory and nonsupervisory personnel, it was found that supervisors excelled in the following characteristics: initiative, dominance, speed of interaction, and adjustment to the interview situation. Henry turned to a projective technique, the Thematic Apperception Test, to supplement interview and test data obtained from 100 successful business executives.[4] On the basis of their responses, he concluded that the successful executives were high in achievement drive, mobility drive, emotional alertness and activity, ability to organize unstructured situations, and tendencies to identify with superiors but not with subordinates.

After numerous psychological investigations of leadership had been conducted, concerted efforts were directed toward synthesizing the results of these studies to discover a personality syndrome universally characteristic of leaders. Stogdill examined 124 leadership studies conducted in both organizational and experimental environments.[5] He

[2] Louis L. Thurstone, *A Factorial Study of Perception,* Chicago, University of Chicago Press, 1944, pp. 140–141.

[3] Eliot D. Chapple and Gordon Donald, Jr., "A Method for Evaluating Supervisory Personnel," *Harvard Business Review,* 24 (Winter 1946), 201–203.

[4] William E. Henry, "The Business Executive: The Psychodynamics of a Social Role," *American Journal of Sociology,* 54 (January 1949), 286–291.

[5] Ralph M. Stogdill, "Personal Factors Associated with Leadership: A Survey of the Literature," *Journal of Psychology,* 25 (1948), 35–71.

concluded: "A person does not become a leader by virtue of the possession of some combination of traits, but the pattern of personal characteristics of the leader must bear some relevant relationship to the characteristics, activities, and goals of the followers." From a synthesis of the literature, Gibb reported that numerous studies of leaders have failed to find any consistent pattern of traits characterizing leaders.[6] Pierce and Merrill likewise stated: "Perhaps one of the chief results of the research is the conclusion drawn that the study of personal characteristics, per se, is only one aspect of the study of leadership."[7]

The consistent failure to find a generalized personality syndrome typical of leaders in any or all leadership settings may have been due to many factors. The following, for example, are the possibilities noted by Gibb: inadequate measurement, lack of comparability of data from different kinds of research, and inability to describe leadership adequately.[8] Because certain of the studies conducted in similar settings produced contradictory findings, and because the studies failed to reveal a universally applicable pattern of traits typical of leaders in all settings, some writers reacted violently and erroneously to the traitist approach. The current view, however, is that several patterns of personality traits serve to differentiate leaders from nonleaders. Investigations are continuing to match personality traits with situations. The extreme reaction to the so-called failure of the traitist approach has abated, and researchers are examining in fresh perspective the relationship of the psychological dimension to sociological, cultural, and other dimensions of leadership in specific situational contexts.

THE SOCIOLOGICAL APPROACH

Recognizing that psychological factors were not entirely sufficient to account for leadership phenomena, some people turned to an examination of sociological factors. The emphasis shifted from analysis of personality traits to a study of roles and relationships—from a concern with characteristics of the individual to a concern with characteristics of the group. Indeed, many of the early situational studies focused on group phenomena primarily and on leadership only incidentally. Basically, the sociological approach maintains that leadership is determined less by the characteristics of individuals than by the requirements of social systems.

[6] Cecil A. Gibb, "Leadership," in Gardner Lindzey, ed., *Handbook of Social Psychology*, Reading, Mass., Addison-Wesley, 1954, p. 889.

[7] Truman M. Pierce and E. C. Merrill, Jr., "The Individual and Administrator Behavior," in Roald F. Campbell and Russell T. Gregg, eds., *Administrative Behavior in Education*, New York, Harper & Row, 1957, p. 332.

[8] Gibb, op. cit., p. 889.

Perhaps the most extensive comparison among groups—designed to distinguish the major dimensions by which groups differ, thereby measuring the impact of the leader—was set forth by Hemphill.[9] He identified such dimensions as size of group, homogeneity of group members, intimacy among the group, and cohesion of the group (pertaining to the group as a unit); and position, participation, satisfaction, and dependence (expressing a respondent's relation to his group). Hemphill found that two dimensions—viscidity (the feeling of cohesion in the group) and hedonic tone (the degree of satisfaction of group members)—correlated more highly with leadership adequacy than did the other dimensions. Guetzkow's investigation of decision-making conferences and Katz, Maccoby, and Morse's study of high- and low-production groups likewise emphasized that working with people in groups is a complicated undertaking and that there are many differences among groups that are of crucial importance to the leader.[10]

Among the methodologies utilized in the situational studies of leadership have been observations of both structured and unstructured groups, interviews with leaders and followers, performance on simulation exercises, analyses of problem-solving and decision-making activities, sociometric choices, and assessments by expert judges. Derived from the studies were generalizations regarding such powerful and useful concepts as potential leadership, permissive leadership, persuasive leadership, and emergent leadership.

It soon came to be recognized that if the analysis of leadership were limited to situational factors, the study of leadership per se would be at a dead end. Conceptually, such issues as the transferability of leaders (e.g., transferring a principal from one school to another school, thereby learning that he can lead in any situation) were difficult to explain. Operationally, such matters as determination of a leader to lead appeared to be denied. There was a gradual drawing away from either traitist or situational approaches, and the emphasis shifted to the analysis of the behavior of leaders.

THE BEHAVIORAL APPROACH

The most recent approach to the study of leadership is the analysis of leadership behavior, which recognizes that both psychological and

[9] John K. Hemphill, *Situational Factors in Leadership*, Columbus, Ohio State University Press, 1949.

[10] Harold Guetzkow, *Groups, Leadership, and Men*, Pittsburgh, Pa., Carnegie Press, 1951; Daniel Katz, Nathan Maccoby, and Nancy C. Morse, *Productivity, Supervision, and Morale in an Office Situation*, Ann Arbor, University of Michigan Press, 1950.

sociological factors, both individual and situational variables, are powerful determinants of behavior. This approach utilizes both types of factors, thereby focusing on the observed behavior of the leader-in-situation. It is not necessarily assumed that leadership exhibited in a given situation will transfer to other situations, but neither is this possibility denied. Methodologically, the research procedures utilized to study the behavior of leaders have included selecting a target population of status leaders (based on formal position held); assessing their leadership behavior utilizing rating scales, interviews, or observations; assessing individual, group, or organizational variables believed to be related to general or specific leadership behaviors; and examining the interrelationships of the personal, situational, and behavioral variables.

In the behavioral approach, an important conceptual distinction is made between leadership and leader behavior. Regarding this distinction, Halpin stated:

> In contrast [to the concept of "leadership"], consider the concept of "leader behavior" and what it implies. First of all, it focuses upon observed behavior rather than upon a posited capacity inferred from this behavior. No presuppositions are made about a one-to-one relationship between leader behavior and an underlying capacity or potentiality presumably determinative of this behavior. By the same token, no a priori assumptions are made that the leader behavior which a leader exhibits in one group situation will be manifested in other group situations. It may be; but the answer to this question is left open for empirical verification rather than incorporated as an implicit assumption into the very terminology we use to define our problem. Nor does the term "leader behavior" suggest that this behavior is determined either innately or situationally. Either determinant is possible, as is any combination of the two, but the concept of leader behavior does not itself predispose us to accept one in opposition to the other.[11]

Halpin also indicated that a further advantage of the concept of leader behavior is the distinction between the description of leadership and the evaluation of leadership:

> In ordinary parlance the term "leadership" is used in an evaluative sense. To say that a man displays leadership implies that this is "good" or "effective" leadership. But the evaluation of what the leader does is only one aspect. . . . The primary task is to describe the behavior of the leader on psychologically meaningful dimensions. If a description of the leader on specific dimensions of behavior and an evaluation of the effectiveness and efficiency of that behavior can be obtained independently, then we can ascertain to what extent each dimension contributes to favorable evaluation. Furthermore, we can determine whether this contribution

[11] Andrew W. Halpin, *The Leadership Behavior of School Superintendents,* Chicago, Midwest Administration Center, University of Chicago, 1959, p. 12.

changes when the source or criterion of evaluation is changed. This separation of the *description* of what the leader does from the *evaluation* of the effectiveness and efficiency of what he does is of signal importance. Because it focuses upon the description of behavior, the leader behavior concept makes it easier for us to distinguish between (a) what the leader does, and (b) how what he does is evaluated. What is more, this distinction also reveals the pertinence of two related questions about the leader's behavior: "As described *by whom?*" and "As evaluated *by whom?*"[12]

Most of the recent studies of leadership utilize the leader behavior approach in which deliberate care is taken to differentiate the kinds of criteria and the sources of information used to describe leaders and those utilized to evaluate leaders. Moreover, there has been a noticeable shift from the simplistic, evaluative view of leadership as a unitary phenomenon to a complex, descriptive view of leadership as a multifaceted phenomenon. Because leadership is so complex, it is essential that we direct our attention to the nature and meaning of leadership.

Definition of leadership

Considerable disagreement exists concerning the meaning of leadership. Those predisposed to a personalistic concept of leadership tend to view it as a one-way influence process, defining it in terms of inferred or observed specific characteristics or combinations of characteristics of individuals. Those predisposed to a situational concept tend to view leadership as an interactive process, defining it in terms of leader-group relationships and interactions. Others who hold an organizational orientation are committed to the view that the incumbents of status positions are ipso facto leaders, their role behavior therefore defining leadership behavior. Others despair of the definitional problem, at least insofar as attempts are made to compare or contrast leadership with other terms, such as management or administration. Still others who have a pragmatic orientation insist that leadership simply consists of that which experts in the field wish to consider, designate, and measure as leadership. Thus it is not surprising to find a plethora of definitions by those presumed to have had firsthand experience with the phenomenon.

There appears now to be some rapprochement among the conceptualizations, and we define leadership as that behavior of an individual which initiates a new structure in interaction within a social system; it initiates change in the goals, objectives, configurations, procedures, inputs, processes, and ultimately the outputs of social systems. The size of the focal social system may range from gross cultures to institutions

[12] Ibid.

within cultures to individuals within institutions or cultures. This definition takes into account effectiveness and efficiency measures, group achievement and group maintenance functions, situational and personalistic determinants, organizational and individual constructs, active and passive relationships, latent and manifest conflicts, formal and informal contexts, means and ends, and similar dichotomous distinctions. Leadership is dynamic, since it involves social systems in action and interaction.

Typically people have tended to apply the concept of social system to large aggregates of human relationships. In Western cultures, moreover, there has been a tendency to view "biggest" as "best." Thus it is understandable that in the search for knowledge about leadership one might turn first to heads of state and next to heads of large organizations —the Peter Principle notwithstanding. But one must be cognizant that leadership is pervasive and is exercised by the man on the street as well as by the so-called exemplars; it is exercised in small social systems as well as large ones.

Issues in the study of leadership

Recurring issues in the analysis of leadership include the locus for leadership, the stages of leadership, the frequency and potency of leadership, and the scope of leadership.

LOCUS FOR LEADERSHIP

The locus for leadership involves the boundaries of the focal social system within which leadership occurs; that is, it indicates whether one is focusing on the classroom, the school, the school district, or the entire community as the social system. Many analyses of leadership tend erroneously to focus almost exclusively on intragroup and intraorganizational relationships while ignoring intergroup and interorganizational —not to mention extragroup and extraorganizational—relationships. The *same* behavior that may be viewed as leadership from an intraorganizational or subsystem point of view may be regarded as *lack* of leadership from an extraorganizational or suprasystem point of view, and conversely. To illustrate this point, let us consider briefly the leadership behavior of a principal faced with a rabidly militant group of citizens who were intent on burning certain books in his school library. Suppose that in the course of several initial confrontations and countless subsequent meetings he was able to change basic community concepts of academic freedom—not to mention their "use" of the library. Viewed from a limited intraorganizational stance, this principal might be characterized as a nonleader engaged in maintenance behavior—trying to keep his library intact. Viewed from an extraorganizational stance, however, the principal's behavior reflected the essence of leadership—changing and restructuring the community's expectations for the school. To reiterate, in addition to the need for clarifying social system boundaries, the need exists for enlarging one's view of the focal social system that is being led.

Other factors related to the locus for leadership include the degree of permanence, complexity, structure, and rewards of the focal social system. Some investigation of leadership—particularly the experimental work—have perforce been conducted utilizing temporary social systems (children's clubs or college sophomores), assigning relatively mundane tasks ("winning" a game or "leading" a discussion), utilizing simplistically structured roles ("presenter-reactor" or "expert-uninformed"), and minimizing reward and accountability (paying participants equally or assuring them in advance that they have nothing to lose).

Although such studies may increase our understanding about leadership within their limited contexts, the findings may be of meager value when transfer is made to enduring, complex, hierarchical, sanction-bearing focal social systems, such as the school. In this regard, one might reflect on the extent to which the notions of "autocratic," "democratic," and "laissez-faire" leadership have been applied in business, governmental, and educational institutions, even though this typology initially was derived from experimental studies of five-member hobby clubs composed of ten-year-olds. This is not to suggest that the principal should be "autocratic"; however, the perceptive principal should be wary of the platitudinous preachments that are derived from an experimental context and proposed as panaceas for leadership in a complex context, such as the school.

STAGES OF LEADERSHIP

The following sequential taxonomy of the stages of leadership may be useful for assessing the dynamics of the leadership process through time:

1. ATTEMPTED LEADERSHIP: acts that include expression of an intention to initiate a new structure for dealing with a problematic state of a social system.

2. ACCEPTED LEADERSHIP: acts that are mutually acknowledged as a tentative solution to a problematic state of a social system.

3. IMPLEMENTED LEADERSHIP: acts that have initiated a new structure in a social system.

4. EFFECTIVE LEADERSHIP: acts that have initiated a new structure and have met the expectations for resolving a problematic state of a social system.

Clearly, not all attempted leadership acts will be accepted; not all those accepted will be implemented; nor will all those implemented be judged as effective. As a broad case in point, let us consider a school wherein the principal has expressed and explored with his staff the desirability of moving from a self-contained classroom structure to one of team teaching. This expressed intention to restructure the school represents the first stage, attempted leadership. Let us next assume that the teachers in the proposed team arrangement acknowledge that the move to team teaching might improve the instructional program. There is agreement: "Yes, we will try team teaching." This represents the second stage; the attempted leadership has been accepted. Next the team teaching arrangement is put into effect; the activities of students and teachers are restructured in terms of the teaching team. The attempted and accepted leadership acts are implemented. The final stage remains—that of determining whether the new structure of team teaching is indeed effective. Thus viewed, the process of leadership is systematic, coherent, and even cyclical. If in the final stage it is determined that the new structure, team teaching, is not effective, a new series of leadership acts must then be attempted, accepted (it is hoped), then implemented, and finally judged again with respect to their effectiveness.

FREQUENCY AND POTENCY OF LEADERSHIP

Frequency of leadership refers to "how often" or "the extent to which" a leader engages in certain types of behaviors. Several of the scales and questionnaires that are utilized to assess leadership ask respondents to indicate whether the principal "frequently," "often," "sometimes," "seldom," or "never" engages in specified behavior. Yet in terms of the foregoing taxonomy of stages of leadership, we may observe that leadership frequency relates primarily only to attempts at leadership. Frequency of attempted leadership represents an essential ingredient in the assessment of leadership, but it does not represent a sufficient assessment. There is considerable evidence to substantiate the conclusion that in many schools the principal frequently attempts leadership acts, but the attempted leadership is never really accepted by the faculty, students, or citizens. Conversely, there is evidence that in other schools the attempted leadership acts of faculty, students, or citizens are never really accepted by the principal—unless, perhaps, they are presented under the guise that they originated with the principal in the first place. Clearly additional research is needed concerning the frequency not only of attempted leadership but also of accepted, implemented, and effective leadership.

Another point should be made with regard to frequency of leadership. In "shadow" or nonparticipant observation studies of principals, in analyses of simulation performance on in-basket exercises, and in summaries of daily logs, diaries, or calendars of principals, the perspicacious analyst is often struck by the absence of behaviors that reasonably could be considered to be leadership in any of its stages. Thus it may be assumed that in some schools there is little latitude for the principal to exercise leadership, or the principal has little inclination to lead—or perhaps both. Such a low frequency of attempted leadership can result in inadequate structures, ineffective procedures, and archaic goals.

In still other schools there is evidence of such frequent and continual attempts at leadership that little attention is given to accepted, implemented, and effective leadership. In such situations faculty members are heard to complain, "I wish that just for once around here we could finish one thing before starting a dozen others." Thus viewed, leadership behavior is neither good nor bad. Excessive, continuous, and frequent changes in an organization's structures, procedures, and goals can result in disorientation, disorganization, and disintegration. Apparently there are desirable upper as well as lower limits to the need for leadership frequency.

Just as frequency is an important aspect of leadership, so is the factor of potency. Potency refers to the extent to which an initiated change represents a significant departure from that which exists (i.e., the magnitude of an initiated change). It is in terms of potency, for example, that a person such as Dewey, who drastically altered the teaching-learning situation, was eminently qualified to be called an "educational leader." In the field of education, a common observation is that the goals, structures, and procedures of the schools have changed very little over the last several decades. Perhaps a safe generalization is that the leadership acts of many educators are of low potency and are limited primarily to tinkering with the organizational structure—"When in doubt, appoint another committee."

SCOPE OF LEADERSHIP

The issue of scope includes concern with the extent to which leadership is viewed as functionally diffuse or functionally specific. As indicated in Chapter 3, which dealt with social systems, individuals in a functionally diffuse relationship are bound to one another such that their mutual obligations are limitless; in a functionally specific relationship, they are limited. Yet the mechanisms whereby a leader-follower relationship changes from one of functional specificity to one of functional diffuseness, or conversely, are by no means clear. Many writers have either ignored or suppressed the diffuse often charismatic relationship that tends to build within a school as people work together over time. Because the school is an intensive institution where people are taught to care about others, we have observed (particularly in elementary schools) that the leader-follower relationship may become quite diffuse. In such situations, for example, it is not uncommon to hear the teachers sincerely say, "We just love our principal." Bureaucratic theory of Weber notwithstanding, recent findings concerning organizational climate reveal that such a diffuse leader-follower relationship may be much more beneficial than it is dysfunctional. Many bureaucratic and impersonal schools need more love in them. Certainly there is a need for additional study of leadership in functionally diffuse relationships.

Leadership scope is also concerned with the breadth and depth of the leadership role. Some authorities tend erroneously to limit the scope of leadership by equating it with a given task, process, or cognitive procedure. That is, such "experts" mount a soap box and flatly declare their biased "insight" in such statements as, "The essence of the principal-ship is *instructional* leadership," or "The *real* leadership role of the principal is decision making," or "The principal who *actually* is a leader is an innovator." The principal who would in fact become a leader might do well to ignore such simplistic conceptions of leadership scope.

Conversely, leadership scope can be interpreted too broadly, resulting in leadership ascription. It does not necessarily follow, for example, that an army general will be an effective President. A "good" teacher, or even a "good" assistant principal, may not make an effective principal. Even so, there is a preoccupation, sometimes at high levels, with image building and image maintenance in what is apparently a deliberate effort to widen, if not manipulate, perceptions of leadership scope. In this regard, principals would do well to examine the extent to which they attempt to be all things to all people. To err in the direction of excessively broadening one's leadership scope is fraught with as many pitfalls as limiting leadership to a given task, such as instruction, a particular process, such as planning, or a given procedure, such as involving others in decision making.

Thus far, some approaches, conceptions, and issues regarding leadership have been discussed. But the central intriguing question is: "How does the principal behave when he is leading?"

The principal and leadership behavior

Analysis of leadership behavior permits examination not only of what one does when he is leading, but also of what types of personal or situational variables bear a positive relationship to or correlation with the different types of leader behavior. Thus the principal may gain insight not only regarding types or styles of leader behavior but also regarding the central question, "What difference does leadership make?"

Most of the research concerning the behavior of leaders in the field of education derives from concepts developed at the Ohio State University and at the University of Chicago. In the Ohio State work the dimensions of initiating structure and consideration behavior were isolated; in the Chicago work the dimensions of nomothetic, idiographic, and transactional behavior of leaders were described.

INITIATING STRUCTURE AND CONSIDERATION BEHAVIOR

Out of the work of the Personnel Research Board at Ohio State University, two dimensions of leadership—initiating structure and consideration—emerged as significant in the description of leader behavior. These two dimensions were originally delineated by Halpin and Winer from a factor analysis of responses to the Leader Behavior Description Questionnaire (LBDQ) of Hemphill and Coons.[13] These dimensions were defined as follows:

> **1.** Initiating structure refers to the leader's behavior in delineating the relationship between himself and members of the work-group, and in endeavoring to establish well-defined patterns of organization, channels of communication, and methods of procedure.
> **2.** Consideration refers to behavior indicative of friendship, mutual trust, respect, and warmth in the relationship between the leader and the members of his staff.[14]

In a study of the leadership behavior of aircraft commanders, Halpin discovered that the effective leaders were those who scored high on both initiating structure and consideration.[15] Hemphill came to a similar conclusion from a study of administrators in liberal arts colleges.[16] In a subsequent study of school superintendents, Halpin secured descriptions of the leadership behavior of school superintendents from the superintendents themselves, from members of their administrative staffs, and from members of their boards of education by administering the LBDQ.[17] Two forms were administered: the "real" form, on which

[13] Andrew W. Halpin and B. James Winer, "A Factorial Study of the Leader Behavior Descriptions," in Ralph M. Stogdill and Alvin E. Coons, eds., *Leader Behavior: Its Description and Measurement*, Columbus, College of Education, Ohio State University, 1957; John K. Hemphill and Alvin E. Coons, "Development of the Leader Behavior Description Questionnaire," in Stogdill and Coons, eds., op. cit.

[14] Halpin, op. cit., p. 4.

[15] Andrew W. Halpin, "The Leader Behavior and Effectiveness of Aircraft Commanders," in Stogdill and Coons, eds., op. cit.

[16] John K. Hemphill, "Patterns of Leadership Behavior Associated with Administrative Reputation in the Department of a College," *Journal of Educational Psychology*, 46 (November 1955), 385–401.

[17] Halpin, *The Leadership Behavior of School Superintendents*, ibid.

respondents described the actual leader behavior of the superintendent; and the "ideal" form, on which they indicated the leader behavior that the superintendent ideally should exhibit.

One of the more significant findings concerning the real or actual leader behavior of the school superintendents was that the staff members and the board members, respectively, tended to agree among themselves in describing the superintendent's leader behavior, but the groups did not agree either with each other or with the superintendents' descriptions. This means that superintendents may behave differently when dealing with the board and when dealing with the staff. It also indicates that in describing leadership one should take into account more than one source of description, since even in viewing the same behavior, two people—tending to see what they are conditioned to see— may give different interpretations.

Results concerning the ideal or desired leader behavior of the superintendents were interesting for both dimensions. Concerning the dimension of initiating structure, the boards believed that the superintendents should be very strong, whereas the superintendents and staffs believed that the superintendents should initiate far less structure than the boards expected. The staffs, in turn, preferred even less structure than the superintendents believed they should initiate. Regarding the dimension of consideration, the superintendents set for themselves higher standards of consideration than either the staffs or the boards set for them. The boards in fact expected the superintendents to show greater consideration to their staffs than the staffs themselves posited as ideal.

Regarding the difference between the real and the ideal or between the actual and the desired leader behavior, most of the superintendents were more likely to fall short of the ideal on the dimension of initiating structure than on the dimension of consideration. Relationships of the real and ideal scores were examined and plotted in terms of both the initiating structure and the consideration dimensions (see Figure 8.1). This quadrant relationship has been particularly useful for analyzing and classifying leadership behavior in terms of the differential leadership styles: "high initiating structure–high consideration," "high initiating structure–low consideration," "low initiating structure–high consideration," and "low initiating structure–low consideration," and for correlating these styles with other measures, such as leadership effectiveness. Results similar to those of Halpin were obtained by Evenson in a study of school principals.[18]

Noting that an outside observer of an interaction can be aware of

[18] Warren L. Evenson, "Leadership Behavior of High School Principals," *National Association of Secondary-School Principals Bulletin,* 43 (September 1959), 96–101.

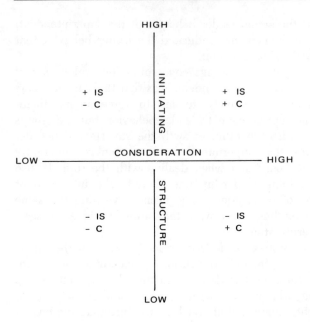

Figure 8.1
Model of initiating structure and consideration as coordinate dimensions of leadership
SOURCE: Adapted from Andrew W. Halpin, *The Leadership Behavior of School Superintendents,* Columbus, College of Education, Ohio State University, 1956, p. 10.

consistently occurring behavior that has not been perceived by the parties to the interaction,[19] the staff associates of the Midwest Administration Center at the University of Chicago conducted an intensive study of the behavior of school superintendents in four midwestern communities.[20] At intermittent periods throughout the school year, staff associates trained in the nonparticipant observation technique visited, observed, and recorded verbal and nonverbal behaviors of the school superintendents in interaction with others. Reports of the observations were prepared and subjected to individual and group analyses, utilizing the leadership dimensions of initiating structure and consideration. The dimensions were found to be very useful for describing leader behavior. For example, the superintendents were initiating such structures as the following: a joint committee of maintenance supervisors and instruc-

[19] John K. Hemphill, "Administration as Problem Solving," in Andrew W. Halpin, ed., *Administrative Theory in Education,* Chicago, Midwest Administration Center, University of Chicago, 1958, reprinted, New York, Macmillan, 1967, p. 96.

[20] James M. Lipham, "Initiating Structure and Consideration," in Staff Associates, eds., *Observation of Administrator Behavior,* Chicago, Midwest Administration Center, University of Chicago, 1959, pp. 27–68.

tional supervisors to establish an in-service program for custodians; a change in responsibility for revising student handbooks from a committee of principals to a representative committee of principals, teachers, and students; and a new procedure for assigning utilization of school facilities during evening hours.

The Midwest Center study found that the consideration dimension possessed both positive and negative components, whereas the initiating structure dimension possessed only a positive component. That is, negative initiating structure was difficult if not impossible to discover. Let us see why this is true. Suppose that a principal attempts to initiate a structure and this structure is accepted and implemented. If subsequent evaluations reveal the implemented structure to be ineffective, it may be logical to assume that the parties involved would bring this deficiency to the attention of the principal. To the extent that he takes a new action to amend the structure, a new series of leadership acts would be attempted. To the extent that the leader takes no additional action in such a circumstance, it may be surmised only that he fails to initiate structure. Thus scores on the dimension of initiating structure may vary from no action to positive action. On the other hand, we know that consideration possesses both positive and negative components. Some behaviors may be scored as highly considerate; others, highly inconsiderate.

The Midwest Center study also revealed that the leadership dimensions of initiating structure and consideration were interactive. Many behaviors could be classified appropriately in both dimensions. Structure was usually initiated with regard to consideration. Concerning this circumstance, Halpin observed:

> The correlation between the two dimensions—consideration and initiating structure—shows that an effective leader can initiate structure without sacrificing consideration. Yet we repeatedly encounter superintendents who fear to take a stand, who hesitate to initiate structure, lest they be accused of being anti-democratic. This is nonsense, for the superintendents who adopt this attitude lose the respect of their staffs; teachers can quickly spot the phony who tries to hide his own ineptness in the soggy oatmeal of a psuedo group-process.[21]

In sum, the results of the Midwest Center study indicated that the dimensions of initiating structure and consideration were interactive, were not of the same order in terms of positive and negative manifestation, and were useful for classifying leader behavior.

Utilizing the two-dimensional or quadrant classification of leadership, many investigators have searched for variables that are significantly and positively correlated with the principal's leadership behavior. In a

[21] Andrew W. Halpin, "The Superintendent's Effectiveness as a Leader," *Administrator's Notebook,* 7 (October 1958), 3.

sample of New York schools, Croghan found that school principals who were high in both initiating structure and consideration were more frequently designated by teachers as leaders of the informal groups within their schools than were principals who were low on the same two dimensions.[22] McGhee reported that in schools in New York where no formal grievances had been filed by the teachers, the principals had higher consideration scores than in schools where formal grievances had been filed.[23] In Alabama schools, Lambert found a direct, positive, and significant relationship between the principal's leader behavior, as measured by the two dimensions of the LBDQ, and teacher morale, as measured by the Purdue Teacher Opinionnaire.[24] Watson found the leadership behavior of the principal to be related to the cohesiveness of the teaching group.[25] A highly cohesive group was associated with leadership behavior of the principal who scored high in both initiating structure and consideration. Studies such as the foregoing have been particularly useful in isolating variables that are meaningfully associated with the leadership dimensions of initiating structure and consideration.

Subsequently, the LBDQ was revised by Stogdill to include assessment of leadership behavior along the following dimensions:

1. Representation—the leader speaks and acts as the representative of the group;
2. Demand Reconciliation—the leader reconciles conflicting demands and reduces disorder to the system;
3. Tolerance of Uncertainty—the leader is able to tolerate uncertainty and postponement without anxiety or upset;
4. Persuasiveness—the leader uses persuasion and argument effectively and exhibits strong convictions;
5. Initiation of Structure—the leader clearly defines his own role and lets followers know what is expected of them;
6. Tolerance of Freedom—the leader allows followers scope for initiative, decision, and action;
7. Role Assumption—the leader actively exercises the leadership role rather than surrendering leadership to others;

[22] John H. Croghan, "A Study of the Relationships Between Perceived Leadership Behavior of Elementary Principals and Informal Group Dimensions and Composition in Elementary Schools," doctoral dissertation, Syracuse University, 1969.

[23] Paul R. McGhee, "An Investigation of the Relationships Between Principals' Decision-Making Attitudes, Leader Behavior and Teacher Grievances in Public Schools," doctoral dissertation, Syracuse University, 1971.

[24] Donald B. Lambert, "A Study of the Relationships Between Teacher Morale and the School Principal's Leader Behavior," doctoral dissertation, Auburn University, 1968.

[25] Betty J. Watson, "A Study of the Relationships Among Selected Aspects of Administrative Behavior and Teacher Group Cohesiveness in the Elementary School," doctoral dissertation, University of Rochester, 1965.

8. Consideration—the leader regards the comfort, well-being, status, and contributions of followers;

9. Productive Emphasis—the leader applies pressure for productive output;

10. Predictive Accuracy—the leader exhibits foresight and ability to predict outcomes accurately;

11. Integration—the leader maintains a closely knit organization and resolves intermember conflicts; and

12. Superior Orientation—the leader maintains cordial relations with superiors, has influence with them, and strives for higher status.[26]

Several studies have utilized the revision of the LBDQ that includes the 12 subscales. Stogdill, Goode, and Day have analyzed the leadership behavior of ministers, community development leaders, U.S. senators, and other governmental and industrial leaders.[27] Jacobs analyzed a sample of Michigan secondary school principals to ascertain whether the leadership behavior of principals of schools high in educational innovation differed from that of principals of schools low in innovation.[28] It was discovered that the principals in schools high in innovation received significantly higher ratings on the following leadership dimensions: (1) initiating structure, (2) predictive accuracy, (3) representation, (4) integration, (5) persuasiveness, and (6) consideration. Jacobs concluded, "One of the important factors in instituting educational change is the leadership behavior of the principal."[29]

In a signal study of the leadership behavior of school principals reported by Anderson and Brown, the LBDQ—Form XII was administered to 170 principals and 1551 of the principals' teachers.[30] Data also were obtained concerning staff job satisfaction, staff ratings of principal's effectiveness, staff estimates of overall school performance, and principal's rating of staff morale. In addition, measures were taken of such situational factors as size of school, type of school (elementary,

[26] Ralph Stogdill, *Manual for the Leader Behavior Description Questionnaire—Form XII*, Columbus, Ohio, Bureau of Business Research, College of Commerce and Administration, 1963, p. 3.

[27] Cf. Ralph M. Stogdill, Omar S. Goode, and David R. Day, "New Leader Behavior Description Subscale," *Journal of Psychology*, 55 (October 1962), 259–269; Ralph M. Stogdill, Omar S. Goode, and David R. Day, "The Leader Behavior of United States Senators," *Journal of Psychology*, 56 (July 1963), 3–8; and Ralph M. Stogdill, Omar S. Goode, and David R. Day, "The Leader Behavior of Corporation Presidents," *Personnel Psychology*, 16 (1963), 127–132.

[28] Jan W. Jacobs, "Leader Behavior of the Secondary School Principal," *National Association of Secondary School Principals Bulletin*, 49 (October 1965), 13–17.

[29] Ibid., 17.

[30] Barry D. Anderson and Alan F. Brown, "Who's a Good Principal?" in Walter G. Hack et al., eds., *Educational Administration: Selected Readings*, 2nd ed., Boston, Allyn & Bacon, 1971, pp. 193–199.

junior high, senior high), and social class of the community; staff characteristics on such personal factors as age, sex, preparation, and experience were also evaluated. Factor analysis of the resulting data revealed that school staffs tended to distinguish three clusters of effective principals, as follows:

> **1.** Principals responding chiefly to system needs (high scores on initiating structure, productive emphasis, representation, and role assumption).
> **2.** Principals responding chiefly to the personal needs of staff (high scores on tolerance of freedom, tolerance of uncertainty, and consideration).
> **3.** Principals responding to the need for effective transaction between the needs of the system and the person (high scores on integration, predictive accuracy, superior orientation, and demand reconciliation).[31]

From the leadership scores, a circular model of leader behavior was constructed by plotting the scores on leadership in each of the schools into one of nine categories on the major axes of "system" orientation and "person" orientation (see Figure 8.2). In terms of the two axes, the leadership of a school could be said to be high on one factor but neutral on the other (sectors 1, 3, 5, 7), high on one factor but low on the other (sectors 4, 8), high on both, or low on both (sectors 2, 6, and area 9). When the data were analyzed, it appeared that staff morale, situational factors, and personal characteristics were not associated any more strongly with one leader type than another. A second grouping of categories, however, carved up the model in terms of leadership frequency. When a principal's factor scores plotted in sectors 1, 2, 3, it was because the staffs claimed that the principal frequently exhibited the leader behaviors measured; in sectors 4 and 8 and area 9, the principal occasionally manifested leader behavior; in sectors 5, 6, or 7, the principal seldom, if ever, manifested leader behavior. Using frequency as the basis of analysis, the authors found that neither the situational nor the personal variables were significantly related to leadership frequency. But the opposite was true of morale. The greater the frequency of leader behavior, the higher staff rating of job satisfaction, overall school performance, and confidence in the effectiveness of the principal.

Concerning the first major finding—that the type of leader behavior exhibited by a principal is relatively unimportant—the authors said, "The study indicates that debate over the relative merits of a 'system' or 'person' oriented approach to a leadership problem is unwarranted. A school staff accepts either form of leadership, so long as strength in one form is not cancelled out by a disproportionately poor showing on the other."[32] The results also indicate that perhaps an unwarranted emphasis has been placed on situational and personal variables, at least insofar as they may erroneously be viewed as impediments to

[31] Ibid., p. 195.
[32] Ibid., p. 198.

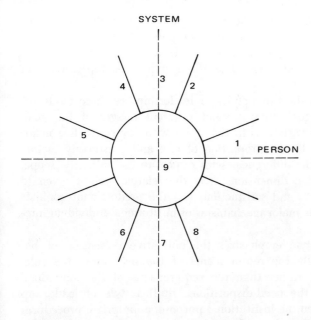

Figure 8.2

Circular model of leader behavior

SOURCE: Barry D. Anderson and Alan F. Brown, "Who's a Good Principal?" in Walter G. Hack et al., eds., *Educational Administration: Selected Readings,* 2nd ed., Boston, Allyn & Bacon, 1971, p. 196.

leadership. Concerning the second major findings of the study, however, the authors concluded, "Who is a good principal? The responses . . . strongly suggest that the good principal—in terms of staff satisfaction, confidence in the principal, and feeling of school success—is simply he who frequently leads his staff."[33]

The types of leader behavior resulting from the factor analysis by Anderson and Brown utilizing the LBDQ are in many ways similar to the nomothetic, idiographic, and transactional leadership types or styles described at the University of Chicago in terms of social systems theory.

NOMOTHETIC, IDIOGRAPHIC, AND TRANSACTIONAL BEHAVIOR

Getzels and Guba originally delineated and defined three leadership styles—nomothetic, idiographic, and transactional.[34] Nomothetic or nor-

[33] Loc. cit.

[34] Portions of the following are drawn from J. W. Getzels and Egon C. Guba, "Social Behavior and the Administrative Process, *School Review,* 65 (Winter 1957), 423–441; and J. W. Getzels, James M. Lipham, and Roald F. Campbell, *Educational Administration as a Social Process,* New York, Harper & Row, 1968, pp. 145–149.

mative refers to emphasis on the sociological or institutional axis of behavior in a social system; idiographic or personal refers to the psychological or personalistic axis of behavior; and transactional refers to alternate emphasis on each. The three styles are represented in Figure 8.3.

In this conception the three styles of leadership are three modes of achieving the same goal; they are not different images of the goal. We may examine the variations in the styles with respect to five major relational elements: (1) the proportion of role and personality factors in the behavior; (2) the differences with respect to the authority, scope, affectivity, and sanction dimensions; (3) the relative weight given to effectiveness, efficiency, and satisfaction; (4) the predominant conflicts dealt with; and (5) the major mechanisms of institutional-individual integration.

The *nomothetic* style emphasizes the normative dimension of behavior and accordingly the requirements of the institution, the role, and the expectations, rather than the requirements of the individual, the personality, and the need-dispositions. In this style of leadership it is assumed that given the institutional purpose, appropriate procedures can be discovered that will implement the purpose by conforming to the "right" procedures. These procedures are therefore included in the role expectations, and every role incumbent must adhere to the expectations. If roles are clearly defined, and everyone is held responsible for doing what he is supposed to do, the desired outcomes will ensue regardless of who the particular role incumbents are, provided they have the necessary technical competence. In the normative style of leadership, the most expeditious route to the goal is seen as residing in the nature of the institutional structure rather than in any particular persons. In a sense, the people fulfilling the roles are as replaceable as the parts of a well-designed machine. In terms of the major variables in the superordinate-subordinate relationship, authority is vested rather than entrusted, the scope of interactions is diffuse rather than specific, the affectivity is universalistic rather than particularistic, and sanctions are extrinsic rather than intrinsic. The predominant conflict that is likely to be dealt with is role conflict, since this is immediately related to the institutional-role-expectation dimension of behavior, and any friction here is seen as threatening the structure of the system. The mode of individual-institutional integration is socialization of personality and adaptation, rather than personalization of role and self-actualization. The standard of administrative excellence is effectiveness more than efficiency.

The *idiographic* style of leadership stresses the personal dimension of behavior and accordingly the requirements of the individual, the personality, and the need-dispositions rather than the requirements of

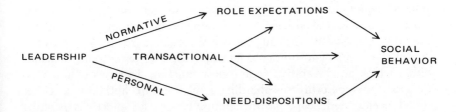

Figure 8.3
Three leadership styles
SOURCE: Adapted from J. W. Getzels and E. G. Guba, "Social Behavior and the Administrative Process," *School Review*, 65 (1957), 436. Copyright © 1957 by the University of Chicago.

the institution, the role, and the expectations. This does not mean that the personal style is any less goal-oriented than the normative style; it means that the most expeditious route to the goal is seen as residing in the people involved rather than in the institutional structure. The basic assumption is that the greatest accomplishment will occur not from enforcing adherence to rigorously defined expectations but from making it possible for each person to contribute what is most meaningful to him. Normative procedural prescriptions of the kind included in the minutely defined roles of the normative style are seen as restrictive and a hindrance rather than as a guide to productive behavior. In terms of the major variables of the superordinate-subordinate relationship, authority is entrusted rather than vested, the scope of expectations is specific rather than diffuse, the affectivity is particularistic rather than universalistic, and sanctions are intrinsic rather than extrinsic. The predominant conflict that is likely to be dealt with is personality conflict, since this is immediately related to the individual-personality-needs dimension of behavior, and any friction is seen as threatening to the functioning of the system. The mode of individual-institutional integration is the personalization of role and self-actualization, rather than socialization of personality and adaptation. The standard of administrative excellence is efficiency more than effectiveness.

The *transactional* style of leader behavior calls attention to the need for moving toward one style under one set of circumstances and toward another style under another set of circumstances. In this sense it is intermediate—indeed, it moves from one style to the other—and is therefore least well defined. Since the goals of the social system must be carried out, it is necessary to make explicit the roles and expectations required to achieve them. And since the roles and expectations are implemented by people with needs to be met, the personalities of these people must be taken into account. But the answer is not simple; it is insufficient to say that one should hew to the middle course between expectations and needs, seeking a compromise between them, for this approach may very well compromise both the institutional role and the individual personality. Instead, the aim throughout is a thorough awareness of the limits of institutional and individual resources and demands within which administrative action must function. In terms of the variables of the superordinate-subordinate relationship, authority is either vested or entrusted, scope is either diffuse or specific, affectivity is either particularistic or universalistic, and sanctions are either extrinsic or intrinsic, depending on the circumstances. There is sensitivity to all types of conflicts—role, personality, and role-personality conflicts being recognized and dealt with. The mode of individual-institutional integration is socialization of personality and adaptation, and personalization of role and self-actualization. The standard of administrative excellence is both effectiveness and efficiency.

One of the early studies that utilized the nomothetic-idiographic-transactional formulation to examine the leadership behavior of school administrators was conducted by Moser.[35] In 12 school systems he conducted intensive interviews with school superintendents and principals and obtained mutual perceptions of their leadership styles. In general, he found that leadership style was meaningfully related to measures of role effectiveness, job satisfaction, and confidence in leadership. Particularly interesting findings concerning the principals were: (1) that the teachers and the superintendent subject the principal to markedly different sets of leadership expectations, and (2) that the principal's behavior varies according to whether he is interacting with superiors or with subordinates. Finding that the principal emphasized nomothetic behaviors (stressing goal achievement, institutional regulations, and centralized authority) in his relations with the superintendent and idiographic behaviors (stressing individual needs and wants, minimum rules, decentralized authority) in his interactions with teachers, Moser concluded, "The principal is in a delicate position as a member of two organizational families."[36]

Whereas Moser examined differences in expectations held for the leadership of the principal *between* groups, such as superintendents and teachers, Moyer studied differences in expectations for the leadership of the principal within a group—specifically, the teaching group.[37] In a study of the type of leadership teachers want, he had teachers react to 80 statements dealing with "leader-centered" and "group-centered"

[35] Robert P. Moser, "The Leadership Patterns of School Superintendents and School Principals," *Administrator's Notebook,* 6 (September 1957), 1–4.

[36] Ibid., 4.

[37] Donald C. Moyer, "Leadership that Teachers Want," *Administrator's Notebook,* 3 (March 1955), 1–4.

behavior by the principal. At the same time, they were asked to rate the personal and professional satisfaction they derived from their working situation. One of his major findings was that the greater the unity within a group in attitudes toward leadership, the higher the satisfaction in the group. When faculties were compared on the basis of their solidarity or homogeneity of attitudes toward leadership, the school faculties high in homogeneity were also high in overall satisfaction derived from the work situation. This result is compatible with Anderson and Brown's finding that congruence in expectations among the members of a group emerges as a factor fully as significant as actual leadership style, which until recently has received the primary attention of researchers.

Improving the principal's leadership

Emanating from the theoretical conceptuals and research studies are several fruitful directions for improving the principal's leadership. First, the principal should take a descriptive, as opposed to evaluative, view of leadership. That is, instead of seeing leadership in a simplistic-evaluative fashion, such as "good" or "bad" leadership, it is more useful to analyze leadership in terms of several interactive and descriptive factors, such as those utilized in the revised LBDQ. Thus analyzed, it becomes possible to evaluate, measure, and subsequently modify leadership behavior in specific ways. In assessing classroom teaching, considerable progress has been made in the analysis of "teaching" behavior; a parallel analysis of "leading" behavior might be productive. Through observations, clinical assessment, simulation exercises, and self-analyses by practicing principals, it should be possible to develop and sharpen considerably our knowledge of the factors used for describing, assessing, and hence improving the principal's leadership.

Second, the principal should take a long-range view of leadership. This would involve examination of the stages of attempted, accepted, implemented, and effective leadership through time, rather than focusing only on frequency of attempted leadership, in many of our current "snapshot" studies of leadership. In analyzing his own leadership behavior, the principal should keep in mind that considerable time may elapse before the ultimate outcomes of a given leadership act can be assessed. Thus the principal not only should be patient, he also must be persistent in his efforts to assess the degree of acceptance, implementation, and effectiveness of his or others' leadership behavior.

A third suggestion is that instead of viewing the determinants, correlates, or outcomes associated with leadership in a simple, "seesaw" fashion, the principal should consider them to be complex, dynamic, and interactive. That is, the variables associated with leadership may be curvilinear, not linear. For example, it typically is assumed that if certain leadership acts result in certain positive outcomes, more of the same leadership acts will result in even greater outcomes. But such may not be the case. Principals should not view leadership in terms of simple pressures and counterpressures, forces and counterforces, and similar linear equilibrium notions.

A fourth guideline for improving one's leadership relates to the need for taking the broad view of organizational relationships instead of the narrow view from inside the organization. The principal needs to recognize that at times a given leadership act may not be equally interpreted as leadership by an intraorganizational constituency, such as the teachers, a supraorganizational constituency, such as the district office personnel, or an extraorganizational constituency, such as parents or citizens. Moreover, there may likewise exist substantial differences in the expectations for leadership within a constituent group. Recognition and acceptance that a given leadership act often endangers the status quo may actually free the principal to act, preparing him in advance to recognize and deal with conflict.

Finally, the principal should recognize that instead of employing only one or two criteria for evaluating leadership, he should utilize multiple criteria. The research on leadership conducted to date indicates that neither now nor in the foreseeable future can one expect to use any single, ultimate criterion for assessing leadership effectiveness. Thus the principal is cautioned against seizing on any one measure, such as staff morale or satisfaction, as *the* criterion for evaluating leadership. Conceivably, it is precisely these "happiness" indices that are jeopardized most by a given leadership act. There is a need for utilizing multiple, perhaps diverse, criteria in evaluating leader effectiveness.

Summary

As an introduction to the analysis of leadership, we discussed the psychological, sociological, and behavioral approaches to the study of the subject. Leadership was defined as that behavior which initiates a new structure in interaction or a change in the goals, objectives, configurations, procedures, inputs, processes, or outputs of a social system. Some issues in the study of leadership, including the locus for leadership, the stages of leadership, the frequency and potency of leadership, and the scope of leadership, were clarified.

Research regarding leadership behavior—classified in terms of initiating structure and consideration dimensions and nomothetic-transactional-idiographic styles—revealed the nature and frequency of the principal's leadership behavior to be systematically related to group homogeneity, job satisfaction, morale, confidence in the principal's leadership, and ratings of the principal's effectiveness. For improving the leadership of the principal, it was suggested that the description of leadership be separated from the evaluation of leadership, that emphasis be given to all stages of leadership, that the variables associated with leadership be viewed as complex and interactive, that leadership be examined from both intraorganizational and extraorganizational views, and that multiple criteria be utilized in evaluating leadership.

SUGGESTED ACTIVITIES

1. Analyze a biographical or autobiographical study of an educational leader and categorize the contradictory traits cited to describe his leadership.

2. Have principals analyze their calendars for a one-week period to obtain a list of their leadership activities. Compare and contrast the lists.

3. Administer a simulation or in-basket exercise and analyze the resultant behavior in terms of frequency, potency, or styles of leadership.

4. Have class or seminar participants provide descriptions of their own leadership behavior using the LBQD—Form XII or any other leadership measure. Score and compare the results along the several dimensions.

5. Administer to teachers and to the school superintendent the "real" or "ideal" forms of a measure of the principal's leadership. Examine the results for systematic differences.

SELECTED REFERENCES

BASS, BERNARD M., *Leadership, Psychology and Organizational Behavior*, New York: Harper & Row, 1960, pt. III.

CARVER, FRED D., and THOMAS J. SERGIOVANNI, eds., *Organizations and Human Behavior: Focus on Schools*, New York, McGraw-Hill, 1969.

CUNNINGHAM, LUVERN L., and WILLIAM J. GEPHART, eds., *Leadership: The Science and the Art Today*, Itasca, Ill., Peacock, 1973.

FABER, CHARLES F., and GILBERT F. SHEARRON, *Elementary School Administration*, New York, Holt, Rinehart and Winston, 1970, chap. 11.

GORTON, RICHARD A., *Conflict, Controversy, and Crisis in School Administration and Supervision: Issues, Cases, and Concepts for the '70's*, Dubuque, Iowa, Brown, 1972, chap. 10.

HALPIN, ANDREW W., *The Leadership Behavior of School Superintendents*, Chicago, Midwest Administration Center, University of Chicago, 1959, reprinted, Macmillan, 1968.

HEMPHILL, JOHN K., "Administration as Problem Solving," in Andrew W. Halpin, ed., *Administrative Theory in Education*, Chicago, Midwest Administration Center, University of Chicago, 1958, chap. 5.

LIPHAM, JAMES M., "Leadership and Administration," in Daniel E. Griffiths, ed., *Behavioral Science and Educational Administration*, Sixty-Third Yearbook, National Society for the Study of Education, Chicago, University of Chicago Press, 1964, chap. 6.

OWENS, ROBERT G., *Organizational Behavior in Schools,* Englewood Cliffs, N.J., Prentice-Hall, 1970, chap. 6.

STOGDILL, RALPH M., *Individual Behavior and Group Achievement,* New York, Oxford University Press, 1959.

Functions of the principalship

THE FIVE CHAPTERS IN THIS SECTION ARE DEVOTED TO THE COMPETEN-CIES REQUIRED IN THE MAJOR FUNCTIONAL CATEGORIES OF THE PRINCIPAL'S ROLE. THE CHAPTERS ARE CONCERNED WITH THE FOLLOWING FUNCTIONS: THE INSTRUCTIONAL PROGRAM, STAFF PERSONNEL SERVICES, STUDENT PERSONNEL SERVICES, FINANCIAL-PHYSICAL RESOURCES, AND SCHOOL-COMMUNITY RELATIONSHIPS. THE PRINCIPAL'S ROLE IS VIEWED AS PROVIDING LEADERSHIP IN THE IMPROVEMENT OF EACH FUNCTION.

CHAPTER 9
The principal and the instructional program

lmost everyone agrees that the principal should be the "instructional leader" of the school. But what does this mean? Elsewhere we have distinguished between the administration of the instructional program, which implies maintenance activities, and the improvement of the instructional program, which connotes leadership activities—that the existing educational program will be altered or changed.[1] Our concern here is less with instructional maintenance than with instructional change, which we view as synonymous with instructional improvement. Although curricular specialists can offer invaluable consultative assistance with instructional change, in the final analysis the principal is the one who is responsible for designing, implementing, and evaluating changes in the instructional program of the school.

In this chapter, instructional improvement is viewed in terms of a general systems approach including four major phases of instructional change. The first phase, assessing program relevance, necessitates the examination of the existing instructional program with both cultural demands and the needs of the learner in mind. The second, planning program improvements, entails the identification of needed changes and competency in choosing the program modifications or alterations that will satisfy particular needs. The implementation of selected program improvements represents the third phase, for which we present a model of the process for orienting the community to curricular change. The evaluation of program change constitutes the fourth phase of instructional improvement, during which attention is given to the types of measures appropriate for evaluating the outcomes of the change. Finally, we summarize the principal's role in instructional development in terms of the basic competencies required of the principal in providing instructional leadership.

[1] James M. Lipham, "Leadership and Administration" in Daniel E. Griffiths, ed., *Behavioral Science and Educational Administration*, Sixty-Third Yearbook, National Society for the Study of Education, pt. II, Chicago, University of Chicago Press, 1964, pp. 119–141.

The systems approach to instructional change

A systematic approach to instructional change inevitably raises the important question, "What categories of behavior are crucial to instructional improvement?" Since many duties and responsibilities are required of the principal, a gestalt of the process of instructional improvement must be provided if one is to prevent the dissipation of time and energy that results from attacking numerous issues in a diffuse or random manner. The systems approach, presented in Chapter 2, possesses particular power and parsimony in that it provides a point of departure for categorizing and analyzing the critical competencies required of the principal in providing instructional leadership.

In utilizing the systems approach to instructional change, we consider both the categories of behavior, conceived according to steps or stages, and the techniques that have proved to be viable at each stage. As Figure 9.1 indicates, the crucial categories of behavior include the following: assessing the relevance of the current program, planning program improvements, implementing program change, and evaluating program outcomes. Competencies of the principal concerning each of these categories are discussed in the paragraphs that follow.

ASSESSING PROGRAM RELEVANCE

Before program change can be initiated, a systematic assessment of the existing curriculum must be undertaken. Such assessment should take into account the changing demands placed by the culture on the schools; simultaneously realizing meeting the needs of individual learners must have primary attention. Formal program evaluation with reliable instrumentation is considered to be an excellent method for assisting in the determination of program relevance.

CULTURAL DEMANDS. Regarding curricular development, Inlow has suggested that cultural values govern all curricular choices and decisions.[2] Certainly if a school program is planned with the intent of reflecting the wishes of a culture or society, Inlow's statement is worthy of consideration. A few trends may be cited to indicate the impingement of cultural demands on the school.

In the chapter dealing with educational values, we indicated that societal demands are changing continually, partly because of myriad technological advances that have prompted people to become extremely mobile. Many wage earners are employed in occupations demanding frequent relocation, which means that the school-age child is frequently

---

[2] Gail M. Inlow, *The Emergent in Curriculum*, New York, Wiley, 1966, p. 43.

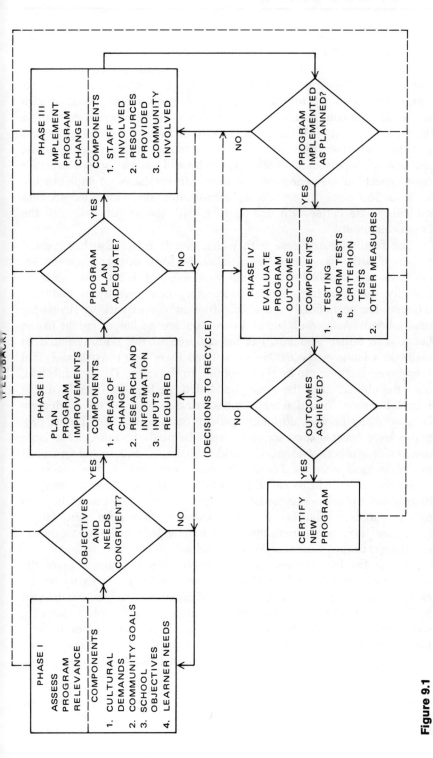

(FEEDBACK)

Figure 9.1
Systems model of the instructional leadership process

uprooted and forced into a new educational milieu. The availability of more lucrative job opportunities in metropolitan areas also has prompted an exodus of families from rural America to urban or suburban areas. Not only has this transmigratory tendency of families caused student adjustment problems to which the school must address itself, it also has made communities and student bodies more heterogeneous than in the past. Coupled with the heterogeneity of these "new nomads,"[3] and resulting also from the necessity of constructing larger schools, is the problem of impersonality within the school. Thus the school program must reflect an awareness of the need for emphasis on individuality while at the same time fostering socialization skills intended to help students relate better with one another, with the school, and with the larger community.

The regularity and ease with which people travel also has created a change in the basic family orientation. To some extent, this condition has been responsible for a general weakening of family ties. Ease of mobility has been instrumental in creating new friendships and new interests for each family member, often at the expense of loosening family bonds. As a result, many basic skills are no longer taught in the home. The father who instructs his children in the skills required to maintain a home or the mother who shows them how to cook, sew, and keep house has come to be the exception to the norm. Driver education, once the obligation of the home, has fallen, perhaps by default, to the school. Even sex education recently has found its way into the curriculum because many families no longer provide such instruction. Lunch programs have become common in the schools, partly because of the large number of mothers who work outside the home, and school breakfast programs have been established in some communities. The extent to which the school will be called on in future years to extend its program to respond to and accommodate changes in American family life can only be surmised. Thus far, educators appear to have been quite willing to initiate services in areas the home has neglected, despite warnings of a danger toward overextension of the school.

, Just as the ten-year period immediately after the launching of the first Russian satellite in 1957 was characterized by an emphasis on science, mathematics, and technology, the succeeding years have witnessed an increasing concern for developing within young people a sense of social awareness. After Sputnik, a variety of critics were quick to fault the American educational system for allowing the Soviet Union to acquire leadership in space exploration.[4] Curricula were criticized as

[3] Alvin Toffler, *Future Shock*, New York, Random House, 1970, pp. 74–94.

[4] Cf. Hyman G. Rickover, *Education and Freedom*, New York, Dutton, 1959; Max Rafferty, *Suffer, Little Children*, New York, New American Library, 1962; Max Rafferty, *What They Are Doing to Your Children*, New York, New American Library, 1964.

being oriented toward life adjustment, with insufficient emphasis on development of intellectual skills. The National Defense Education Act, which earmarked large sums of money initially to provide in-service training for teachers of science, mathematics, and foreign language, as well as to equip counselors better to identify future scientists, was prompted by a national concern over professional training programs in the fields named. Undoubtedly this act had a significant effect on curricular determination at every level of education.[5] Conant's comprehensive studies of the junior and senior high schools throughout the country also prompted considerable curricular revision and likewise stressed the need for strong mathematics, science, and foreign language programs.[6] Moreover, the necessity for early identification of students with special talents in these disciplines was emphasized.

In 1965 Congress passed the Elementary and Secondary Education Act, which allocated $1 billion for improving education for the disadvantaged. By this time the national priorities had changed and prime concern was devoted to the provision of equal opportunities for all students, as well as the need to coexist happily with others in an age when technology had thrust diverse groups of individuals into common surroundings. More recently, additional societal demands have surfaced —the need to develop means with which to control our deteriorating environment and the need for emphasis on preparation for satisfying and productive careers—ideally in an era of peace.

Although each of these changes in societal priorities has been instrumental in generating alternatives to existing instructional programs, every community has a substantial number of citizens who are dedicated to maintaining the status quo or ensuring that traditions are preserved. The attitude, "What was good for me is good for my kids," is surprisingly prevalent in many sections of the country, and of course any program not concentrating specifically on the three Rs is castigated by several subpublics. Such citizens often are extremely vocal and influential, and their cause has been fueled by the number of problems evident in today's schools, as compared with their own school years when strict discipline was enforced and willing compliance expected.

Even the most conscientious efforts to ensure curricular responsiveness to cultural demands will sometimes prove frustrating in our complex and constantly changing society. Nevertheless, it is an obligation of the

---

[5] Roald F. Campbell and Robert A. Bunnell, *Nationalizing Influences on Secondary Education*, Chicago, Midwest Administration Center, University of Chicago, 1963.

[6] James B. Conant, *The American High School Today: A First Report to Interested Citizens*, New York, McGraw-Hill, 1959; James B. Conant, *The Comprehensive High School: A Second Report to Interested Citizens*, New York, McGraw-Hill, 1967; James B. Conant, *Recommendations for Education in the Junior High School Years: A Memorandum to School Boards*, Princeton, N.J., Educational Testing Service, 1960.

principal to assess constantly the expectations held in the culture for the school as an institution, thereby capitalizing on societal pressures to ensure a contemporary curriculum. Relevant activities of the principal in this regard include such personal activities as reading, attendance at professional meetings, or enrollment in courses and seminars devoted to developing an understanding of cultural demands on the school. Professional role activities in this domain include the initiation of alterations in the goals and objectives of the school and school district, the interpretation to the staff of the need for change, and the influencing of educational policy at state and local levels in response to societal demands.

LEARNER NEEDS. The needs of the learner constitute one of the most basic considerations in curricular planning.[7] Although the needs of learners have been classified in many ways, they may be analyzed according to two overall categories—needs of learners in general and needs of learners in the local community.

Regardless of the magnitude of societal pressures influencing the instructional program, learner needs must be accorded primary importance if the curriculum is to be relevant for the consumers of the program. We indicated in Chapter 4 that according to the composite framework of Downey, Seager, and Slagle, the task of public education can be categorized within four distinct dimensions: intellectual, social, personal, and productive.[8] Although public expectations for the schools typically have suggested primary concentration on the intellectual dimension, currently there is strong support for ensuring within the productive dimension that each student not intending to further his formal education will leave high school equipped with a job-entry-level skill. In accordance with this view, the federal government provides considerable sums of money to support vocational and career education programs in the schools. Vocational programs at the secondary level include numerous cooperative and work-study programs that offer students opportunities to relate in practice what has been discussed in theory in the classroom. We concur that such programs are valuable and certainly represent an emerging focus for learning opportunities; however, care must be taken in designing such programs to ensure the placement of students into meaningful work experiences. It is hoped that the increased availability of funds for work-study, vocational, and career education programs will not result in an undue emphasis on the productive dimension.

[7] Ralph W. Tyler, *Basic Principles of Curriculum and Instruction*, Chicago, University of Chicago Press, 1950.

[8] Lawrence W. Downey, Roger C. Seager, and Allen T. Slagle, *The Task of Public Education*, Chicago, Midwest Administration Center, University of Chicago, 1960.

Because of the importance attached to earning a college diploma, the intellectual needs of students continue to receive considerable stress in the schools. The expectation prevails that a high school graduate should be prepared to hold a responsible job or be assured of a successful college career. Even so, if more attention were directed toward need fulfillment in the social and personal dimensions, students undoubtedly would be better prepared psychologically and emotionally to cope with future academic and vocational problems.[9] With knowledge expanding so rapidly, and with job responsibilities becoming more technical and so much more demanding that further training is required, it is doubtful whether schools can ever ensure a product that is guaranteed to succeed either in college or in jobs. A basic ingredient of such success, however, requires continued emphasis on the social and the personal dimensions, as well as on the intellectual and productive dimensions.

Another trend in education has recently emerged. Some now insist that "kindergarten is too late" and that nursery and preschool education are required to capitalize on the time of life when a large portion of one's basic intelligence is being formed.[10] Moreover, the traditional kindergarten philosophy of providing young children with a variety of delightful socializing experiences has been transformed into a "no-nonsense" approach, with emphasis shifting from the affective and psychomotor domains to the cognitive. In response to this transition, some parents are attempting to offer preschool instruction in the home; others are enrolling their children in day-care centers and nursery schools. Contributing to this increased early emphasis on cognitive learning have been television programs, such as "Sesame Street" and "The Electric Company," which have exposed children throughout the country to the joys of learning. Certainly this generation, to whom learning has been a delight, will not be content with traditional peda-gogical methods and materials; indeed, today's children have become conditioned to expect diversified teaching techniques and imaginative curricula.

While the identification of the needs of learners in general is an important consideration in the improvement of the instructional pro-gram, the analysis of the unique needs of the learner in the local com-munity is mandatory. For example, the needs of a maturing student in Chicago, Illinois, undoubtedly differ substantially from those of a stu-dent in Tifton, Georgia. Ultimately, the goal of any curriculum is to provide a program that can be tailored to the needs of each student, thereby ensuring individualized instruction. A first step toward achieving

[9] William Glasser, *Schools Without Failure*, New York, Harper & Row, 1969, pp. 12–14.

[10] Esther P. Edwards, "Kindergarten Is Too Late," *Saturday Review*, 51 (June 1968), 68–70, 76–78; *Preschool Breakthrough: What Works in Early Childhood Edu-cation*, Washington, D.C., National School Public Relations Association, 1970.

this goal is to focus on the local community and the local school population to ascertain, with the assistance of everyone concerned, significant and differentiated needs of learners within the community.

RELATING OBJECTIVES TO STUDENTS. Of course, the needs of society and those of the community must converge in the instructional program in terms of the needs of the individual learner. Many years ago, Hopkins posited the following criteria for use in considering whether suggested learning experiences warrant incorporation in the school program:

1. The experience must begin with and continue to grow out of the real felt needs of pupils.

2. The experience must be managed by all of the learners concerned —pupils, teachers, parents, and others—through a process of cooperative democratic interaction.

3. The experience must be unified through evolving purposes of pupils.

4. The experience must aid each individual to increase his power to make intelligent choices.

5. The experience must aid each individual to mature his experiences by making progressive improvements in the logic of such experiences.

6. The experience must increase the number and variety of interests which each individual consciously shares with others.

7. The experience must help each individual build new and refine old meanings.

8. The experience must offer opportunity for each individual to use an ever-increasing variety of resources for learning.

9. The experience must aid each individual to use a variety of learning activities compatible with the variety of resources.

10. The experience must aid each individual creatively to reconstruct and expand his best past experience in the developing situation.

11. The experience must have some dominating properties which characterize it as a whole and which usually give it a name.

12. The experience must close with a satisfactory emotional tone for each participant.[11]

Hopkins' criteria emphasize the importance of relating the objectives of the instructional program to the needs of students. Each learning experience within the curriculum must be planned with the objective of relating to student needs. Within the last decade, there has been considerable emphasis on stating instructional objectives in terms of learner behavior as one means for ensuring a planned, purposeful, and relevant program of studies.[12]

Considerable progress has been made recently in the individualiza-

[11] Levi Thomas Hopkins, *Interaction: The Democratic Process*, Lexington, Mass., Heath, 1941, p. 218.

[12] Robert F. Mager, *Preparing Instructional Objectives*, Palo Alto, Calif., Fearron, 1962.

tion of instructional programs in terms of learner needs. The individualization of instruction is a task of considerable magnitude, requiring
changes in traditional organizational structures, teaching roles and
responsibilities, instructional methods and materials, and the utilization
of time and resources. Several prototypic programs have been designed,
however, to provide direction for schools in their efforts to individualize
instruction. One example is the work being done at the University of
Wisconsin Research and Development Center for Cognitive Learning.[13]
Principals should keep abreast of such programs, which provide guidance in relating instructional objectives to the needs of students.

FORMAL PROGRAM EVALUATION. Having taken into consideration cultural
demands and local learner needs and having followed the careful formulation of specific curricular objectives, one often finds it desirable to
utilize formal evaluation as a means for examining the existing school
program. Such an evaluation serves, among other things, to appraise
the degree to which existing learning experiences relate curricular objectives to student needs. The use of a prepared evaluation instrument,
such as the *Evaluative Criteria* published by the National Study of
Secondary School Evaluation, can be of immeasurable value in program
assessment.[14] Even though these instruments focus ordinarily on the
quality and quantity of inputs to the school, such as personnel and
facilities, the relevance of processes and the success of program outputs
in relation to the school's philosophy and objectives also are stressed.
This type of instrumentation lends itself to quick quantification and
qualification of data and provides a proven format for the evaluation.
Although most of our evaluative instruments pertain specifically to
secondary schools, significant efforts have been expended recently in the
development of suitable evaluative criteria for the elementary school.[15]

The benefits accrued from formal program appraisal through the
use of a standard evaluative instrument are manifold. When planned
and coordinated properly, the exercise itself can serve to increase the
rationality of program goals and to enhance faculty identification with
the goals. Through an interdisciplinary approach to committee assignments (e.g., whereby science teachers participate in the evaluation of
the English curriculum or primary teachers help evaluate the upper

[13] Herbert J. Klausmeier et al., *Individually Guided Education and the Multiunit Elementary School, Guidelines for Implementation,* Wisconsin Research and
Development Center for Cognitive Learning, University of Wisconsin, Madison, 1971.

[14] National Study of Secondary School Evaluation, *Evaluative Criteria,* 4th ed.,
Washington, D.C., 1969.

[15] Center for the Study of Evaluation, *Elementary School Evaluation Kit,* Boston,
Allyn & Bacon, 1973.

elementary curriculum), staff members escape from the provinciality that results from interest only in their particular subject or grade-level specialization. When priorities for improvement subsequently must be established, resistance to change is often minimized if the faculty is well informed of the goals, problems, and needs of each curricular area in the school.

After a comprehensive assessment has been made of the school's program by the professional staff, parents, and students, a distributed report of the findings is obligatory. The evaluation does not terminate here, however. At this point, external appraisal is often desirable to substantiate, amend, or refute the findings resulting from the internal appraisal. If a high school is a member of a regional accrediting association, assistance with such external evaluation is often provided periodically. Any elementary or secondary school desiring external appraisal and not holding membership in an accrediting association may seek such assistance from the State Department of Education, state or regional professional associations, university specialists, or neighboring educators.

As a consequence of the internal and external appraisals, typically a list of recommendations is generated and classified according to those that are immediately attainable and those that are attainable only after a substantial expenditure of money or major changes in physical or personnel resources. Priorities must be established for each recommendation, and plans must be devised for either expeditious or long-range adoption and implementation. The entire formal evaluation process should be repeated several years later. In this manner a relevant curriculum becomes a distinct probability.

PLANNING PROGRAM IMPROVEMENTS

The planning of program improvements involves the specific delineation of areas of needed change, the use of information and research for the development of alternatives, and the analysis of the inputs required for each alternative. Too frequently, new programs are adopted without attention to research information relating to the programs and without a synthesis of input from each relevant reference group. The paragraphs that follow contain specific suggestions for enhancing the planning of program change.

AREAS OF NEEDED CHANGE. Any self-evaluation, complemented by an external appraisal, will reveal legitimate areas of needed change or improvement. In this regard, however, some principals have been guilty of uncritically adopting and replicating programs that have received acceptance or publicity in other districts.[16] If, for instance, it has been determined after evaluation that a school's traditional student schedule constrains curricular offerings, the adoption of a flexible-modular schedule, which emphasizes greater student freedom, is sometimes suggested. Many school buildings, however, are not able to accommodate a flexible-modular schedule based partly on the presumption that spaces are provided wherein students can make productive use of "unscheduled" time. During his unscheduled time, for instance, a student should have available to him a variety of individual learning opportunities in open labs or learning stations on a daily or weekly basis. A school without the flexibility to accommodate individual student exploration and without the capacity to adjust student schedules on a daily or weekly basis probably should consider alternative options for flexible student programming. Many so-called flexible-modular schedules are, in fact, quite inflexible once they have been developed and therefore might be labeled more realistically "variable" schedules. Bush and Allen, Wiley and Bishop, and Manlove and Beggs all treat these concepts thoroughly, giving theoretical foundations, planning and implementation strategies, and evaluation techniques.[17]

Team teaching, through horizontal or vertical differentiation of teaching responsibilities, is another popular practice suggested frequently as a solution to an inadequate curriculum. Through an emphasis on the unique talents and training of each team member, a complementary unit of professionals and paraprofessionals can be organized in an effort to maximize the contribution of each individual. Once again, however, a word of caution is in order. Effective team teaching requires common planning time, flexible facilities, and interpersonal compatibility among team members. Without these ingredients, its potential effectiveness will be minimized.

Still another device purporting to improve learning experiences is homogeneous ability grouping of students. The research evidence, however, is inconclusive concerning the value of any type of grouping scheme.[18] We do not choose to argue either for or against homogeneous

[16] Herbert A. Thelen, "New Practices on the Firing Line," *Administrator's Notebook*, 12 (January 1964), 1–4.

[17] Robert N. Bush and Dwight W. Allen, *A New Design for High School Education: Assuming a Flexible Schedule*, New York, McGraw-Hill, 1964; W. Deane Wiley and Lloyd H. Bishop, *The Flexibly Scheduled High School*, West Nyack, N.Y., Parker, 1968; Donald C. Manlove and David W. Beggs, III, *Flexible Scheduling Using the IndiFlexS Model*, Bloomington, Indiana University Press, 1965.

[18] Harold G. Shane, "An Annotated List of 40 Grouping Plans," in Maurie Hillson and Ronald T. Hyman, eds., *Change and Innovation in Elementary and Secondary Organization*, New York, Holt, Rinehart and Winston, 1971, pp. 204–212.

tracking or any other form of ability grouping, but we do advise against homogeneous grouping unless the following provisions are incorporated:

1. Extreme care, based on comprehensive objective criteria, is used in the assignment of students.

2. Proper instructional materials and properly trained professionals are available for *all* groups.

3. Provision is made for prompt transfer of students from one group to another when misidentification of ability becomes apparent.

These practices—variable scheduling, team teaching, and ability grouping—are cited only as examples of current practices intended to focus more realistically on the needs of students, or, in the academic vernacular, to "individualize instruction." None of the plans is without a vocal and supportive following, and certainly each has its merits. Rather than copying an innovative practice that is widely acclaimed or that seems to work in a neighboring school, however, the principal would do well to determine what program and student objectives his particular school hopes to achieve, then design revisions that serve those purposes. This strategy assumes that personnel, facility, and financial constraints of the school will be considered in the planning, since failure to do so is disastrous. In this regard, we are reminded of the thoughtless principal who mandated overnight that henceforth his school would be a school without failure. Subsequently, one of his teachers commented somewhat as follows: "Boy, we've had some failures around this place before, but none so great as our failure to understand the meaning of failure before deciding to have a school without any."

It should be remembered, also, that the degree to which any plan to individualize instruction is successful depends primarily on what transpires between the teachers and the learners on a day-to-day basis. Team teaching, flexible scheduling, ability grouping, or any other device will be unsuccessful unless the teacher is concerned with the individual learner. In this regard, even the most traditional curriculum (e.g., the self-contained classroom) can offer individualized instruction if the teacher has the inclination, the capacity, the expertise, the materials, and the time to provide it.

RESEARCH AND INFORMATION. As stressed in Chapter 7, any decision-making process, particularly decisions to alter the curriculum, necessitates the collection, tabulation, and analysis of relevant information from several sources. No plan for instructional change is any stronger than the information base that supports it. Therefore, consideration must be given to some of the basic sources of information.

Opinion polls and need surveys represent popular methods of data collection and, if conducted properly, are beneficial in analyzing community, teacher, and student needs and opinions. Many universities and state departments of education have staff personnel who specialize in surveys of school and community alike. Some school systems prefer to engage in their own surveys, but care should be taken in such cases that the studies are objective.

Students, both past and present, harbor a fund of information regarding the appropriateness of the curriculum. Follow-up studies and personal contact with graduates provide essential data to be considered prior to initiating major program improvements. Unfortunately, however, during the past several decades little progress has been made in either the content or the methodology of follow-up studies as a viable means for program change.

In addition to conducting follow-up studies of students who have progressed to the next level, one should recognize that current students represent not only a captive but also a willing group of respondents that, for reasons unknown, are all too frequently ignored in curricular planning. Inclusion of data from this valuable information source will serve greatly not only to legitimize but also to facilitate the implementation of subsequent program changes.

The research journals, reports, and abstracts of the professional literature represent another virtually untapped source of information for curriculum planners at the building level. A never-ending supply of research evidence is being generated in universities, research centers, and regional laboratories,[19] but either the information is viewed with skepticism by practitioners or else it is not being relayed in meaningful terms. Thus the principal, as a scholar, must provide the linkage between the knowledge producers in the universities and the knowledge utilizers in elementary and secondary classrooms. In addition to serving as a synthesizer and communicator of knowledge, the principal also should encourage the staff to engage in professional development activities.

As a brief aside, we might cite the Eight-Year Study as a classic example of the reluctance of educators and others to credit the value of research.[20] After carefully matching and studying 1475 pairs of students from conventional and experimental schools, the authors concluded that success in college is not dependent on the selection of a sequence of certain high school courses labeled "college preparatory." Although the study was completed in 1940, most high schools still offer "college" tracks, and bright students displaying college potential are encouraged or even forced into these tracks with the justification that the courses are

[19] Cf. Educational Resources Information Center (ERIC) Document Reproduction Service, Bethesda, Md.

[20] C. D. Chamberlain et al., *Adventure in American Education, vol. IX; Did They Succeed in College?*" New York, Harper & Row, 1942.

necessary for college entrance and success. Even though a large number of colleges and universities no longer specify certain courses for admission, the folklore of a "college preparatory" curriculum still prevails.

Possibly the most important source of data collection for curricular development is in the classroom. Listed below are the major categories of evaluative instruments that can be utilized by a building staff to provide useful information for program planning prior to program alterations:[21]

Mental ability tests	Interview schedules
Achievement tests	Observation schedules
Anecdotal records	Personality inventories
Appreciation tests	Rating scales
Aptitude tests	Sociometric devices
Aptitude inventories	Interest inventories

Teacher acceptance and support for a plan to collect a wealth of data within the classroom depend, of course, on the use to which the information will be put. Individual, class, and school profiles should be constructed and made available to all professionals to supply basic information about the needs, interests, strengths, and weaknesses of the student body as a whole and of each student in particular.

INPUTS REQUIRED. As Figure 9.2 indicates, Saylor and Alexander emphasized a cooperative approach to the planning of instructional improvement.[22] They stressed the need for careful communication between groups and for the coordination of group efforts. The coordination function, and those of stimulation and facilitation, are performed by the principal, whose influence is crucial to the success of the entire process. The principal must make certain that all groups have formulated objectives within their province to provide input. In the planning process, for instance, student and community groups would be expected to identify needs and objectives, whereas the faculty group would be concerned not only with needs and objectives but also with the technical aspects of program implementation. The model also illustrates that planning receives final approval within each learning group, thus reinforcing the earlier point that the success of any program improvement or innovation is dependent on the receptivity it is accorded in the individual classroom.

[21] Ronald C. Doll, *Curriculum Improvement: Decision-Making and Process,* 2nd ed., Boston, Allyn & Bacon, 1970, p. 365.

[22] J. Galen Saylor and William M. Alexander, *Curriculum Planning for Modern Schools,* New York, Holt, Rinehart and Winston, 1966.

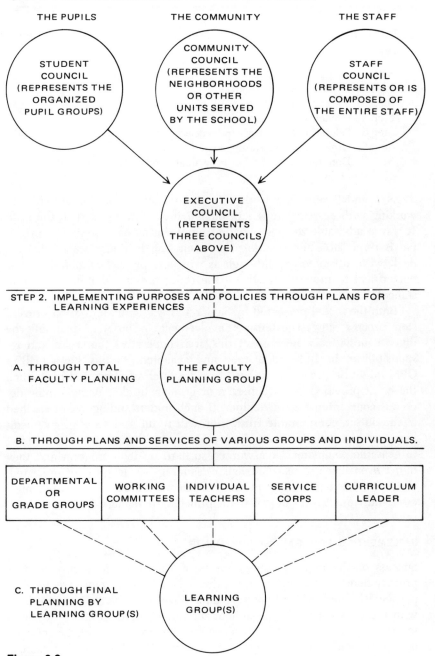

STEP 1. PLANNING CURRICULUM PURPOSES AND POLICIES

THE PUPILS   THE COMMUNITY   THE STAFF

STUDENT COUNCIL (REPRESENTS THE ORGANIZED PUPIL GROUPS)

COMMUNITY COUNCIL (REPRESENTS THE NEIGHBORHOODS OR OTHER UNITS SERVED BY THE SCHOOL)

STAFF COUNCIL (REPRESENTS OR IS COMPOSED OF THE ENTIRE STAFF)

EXECUTIVE COUNCIL (REPRESENTS THREE COUNCILS ABOVE)

STEP 2. IMPLEMENTING PURPOSES AND POLICIES THROUGH PLANS FOR LEARNING EXPERIENCES

A. THROUGH TOTAL FACULTY PLANNING

THE FACULTY PLANNING GROUP

B. THROUGH PLANS AND SERVICES OF VARIOUS GROUPS AND INDIVIDUALS.

DEPARTMENTAL OR GRADE GROUPS	WORKING COMMITTEES	INDIVIDUAL TEACHERS	SERVICE CORPS	CURRICULUM LEADER

C. THROUGH FINAL PLANNING BY LEARNING GROUP(S)

LEARNING GROUP(S)

Figure 9.2

Organization of the individual school for curriculum planning

SOURCE: J. Galen Saylor and William M. Alexander, *Curriculum Planning for Modern Schools*. Copyright © 1966 by Holt, Rinehart and Winston, Inc. Copyright 1954 by J. Galen Saylor and William M. Alexander under the title *Curriculum Planning for Better Teaching and Learning*. Reprinted by permission of Holt, Rinehart and Winston, Inc.

Listed below is the seven-step process to curriculum planning offered by Taba:

Step 1: Diagnosis of needs
Step 2: Formulation of objectives
Step 3: Selection of content
Step 4: Organization of content .
Step 5: Selection of learning experiences
Step 6: Organization of learning experiences
Step 7: Determination of what to evaluate and of the ways and means of doing it[23]

Steps 1 and 2 represent leadership responsibilities of the principal in working with citizens; steps 1 through 7 involve working with the staff. It is also advisable to solicit student input during each step. The principal is responsible for ensuring that each step in the process has been dealt with satisfactorily, although as with any process formulation, it is not critical to proceed exactly in the order prescribed if local circumstances dictate otherwise.

Both the model presented by Saylor and Alexander and Taba's seven-step process suggest extensive involvement in program planning by diverse individuals. Because of this, it is imperative that roles and responsibilities be fully understood and accepted. At this stage PERT/CPM might be effectively utilized to indicate clearly how and how much the input provided by each person or group will alter or determine decisions concerning the curriculum. If such understanding is not reached at the outset, considerable frustration will result and some group members may resent the ultimate product. In such situations it is not unusual to hear the complaint, "We worked so hard on that program and they didn't even listen to us." Curricular planning is a lengthy, complicated, and specialized process requiring considerable input from many interested individuals, who all look to the principal for leadership.

IMPLEMENTING PROGRAM IMPROVEMENTS

Success of the implementation phase of the curriculum improvement process depends largely on the principal's ability to motivate others—particularly the faculty—to accept, internalize, and behave in accordance with the program plan. Throughout the implementation effort, attention must be given to such maintenance functions as the selection of new equipment and supplies necessary to accommodate the intended change. Finally, the principal must provide leadership in orienting the community to the program change.

[23] Hilda Taba, *Curriculum Development: Theory and Practice,* New York, Harcourt Brace Jovanovich, 1962, p. 12.

MOTIVATING OTHERS TO CHANGE. The extent to which an organization is amenable to change depends partly on the leader's ability to motivate each organizational participant to internalize the proposed change. The development of skills, strategies, and techniques to motivate organizational incumbents to change has always been a problem for leaders.

Bennis has offered the following four points for consideration in the change process:

1. The *client-system* should have as much understanding of the change and its consequences, as much influence in developing and controlling the fate of the change, and as much trust in the initiator of the change as possible.

2. The *change effort* should be perceived as being as self-motivated and voluntary as possible. This can be done through the legitimization and reinforcement of the change by the top management group as well as by the significant reference groups adjacent to the client-system. This can also be done by providing as much true volition as possible.

3. The *change program* must include emotional and value as well as cognitive (informational) elements for successful implementation. It is doubtful that relying solely on rational persuasion (expert power) is sufficient. Too often rational elements are denied or rendered impotent because they conflict with a strongly ingrained belief, consciously or unconsciously held. Intellectual commitment is a first step, but not a guarantee to action. Most organizations know what ails them or what could help them; the problem is utilization.

4. The *change-agent* can be crucial in reducing the resistance to change by providing consultation and psychological support during the transitional phase of the change. As I have stressed over and over again, the quality of the relationship is pivotal to the success of the change program. As long as the change-agent acts congruently with the principles of the program and as long as the client-system has a chance to test his competence and motives (his own and the change-agent's), he should be able to provide the support so necessary during the risky phases of change.[24]

As Bennis stated, understanding of the change is not sufficient; implementation requires internalization—"a process which leads to automatic self-generation and integral functioning."[25] As social systems theory indicates, there must be a fusion of the goals of the organization and the goals of the individual.

We indicated in our earlier discussion of decision making that employees often support changes in whose initiation they were involved personally. Since some faculty members may not have played a significant role in the generation and planning of specific changes in a school's pro-

[24] Warren G. Bennis, *Changing Organizations: Essays on the Development and Evolution of Human Organizations,* New York, McGraw-Hill, 1966, pp. 176–177.

[25] Ibid., p. 175.

gram, however, motivation becomes a major problem. An accurate diagnosis of the latent and manifest causes of the resistance to change, such as loss of power or prestige, will permit an administrator to concentrate on causes rather than symptoms and should result in the creation of a plan to lessen the resistance.[26]

The principal also should be aware that change is more likely to occur in open than in closed organizational climates, hence the importance of assessing the variables of his own behavior that might be modified to improve the organizational climate within the school. Finally, in terms of decision theory, the principal should recognize that whereas a heuristic decision-making mode is called for in the initial stages of curricular change, a routinized—if not negotiated—mode is likely to be in order as one moves toward the implementation of change. Thus in motivating others to implement planned change, the principal needs not only to be skilled in interpersonal relationships but also to be flexible in his decision-making styles.

MATERIAL RESOURCES REQUIRED. Most major curricular changes require modifications in material as well as in personnel. Decisions concerning the provision of instructional equipment and supplies often present serious problems for the principal—particularly if the proposed curricular change is experimental and requires substantial outlay. Advances in both content and technology have flooded the market with a wealth of audiovisual and printed materials designed to assist in the teaching-learning process. School principals, besieged by teacher requests for supplies and beleaguered by enterprising salesmen, must exercise caution in the purchase of equipment and supplies. This caution should lead to the identification of learning resources characterized by: (1) relevancy, (2) usability, (3) accuracy, and (4) economy.[27]

Relevancy depends on the relationship of the resource to the particular goal-seeking activity, whereas usability is determined by accessibility and appropriateness for an age group. The astronomical expansion of knowledge makes the criterion of accuracy especially difficult to monitor, but care should be exercised to exclude biased and erroneous materials. Economy possibly is the most difficult characteristic to measure. Price tags are easily compared, but economy must take into account the ability to accomplish successfully the intended curricula change, as well as factors of consummality. Texts, library books, and other resource materials

---

[26] Cf. Alvin Zander, "Resistance to Change—Its Analysis and Prevention," in Warren G. Bennis, Kenneth D. Benne, and Robert Chin, eds., *The Planning of Change*, New York, Holt, Rinehart and Winston, 1961, p. 546; Dan C. Lortie, "Change and Exchange: Reducing Resistance to Innovation," *Administrator's Notebook*, 12 (February 1964), 1–4.

[27] Saylor and Alexander, op. cit., pp. 469–471.

that are purchased and remain unused represent a financial waste that no school can afford. Yet effective materials are essential to promoting learning and thus represent a sound investment. The principal and the staff must first reach agreement on categorizing resources according to cost-effectiveness or cost-benefit criteria before priorities can be established and specific materials ordered for a program.

ORIENTATION OF THE COMMUNITY TO CHANGE. Orientation of the community to proposed changes in the school program represents a special problem that principals have attacked with varying degrees of success. There is no question that community acceptance, or at least understanding, of a new program is vital. In years past, educators have expected the community to accept any and all program revisions that, by educator acknowledgment, presumably would improve learning opportunities for students. In many communities today, however, such willing acquiescence is no longer the norm, hence it is important that principals endeavor to communicate accurately and clearly—particularly with citizens who are unaccustomed to educational terminology.

The field of education is generally lacking in an adequate descriptive and compehensive vocabulary, such as in the field of medicine, and many citizens, even the well educated, express considerable confusion over educators' use of terms. In program changes, citizens and parents basically are interested in knowing how the objectives, procedures, or results in a new program will differ from, and presumably improve, the existing program. The mistake most frequently made by principals in communicating with the public is getting caught up in explaining the fine points or details of a proposed change while ignoring the major change itself— not to mention the intended results of the change. In this regard we are reminded of the parent who made the following comment after hearing the principal and teachers ramble for nearly two hours at a PTA meeting about a proposed curricular change: "Before I came I thought I knew what they were going to do. Now I don't know, and I don't think they do either."

In Figure 9.3 we offer a model depicting a procedure that can minimize citizen confusion and create acceptance, or at least understanding, of a new program. First, a summary of the present curricular plan should be presented, together with the results that plan has been achieving (sets A and B). Next the proposed environmental changes leading to a new curricular plan appear. Then aspects of the new plan, including such items as scheduling techniques, grouping practices, or new materials, also should be explained (set C). Specifically, the intended results within the cognitive, affective, and psychomotor domains (set D) should be stated in a vocabulary that parents can understand (e.g., mental, attitudinal, and physical changes in students). Results common to both

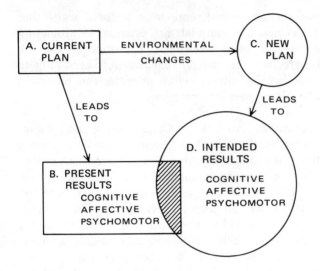

Figure 9.3
Model for orienting the community to curricular change

plans (intersection of sets B and D) will pose a less serious problem in orientation than the discrepant or even unanticipated results represented by the unshaded portion of set D. A community that fully understands the new program and its intended results will be more supportive of the program and less inclined to criticize results in set D that may differ from those initially identified.

EVALUATING PROGRAM CHANGE

Having involved the staff and the community in implementing an instructional change, the principal must evaluate the curricular changes that have been implemented. Although there are several appraisal or assessment models for evaluating program outcomes, the evaluation model developed at the Center for the Study of Evaluation at the University of California at Los Angeles is particularly useful.[28] In this model, a clear distinction is made between process evaluation and outcome evaluation. As indicated in Chapter 2, process evaluation directs attention to analyzing the success with which a program procedure is being implemented in the educational setting for which it was intended. It also is concerned with appraising the value of the new program with respect to measurable gains in pupil performance. If a need for program modification is apparent during process evaluation, appropriate adjustments can be made.

[28] Stephen Klein, Gary Fenstermacher, and Marvin C. Alkin, "The Center's Changing Evaluation Model," *Evaluation Comment*, 2 (January 1971), 9–12.

Unfortunately, principals generally have given little systematic attention to process evaluation; instead they have tended to focus on summative or outcome evaluation.

After a program change has been introduced into the school and after process evaluations have been performed, decisions must be made regarding the overall worth of the program. Referred to as outcome evaluation, this process establishes a rationale for: (1) continuing the program with or without modifications, (2) expanding the program, or (3) terminating the program. Central to outcome evaluation is a determination of the improvement of student behavior or performance, which in the final analysis is the purpose of any instructional program.[29] In conducting outcome evaluation, two types of tests—norm-referenced and criterion-referenced—are often utilized.

Norm-referenced tests are useful in ranking students in terms of their ability, knowledge, or attitudes; they provide a good basis for comparing students with other groups—for example, the students in one school with those in the state or nation, through using norm and percentile tables.[30] Unfortunately, however, norms refer to reference groups and do not indicate the total of what the student has or has not learned. Second, norm-referenced tests are not likely to measure the exact set of objectives called for in a specific educational program. For example, a score on a mathematics test may represent a composite of 10 objectives, only four of which are in common with a particular program that has been implemented.

Criterion-referenced measures complement their normative counterparts by describing (1) the specifics of the program objectives and (2) what a test score means in reference to a performance standard. The use of criterion-referenced measures would be laudable if one knew how to determine what criterion levels to specify, or what performance level for an individual student constitutes objective attainment and how to interpret the results if the objectives are not achieved. To illustrate the latter point, suppose that employing a new fourth grade mathematics unit led to 30 percent of the students attaining all the unit's 20 objectives, 50 percent attaining 15 objectives, and only 20 percent achieving 10 objectives. The principal might be quite impressed. But would he still be impressed if he learned that most of the students could achieve 10 of these objectives prior to taking the instructional unit? Norm-referenced measures would help to clarify the actual utility and significance of a program, since such norms help to establish individual objectives for students. This is not a limitation of the criterion-referenced measure per se but of the way most of these measures are developed, scored, and interpreted.[31]

---

[29] Garth Sorenson, "Evaluation for the Improvement of Instructional Programs, Some Practical Steps," *Evaluation Comment,* 2 (January 1971), 13.

[30] Klein, Fenstermacher, and Alkin, op. cit., 3.

[31] Ibid., 3.

The obvious conclusion is that a combination of the two types of measures is needed. The idea is to include the calibration of item difficulty and normative scores in the development and interpretation of criterion-based measures. A final point should be emphasized. Since performance objectives are established with respect to individual student characteristics, the assessment of program effectiveness should be based on a composite of individual student performance evaluations, rather than an assessment of the program or the student's performance on the basis of a single set of program objectives.

As the model of curricular change in Figure 9.1 indicates, instructional improvement is a cyclical process that is dependent on formal evaluation for vitality at each stage in the process. Within this process, recycling can occur following evaluation of program relevance, evaluation of program planning, evaluation of program implementation, or evaluation of outcomes. The principal's involvement is most extensive at the decision points (diamonds in Figure 9.1), for it is he who has the ultimate responsibility for determining the proper course of action at each appropriate stage.

Whereas the importance attached to process evaluation is unique to the UCLA model, outcome evaluation has been detailed at length by various writers. Beauchamp has listed four dimensions to be considered in outcome evaluation:

1. Evaluation of teacher use of the curriculum
2. Evaluation of the design
3. Evaluation of pupil outcomes
4. Evaluation of the curriculum system[32]

Although favoring an extensive array of objective measures with which to assess the aforementioned dimensions, Beauchamp also stressed the need to include subjective evaluation, especially from teachers.

In a lengthy discussion of the qualitative dimensions of outcome evaluation, Doll has suggested the following general questions as guides:

1. How has pupils' learning improved as a consequence of initiating and continuing this program?
2. How has the behavior or performance of classroom teachers improved?
3. How have the attitudes of teachers toward learners, learning, and teaching improved?
4. How have the procedures which have been used in changing the curriculum proved effective in creating desirable change?[33]

[32] George A. Beauchamp, *Curriculum Theory*, 2nd ed., Wilmette, Ill., Kagg, 1968, p. 137.

[33] Doll, op. cit., p. 395.

The first dimension—assessing the improvement in pupil learning—most assuredly is the primary consideration in determining the value of the instructional change. It is the most important criterion and also the most difficult to measure.

Several evaluative techniques in addition to norm-referenced and criterion-referenced tests are useful for assessing changes in pupil behavior. The following list, suggested by Saylor and Alexander, might be utilized to evaluate student progress in relation to preestablished behavioral or performance objectives:

1. CASE STUDIES: Comprehensive studies of individuals' behavior.

2. CONFERENCES: With parents, other teachers, employers, and so on—to secure data regarding an individual's behavior in situations not observed by the teacher.

3. DIARIES AND LOGS: Kept by learners and analyzed by the teacher to secure various items of information.

4. GROUP EVALUATION OF INDIVIDUALS: Through rating scales and sociometric techniques to secure evidence from his peers as to an individual learner's acceptance and performance.

5. INTERVIEWS WITH LEARNERS: To get information about their performance, understanding, and other items of behavior.

6. INVENTORIES OF MANY TYPES: To give information about such items as personality traits, outside activities, reading and listening habits, and use of time.

7. OBSERVATION OF PUPILS: In various situations to determine behavior of a specific nature.

8. PERFORMANCE TESTS: Including creative work, group productions, physical skills, and similar items of behavior best tested through observation of performance.

9. PICTURES, STILL AND MOTION: For later observation of performance, appearance, and so on.

10. RATING SCALES: Used by teacher, pupils, and others to estimate behavior on such varied traits as courtesy, speech, and legibility of handwriting.

11. RECORDINGS: Of individual voices and group discussion for later analysis.

12. RECORDS OF MANY TYPES: Achievement, anecdotal, attendance, autobiographical, cumulative, disciplinary, health, library, participation (in activities, discussion, elections), tests, and time studies.

13. SELF-ANALYSIS: Made by learners on checklists, rating scales, questionnaires, problem situations, and general questions.

14. WRITTEN TESTS: Standardized, teacher-made, group-made, to test information and skills.[34]

Although the evaluation process is a time-consuming endeavor, thoroughness and accuracy are necessary if intelligent decisions regarding

[34] Saylor and Alexander, op. cit., pp. 586–587.

recycling, termination, or expansion of a program are to be made. Whereas the principal typically is responsible for the ultimate decision to modify, terminate, or expand a program, the responsibility for conducting continuous evaluation rests with many individuals. The principal's role is to ensure that evaluative techniques are appropriately chosen and conscientiously administered. Then, when he is fortified with data from myriad evaluative sources, his role as decision maker in determining the eventual fate of a program improvement becomes rational and manageable.

Competencies in instructional improvement

In summary, let us review some of the major competencies required of the principal in providing instructional leadership. Although the leadership role of the principal is highlighted in the competencies, the stages of attempted, accepted, implemented, and effective leadership indicate that many others will be appropriately involved. Other writers have utilized different conceptual schemes for categorizing the competencies,[35] but we again find it instructive to take the four phases of the systems approach to instructional change as a taxonomic classification of the competencies.

PHASE I. ASSESSING PROGRAM RELEVANCE

Competency No. 1.   The principal studies and interprets the trends in the society that demand curricular change.

Competency No. 2.   The principal delineates the general needs of learners that are basic to the instructional program.

Competency No. 3.   The principal directs the assessment of the needs of learners that are unique to the school and community.

Competency No. 4.   The principal integrates the goals and objectives of the school with the needs of the learners.

Competency No. 5.   The principal conducts a formal assessment of the adequacy of the current program for meeting objectives and learner needs.

PHASE II. PLANNING PROGRAM IMPROVEMENTS

Competency No. 6.   The principal examines and interprets alternative programs, procedures, and structures for improving the instructional program.

[35] Kenneth E. McIntyre, "Administering and Improving the Instructional Programs," in Jack A. Culbertson, Curtis Henson, and Ruel Morrison, eds., *Performance Objectives for School Principals*, Berkeley, Calif., McCutchan, 1974.

Competency No. 7.   The principal utilizes research and information in formulating viable alternatives for change.

Competency No. 8.   The principal involves others in the development of instructional alternatives.

PHASE III. IMPLEMENTING PROGRAM IMPROVEMENTS

Competency No. 9.   The principal allocates and assigns the staff to accomplish instructional goals.

Competency No. 10. The principal inventories, acquires, and assigns the materials, equipment, and facilities to accomplish instructional goals.

Competency No. 11. The principal explains the instructional change to parents and the community.

PHASE IV. EVALUATING PROGRAM CHANGE

Competency No. 12. The principal examines and recommends instrumentation for evaluating program processes and outcomes.

Competency No. 13. The principal collects, organizes, and interprets data concerning the present as compared with the previous performance of students.

Competency No. 14. The principal certifies the viability of the program or initiate subsequent change in the newly established instructional program.

Summary

In this chapter we suggested that a major responsibility of the principal is providing leadership in instructional improvement or change. Utilizing a systems approach, we posited four essential phases of instructional improvement: assessing program relevance, planning program improvements, implementing program improvements, and evaluating program change.

The first phase includes attention to societal demands and learner needs, which are both in a state of continuous change. The second phase, implementation of program improvements, entails careful attention to motivating others, particularly the staff, to change. The proper orientation of the community also was viewed as essential, since the success or failure of new programs often depends directly on community acceptance. The final phase of the process includes the use of adequate assessment procedures, including process evaluation and outcome evaluation, to determine the effect of a new program. Ultimately, the gain in pupil growth, as measured by a variety of techniques, was seen as the single most important determinant in measuring the value of any program change.

The chapter concluded with a delineation of 14 basic competencies required of the principal who would be an effective instructional leader.

SUGGESTED ACTIVITIES

1. Using Section 4 of the *Evaluative Criteria* as a guide, assess the quality of the instructional program of a school with which you are familiar.

2. Take a position with regard to a plan for grouping of students. Present a paper substantiating this position through reference to research studies.

3. Utilize the *Task of Public Education* questionnaire in a community to determine parent, teacher, or student expectations for a particular school. Compare the results with those presented in Chapter 4.

4. Design an appropriate educational program for a school in 1985 of any one of the following:
   a. 650 elementary students
   b. 1000 middle or junior high students
   c. 1500 high school students
Stress and justify the major instructional changes that will characterize schools of the 1980s.

5. Apply the model of instructional change to a particular program and determine which measures are essential for both process evaluation and outcome evaluation.

SELECTED REFERENCES

ALEXANDER, WILLIAM M., ed., *The Changing Secondary School Curriculum*, New York, Holt, Rinehart and Winston, 1967.

BLOOM, BENJAMIN S., THOMAS J. HASTINGS, and GEORGE F. MADAUS, eds., *Handbook on Formative and Summative Evaluation of Student Learning*, New York, McGraw-Hill, 1971.

FABER, CHARLES F., and GILBERT F. SHEARRON, *Elementary School Administration: Theory and Practice*, New York, Holt, Rinehart and Winston, 1970, pp. 143–206.

FEYEREISEN, KATHRYN V., et al., *Supervision and Curriculum Renewal: A Systems Approach*, New York, Appleton, 1970, pp. 115–225.

GOODLAD, JOHN I., *School, Curriculum, and The Individual*, Waltham, Mass., Blaisdell, 1966.

HANSEN, JOHN H., and ARTHUR C. HEARN, *The Middle School Program*, Skokie, Ill., Rand McNally, 1971.

KRUG, EDWARD A., *Curriculum Planning*, rev. ed., New York, Harper & Row, 1957.

MCINTYRE, KENNETH E., "Administering and Improving the Instructional Program," in Jack A. Culbertson, Curtis Henson, and Ruel Morrison, eds., *Performance Objectives for School Principals*, Berkeley, Calif., McCutchan, 1974.

NATIONAL STUDY OF SECONDARY EDUCATION, *The Curriculum: Retrospect and Prospect, 70th Yearbook,* Chicago, University of Chicago Press, 1971.

SAYLOR, J. GALEN, and WILLIAM M. ALEXANDER, *Curriculum Planning for Modern Schools,* New York, Holt, Rinehart and Winston, 1966.

TRUMP, J. LLOYD, and DELMAS MILLER, *Secondary School Curriculum Improvement,* Boston, Allyn & Bacon, 1968.

WILSON, L. CRAIG, *The Open Access Curriculum,* Boston, Allyn & Bacon, 1971.

CHAPTER 10
The principal
and the staff

The role of the principal in providing leadership to the professional staff has changed drastically during recent years. As schools have become larger, for example, opportunities for the principal and the teachers to interact have become less frequent and interpersonal relationships have become more formalized. Professional negotiations also have altered substantially the traditional power relationships in the bureaucratic structure of the school.[1] These factors, together with more demanding certification requirements and improved teacher training programs,[2] have generated a feeling of autonomy and self-reliance among teachers who no longer will tolerate a paternalistic principal—even the benevolent one who views himself as the spokesman for "his faculty." This emerging professionalism of teachers holds numerous implications for the leadership role of the principal. The principal who would be the leader of the staff, therefore, must embark on a well-planned staff personnel program designed to enhance the effectiveness and the efficiency of each staff member.

Role theory, which is concerned with the effectiveness and efficiency of each staff member, offers a particularly productive perspective for viewing the principal's functions in orchestrating the complementary components of a well-planned staff personnel program. Because instructional improvement and staff development are intimately entwined, again we are concerned less with the maintenance activities than with the leadership activities of the principal in this domain. These activities may be grouped according to the following five functions: (1) the identification of new staff members—assessing the degree of congruence of the values of the community and objectives of the school with the personal values, needs, and abilities of each prospective staff member; (2) the orientation of new staff members—conducting activities that clarify the major institu-

---

[1] Timothy M. Stinnet, Jack H. Kleinmann, and Martha L. Ware, *Professional Negotiation in Public Education,* New York, Macmillan, 1966; Myron H. Lieberman and M. H. Moskow, *Collective Negotiations for Teachers,* Skokie, Ill., Rand McNally, 1966.

[2] National Commission on Teacher Education and Professional Standards, *A Manual on Certification Requirements for School Personnel in the United States,* Washington, D.C., National Education Association, 1970.

tional role demands; (3) the assignment of staff—ensuring maximum compatibility between the demands of the role and the needs of the individual; (4) the improvement of staff—conducting activities that expand and improve both the role and the abilities of the individual; and (5) the evaluation of staff—assessing the degree to which individuals are performing in accordance with expectations held for the expanded role. Leadership activities of the principal in each of the staff personnel functions are presented in outline form in Figure 10.1 and are described in detail in the sections that follow. The chapter concludes with another set of basic competencies required of the principal in providing leadership to the staff.

Identification of new staff members

Central to the personnel function of any school organization is the identification of professionally qualified personnel who possess the requisite values, attitudes, and abilities to contribute significantly to the realization of organizational goals, while feeling that they are attaining their individual goals. No school can hope to move forward, striving always to expand and refine programs, without a systematic method for identifying prospective teachers, counselors, and other certificated and noncertificated staff members.

Because of teacher mobility, few school systems enjoy the luxury of staff permanence. Even during times of economic stress, teachers continually are seeking more attractive positions both within and outside the field of education. Excellent teachers tend to be upwardly mobile, and this drive can prompt restlessness if promotions or alternatives for role renewal are not forthcoming. Moreover, creative teachers are eager to experiment and to digress from the ordinary. Such a desire can be satisfied in part through their appropriate placement in a dynamic school setting, but occasionally a complete change of environment in a different school system may be necessary.

Administrators must recognize that teacher resignations do not necessarily represent an indictment of recruitment or selection policies and procedures. On the contrary, carefully planned and administered recruitment procedures will often produce quality educators whose need-dispositions may not easily be satisfied through experience in a particular school or school district. In contrast, shoddy recruitment practices can produce a sedentary staff, thereby negating the advantages associated with the employment of new personnel with new ideas. Certainly a degree of permanence is desirable in any organization, but principals have tended to overemphasize the benefits of maintaining a stable staff to the point that low staff turnover statistics are sometimes cited erroneously as

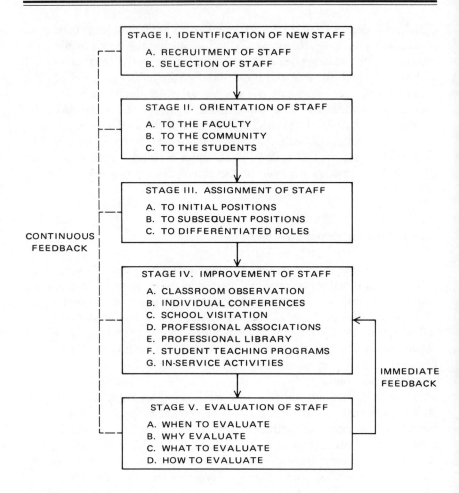

Figure 10.1
Model of the principal's leadership role in staff personnel functions

an index of organizational excellence when in fact the exact opposite may be true. Ironically, the school systems that are the most selective in the employment of staff often experience considerable turnover.

For the present, at least, there appears to be no shortage of teachers. Perhaps indicative of the trend, the 1966–1967 *Education Index* listed two dozen articles related to teacher recruitment. Only three articles were listed for 1972–1973. In urban and suburban areas, especially, job opportunities for elementary and secondary teachers are less plentiful in the 1970s than in the 1960s.[3] Traditionally, urban environments have repre-

---

[3] "Graduates and Jobs: A Grave New World," *Time,* 97 (May 1971), 49–52.

sented more attractive locations for prospective teachers because of higher salaries, increased social opportunities, and proximity to universities and cultural events. Since many urban areas are no longer as attractive, the more remote school districts are now receiving applications from larger numbers of qualified candidates.

The rapid reduction of the teacher shortage can be traced to several factors. Higher salaries and extended fringe benefits have permitted the teaching profession to compete with other occupations in attracting quality candidates.[4] Since the mores of our culture no longer mitigate severely against the married woman who is employed, it is becoming commonplace for one household to include two wage earners as teachers. Thus the advantages of a nine-month working year can be capitalized on, with husband and wife enjoying concurrent vacations.

Irrespective of monetary considerations, teaching is becoming a more attractive profession for other reasons. For young people who possess the postemergent values of social responsibility and moral commitment, teaching offers opportunities to be of genuine help to youth. The desire to help others represents an important consideration for college students in planning a worthwhile career; teaching offers a means of satisfying that desire.

Not to be overlooked in analyzing the abundance of teachers is the declining birthrate. Economic uncertainty, awareness of the population explosion, and advances in techniques of birth control all have contributed to a diminution in the size of American families. Large families are no longer the vogue, and young marrieds have been inclined to postpone child-rearing obligations until their financial status is somewhat secure.

Finally, citizen disenchantment with the output of the schools and the increasing burden of financing the schools have resulted in the defeat of numerous school levies and operational millages. In an attempt to maintain a degree of solvency, some boards of education have been forced to increase pupil-teacher ratios, thereby flooding the market with teachers. Closely allied are taxpayer demands that school districts become more accountable, and, in an attempt to placate, some boards have approved reductions in staff as a cost-saving device.

Whereas it might be expected that the influx of prospective teachers would simplify the personnel function for principals, quite the opposite is true. In the past, during times of the acute teacher shortage, administrators allowed themselves to develop sloppy recruitment and selection procedures because limited numbers of candidates were available. On-the-spot hiring, temporary certification, and misassignment were commonplace—even accepted as necessary or legitimate personnel practices.

---

[4] "The American Public School Teacher," *Research Report 1967-R4,* National Education Association, Washington, D.C., 1967.

With the recent increase in the availability of competent teachers, it is imperative that personnel practices be refined to secure the employment of the best available candidates. Excellent candidates will always be in demand; only through conscientious recruitment and selection efforts will a high-calibre candidate be contracted.

Recruitment and selection of staff

The identification of prospective staff members consists of two complementary phases, and each is unique. The recruitment phase is concerned with establishing a pool of potentially acceptable candidates; the selection phase is concerned with the elimination of candidates whose values, interests, needs, and abilities, having been carefully analyzed, fail to satisfy the requirements for a particular role. A principal's role in the recruitment and selection functions may vary considerably depending on the size of the school system, yet his involvement in the process is crucial.

RECRUITMENT OF STAFF

Establishing a list of prospective employees is a task ordinarily associated with the central office. In large school systems a separate division of staff personnel services has the primary responsibility, whereas in small systems the superintendent assumes or may delegate this function.

Recruitment cannot begin until building principals have assessed their staffing needs for the forthcoming year and have communicated their requests to central office personnel, who may use a variety of techniques in accumulating an adequate number of qualified applicants. Brochures describing the school system and the community, along with data about salary ranges and opportunities for advancement, have been quite effective in attracting interested teachers.

Periodic, prearranged visits by school district personnel to college and university placement offices are an integral part of the recruitment program and should not be neglected simply because of an apparent teacher surplus. In the absence of a personnel director, building principals frequently must visit university placement offices to recruit teachers for the entire system. This practice is not advisable as a rule, because principals may not be aware of the personnel requirements in other buildings; moreover, they do not have sufficient time to prepare for and accurately evaluate their placement agency contacts. Finally, and most importantly, danger exists that the distinctiveness of the two functions—recruitment and selection—may become obscured if principals' involvement in the recruitment process extends further than identifying the positions that will be vacant. Means other than the recruitment interview should be found to provide the principal with productive college and university contacts.

SELECTION OF STAFF

The recruitment and selection functions become clouded if the selection of personnel is not consummated at the building level. Statutory requirements usually specify that the ultimate prerogative of employment rests with the board of education's acting on recommendations from the school superintendent. Such approval, however, may be little more than perfunctory. No one is in a better place than the principal to assess the role demands within the school and to select employees whose need-dispositions are congruent with these demands. As the educational leader of the school, the principal is responsible for assisting each staff member, through a carefully planned program of supervision, to realize his ultimate potential. In that respect, the initial selection of a quality staff is paramount.

The decision to engage in a contractual relationship with a teacher means that the school district is obliged to provide every conceivable resource to help ensure that the contracted teacher will experience success. Careful selection practices will minimize the time and money required to fulfill that responsibility. By direct contrast, some administrators believe that selection is not as crucial because dismissal is relatively easy until teachers have attained tenure status. But dismissal is always costly for the system and for the teacher, and it often has an adverse effect on staff morale and student achievement. In nearly every instance, dismissal proceedings represent an indictment of selection, supervision, or evaluation practices.

The selection of quality staff members is no simple assignment. Teaching is a complex profession, and educators are constantly groping for more sophisticated methods of assessing a person's potential to achieve a positive impact on student growth and achievement by his interactions with students and others. The building principal, because of his daily contact with the total learning environment, is the individual best qualified to assess the extent to which the expectations of a given role are likely to be met by a particular individual. Meaningful participation in the selection of staff, therefore, is a right of the principal that should not be denied.

After the recruitment process has narrowed the number of applicants to a select few, each candidate should be invited to meet with the principal, preferably in the school and at the convenience of both parties. Prior to this meeting, the principal will have had the opportunity to review comments from the recruitment interview, and the candidate will be able to acquire information about the school system. Under these circumstances, the principal can dispense with generalities in the selection interview and concentrate on an in-depth appraisal of the candidate's philosophy, goals, needs, and potential. Equally important at this stage is provision for the candidate to assess the appropriateness of the assignment in terms of his own expectations so that he is equipped to make a sensible choice if a contract is tendered. Free interchange of information between principal and applicant during the selection interview will better prepare each to make an intelligent decision.[5]

After he has met with each of the applicants, the principal must decide which candidate will most nearly satisfy the expectations held for the position. A common failing of principals in this regard is to select teachers whose philosophy of education is closely identified with their own or other faculty members'. Staffing a school with "my kind of teacher" seems to be a career goal of some principals, and having accomplished this, they pride themselves on a smoothly functioning operation. The negative impact of such an orientation, however, is worth consideration. To staff a building with teachers espousing identical philosophies and utilizing similar teaching procedures generates the likelihood of a strict adherence to the status quo. Faculty meetings and curricular councils can become sterile because of the lack of challenge from professionals holding dissimilar value orientations. If only to foster innovation, some degree of philosophic disequilibrium should exist within a school.[6]

Students also can benefit from association with teachers of varying values, personalities, and instructional techniques. Due to increasing mobility of American families, school populations are no longer homogeneous in composition but represent instead a microcosm of society. Within this microcosm is a diverse array of student interests, talents, and abilities. For example, some students relate best to a traditional teacher who may utilize a formal instructional methodology, whereas others respond best to a postemergent teacher who may utilize less structured teaching techniques.[7] Thus the assemblage of divergent personality types within a building creates an environment with which most of the students can identify.

Accurate assessment of teaching potential is an arduous task. Prior to making a final determination, the principal should accumulate a variety

[5] John L. Morris, "Interview: Guidelines for Making It a More Effective Hiring Device," *Clearing House,* 46 (September 1971), 35–39.

[6] William M. Martin, "Role Conflict and Deviant Adaptation as Related to Educational Goal Attainment: A Social Systems Approach," doctoral dissertation, University of California, Los Angeles, 1970.

[7] Gale W. Rose, "Organizational Behavior and Its Concomitants in Schools," *Administrator's Notebook,* 15 (March 1967), 1–4.

of information giving insight into the character and capabilities of each candidate. Transcripts, letters of recommendation, related experiences, ratings during practice teaching, analysis of the recruitment interviews, feedback from interviews with lead teachers or department chairmen, and other useful data must be considered in attempting to identify a potentially successful candidate who will contribute to the achievement of both organization and individual goals. Conscientious efforts in this endeavor will minimize chances of faulty selection and should serve eventually to enhance the morale of the faculty as they begin to realize that the hiring of replacements is a systematic and careful procedure.

Orientation of staff

The orientation of new staff members, sometimes referred to as "induction," is a continuous process that begins with the recruitment interview and lasts throughout an employee's professional association with the school district.[8] Orientation has as its major purpose the transmission and understanding of the major demands of the role as viewed by the principal, other teachers, students, and the community. During the recruitment interview, the candidate is encouraged to ask questions about the school. This information, together with any printed materials, serves as an initial orientation to the district. The recruiter himself may be scrutinized by the candidate, since he represents the district through his verbal and nonverbal behavior.

During the selection process, the candidate also should be invited to spend time with the building principal, department heads or unit leaders, teachers, students, and others in the school. Throughout these contacts, the candidate is orienting himself to the school, trying to determine whether he will accept an offer of employment. The formal orientation process, a responsibility of the building administrator, begins following acceptance of a contract and is directed toward increasing the new employee's knowledge of the expectations held for him by the teaching and administrative staff, the students, and the community.[9]

Many well-intended orientation programs are unfortunately confined to a one-day gathering prior to the opening of school, when newly hired professional staff members are required to report early and are expected, as passive participants, to familiarize themselves with the functions and responsibilities of various organizational components. A more valuable

[8] William B. Castetter, *The Personnel Function in Educational Administration*, New York, Macmillan, 1971, pp. 214–231.

[9] Samuel Hill, "The Development of Criteria for Orientation Programs for New Teachers," doctoral dissertation, University of Virginia, 1961.

orientation program would begin in the spring and continue through summer and fall, thus providing the new employee sufficient time to familiarize himself with the staff, the students, and the community.

ORIENTATION TO THE STAFF

As soon as possible, a new teacher should have opportunities to become acquainted with the members of the faculty with whom he will be working. The teaching staff should accept primary responsibility for this portion of the orientation program which, in a school with many teachers, may continue throughout the first school year. Although new teachers may be quite apprehensive, the staff can countervail these feelings by generating a spirit of acceptance. A new teacher who is aware of each faculty member's unique role in the accomplishment of the school's purposes will be able to identify more readily with the staff and the school.

As we stated earlier, implicit in the tendering of a teaching contract is the objective that the administrative staff will make every effort to assure a successful career for the teacher. Part of the orientation process, then, consists of identifying for the new teacher the function of each administrator at both building and central office levels. Regardless of the size of the system, new teachers should have the opportunity to meet with key administrators and supervisors to sharpen perceptions concerning the assistance that can be furnished by central office personnel.

ORIENTATION TO THE COMMUNITY

Teachers were once expected, or at least encouraged, to reside within the school district in which they were employed. The advantages accruing from this practice are obvious. Through increased association with residents, teachers gain insight into community value orientations, parental expectations for the school, and student concerns and problems. As residents of the community, teachers frequently become involved in a variety of civic functions and find numerous leadership opportunities. Not only is this type of involvement beneficial in fostering positive community attitudes toward the school, it also accommodates the need for social interaction that is characteristic of many teachers.

However, for a variety of reasons—desire for privacy, lack of congruence between community and teacher value systems, emphasis on freedom of choice, and relative ease of travel—many of today's teachers, especially in urban areas, no longer choose to live within the district or the attendance area of their schools. Providing a meaningful community orientation for this type of teacher is very difficult, since some tend to disassociate themselves from the community except during the school day. Through formal and informal community contacts, initiated and coordinated by the principal, teachers should be encouraged to become meaningfully involved in community activities and affairs.

In less populous regions and in schools with active parents' associations, orientation is often provided by interested members of the community; the principal merely facilitates the process. In urban areas and in larger schools where the school's community is not readily identifiable, the principal ordinarily is required to assume the responsibility of orienting the new teacher to the community. Especially important is an identification of the human and physical resources the teacher may wish to utilize during the school year. As the interests of new teachers become apparent to the principal, he should be prepared to suggest organizations, associations, clubs, and social groups in which the faculty may be interested. Despite the potential for interrole conflict on the part of the teacher, community involvement should be encouraged because an active, involved teaching staff can be instrumental in increasing cohesiveness among the various community reference groups, as well as congruence in expectations between the community and the schools.

ORIENTATION TO THE STUDENTS

Often overlooked in the orientation program is provision for the new teacher to become acquainted with the student body. Many times the entire student population is categorized according to generalizations relating to academic orientation or socioeconomic status, and teachers are expected to adjust accordingly. For example, if an applicant raises a question in the employment interview about the academic motivation of the student body, he may receive an answer such as "65 to 70 percent normally go on to college," or "75 percent of our families are upper-middle class." With such statistics, the orientation to the student body presumably is concluded. Instead, the candidate ideally should meet with representative groups of students before signing a contract, thereby judging for himself whether he would be comfortable in a given school. Too often, teachers generalize achievement and behavioral expectations for students based on the type and location of the community without considering the heterogeneity that exists within any student body.

After a contractual agreement has been reached, continued opportunities to meet and talk with students should be provided; in this way the new employee will develop considerable insight into the goals, need-dispositions, strengths, and weaknesses of the entire student body before he begins to teach. During the school year, orientation to the students continues through involvement in the classroom and with the cocurricular program, which allows teachers to observe and work with students in a relaxed, and often less threatening, environment. In addition, new teachers should be encouraged to work with students in community organizations to obtain a more complete perception of student values, interests, and abilities.

Assignment of staff

The major purpose of the assignment process is to ensure a maximum degree of congruence between the expectations for the position vacancy and the personal characteristics of the teacher. Although the probability of assuring appropriate teaching assignments will be maximized if the recruitment and selection processes are treated conscientiously, instances of misassignment of experienced as well as new faculty members must be detected and rectified. If the number of new positions to be filled is minimal, the assignment of teachers is a direct function of the selection process. Often, however, the assignment problem is compounded because the principal may have several teachers to assign in identical or related fields. In the assignment or reassignment process, it is essential that both the major expectations for the institutional role and the personal needs, dispositions, and abilities of the teacher be fully explored and mutually understood.

Figure 10.2 schematically depicts the dynamics of the staff assignment process. In this model, based on role theory, the three essential components to be considered are as follows: the principal's perceptions of the teaching assignment (point A in the diagram); the teacher's perceptions of the teaching assignment (point B); and the teacher's values, abilities, and needs as an individual (point C). Line AB represents agreement between the principal and the teacher about the major parameters of the role; line AC represents the principal's visualization of the degree of role-personality congruence or the compatibility between the role and the teacher; and line BC represents the teacher's perceived estimate of self-role congruence or compatibility. The dotted lines, AA', BB', and CC', represent joint exploration and communication in private conferences concerning the mutual expectations held for the teaching assignment, as well as perceptions of the teacher as a person that are held by both the principal and the teacher. Ideally, these variables will converge during the assignment process (represented by the smaller area of triangle A'B'C') to enhance the role-personality compatibility of the teacher. In such conferences it is essential that openness of communication be maintained to permit consideration of all relevant role and personality elements. After the assignment is made, the role-personality relationship should continue to converge, facilitating a satisfying relationship between the demands of the organization and the needs of the teacher.

PRINCIPAL'S PERCEPTIONS
OF THE TEACHING
ASSIGNMENT

TEACHER'S PERCEPTIONS
OF THE TEACHING
ASSIGNMENT

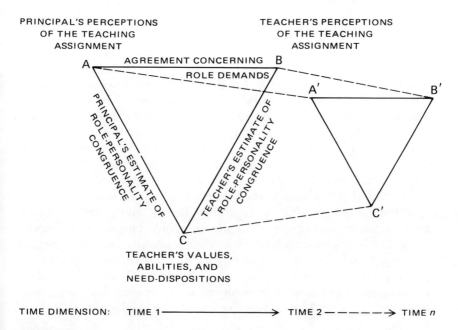

AGREEMENT CONCERNING
ROLE DEMANDS

PRINCIPAL'S ROLE-PERSONALITY CONGRUENCE

TEACHER'S ESTIMATE OF ROLE-PERSONALITY CONGRUENCE

TEACHER'S VALUES,
ABILITIES, AND
NEED-DISPOSITIONS

TIME DIMENSION: TIME 1 ————————————→   TIME 2 — — — — — → TIME n

Figure 10.2
Dynamics of the staff assignment process

ASSIGNMENT OF NEW TEACHERS

Several legal and policy constraints guide the principal's actions in the assignment of new teachers. State certification standards serve as a controlling influence to some extent, but usually they are broad enough to allow considerable flexibility at both elementary and secondary school levels. For example, elementary teachers are not ordinarily certificated by grade level (first, fourth, or fifth) but for a cluster of grades (primary or upper elementary), or typically, for all elementary grades. Similarly, certification at the secondary level is granted in some states by broad fields. Certification in science, for example, might qualify one to teach courses in physics, chemistry, biology, general science, or other fields. Standards adopted by regional accrediting agencies also restrict teacher assignment practices, since association standards sometimes exceed those set for state certification. At the district level, additional requirements may be set through professional negotiations with teacher groups. The principal must be thoroughly familiar with the legal, policy, and procedural limits that regulate assignment practices.

If a new teacher is expected to be successful during his first year, the scope of his role should be reasonable. The practice of awarding the more advanced or "faster" sections to experienced staff members, thereby burdening the new teacher with less advanced or "slower" sections, represents a poor personnel practice that can demoralize a beginning teacher. A more defensible guideline for assigning classes, sections, or students is to allow the new teacher to have instructional opportunities similar in scope to those provided the experienced teachers. Extensive extra duty assignments for new teachers also should be discouraged. Too often, a new faculty member is "awarded" the student council advisorship, safety patrol sponsorship, lunchroom supervision, committee assignments, or other arduous tasks, thereby engendering considerable intrarole conflict because of the inordinate time demanded. Certainly new teachers should assume a fair measure of extra assignments, but not so many that their classroom effectiveness is jeopardized.

Although the principal is responsible for regulating the breadth of the professional role of a new teacher, he should be assisted by experienced faculty members whose responsibilities to the profession include appropriate induction of new colleagues. In some schools, district-wide policies also are helpful in reducing the teachers' interrole conflicts through restrictions on outside employment, supervision of student teachers, or college attendance during the first year of employment.

REASSIGNMENT OF TEACHERS

During the school year it may become apparent that a teacher has been misassigned and might perform at a more acceptable level in another class or section, or even in another school. Teachers who become aware of severe role or role-personality conflicts sometimes tell the principal about their predicament. Serving as a deterrent to such confidences, however, is the natural reluctance to share one's frustration with those who have authority to judge the effectiveness of role performance. Reassignment to correct an apparent misassignment is a delicate matter and should be consummated only after extended consultation with the faculty member involved and with others who may be affected. This course of action is suggested only if the building principal is fairly certain that a change of assignment within the school or to another school will enhance the effectiveness and efficiency of the teacher. Under no circumstances is this procedure to be used if the teacher has demonstrated that he has limited potential for improvement in his role performance. In such cases, dismissal proceedings incorporating legal guidelines are appropriate. Teacher tenure regulations notwithstanding, the principal who passes ineffective teachers on to his colleagues, pretending that reassignment is a panacea for ineffective performance, is guilty of unprofessional conduct.

Less critical, but more frequent, are reassignment requests originating from experienced, competent faculty members who seek a change. Such a request may be prompted by many desires: to apply additional training that has been received, to explore new interests, or to move to what is perceived as a more desirable school. The authorization for intraschool transfers typically rests with the principal, and it may be granted if the principal and the teacher are convinced that the morale and productivity of the individual and the school will not be affected adversely. Inter-school transfers, however, including transfers mandated at the district level, should receive the approval of the receiving principal, as well. The latter should be permitted to learn about the circumstances surrounding the transfer, and he should have the opportunity to interview and observe the teacher in the classroom before reaching a decision. This procedure is especially critical when a teacher is seeking a change in organizational grade levels, such as a transfer from a middle school to a high school or to an elementary school. Success as a teacher at one level does not guarantee success at a different level.

Through the acquisition of additional graduate training, some teachers are able to gain specialized certification, thereby qualifying for positions substantially different from their original assignments. Counselors, instructional media personnel, special education teachers, vocational education coordinators, administrators, and similar professionals are usually recruited from the ranks of experienced teachers who have completed advanced degrees in their fields of specialization. For staff morale purposes, vacancies in these positions at the building level are often filled from within the school; but the principal again must be cautioned against assuming that a successful classroom teacher will perform equally well in several of the aforementioned specialities. By arbitrarily removing from consideration for these positions all teachers from another school or school system, the principal is neglecting his responsibility to staff his building with the best available candidates.

DIFFERENTIATED STAFFING ASSIGNMENTS

School staffs that are differentiated in a hierarchical scheme according to the roles and responsibilities of each teacher represent a unique staffing challenge for the principal.[10] In such arrangements, a team, unit, or group approach to teaching is employed, and a teacher is required to work very closely with members of his own team in planning, implementation, and evaluation. Accordingly, the principal must be informed about the personalities within each team, and he must seek their assis-

[10] *Unit Operations and Roles,* Institute for the Development of Educational Activities, Melbourne, Fla., 1970; *Principal's Handbook,* Institute for the Development of Educational Activities, Melbourne, Fla., 1971.

tance in identifying the type of person who will enhance rather than hinder team progress.[11] The principal, because of his relative objectivity, must exercise the prerogative of final selection and must later provide orientation sufficient to assist the new teacher in becoming a contributing member of the team.

Selecting teachers for more prestigious positions within differentiated staffs is a difficult administrative responsibility. Titles such as team leader, unit leader, master teacher, or resource teacher carry more responsibilities than are required of the typical teacher. Some compensation is awarded ordinarily through a block of released time to complete the responsibilities or through a salary differential. To date, however, these two compensatory practices have not been sufficiently attractive to entice some capable individuals, who are reluctant to assume added responsibilities at the expense of spending less time with students. In those instances, selection of teachers for staff leadership positions can be frustrating to the principal because his identification techniques, however well planned and executed, will have been fruitless. To overcome the reluctance of teachers with recognizable leadership skills to accept positions of responsibility, principals must convince them of the inherent opportunities to have more extensive impact on students while fulfilling the leadership roles.

A variety of models for staff differentiation have been developed and tested.[12] Again, however, we caution against the uncritical acceptance and installation of a differentiated staffing model as a panacea. For example, attention must be paid not only to staff abilities, attitudes, interests, and compatibility, but also to the adequacy of the school building, the availability of supplies and materials, and community understanding and support for the program. Teacher in-service training, building remodeling, and community involvement can enhance the possibility of a successful endeavor; but modifications in any plan may be necessary, especially if the leadership potential within the staff is too limited at a given point to satisfy the intent of the plan.

Whereas assigning a teacher to a team and designating the teacher's

[11] Robert D. Gilberts, "The Interpersonal Characteristics of Teaching Teams," doctoral dissertation, University of Wisconsin, 1961.

[12] Cf. James L. Olivero and Edward G. Buffie, eds., *Educational Manpower*, Bloomington, Indiana University Press, 1970; J. W. Keefe, "Differentiated Staffing: Its Rewards and Pitfalls, Trump Plan and Allen Plan," *National Association of Secondary School Principals Bulletin*, 55 (May 1971), 112–118; Dwight W. Allen, "Differentiated Teaching Staff," *California Education*, 3 (June 1966), 12–15; W. D. Hedges, "Differentiated Teaching Responsibilities in the Elementary School," *National Elementary Principal*, 47 (September 1967), 48–54; Herbert J. Klausmeier et al., *Individually Guided Education and the Multiunit School: Guidelines for Implementation*, Madison, Wisconsin Research and Development Center for Cognitive Learning, University of Wisconsin, Madison, 1971.

role in the hierarchical structure of the team are responsibilities of the building principal, the delineation of intrateam roles is ordinarily a team responsibility. Some teachers are more effective in large group instruction; others, in small group work. Staff assignments should be made in accordance with such personalistic factors. The principal, through supervision, should make certain that the role responsibilities have been assigned logically and equitably. The principal also should understand the potential for latent role and personality conflicts within a team. When conflicts become manifest, he should adjudicate them with dispatch, thus enhancing the complementarity in role-personality relations within the teaching team.

Considerable excitement and enthusiasm have been generated in buildings utilizing differentiated patterns of staffing. However, such positive attitudes can be dissipated quickly if adequate administrative time is not devoted to specifying role expectations, formulating teams, and replacing team vacancies with personnel whose interpersonal needs and dispositions are compatible with other team members and with the team teaching role.[13] In essence, team teaching and other subunit forms of organization simply reveal in microcosm the cruciality of effective recruitment, selection, and placement practices within the school.

Staff improvement

As with program improvement, the improvement of the teaching staff comprises leadership techniques and procedures designed to change the teacher's role performance. Classroom visits, observations, and conferences constitute the core of the staff improvement program. Other components include school visitations, professional associations, the professional library, student teaching supervision, and in-service educational programs.

As indicated earlier, teachers today are better prepared than ever before. Their knowledge of subject matter and their familiarity with pedagogical principles and techniques are generally sound. Despite increased preparation, however, many teachers experience difficulty in relating to today's youth, who have become more curious, more sophisticated, and more demanding in their approach to learning, thereby complicating the teaching function. As one principal observed, "The minute new teachers report to my school, already they are outdated." A major challenge to the principal's leadership, therefore, is to provide a con-

---

[13] William C. Schutz, *FIRO: A Three-Dimensional Theory of Interpersonal Behavior,* New York, Holt, Rinehart and Winston, 1958.

tinuous, systematic program of professional improvement to enhance the effectiveness and the efficiency of teachers within the classroom.

Several impediments to providing leadership in staff improvement should be recognized at the outset. The first concerns recency of classroom experience of principals. Although in an earlier era building administrators were recognized as the "principal" teacher, present principals often have been disassociated from classroom teaching for so long that they no longer feel competent in the instructional function. Except in small schools, the principal is seldom involved in teaching. Ordinarily, he has served previously as assistant principal for several years, and his experiences in that position may not have been directly relevant to the acquisition of expertise in teaching. The longer an educator remains in the position of principal, the harder he must work to remain abreast of recent developments in the teaching-learning process.

Another impediment to the principal's involvement in instructional improvement is the lack of sufficient administrative assistance.[14] The role of the principal has become one of the most demanding in the field of education in terms of time and responsibilities; and unless adequate supportive administrative and specialized help is provided, the principal's time can be consumed with maintenance rather than leadership activities. To be successful, the program of staff improvement must receive primary attention from the principal—attention that requires both competence and time. It is unfortunate that some principals, especially in large schools, have chosen to divorce themselves from direct involvement with the instructional program. In such schools, an assistant principal sometimes has major responsibility for instructional and staff improvement. In schools with differentiated patterns of staffing, for example, team leaders often are instrumental in helping their team or unit members—based on the rationale that they are closer to the classroom and are capable of rendering more expert assistance. But the principal must remember that whereas direct implementation of the program may be delegated to others, it is he who is ultimately responsible for the success or failure of both instructional and staff improvement.

Another limitation to leadership in staff improvement is the erroneous assumption that the principal should be technically competent in all teaching fields. Some teachers hesitate to accept the assistance of the principal who, as a generalist, may be relatively uninformed about recent content and technological developments in a specific curricular field. In this regard, however, the principal should be able to mobilize and capi-

[14] *The Elementary School Principalship in 1968,* Washington, D.C., Department of Elementary School Principals, National Education Association, 1968, pp. 46–52; J. Lloyd Trump et al., "Principal's Role in Improving Instruction," *National Association of Secondary School Principals Bulletin,* 51 (May 1967), 77–90.

talize on the services of subject supervisors and coordinators from outside and inside the school district. In larger districts, central office consultants can be a valuable resource for the principal; but unless their roles have been closely defined as supportive or consultative, considerable role conflict may exist regarding who is responsible for providing leadership in staff improvement. It is our view that the primary responsibility for a teacher improvement program rests with the principal because of his immediate availability, his understanding of the needs of the teachers and the student body, and his knowledge of consultative resources that may be made available to assist teachers through a variety of staff improvement programs.

CLASSROOM VISITATION

At the very core of any plan to improve instruction is a well-planned and systematic program of classroom visitation.[15] For the principal to be of assistance to any teacher, he must know what goes on in the classroom. Of course the principal receives informal and indirect feedback concerning the climate of instruction and the quality of teaching from students, parents, and other teachers and from his observations as he moves through the building, but these cannot substitute for direct visits, observations, conferences, and consultations with each teacher.

As Argyris has stressed, all organizational role incumbents desire increased opportunities for variety, creativity, and complexity in their role responsibilities.[16] Few teachers have to be convinced of the importance of classroom visitation as a means for helping them achieve increased role effectiveness. Classroom visits should be designed within a framework that permits differences in teaching methodologies, emphasizes creative approaches to teaching, and recognizes effective teaching performance.

Some principals, even though they acknowledge the value of classroom visitation, are reluctant to engage in a systematic program whereby all faculty members are visited periodically; instead, they rely on the premise that they are "on call" if the teachers request assistance. Such behavior would be defensible if all teachers were adept at self-diagnosis and if they were disposed to alert administrators to self-identified deficiencies. In reality, however, the more competent teachers often dominate the principal's time, since they are quick to seek approval of the administration for their successful efforts. Meanwhile, the teachers most in need of help keep plodding along, ignored.

[15] *Evaluation of Classroom Instruction, Research Report 1964-R-14*, Washington, D.C., National Education Association, 1964.

[16] Chris Argyris, *Integrating the Individual and the Organization*, New York, Wiley, 1964.

Analogous to the "on-call" syndrome is the antiquated "open-door" mode, which for many years was considered an excellent leadership style. Subscribing to this view, a principal typically waited for problems to develop and then, in a congenial, friendly manner, welcomed discussion of these problems, usually in his office. The modern principal cannot afford to be trapped into this mode of operation. Instead, he should be out of his office engaged in direct observation, diagnosis, and interaction concerning every phase of the school program. Contemporary transactional leadership styles necessitate an "open mind" rather than an "open door" policy.

The program of classroom visitation involves several facets, including the following: preparation for the program, previsit conferences, observation visits, and postvisit conferences.

PREPARING THE FACULTY. A new principal, or a principal recognizing for the first time the necessity and importance of classroom visitation, must exercise great care to create within the staff a receptive climate for the visitation program. This is especially important in schools where previous poor practices have conditioned the teachers to accept the "snoopervisory" role of the principal as a necessary misfortune. The principal should assure the staff that any supervisory program has as its main objective the cooperative assessment and enhancement of teaching effectiveness and efficiency and that he subsequently will deploy sufficient resources to maximize the potential of each teacher. Obviously, these objectives are predicated on the assumption that all teachers possess untapped potential and the principal and the individual teacher working in concert can provide the conditions whereby that potential may be realized. For teachers who view classroom visitation as a device ordinarily employed by principals to determine whether new teachers should be granted tenure or whether other teachers should be granted merit, this alternative viewpoint is refreshing.

A principal who incorporates within his philosophy of instructional improvement a commitment to cooperation between administrator and teacher should feel less apprehensive about classroom visitations. He must not feel impotent merely because his training and experience have not included each of the grade levels and subject fields of the faculty. His purpose is not to explain "how to teach" but to identify with the teacher means by which instructional effectiveness can be improved. When the staff becomes aware of this purpose, the chances of the principal's being perceived as a threat to their professional status should be lessened.

THE PREVISIT CONFERENCE. Before observing the teacher in the classroom setting, the principal must engage him in a previsit conference to identify cooperatively the goals, objectives, and purposes of a particular unit of instruction. The behavioral or performance objectives for the learners should be reviewed,[17] and the methodology for attaining these objectives should be discussed and analyzed. Behavioral objectives are particularly helpful because they emphasize what is to be learned rather than what is to be taught. Depending upon the objectives of the unit, an appropriate observational methodology should be analyzed and agreed upon mutually.

Objective assessment and classification of the verbal and nonverbal behavior of classroom participants through use of an interaction analysis instrument permit a teacher to compare what he wants to accomplish with a nonthreatening objective summation of his spontaneous behavior.[18] Such analysis, therefore, might be appropriate.[19] If the teacher and principal are concerned about style of presentation and mannerisms, a videotape recorder can be of considerable value. Finally, an exceptionally useful supervisory approach involves the use of microteaching techniques, which enable a teacher to view a model of a particular teaching skill, practice the skill in the teaching situation, critique the results, and practice the skill again, if warranted.[20] If objectives are written in measurable terms, the effectiveness of a lesson or unit can be judged partially through student performance. Regardless of the observational techniques deemed appropriate for a particular unit, the principal is obliged not to introduce new or extraneous assessment procedures during the visit.[21]

Depending on the teaching unit and the types of observational tools to be applied, the length of the observation visit may vary. Too frequently, only a single class session or part of a class session is observed, when in reality an accurate appraisal of teaching effectiveness would require a longer period of time. During the previsit conference, the teacher and principal should decide on the time and duration of the visit and establish a time for the postvisit conference, which should be held as soon as possible following completion of the observation.

The previsit conference can be instrumental in allaying teacher apprehension of the forthcoming visit and can provide the principal with

[17] Norman E. Gronlund, *Stating Behavioral Objectives for Classroom Instruction,* New York, Macmillan, 1970.

[18] Edmund J. Amidon and John B. Hough, *Interaction Analysis: Theory, Research and Application,* Reading, Mass., Addison-Wesley, 1967.

[19] Cf. Ned A. Flanders, *Analyzing Teaching Behavior,* Reading, Mass., Addison-Wesley, 1970.

[20] W. D. Johnson, "Microteaching: A Medium in Which to Study Teaching," *High School Journal,* 51 (November 1967), 85–92.

[21] William H. Lucio and John D. McNeil, *Supervision—A Synthesis of Thought and Action,* 2nd ed., New York, McGraw-Hill, 1969, p. 250.

an orientation to the staff member's approach to teaching—a necessary ingredient if the observation and feedback are to be effective. This, of course, is in direct contrast to the utilization of random classroom visits as a primary means for identifying instructional problems. The principal who "drops in" to classrooms unannounced is at a distinct disadvantage. He is able neither to assess accurately the objectives of a lesson nor to judge adequately the effectiveness of the teacher.

THE OBSERVATION VISIT. If the principal and the teacher have agreed on the objectives of the unit of instruction, the method of assessing the effectuation of the objectives, and the time and duration of the observational visit during the previsit conference, the actual observation should not be disturbing to the teacher. The principal should remain inconspicuous during the visit, avoiding involvement in the lesson. When students and teachers become accustomed to periodic classroom visits by the building administrator, they soon respond as though the class were not being observed. Important, too, is the realization for students that the principal visits the classroom because he is vitally concerned about their educational development and that he is not merely the "enforcer of rules." A visible principal is perceived by both teachers and students as a concerned and interested principal.

If videotaping is not used, the checklist has several advantages as an observational tool. Teacher behavior can be coded systematically, and the completed instrument provides an objective assessment of the teacher's performance. During the postobservation conference, the completed instrument is a logical point of departure for a mutual appraisal of teaching effectiveness. Conversely, if the checklist is quite extensive and demands considerable attention during the visit, opportunity for free observation will be limited. Extensive writing should be avoided during the visit because of the anxiety it may create for students or the teacher. The principal may wish to allow time immediately following the visit to commit to writing salient features of the observed lesson. This practice is especially critical if a checklist is not utilized.

The principal also should carefully refrain from giving nonverbal cues relating to the effectiveness of the observed lesson. In this regard we are reminded of the following comments made by one of our youngsters: "The principal visited our class today for a whole hour! I thought things were okay, but he must not have thought so because he frowned and scowled the whole time."

THE POSTVISIT CONFERENCE. The postvisit conference, conducted as soon as possible after the visit, is for the mutual determination of the effectiveness of the lesson in terms of the preestablished goals. Just as the principal reserves time directly following the observation to write down his reactions to the visit, the teacher, too, should be given time to reflect on the students' responses during the lesson. Often teachers are adept at analyzing the effectiveness of their own instructional techniques and may be able to provide a self-evaluation that is quite objective and insightful.

If it is determined that the presentation failed to accomplish the stated objectives, two courses of action are apparent. Careful analysis of the objectives may reveal that they were inappropriate for the purpose of the particular unit; in that case the objectives could be restated and these aspects of the unit could be repeated and again observed.[22] If, however, the objectives were logical and deemed attainable, the teacher should be assisted in identifying and utilizing additional resources to accommodate the task. The principal may wish to make suggestions about performance and enlist the assistance of central office or outside curriculum consultants to furnish special expertise for the teacher. At this juncture, consultant knowledge of the appropriateness of objectives and of the methodology to attain those objectives can be indispensable.

The postvisit conference has as its goal the formulation of a plan for improving the teacher's effectiveness in the classroom. As instructional leader, the principal is responsible for the development and coordination of the plan, but his degree of personal involvement may vary depending on the size of the school system and on the available resources. In a small school system, lacking varied resources ordinarily found in larger systems, the principal's direct involvement may be extensive.

The plan just outlined for improving instruction through use of classroom observation requires an extended commitment of time from the principal. This commitment is vital, moreover, if staff attitudes toward the observation process are to be favorable. Superordinate administrators sometimes must be convinced of the importance of this responsibility and, if adequate supportive administrative help is not provided, priorities must be established reflecting the importance of the staff improvement dimension of the principal's role. Since personnel costs consume the largest share of a school's budget, and since student learning is the first order of business for any school, the improvement of instruction should receive top priority from the principal, who is ultimately accountable for organizational effectiveness and individual efficiency. To implement a systematic method of classroom observation constituting the nucleus of the staff improvement program, the principal must have sufficient time and assistance at his disposal. To deny him such resources is to minimize his potential as an instructional leader.

ADDITIONAL COMPONENTS OF THE STAFF IMPROVEMENT PROGRAM

Although the classroom observation process represents the principal ingredient of a staff improvement program, concentration on this aspect

[22] Lucio and McNeil, op. cit., pp. 249–250.

at the expense of other pertinent components would be unfortunate. Listed below are additional elements of a comprehensive program designed to improve teaching performance:

1. Intraschool and interschool visitation
2. Professional organizations
3. The professional library
4. Student teacher programs
5. In-service programs

INTRASCHOOL AND INTERSCHOOL VISITATION. Teacher training institutions, with their emphasis during the clinical experience on "learning by doing," typically give the neophyte few opportunities for observation of professionals other than the supervising teacher. During contractual employment, the restrictiveness of teaching assignments also serves as a deterrent to peer observation, except in schools that have adopted differentiated staffing arrangements.

The value of an intraschool visitation program is clear. Teachers are exposed to varied styles of teaching behavior and can discuss, with those observed, the perceived merits of particular methods, materials, and procedures. In this way the teacher gains access to several viable role models. Instructional techniques that have resulted in enthusiastic student response are often emulated and subsequently diffused throughout the school. Also, teachers become more aware of total school and subunit goals, thereby developing a greater degree of empathy with others and a stronger identification with the total mission of the school.

Opportunities also are provided in intraschool visitation to view students in contrasting academic environments. Since students perform at varying levels, depending on teacher expectations and the type of instruction to which they are exposed, intraschool observation enables a teacher to understand better the learning processes of individual students. Such understanding is helpful in planning programs of individualized instruction.

The interschool visit (both within and outside a school district) is also a valuable method for alerting teachers to successful organizational patterns, instructional arrangements, educational materials, and teaching techniques. In many forward-looking school systems, teachers are entitled to at least one interschool visitation day per semester or year. Such programs possess merit for both the sending and the receiving schools. Teachers in the receiving school are able to share knowledge and experiences with understanding colleagues. Teachers from the sending school are likewise exposed to fresh ideas, which they subsequently can disseminate in their school.

Although in many of the interschool visitation programs the teacher is required to visit a comparable teaching site and position, consideration should be given, as well, to instituting teacher exchanges between vertical organizational levels. Ordinarily, neither secondary nor elementary teachers are cognizant of the goals, methodologies, and role expectations at organizational levels other than their own. These exchanges can serve to enhance vertical curricular planning and implementation.

PROFESSIONAL ORGANIZATIONS. Through membership in professional organizations related to their instructional fields, teachers are able to keep abreast of the latest developments and research findings and are provided with numerous occasions to be of service to the profession. Opportunities exist within organizations for the development of leadership skills, and teachers should be encouraged to avail themselves of these opportunities.

If possible, and especially when positions of leadership have been assumed by faculty members, professional leave time should be granted to teachers for participation in organization meetings, and there should be appropriate public acknowledgment of the leadership involvement. Reviews of conferences, institutes, and workshops should be duplicated and distributed to other faculty members; meetings of particular relevance might be discussed during staff meetings.

THE PROFESSIONAL LIBRARY. During pre-service training, prospective teachers become accustomed to utilizing a wealth of information pertaining to professional education. After graduation, however, the teacher may locate in a district that is far from a major education library. An adequate professional library within the school can help teachers keep track of current developments and research in the field of education. Continuous exposure to new ideas will give faculty members fresh insights into their own effectiveness.

School librarians can be of considerable help in providing an adequate professional collection. They should assume responsibility for assembling professional materials, as well as for reproducing and distributing pertinent research articles to the staff. A separate financial account for the professional library should be established. Provisions for a professional library are sometimes specified in negotiated teacher–school board master agreements; but too frequently the provision is satisfied by the acquisition of a few books, perfunctorily selected. The principal and the staff must view the establishment and maintenance of a quality professional library as an integral part of the total program of professional improvement.

STUDENT TEACHER PROGRAMS. Possibly the most important component of the pre-service teacher training program is the clinical experience, usually referred to as student teaching, practice teaching, or intern teaching.[23] Of course the success of student teaching programs depends on the willingness of schools to provide training stations supervised by critic teachers who are competent in diagnosing a student teacher's growth. Many school districts have capitalized on the advantages of early identification of potentially dynamic teachers by rewarding outstanding student teachers with offers of full-time employment. The major benefit of student teaching, however, is the exchange of ideas that occurs between faculty members and student teachers, who often bring vitality and fervor to teaching. Since the student teachers' idealism has not yet been tempered by the realities of practice, their enthusiasm can be instrumental in creating a more favorable learning climate within the school.

Direction of the student teacher training program should receive careful supervision by the principal. The staff members selected as critic teachers should realize that the legal responsibility for instruction rests with the contracted teacher, even though the student teacher may be delegated to do some instruction. The education of students, not the training of prospective teachers, is the first priority of the school; therefore, the critic teacher is expected to supervise continually the planning, implementation, and evaluation efforts of the trainee. Experienced teachers who accept the responsibility of supervising a student teacher but fail to provide continuous assistance and direction are guilty of malpractice. Parents and students have a right to expect that classroom learning activities will be either conducted or carefully directed by the certificated professional legally assigned to the class or section.

Providing meaningful training experiences for student teachers entails considerable effort by principals and teachers. The major justifications for this increased expenditure of time and effort are (1) that the exchange of ideas between trainees and teachers will be beneficial to the school, and (2) that performance standards for teachers will be continuously upgraded in the future.

IN-SERVICE EDUCATION. There is little agreement regarding the elements that constitute an in-service education program. Some erroneously limit the concept to activities involving an entire staff or school system. For example, negotiated agreements often contain provisions for a stated number of in-service days, thereby implying that in-service programs focus on group rather than individual growth. This specialized usage of the term "in-service" is unfortunate because it implies that the in-service needs of teachers can be satisfied through organized group involvement.

[23] James Bryant Conant, *The Education of American Teachers*, New York, McGraw-Hill, 1964.

Consequently, teachers and administrators often refer to an "in-service day" when the total faculty meets to attack a problem or to be exposed to ideas, innovations, or research. Even less effective are in-service meetings that drag into the dinner hour because they were scheduled on top of the regular school day, largely as an ancillary program.

In our view, in-service education includes all professional development activities in which one engages after initial certification and employment and does not conclude until there is a termination of services. It is primarily an individual matter. Hence the insights necessary for professional improvement are obtained from such sources as one's professional interactions with administrators and other organizational role incumbents, as well as the personal pursuit of more effective instructional techniques through travel and enrollment in courses.

Ideally, the in-service program should focus on remedying identified weaknesses in an individual's pre-service program. The new teacher and the principal together should identify a corrective course of action in terms of individual needs. Thus in-service education complements rather than duplicates pre-service programs. On occasion, an entire staff recognizes a common pre-service preparation deficiency or needs to be updated concerning emerging theory and practice. In such instances, the involvement of the faculty in identifying, planning, and conducting relevant programs is essential. The principal, as leader of the staff, assists in the identification of needs and the provision of programs to meet those needs.

Staff evaluation

The evaluation of teaching personnel involves judging the extent to which the procedures and processes utilized are accomplishing the specified outcomes. Therefore, both staff evaluation and instructional evaluation are aspects of the total evaluative process. In the preceding chapter, instructional evaluation focused specifically on assessing change in the behavior of the learners; in the sections that follow, we concentrate on assessing change in the behavior of the teachers.

The process of staff evaluation includes attention to the following: (1) the timing of evaluation—"when" to evaluate; (2) the purposes of evaluation—"why" evaluate; (3) the information to be collected—"what" to evaluate; (4) the instruments to be utilized—"how" to evaluate.

WHEN TO EVALUATE

Educators have been told for so many years that evaluation is a continuous process, that unfortunately it has become a meaningless incantation. Yet surely staff evaluation is a never-ending process that begins with the initial contract and continues through termination of employment. Although principals continually form impressions of the competency of teachers, all too often they ignore these process judgments, tending to equate staff evaluation with the mandatory if not perfunctory completion of an evaluative form that expresses summary judgments of outcomes at the end of year.

Instead of viewing staff evaluation as a single entity, the principal should see it as consisting of multiple activities. For example, the principal and the teacher should meet early in the school year to review the goals for the year and the expectations for the teacher. Then evaluative sessions are necessary throughout the year to determine how well proposed goals are being achieved, expectations met, and individual needs fulfilled. Final evaluation, near the close of the school year, is therefore summative and will produce less discord, since formative evaluation already has been employed. In subsequent years, new goals and expectations will be proposed, to allow the teacher to continue to grow professionally and personally.

Bolton has developed a particularly useful model depicting the evalu-

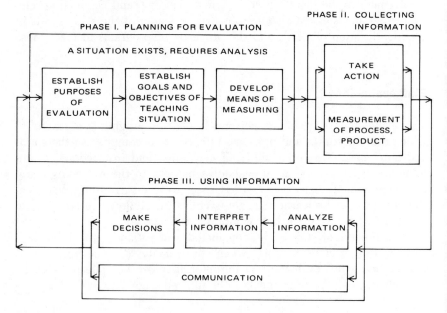

Figure 10.3

Evaluation of school processes and products: a three-phase, cyclical process

SOURCE: Dale L. Bolton, "Evaluating School Processes and Products: A Responsibility of School Principals," in Jack A. Culbertson, Curtis Henson, and Ruel Morrison, eds., *Performance Objectives for School Principals*, Berkeley, Calif., McCutchan, 1974.

ation of school processes and products as a three-phase process (see Figure 10.3).[24] Because judgments are based on information collected and because this information should be purposeful, he suggests that evaluation consists of the following phases:

Phase I.   PLANNING FOR EVALUATION—which involves analysis of a specific situation, establishment of purposes for evaluation, setting of specific goals and objectives, and deciding on means for measuring the processes used and the eventual outcomes;

Phase II.   COLLECTING INFORMATION—which involves observation and monitoring of the activity planned; and

Phase III. USING INFORMATION—which includes communication regarding the analysis and interpretation of information as well as making decisions regarding next steps to be taken.[25]

As indicated throughout this chapter, these phases are sequential and cyclical, repeating themselves in iterative fashion, each building on information and activities of the prior phase. Thus the information analyzed during each phase serves as the basis for the next. Moreover, the final phase (reviewing the situation and resetting goals) serves as a natural prelude to the first and to repetition of the entire cycle.

WHY EVALUATE

Since the single salary schedule ensures equal monetary rewards for staff members (depending on years of training and experience) regardless of the quality of their performance, the skeptic may ask, "Why evaluate?" Although teacher evaluations are not ordinarily used to determine salary increases, even though such a plan has considerable merit, there are numerous compelling reasons why principals should implement a viable program of performance appraisal. Bolton has stated that the major reasons for evaluation include the following:

1. To change goals or objectives
2. To modify procedures
3. To determine new ways of implementing procedures
4. To improve performance of individuals
5. To supply information for modification of assignments
6. To protect individuals or the school system
7. To reward superior performance
8. To provide a basis for career planning and individual growth and development

[24] Dale L. Bolton, "Evaluating School Processes and Products," in Jack A. Culbertson, Curtis Henson, and Ruel Morrison, eds., *Performance Objectives for School Principals,* Berkeley, Calif., McCutchan, 1974.

[25] Ibid.

9. To validate the selection process
10. To facilitate self evaluation.[26]

Bolton further suggested that many problems may be avoided by openly discussing all purposes, rather than allowing some to be considered as a hidden agenda, only to emerge during the decision phase of the evaluation process.[27] Moreover, the goals of the individual teacher must be compatible with the teaching unit or department; these must be compatible with schoolwide goals, which must be compatible with school district goals, if the system is to operate rationally. Therefore, agreements must be reached on the appropriateness of goals and the purposes for evaluation. In reaching such agreement, the communicative distance between and among complementary organizational role incumbents should be reduced through free, open, and frequent discussions of "why evaluate."

WHAT TO EVALUATE

As our friend and colleague, the late Arvil S. Barr, used to say, "If we could just reach agreement on what to evaluate, then merit pay for teachers would be a simple matter." What to evaluate is a perennial problem to which educators have directed sustained research efforts without reaching a satisfactory consensus.[28] There is much debate over the nature of the stereotypic personalistic syndrome required for effective and efficient teaching, and this concern is appropriate if the idiographic dimension of behavior is to be maximized. By the use of a personalistic or traitist approach, however, agreement has been reached in many schools about the desirable personal qualities for a teacher in that school.

Generally, it is agreed that ability to teach is the most important criterion.[29] Everyone defines this ability in his own way, but we do know that the specific behaviors on a teacher rating scale are much less important than the cooperation that has occurred between the principal and the teachers in choosing, defining, describing, and devising a means for assessing the behaviors. Often, too, in addition to teaching effectiveness (however defined), the personal qualities, nature of interpersonal involvement, and extent of professional growth are evaluated.

[26] Ibid.

[27] Ibid.

[28] Cf. Arvil S. Barr et al., "Measurement and Prediction of Teacher Effectiveness," *Review of Educational Research*, 25 (June 1955), 261–269; Arvil S. Barr, "Teaching Competencies," *Encyclopedia of Educational Research*, rev. ed., New York, Macmillan, 1950, pp. 1453–1454.

[29] *Evaluating Teaching Performance*, Bethesda, Md., ERIC Clearinghouse on Educational Administration, 1971.

HOW TO EVALUATE

Once the principal and the teachers have agreed about what to evaluate, the determination and utilization of instrumentation for evaluation are relatively simple matters. Rating scales and checklists have proved to be appropriate, but of course the items must be agreed on in advance. Moreover, the scales should be flexible enough to include the evaluation of such specialized staff members as counselors and athletic coaches, whose services do not always lend themselves to the use of the instruments designed for teachers.

Whenever a principal is uncertain of a teacher's capabilities or contributions, he may tend to cluster the ratings near the midpoint of the scale. Central tendency can be avoided, however, through greater familiarity with the teacher's behavior or by using a group appraisal system that includes other administrators, unit leaders, or teachers in the building. Group evaluative procedures, including assessments by assistant principals and department heads, have been effective in some schools because they lessen the impact of one person's bias.

The use of rating scales merits another caution. In an attempt to balance the number of high evaluations with low evaluations, some principals tend to score inexperienced teachers lower than those with more experience. Such appraisals may, of course, be accurate. Too often, however, beginning teachers receive low ratings with the unjustifiable excuse that they "still have a good deal to learn," thereby implying erroneously that experienced teachers have developed to their full potential. This mode of rating is inaccurate and should be avoided.

An additional flaw to be guarded against is the "halo effect"—the inclination to rank all items for one teacher favorably because of one outstanding characteristic. In rating, principals should pay careful attention to each individual item. A teacher's demonstrated superiority in one or two categories should not mask the need for improvement on other items. It is equally important that the principal avoid the tendency to attribute merit on the basis of factors other than those on the scale. For example, the principal often forms close and lasting friendships with teachers over time; but evaluations of role performance should not be unduly influenced by such relationships.

Appraisal of the total performance of a staff member is a difficult, time-consuming undertaking. Some teachers address themselves to the challenges of their profession with a flair that attracts attention to their endeavors. Others, equally effective but more reserved, always perform in a quiet and competent manner—almost unnoticed by the principal. Close attention to the procedures utilized for evaluation should result in an even mode of application to the entire staff.

Regardless of the problems connected with staff evaluation, informed decision making dictates its necessity. If staff members participate actively in determining "why," "when," "what," and "how" to evaluate, the process should result in higher quality decisions when the data are utilized for staff improvement.

Competencies in improving staff personnel services

Several specific competencies are required of the principal in providing effective leadership of the staff. These competencies, which relate to each stage of the staff personnel function, are set forth below:

STAGE I. IDENTIFICATION OF NEW STAFF

Competency No. 1.   The principal defines the specific role requirements for each position vacancy.

Competency No. 2.   The principal interviews and selects from identified candidates the staff member best qualified for each position and recommends appointment.

STAGE II. ORIENTATION OF STAFF

Competency No. 3.   The principal coordinates the orientation of new staff members to the school system, the staff, the student body, and the community.

STAGE III. ASSIGNMENT OF STAFF

Competency No. 4.   The principal assesses the degree of congruence between expectations for the role and the need-dispositions of the individual.

Competency No. 5.   The principal assigns new staff members to optimize the achievement of both organizational goals and the goals of individual staff members.

Competency No. 6.   The principal reassigns experienced staff members to positions and roles to permit the attainment of organizational and individual goals.

Competency No. 7.   The principal articulates and coordinates individual and subunit goals and programs with school and school system goals and programs.

STAGE IV. STAFF IMPROVEMENT

Competency No. 8.   The principal engages in development activities designed to update his professional knowledge and skills related to educational and administrative processes.

Competency No. 9.   The principal conducts a systematic program of staff improvement through classroom observation and conferences with staff.

Competency No. 10. The principal organizes such staff improvement activities as school visitation, professional activities, the professional library, student teaching programs, and in-service activities.

Competency No. 11. The principal guides each staff member toward selective involvement in staff improvement activities.

Competency No. 12. The principal assesses group and individual in-service educational activities and recommends ways of improving them.

STAGE V. EVALUATION OF STAFF

Competency No. 13. The principal involves the staff in reaching agreement on the purposes of evaluation and the procedures to be utilized.

Competency No. 14. The principal collects, organizes, and analyzes data concerning the processes and products of teaching.

Competency No. 15. The principal bases his decisions on specific evaluative data.

Summary

In this chapter, a carefully designed program to enhance the role performance of each staff member was posited as a major leadership responsibility of the principal. Five basic components or stages of a viable staff improvement program were presented and discussed. Staff identification was viewed as including the dual activities of recruitment and selection. The principal's involvement in selection of staff was described as a crucial first step in the staff personnel function. The orientation of new teachers was defined as including activities designed to assist the staff to become familiar with significant others—teachers, students, and the community—for all share in the orientation process. The third stage, staff assignment, was considered in terms of role theory, wherein one tries to maximize the degree of compatibility between the normative demands of the organization and the personal values, needs, and abilities of the individual. There was considerable emphasis on the core of the staff personnel program—the improvement of staff—and practical suggestions were made concerning classroom visits and conferences, school visitations, professional organizations, the professional library, student teacher programs, and other in-service activities. The final component, evaluation, was viewed in terms of a theoretical model designed to indicate "when," "why," "what," and "how" to evaluate staff performance.

The chapter concluded with a list of 15 competencies required of the principal in providing leadership to the staff.

SUGGESTED ACTIVITIES

1. Visit a college or university placement office, and with the help of placement officials, identify school systems or employers who utilize effective recruitment procedures. What contributes to the effectiveness?

2. Interview a college supervisor of student teaching to determine his expectations for an excellent program of clinical experiences for teachers.

3. Compare the performance appraisal systems in business and industry with those used in elementary and secondary education.

4. Utilize a classroom interaction analysis instrument to code the verbal interaction between teacher and students in a classroom. Analyze the results, and if possible discuss them with the teacher.

5. Develop or critique an instrument to evaluate a year's performance of a teacher in a school of your choosing. Distribute the instrument to classmates for criticisms, comparisons, and suggestions.

SELECTED REFERENCES

BOLTON, DALE L., "Evaluating School Processes and Products," in Jack A. Culbertson, Curtis Henson, and Ruel Morrison, eds., *Performance Objectives for School Principals*, Berkeley, Calif., McCutchan, 1974.

CASETTER, WILLIAM B., *The Personnel Function in Educational Administration*, New York, Macmillan, 1971.

EYE, GLEN G., and LANORE A. NETZER, *School Administration and Instruction*, Boston, Allyn & Bacon, 1969.

FAWCETT, CLAUDE W., *School Personnel Administration*, New York, Macmillan, 1964.

FLANDERS, NED A., *Analyzing Teaching Behavior*, Reading, Mass., Addison-Wesley, 1970.

GWYNN, JOHN MINOR, *Theory and Practice of Supervision*, New York, Dodd, Mead, 1965.

HARRISON, RAYMOND H., *Supervisory Leadership in Education*, New York, American Book, 1968, pp. 253–298.

LUCIO, WILLIAM H., and JOHN D. MCNEIL, *Supervision: A Synthesis of Thought and Action*, 2nd ed., New York, McGraw-Hill, 1969.

SERGIOVANNI, THOMAS J., and ROBERT J. STARRATT, *Emerging Patterns of Supervision: Human Perspectives*, New York, McGraw-Hill, 1971, pp. 105–154.

UNRUH, ADOLPH, and HAROLD E. TURNER, *Supervision for Change and Innovation*, Boston, Houghton Mifflin, 1970.

WILES, KIMBALL, *Supervision for Better Schools*, 3rd ed., Englewood Cliffs, N.J., Prentice-Hall, 1967.

CHAPTER 11
The principal and the students

The change in student attitudes from passive acceptance to active involvement in decisions concerning their educational growth has altered considerably the traditional role of the principal vis-à-vis the students. In some communities, for example, student representatives are now elected to the board of education. In other schools, students are contributing members of curriculum councils and committees. Still elsewhere, the principal's office is the target for student conduct that in less strident times would have been considered atypical, if not inappropriate. These and other active manifestations of student values and needs create powerful internal demands for change in the school and the student's role in it. At the same time, external demands are being made by many citizens for institutional stability (or even rigidity) to alter student values, roles, and behavior. As the leader of the school, the principal must initiate changes in the organization to ensure that both the needs of the students and the needs of the community are met.

Nowhere is change in the student role more evident than in recent court rulings—particularly those related to the sacred American value of individualism. Especially notable for the principal are interpretations of compulsory school attendance laws and regulations governing student control and discipline, due process, and freedom of expression. It is important, therefore, that principals understand, accept, and behave in accordance with current legal definitions of their students' Constitutional rights and privileges.

In this chapter we first stress that the principal must develop a greater understanding of today's students. Values theory provides one basis for developing such understanding. Next it is stressed that the principal must take significant steps to involve students actively and meaningfully in educational planning and programming. Decision theory is the basis for planning such involvement, and the cocurricular program and student government are ready vehicles. Then we note the need for improving the guidance and other student personnel services. The principal's role in initiating needed improvements can be examined on the basis of leadership theory. The chapter concludes with a review of societal values as expressed in court decisions on student rights, of which the principal should be aware.

Student-school values

It was indicated in Chapter 4 that today's postemergent secular values, which are subscribed to by many students, may be broadly described in terms of an ethic of social responsibility, relevance, personal authenticity, and moral commitment.[1] In a word, today's student is "with it." Concerns about world conditions, one's fellow man, "for real" behavior, and social injustice immediately become the criteria against which the policies, programs, and personnel of the schools are assessed by students. Historically, however, the schools have operated with the view of students as lower organizational participants—placid recipients of educational programs conceived, organized, and implemented by those who give little attention to student values, concerns, suggestions, or advice. Small wonder, therefore, that during the 1968–1969 school year alone more than 2000 high schools experienced walkouts, sit-ins, boycotts, and other manifestations of student dissatisfaction and unrest.[2] Although such incidents of student activism have abated, the phenomenon is symptomatic of the need for greater understanding of mutual value orientations between the students, on the one hand, and the school, on the other.

Figure 11.1 schematically represents some of the major value interactions of the student and the school as an institution. The model is a somewhat inaccurate oversimplification, since the values of the school as an institution are reflected in the policies, goals, and objectives of the school, as well as in the individual values held by such school personnel as the principal and the teachers. Moreover, the dynamic relationship exists potentially not for all students and all staff members but in dyads between each student and each staff member. Even so, it may be instructive to examine the composite major relationships.

The line between A and B in Figure 11.1 represents the difference between the actual values held by the students and those espoused by the school. In some schools this difference may be small indeed—as in the elementary compared with the secondary school or in the rural compared with the urban school. Typically, however, the values of the school as an institution may vary considerably from those of the students, as a comparison of the values of students and teachers revealed in Goldman's study.[3]

Concerning the mutual perception of values, to reduce intraceptive

---

[1] J. W. Getzels, "On the Transformation of Values: A Decade After Port Huron," *School Review*, 80 (August 1972), 505–519.

[2] James E. House, "Can the Student Participate in His Own Destiny?" *Educational Leadership*, 27 (February 1970), 442–445.

[3] Samuel Goldman, "Sub-Public Perceptions of the High School Graduate and the Roles of Institutions in His Development," doctoral dissertation, University of Chicago, 1961.

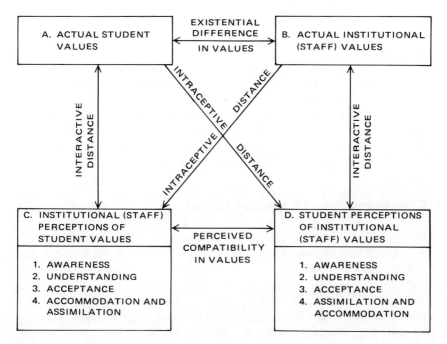

Figure 11.1
Student-institutional value relationships

distance one must first become aware of the value orientations of others. The principal and the staff, for example, should assess the extent to which behavioral manifestations of students are representative of prevailing and underlying themes in the student peer culture of the school. Increased awareness often leads to increased understanding and acceptance of the value positions of others. The desire for acceptance "as one is" is a powerful force acting on staff and students alike. Principals and teachers who cannot be accepting of students should ask themselves whether they are in the right profession, since the school as a public institution requires and encourages the expression of divergent values and perspectives. A reasonable degree of acceptance serves as a natural prelude to value accommodation by the staff and value assimilation by students.

The mutual intraceptive distances can be reduced through increasing the nature and degree of interpersonal interaction between the staff and the students. Students, for example, typically desire a principal who is visibly available for consultation, interpretation, and explanation of school policy, as well as for giving friendly advice. The traditional student image of the principal as chief disciplinarian, enforcer of archaic policies, or maintainer of the status quo can be altered by a principal who conscientiously works to reaffirm his interest in and empathy with students. As a leader he must fully understand the values of the student body as a basis for evaluating the appropriateness of school objectives and programs, and he must initiate changes based on this understanding. Such understanding necessitates continuous formal and informal interaction among members of the student body, the principal, and the total staff. In this way, the perceived compatibility in values may be increased —shortening line CD. As the research on values has revealed time and again, conflict within a social system such as the school is due less to basic differences in value positions than to the fact that values are misrepresented, misperceived, and misunderstood.[4]

Student involvement in decision making

Our research on the decision-making structure of the schools reveals that of all the important reference groups within the school, the students are the least involved in the making of major educational decisions.[5] Student participation in decision making has been limited concerning not only the content of decisions to be made but also the type or extent of involvement. Regarding the content of decisions, students particularly desire additional involvement in decisions having to do with improvement of the educational program, as well as improvement of staff and student personnel services. Regarding involvement, students wish to provide information more systematically and participate at the higher levels of formulating alternatives and recommending alternatives. The principal who understands today's students immediately recognizes that their demands for significant involvement in the educational decision-making process are a natural outgrowth of their basic value orientations, rather than a phenomenon to be decried or denied.

Although occasionally student demands for greater involvement in the educational process have seriously disrupted that very process, a review of the literature reveals that their demands focus on decisions concerning the following:[6]

---

[4] Cf. Max G. Abbott, "Values and Value-Perceptions in Superintendent–School Board Relationships," *Administrator's Notebook*, 9 (December 1960), 1–4; Gale W. Rose, "Organizational Behavior and Its Concomitants in Schools," *Administrator's Notebook*, 15 (March 1967), 1–4.

[5] Glen G. Eye et al., *Relationship Between Instructional Change and the Extent to Which School Administrators and Teachers Agree on the Location of Responsibilities for Administrative Decisions*, U.S. Office of Education, Cooperative Research Project 1913 (5-0443), Madison, University of Wisconsin, 1966; Gordon E. Wendlandt, "Faculty Involvement in the Decision-Making Process and Experience in Collective Negotiations," doctoral dissertation, University of Wisconsin, 1970.

[6] Cf. John Birmingham, ed., *Our Time Is Now: Notes from the High School Underground*, New York, Praeger, 1970; Samuel S. Brodbelt, "The Problem of

1. Involvement in the formulation of rules and policies that affect them.

2. Involvement in the adoption, revision, and improvement of the instructional program.

3. Involvement in the evaluation and improvement of the professional staff.

4. Involvement in the planning and implementation of the cocurricular program.

The principal must lead in the initiation of new structures and in the alteration of established structures so that students may become involved in the mainstream of decision making. Formal representation at faculty meetings, curriculum councils, and board of education meetings has been utilized successfully in many communities to give students opportunities to increase their understanding of the workings of the educational enterprise. In addition, such mechanisms have afforded students opportunities to express their points of view. Unfortunately, the structural format of most adult meetings usually serves as a deterrent to maximum participation from students who at times are impetuous. Therefore, the principal should encourage positive student involvement in informal, less structured settings as well. When students realize that their suggested alternatives are of sufficient quality and import to receive consideration from the school board, the administration, and the faculty, serious confrontation—particularly over procedural matters —is less likely to occur.

With the help of the courts, and through their own initiative, students have reestablished the premise that the focus of the educational process converges on them. As indicated in Chapter 9, which dealt with the educational program, there are several appropriate mechanisms for involving students in decisions concerning improvement of the school's curriculum. The cocurricular program and student government are areas readily lending themselves to active student involvement in decision making.

Growing Dissent in the High Schools," *High School Journal,* 53 (March 1970), 363–371; Gordon Cawelti, "Youth Assesses the American High School," *PTA Magazine,* 62 (May 1968), 16; David A. Kula, "Protest in Black and White; Student Radicals in High Schools," *National Association of Secondary School Principals Bulletin,* 54 (January 1970), 72–85; Louis Panish and Edgar A. Kelley, "The High School Principal: Proactive or Reactive Roles?" *Phi Delta Kappan,* 54 (October 1970), 90–92; J. Lloyd Trump, *Antidotes for Student Unrest in American High Schools,* Washington, D.C., National Association of Secondary School Principals, 1970; Gilbert R. Weldy, "Building Democratic Values Through Student Participation," *National Association of Secondary School Principals Bulletin,* 54 (May 1970), 72–79; Jacob B. Zack, "Restless Youth—What's the Message?" *National Association of Secondary School Principals Bulletin,* 54 (May 1970), 146–158.

THE COCURRICULAR PROGRAM

Despite the broad expectation of citizens and educators alike that the schools should stress the intellectual tasks of public education,[7] the inclusion of additional learning opportunities within the total school program is generally accepted and in many communities is enthusiastically supported. Providing students with opportunities to meet their own needs, to develop new interests, and to capitalize on existing talents is the primary aim of cocurricular activities, which can serve in many ways to reinforce the instructional program.

By definition, cocurricular activities include those experiences not ordinarily identified with the traditional program of studies but authorized or sponsored by the school in an attempt to broaden student participation and learning by capitalizing on available human and physical resources. The term "cocurricular" often is made synonymous with "extracurricular" or merely "student activities." Cocurricular seems to be more appropriate, however, because one of the major purposes of the program is to reinforce and expand on curricular learning experiences. To label such a program "extracurricular" establishes the inference that the activities are superfluous to the educational mission of a school and are therefore a ready target for discard in times of fiscal crisis. Principals must insist that the cocurriculum is a viable and necessary means for increasing student identification with the goals of the school. Consequently, it represents an invaluable resource, not only for students wishing to avail themselves of additional, often less structured activities, but also for students who have difficulty in relating to the school's formal learning program.

The scope of cocurricular programs varies immensely, depending on such factors as age and interests of students; size, resources, and geographic location of school; and the ability of the students to participate in and give direction to the program. The following types of activities, however, are ordinarily included within the offerings:

1. Assemblies
2. Class organizations
3. Clubs
4. Dramatic arts
5. Graduation activities
6. Honor societies

---

[7] Lawrence W. Downey, Roger C. Seager, and Allen T. Slagle, *The Task of Public Education,* Chicago, Midwest Administration Center, University of Chicago, 1960; Marvin J. Fruth, Dennis W. Spuck, and Howard E. Wakefield, *Opening the Door,* Madison, Cooperative Educational Research and Services, University of Wisconsin, 1972.

7. Interscholastic and intramural athletics
8. Music activities
9. Prevocational groups, such as FFA, FTA, and FHA
10. Outdoor education
11. Publications
12. Safety patrols
13. Social activities
14. Speech and debate activities
15. Student council

Although the list is by no means exhaustive, it serves to identify typical components of the cocurricular offerings. As is readily apparent, many of the activities contribute immeasurably to the development of worthy leisure-time skills, interests, and appreciations—a necessary consideration in an era when the work week is being shortened and Americans have increased amounts of leisure time. As indicated in our earlier discussion of the task of public education, the preparation of citizens for constructive use of their leisure time has long been viewed as a major responsibility of the school. The cocurricular program can be instrumental in the accomplishment of that objective.

The role of cocurricular activities extends beyond contributing to students' personal development to fostering social development. Participation in cocurricular activities helps fulfill the need for social interaction. Students are eager to seek new friendships and to obtain peer acceptance. In the nonconstrained environment that characterizes most cocurricular experiences, numerous opportunities exist to establish and strengthen interpersonal relationships. These relationships are often instrumental in bringing about a more positive attitude toward the school. For example, studies of high school students have revealed that their greatest satisfaction with the school results from experiences outside the traditional curriculum—from athletics, clubs, and student interest groups.[8] The next most frequently mentioned source of satisfaction is that of good relationships with peers and with interested teachers. Thus the cocurricular program is a vital source of student satisfaction—an essential ingredient of school morale.

In yet another major aspect of student development—the biological or physical dimension—such cocurricular activities as intramural and interscholastic athletics play a major role. Establishing the proper emphasis on these and other student activities to ensure a comprehensive program is an important, though difficult, administrative function.

[8] Cf. Louis Harris, "What People Think About Their High Schools," *Life*, 66 (May 1969), 23–39; H. L. Willis and Gerald Halpern, "A Survey of How Students Perceive Their High Schools," *Education Canada*, 10 (June 1970), 29–33.

The principal may be hampered in his efforts to provide a meaningful cocurricular program because of a variety of pressures and conflicts in expectations to which he must respond if the program is to be well received. Since students, community, teachers, and central office personnel all have preconceived values and expectations regarding the cocurricular program, the roles of these four reference groups are discussed separately.

ROLE OF STUDENTS. The most important reference group to which the principal must respond when planning the cocurricular program is the student body. Few would suggest that the wide range of student need-dispositions can be met merely by making knowledge available through a formal program of curricular offerings. And given the opportunity, students will quickly identify their needs and interests. Just as the instructional program must allow for individual student differences, the cocurricular program must be established on the premise that each student is unique and deserves psychological, social, and physical experiences tailored to his uniqueness.

Too frequently, the student activities in one school duplicate those of another, even though the schools are located in vastly different communities. This circumstance not only limits the creativity of students, it also encourages the adoption of activities having goals that may be inconsistent with the purposes of the school or incompatible with the needs of a particular student body. A more logical approach to designing a successful cocurricular program is to enlist the assistance of students in assessing currently unmet student needs. From this point, they can identify alternatives by which these needs might receive attention through an expanded or revitalized cocurricular program.

After the systematic needs assessment has been conducted, the students may become primarily responsible for formulating and recommending alternative activities that are in keeping with the school's philosophy and objectives. Even in the most conservative or traditional schools, student involvement in designing cocurricular programs consistent with their needs, values, and interests is initially less threatening to teachers and parents than immediate student involvement in other decision-content areas. In effect, therefore, the planning and implementation of the cocurricular program represents an appropriate "point of entry" for significant student involvement, which subsequently can be expanded to other major decision functions, as well.

After refinement and review of the student recommended activities, it is decided which activities are to be added or which changes are to be implemented. Like the curriculum, the cocurriculum should be continuously and systematically evaluated. If an activity proves to be unworkable or if it is not serving the intended need, alternative activities can be devised, implemented, and subsequently evaluated.

ROLE OF THE COMMUNITY. When taxpayer support for school operation is less than enthusiastic, the entire educational program of a school is under close scrutiny from citizens. Although educators typically welcome increased community involvement, particular problems are posed when the basic community concern is to cut costs. Raises in staff salaries, together with increased operational costs, have served to arouse taxpayer concern about all school programs. Not only has the appropriateness of innovative curricular programs been questioned by the citizenry, but, as always, the value of cocurricular offerings—especially those that are not self-supporting—is challenged. In some school districts, threats to abolish athletics, intramurals, concerts, clubs, and other activities have been used with some success as leverage to secure passage of budgets or operational referenda. When the budgets are defeated, however, the campaign threats tend to become a reality. In our judgment, such practice is questionable unless it is based on a thorough review of all possible alternatives for cost reduction.

Of course community interest in the cocurricular program is not always prompted by fiscal concerns. A real question exists regarding how far the school should go in providing for specialized interests, talents, and needs of adults, as well as students, other than through the traditional instructional program. There is little doubt that certain school-sponsored cocurricular activities (e.g., athletics, music, art, drama) in some communities receive emphasis far out of proportion to that accorded the instructional program. Although community involvement in the school should be encouraged, care must be exercised to ensure that student participation in cocurricular activities is not exploited. We are reminded of the plight of a secondary principal who remarked, "This community is split right down the middle in terms of 'music boosters' and 'athletic boosters.' I wish we had some 'school boosters.'"

In still other communities, there may be apathy to both the cocurricular and the curricular programs of the schools. In such situations, the opportunities for student interest expansion and talent development implicit in program enrichment can be stressed as basic and legitimate reasons for the development of a diverse student activity program. In addition, data can be obtained and made available to citizens concerning the positive holding power of many cocurricular activities, particularly for potential student drop-outs. Often the principal, working with teacher sponsors of the various activities, is able to convince the community of the soundness of the activity program through planned parent involvement. Also, human resources available within the community should be tapped for appropriate assistance with the program, not only to vitalize each activity but also to promote sound school-community relations. In this respect, the coordination of a ʳound school-community relations program, as discussed in detail in Chapter 13, is the responsibility of the principal as he strives to reinforce the positive impact of student participation in both curricular and cocurricular activities.

ROLE OF THE TEACHING STAFF. A frequent and very successful practice is that of requiring a member of the instructional staff to agree to serve as a cocurricular advisor or sponsor before the activity can be approved by the school. The sponsor is typically expected to interpret school policy, offer guidance and direction, and ensure that the activity operates in accordance with the philosophy and goals of the school. Inherent in activity sponsorship, however, are some obvious problems. Certain teachers, because of their ability to establish rapport with students, their youth, or their multiplicity of interests, are identified readily by students as prospective sponsors. Even the most dedicated teachers are aware, however, that overextension in this area may on occasion conflict with their primary role as a classroom teacher. Because of this potential for role conflict, some teachers are hesitant to accept invitations for such involvement. The principal can help to minimize this circumstance if he shows that he places high priority on the cocurricular program by displaying a personal interest, appearing at activity functions, and remaining abreast of each activity.

Although many teachers welcome the opportunity to become acquainted with students in informal settings, the principal should not assume teacher interest in all cocurricular offerings. The assignment of staff to cocurricular activities should be made with concern for not only compatibility between teacher needs and the activity but also for compatibility between teachers and students. Students might well participate in making such assignments by nominating sponsors. In summary, the principal's assignment of staff to cocurricular activities should receive the same care and attention that are given to classroom assignments.

Teacher reaction to pressure from administrators and students for increased participation in cocurricular activities has emerged formally in districts with negotiated agreements. Definite guidelines that strictly define the teacher's day and require appropriate financial compensation for specific activity sponsorship have been negotiated in many districts. Thus the principal's discretionary power to make cocurricular assignments based entirely on student and teacher interests has been curbed. Certainly, any cocurricular assignment that requires substantial teacher time is worthy of financial compensation. Even so, teachers should be encouraged to offer their professional services and talents in a variety of activities, to gain a more thorough understanding of their students, as well as to improve school-community relations.

ROLE OF THE DISTRICT OFFICE. Pressured by the community's legitimate demand for fiscal austerity, the school board sometimes is reluctant to allocate the funds necessary to support the cocurricular program. This reality has prompted the need for engaging in fund-raising activities by school-sponsored clubs as a means of basic survival. Although such activities can be justified partly through their emphasis on group interaction and cohesion, a concentration on fund-raising activities soon obscures the real purposes for a group's existence. Moreover, a profusion of such activities may become highly dysfunctional and can create considerable ill will both within the school and toward the school on the part of citizens.

To legitimize the establishment of an adequate cocurricular program and to assist in the attainment of program objectives, financial support from the school district's operating budget is essential. The principal's philosophical position in this matter is crucial. He must resolutely insist that the cocurricular program is an integral part of the total school offerings and is, therefore, deserving of adequate financial support.

STUDENT GOVERNMENT

Student councils have been much maligned in recent years for their alleged inability to effect change when their constituency has cited definite needs for improvement. Some insist that to change student government and make it a viable means of student involvement we ought first to renounce student councils for "the hoaxes they are."[9] Accusations regarding the close identification of such bodies with the school's power structure or the "establishment," their lack of commitment, and their inability to represent the total student body have been justified in some respects. Too frequently, the student council is saddled with an archaic constitution and operating procedures that preclude effective fulfillment of its role and function.

Marich compared the types of activities sponsored by councils over a ten-year period.[10] He found that although the activities were quite diverse in the 1968–1969 school year, the two most frequently sponsored

[9] Mark A. Chesler, "School Crisis and Change," in Richard L. Hart and J. Galen Sayor, eds., *Student Unrest: Threat or Promise?* Washington, D.C., Association for Supervision and Curriculum Development, 1970, p. 117.

[10] Milan Marich, Jr., "Investigation of Changes in Selected Student Council Activities in Michigan Secondary Schools," doctoral dissertation, University of Michigan, 1970.

activities—social functions and student assemblies—were the same as those reported by Weaver a decade earlier.[11] Sponsoring dances, monitoring halls, and conducting bake sales are a few of the relatively unimportant yet typical activities in which this potentially powerful group of elected leaders has tended to engage. Although such activities may be of value, they typically can be effectively delegated by the council to other groups.

Perhaps the principal has been unwittingly responsible for the misdirection of student talent and energy, for too often the student council has been used as a means of achieving organizational ends at the expense of the satisfaction of student needs. If the principal hopes to maximize the potential of student government, he must encourage its active participation in the identification and solution of significant school problems. This type of participation requires the adoption of an effective operational framework for the council, whose components include representation, sponsorship, time, physical resources, and training.

REPRESENTATION. If the council intends to speak for all students, it must extend its representation to all. Arbitrary requirements, such as grade point averages, serve only to antagonize and isolate that group which, for all practical purposes, has been disenfranchised. Students who are unable or who have chosen not to achieve at normative academic standards will be unwilling to identify with a student council whose members have attained a stipulated grade point average. Considerable potential for leadership exists within the ranks of students who are low achievers. To suppress their desire to work within the established framework will serve only to increase their alienation and encourage them to form splinter groups implicitly or explicitly dedicated to undermining the council's work. If one subscribes to the sacred American values of democracy, individualism, and equality, the denial of equal representation in student government is indefensible.

SPONSORSHIP. For several reasons, sponsorship of the student council has not been an attractive position for teachers. The role requires many hours of dedicated work and the capacity for creative leadership. The advisor's ability to assess and guide student action is critical to the ultimate success of the council, requiring keen insight into student values, as well as skills in group processes. With these traits as prerequisites for effectiveness in the advisor role, it is unfortunate that in many schools the sponsorship of the council is arbitrarily or expeditiously shifted from one staff member to another.

---

[11] Donald C. Weaver, "Primary Aims and Appropriate Activities of Michigan Public Secondary School Student Councils," doctoral dissertation, University of Michigan, 1961.

The principal must exercise care in his selection of a council advisor, arriving at a decision only after review of the demands of the role in conjunction with the need-dispositions, training, and experience of prospective sponsors. Since any choice that is opposed by the council will prove to be unsatisfactory, student involvement in making this decision is an obvious necessity.

TIME. A council that is expected to be a problem-solving and decision-making group must be assigned a significant block of time in which to function. One period per day, within the framework of a six- or seven-period school day, may be appropriate for larger schools and might be necessary in smaller schools with serious problems. In other schools, two or three class periods per week may represent an adequate time allotment.

A time commitment of one period per day would probably warrant the granting of one unit of credit for participation. Ordinarily social studies credit may be awarded at the secondary school level, provided proper consideration is given to the development of problem-solving skills and leadership techniques while the school is being analyzed as a social system. With so much time, the council should be able to discard the ignominious but omnipresent suggestion box and employ, instead, appropriate survey and political techniques to identify student concerns and to design and implement programs to deal with these concerns.

PHYSICAL RESOURCES. A problem-solving group, to be effective, requires an environment conducive to group activity. To ensure maximum effectiveness of the council, an appropriate work space should be provided, including the necessary office and duplicating facilities. Access to data processing equipment also can facilitate the analysis and solution of identified problems. The availability of adequate physical resources will greatly increase the productivity of the council.

TRAINING. The preceding suggestions are practical insofar as there exists within the council the necessary leadership to amplify its effectiveness. An advisor who has leadership skills and is trained in group processes can be invaluable in developing these skills in council members. Important also is student attendance at state or regional workshops designed to develop leadership qualities. For example, for several years the University of Michigan has sponsored intensive, week-long institutes for selected students identified by their schools as prospective leaders. Included among topics of exploration are problem-solving methods, dynamics of large and small groups, communication theory, evaluation strategies, social survey techniques, and decision-making theory. This type of training is imperative if the council aspires to become an organization dedicated to continuous school improvement through responsible leadership.

In summary, effective and meaningful student participation in student government is important for several reasons. First, the inherent value of student involvement in decisions that affect them is ethically appropriate. Second, such participation is educationally sound. Third, if current research is correct, student involvement in decision making also is politically wise, in terms of preventing student unrest. Although the political reason may appear to be manipulative, it is not. As indicated in Chapter 8, involvement may range from providing information to developing possible alternatives to recommending an alternative to making a decision. The principal who is aware of these stages can plan for increases in student involvement on the appropriate decisions and at the proper stages, to benefit both the school and the students. Factors to be considered include age and maturity of the students, community values and expectations, organizational constraints, and staff and student values and need-dispositions. In conclusion, we simply observe that like any other group in society with political demands, students who lack appropriate institutional structures for effective participation will become alienated.[12] The principal who would be a leader, therefore, will be actively engaged in initiating change in established structures or in establishing new structures for student participation in decision making, not only in student government but in guidance and other functional areas, as well.

The improvement of guidance services

The guidance program is central to the effectiveness of the school as a social system and to the efficiency of the student as an individual. In the model in Figure 11.2, the student is the focal point of the five basic guidance services provided, since his benefit is the program's *raison d'être*. Although teachers, administrators, employers, colleges, and parents all benefit indirectly from the guidance services, the basic purpose of the guidance program is to increase the student's feelings of satisfaction, belongingness, identification, and achievement, both in present and projected life situations. With this objective in mind, the function of the principal in the improvement of guidance services is to remove the constraints or impediments that prevent the counselor from being of maximum service to students.

[12] John M. Meyer and Richard Rubinson, "Structural Determinants and Student Political Activity: A Comparative Interpretation," *Sociology of Education*, 45 (Winter 1972), 23–46.

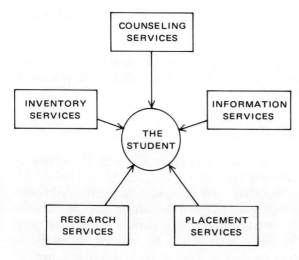

Figure 11.2
Scope and focus of the guidance program

Studies of the actual and the idealized expectations for the guidance counselor's role generally reveal that the counselor spends more time with student scheduling, testing, and other record-keeping functions than ideally should be the case.[13] Correspondingly, counselors spend much less time than they should with individual students, teachers, and parents. Moreover, there is firm evidence that expectations for the counselor's role held by both administrators and teachers are at considerable variance with the expectations held by the guidance personnel themselves. As organizational superordinate, the principal is responsible for developing a greater understanding of priorities for the counselor's role; as an organizational specialist, the counselor is responsible for contributing to such understanding, both in his utilization of time and in his interactions with principal, staff, and students. Moreover, in pre-service preparation programs for both principals and counselors, it is incumbent on university departments of guidance and departments of educational administration to structure required or elective courses to enhance mutual understanding between these professional organizational role incumbents.

Whereas in larger schools the guidance services usually are organized and provided by a full-time specialist or group of specialists, in smaller secondary schools and in some elementary schools, the principal may

[13] Cf. Robert J. Nejedlo, "Value Orientations and School Counselor Role Expectations," doctoral dissertation, University of Wisconsin, 1964; Siegfried C. Dietz, "Principals' Attitudes Toward Counselor Role and Function," *National Association of Secondary School Principals Bulletin,* 56 (April 1972), 72–75.

have to assume guidance duties. In all cases, the principal must give leadership in coordinating the inputs of all who play integral parts in the guidance of students.

The major functions of the guidance program include the inventory service, the information service, the counseling service, the placement service, and the research service.

THE INVENTORY SERVICE

The inventory service includes activities connected with the obtaining and collecting of all relevant data about the individual student—his needs, values, abilities, interests, achievements, and goals. Although certain activities (e.g., testing and record keeping), may be partially delegated to teachers or clerical aides, the inventory service is vital to a sound guidance program. Included in the student inventory or personal record are pertinent demographic data, standardized test results, yearly progress reports, anecdotal records, reports of parent-teacher contacts, summaries of cocurricular experiences, and any other information necessary for developing an understanding of each student.

Incumbent on the principal and the guidance staff is the responsibility for developing policies governing the assemblage, tabulation, maintenance, and dissemination of information included in student records. Procedures should be adopted both to ensure privacy and to make certain that items of short-term value are discarded periodically.[14]

THE INFORMATION SERVICE

The information service—including personal, social, career, and academic information—is effected through individual and group contacts and by making available in the guidance offices, library, or media center a wide variety of pertinent and current materials. A well-stocked collection of such materials housed in a guidance center is of considerable value to students and can facilitate the utilization of other guidance services. In addition to being familiar with the materials, the guidance counselor should possess current knowledge that will enable him to interpret the materials—concerning not only schools and colleges, but vocations and careers as well.

Work-study programs, internships, and summer work experiences give the counselor valuable firsthand experience for interpreting factual information. Many schools regularly receive a wealth of information

[14] *Guidelines for the Collection, Maintenance, and Dissemination of Pupil Records,* A Report of a Conference on the Ethical and Legal Aspects of School Record Keeping, New York, Russell Sage Foundation, 1969, pp. 1–47.

from colleges and universities, professional and labor organizations, the military, business, and industry—in addition to updated career information monographs and publications that come via subscription. Unfortunately, the concern in some schools appears to be more with developing accurate filing systems for the information than with getting the information into the hands of students. It is especially important that information for students be presented objectively, since counselors exert more influence than they perhaps realize on student decisions concerning colleges and careers.[15]

To augment national or statewide information, many schools have conducted surveys of local educational and employment opportunities. Students often become enthusiastically involved in such studies, since in the process they not only gain valuable educational and social experiences, they also derive considerable satisfaction from contributing to the informational services available to all students.

THE COUNSELING SERVICE

The counseling interview is the heart of the guidance program, for in this setting the relevant data about the individual student and the relevant information bearing on the student's concerns are synthesized and merged in a process of self-understanding, growth, and development. In fact, the counseling service is so intrinsic to the total guidance program that the terms "counseling" and "guidance" are often used synonymously. Because the counselor-counselee relationship is of crucial importance, it is imperative that each professional counselor have completed advanced training and clinical experiences in counseling techniques and methodology. Certain guidance services may be delegated to paraprofessional or clerical personnel, but the counseling service cannot. The counselor must view group and individual counseling with students, teachers, and parents as a primary function of his role.[16]

To compensate for their lack of classroom contact with students, counselors should be encouraged to have as much informal verbal and visual contact with students as possible. The establishment of rapport between counselor and student is necessary for productive counseling interviews. Rapport can often be strengthened by student awareness that the counselor's information about him is not confined merely to secondary sources. If a counselor expects to be of help to a student who is groping for solutions to academic, psychological, social, or voca-

[15] Aaron V. Cicourel and John I. Kitsuse, *The Educational Decision Makers*, Indianapolis, Bobbs-Merrill, pp. 135–146.

[16] Jon Carlson and John J. Pietrofesa, "A Tri-Level Guidance Structure: An Answer to Our Apparent Ineffectiveness," *Elementary School Guidance and Counseling*, 5 (March 1971), 190.

tional problems, he must try hard to become personally acquainted with each student's values, needs, and abilities. Although such efforts are time consuming, they lead to the essential advice that applies to counselors as well as to principals: "Get out of the office and into the school."

THE PLACEMENT SERVICE

At the elementary and middle school levels, the placement service is primarily concerned with in-school placement and student scheduling. At the senior high school level, the placement service entails in-school scheduling, as well as part-time, work-study, and post-high school placement. In an era of flexible and individualized programming of students, principals have come to depend increasingly on counselors for assistance with the student scheduling function—not merely for filling out "add-drop" cards but for help in basic curricular and cocurricular planning and decision making. In many comprehensive schools, however, the in-school placement function should be reexamined to ensure that the time of both administrators and counselors is being utilized wisely. Teachers need to become more involved in this function.

At the high school level, the counselor not only coordinates placement activities but also maintains continuing contact with business, industry, education, military, and labor representatives who utilize the product of the schools. Active involvement of the principal in the placement service is vital to the program of school-community relations—through major participation in policy and advisory committees and through minor participation in providing routine recommendations and answering requests for information.

To assist secondary school students in identifying postgraduation possibilities, guidance personnel employ a variety of techniques. These include sponsoring college visitations; hosting representatives from business, education, labor, industry, and the military; and inviting graduates of the school to visit formally and informally with students. With career opportunities changing and expanding so rapidly, it is imperative that various methods be employed to increase the career awareness, exploration, and entry-level skills of all students.

Educators often are frustrated in their attempts to help students make their post-high school plans objectively because of pressure from parents whose goals for their children may be unrealistic and overly ambitious. This problem can be minimized through open communication between the school staff and parents regarding the aptitudes, abilities, achievements, and interests of the student in his years of formal schooling. In many communities, such open communication and counseling is needed during the middle and elementary school grades as well as during high school.

The placement service is particularly relevant to the drop-out. Regardless of the attractiveness of the school milieu and irrespective of efforts designed to prevent them from leaving the school, some students choose to terminate their formal education prior to graduation. These young men and women need initial assistance in locating suitable jobs. Moreover, the school has an obligation to maintain continuing contact with each former student to offer professional aid and programs of reeducation for as long as possible.

THE RESEARCH SERVICE

Important to the ultimate success of any school is the research service, which centers on the collection, tabulation, and presentation of data regarding current students, those who have entered college or the world of work, and those who have otherwise terminated their formal contact with the school. The data available from students are invaluable for assessing the school's capacity to fulfill its stated goals. As shortcomings in the school are identified, corrective measures can be taken to eliminate the deficiencies, thereby assuring a program of greater relevance for current and future students. Counselors and administrators must recognize the valuable contributions to be realized from systematic and continuous research, and they must accord this service top priority to permit existing programs to be intelligently altered and future programs wisely planned.

Germane also to the research function is the continuous evaluation of the scope and quality of the guidance program itself. Principals should see that students, teachers, and parents are surveyed to obtain their actual and ideal expectations and their evaluations of the effectiveness of the guidance program. This strategy can supply useful feedback regarding the guidance services that are available or should be improved.

IMPEDIMENTS TO AN EFFECTIVE GUIDANCE PROGRAM

In summary, the positive impact of a well-organized, vertically articulated guidance program has been realized in too few schools. For a variety of reasons, students and teachers have not adequately availed themselves of the five basic services of the guidance program. Among the prohibiting factors that tend to neutralize the effectiveness of the guidance program are the following:

1. The ratio of guidance counselors to students has been unrealistic. If the counselor is expected to give professional assistance, the number of students for whom he is responsible must be a manageable one. Suggested ratios have been offered by a variety of experts, but for the most

part the guidelines of the regional accrediting associations have been a major determining factor. Most associations recommend that member schools maintain a student-counselor ratio of 500:1 or less.[17] Although some schools recognize the need to reduce this ratio, unfortunately others view it as a guideline for quality, rather than the minimum standard that it is.

A suggested ratio might be appropriate for smaller schools or those serving communities of similar socioeconomic conditions, shared values, and congruent expectations. As the size of the school and the diversity of the students increase, however, there is a dramatic need to reduce the student-counselor ratio. Instead of determining the student-counselor ratio through compliance with an arbitrary or minimum standard, the principal should conduct a critical evaluation of the guidance department's effectiveness in terms of stated goals. Ratio adjustments can then be made in terms of need.

2. Too few counselors are employed at the middle and elementary school levels. Although some districts maintain a student-counselor ratio in the middle school comparable to that of the senior high school, other districts have only token guidance services in grades six through nine, even though this age group is undergoing a critical period of development and adjustment.

At the elementary level especially, recognition of a need to include the services of a professionally trained guidance counselor has been slow in materializing. Elementary school personnel who espouse the self-contained classroom concept have been reluctant to accept the need for guidance personnel, arguing instead that a counselor can do little to assist the classroom teacher who supervises the students during most of the school day. The increasing flexibility, diversification, and individualization of elementary school curricula and the emerging emphasis on career awareness, however, magnify the need for guidance counselors in the elementary school. Moreover, one of the most significant developments in recent years is the acceptance of the position that guidance in the elementary schools is developmental rather than remedial and should be made available to all students.[18]

3. Students and teachers often are unaware of or fail to take advantage of the full array of guidance services offered. Many students do not meet with a counselor alone until the high school years, and then the meeting may be prompted by deviant student behavior. To mini-

[17] North Central Association of Colleges and Secondary Schools, *Policies and Criteria for the Approval of Secondary Schools,* Chicago, 1970.

[18] Oscar Bedrosian et al., "Pilot Study to Determine the Effectiveness of Guidance Classes in Developing Self-Understanding in Elementary School Children," *Elementary School Guidance,* 5 (December 1970), 124–134.

mize this negative image, counselors should be encouraged to have a variety of helpful formal and informal contacts with students in curricular and cocurricular programs. These contacts are necessary to establish an atmosphere of trust and understanding to allow students to become aware of, understand, and utilize the guidance services.

Teachers also are often reluctant to utilize guidance personnel in helping them better to understand each student. To dispel such reluctance, the principal must facilitate the integration of guidance services with instructional services through planned activities that reduce the communicative distance between teachers and counselors.

4. Some administrators have inappropriately assigned certain administrative functions to guidance personnel, thereby contributing to teacher, student, and parent perceptions of counselors as being quasi-administrators. For example, in most schools some responsibility for resolution of discipline and truancy problems has been delegated to counselors, who do in fact need to be involved in these problems. However, the principal should recognize that the assignment of such duties creates an untenable interrole conflict for the counselor. As a dean of students once said, "First I'm supposed to guide them; then I must suspend them."

5. Physical proximity of the counseling suite to the administrative offices also has contributed to confusion and conflict in the counselor's role. Although the counselor's immediate availability to the principal may be of considerable practical utility, too often it results in the assignment of sundry routine tasks to counselors. In schools too small to justify subordinate administrative help, this problem has been magnified when the counselor becomes identified, either officially or unofficially, as "second in command." In some instances, counselors have promoted this image because of their desire to be of service to the school. Moreover, many administrators have been selected from the counseling ranks, and counselors aspiring to administrative positions do not view this close association with the administration as particularly disturbing. But to identify positively the guidance department's primary goal of service to students, it is appropriate that the guidance offices be physically apart from the administrative complex. In addition, counseling and administrative staffs must work closely together to define, clarify, and communicate to others their exclusive as well as their mutual role responsibilities.

6. A final impediment to the full utilization of guidance services is the lack of coordination of guidance services with the other specialized student personnel services. In many school districts the services of school nurses, psychometrists, psychologists, social workers, police liaison officers, and a host of other governmental and volunteer workers converge appropriately on the student at the operational level of the school. Thus

far, however, there has been a failure to deal meaningfully with many social problems (e.g., shoplifting, drug abuse, truancy, vandalism, and venereal disease) whose solutions demand that closer working relationships be established among teachers, counselors, and other student personnel specialists inside and outside the school.

Systematic case studies and case conferences have been utilized successfully to assist the individual student. Unfortunately, however, in most schools the case study is used for the analysis of deviant student behavior, even though each teacher and each student personnel specialist can contribute much to improving the student-organization relationship for all students. Institutes, workshops, and conferences are other mechanisms for increasing the understanding of mutual role and personality relationships among teachers, counselors, and other student personnel workers. The principal, as a leader, must initiate the appropriate structures within the school for orchestrating the contributions of each staff specialist toward the attainment of school and individual student goals.

The student and the school organization

The values of the larger society expressed in constitutional provisions, laws, court decisions, and administrative regulations all serve to delimit and define the relationship of the student to the school organization. Currently, several trends are altering considerably the legal status of the student. The changes having greatest implications for the principal-student relationship relate to compulsory school attendance, discipline, freedom of expression, freedom from search and seizure, and due process; the principal should know and understand each of these areas.

COMPULSORY SCHOOL ATTENDANCE

Laws and regulations governing compulsory school attendance contribute to the uniqueness of the school as a social system. As Miller and others have observed,

> . . . the public school would seem to say to all comers—the rich and the poor, the black and the white, the tall and short, whatever array live within the school district boundary line—that whoever you are or whatever you are, the school will take you. . . . The history of public schools in general has been one of continued effort to develop the means of meeting the needs of all such human individuals. In such a context there should be more concern that schools be fit for pupils than that pupils be fit for the schools.[19]

[19] Van Miller, George B. Madden, and James B. Kincheloe, *The Public Administration of American School Systems,* New York, Macmillan, 1972, p. 108.

Prior to 1901 securing compliance with school attendance regulations was considered to be primarily a parental responsibility, even though the state was obligated to provide a public school system. To illustrate, in *Rulison* v. *Post*, the court declared:

> Parents and guardians are under the responsibility of preparing children intrusted to their care and nurture, for the discharge of their duties in after life. Lawgivers in all free countries . . . have deemed it wise to leave the education and nurture of the children of the State to the direction of the parent or guardian. . . . The State . . . leaves it to the parents and guardians to determine the extent to which they will render it available to the children under their charge.[20]

In another Illinois case, shortly thereafter, the court concurred by stating: "The policy of our law has ever been to recognize the right of the parent to determine to what extent the child should be educated."[21]

There was increasing concern, however, that under this system "the child, at the will of the parents, could be allowed to grow up in ignorance, and become a more than useless member of society."[22] In 1901 the Indiana Supreme Court settled the question of constitutionality of compulsory attendance laws in the following statement:

> The natural rights of a parent to the custody and control of his infant child are subordinate to the power of the state, and may be restricted and regulated by municipal laws. One of the most important natural duties of the parent is his obligation to educate his child, and this duty he owes not to the child only, but to the commonwealth. If he neglects . . . to do so, he may be coerced by law to execute such civil obligations. . . . Statutes making it compulsory upon the parent, guardian, or other person having custody and control of children to send them to public or private schools . . . have not only been upheld as strictly within the constitutional power of the legislature, but have generally been regarded necessary to carry out the express purposes of the constitution itself.[23]

A great deal of administrative time at the building level is devoted to ensuring student compliance with compulsory attendance laws. This expenditure of time is legally binding and, more important, it is administratively significant. For of all social institutions, only the school seeks to locate each person, by name and circumstance, with the intention of offering individual benefits. This effort to find and subsequently accept each individual in the American society makes the school a coercive, yet normative, social system.

Nationwide acceptance of the value of compulsory attendance laws has burdened the principal with much administrative and clerical work

[20] *Rulison* v. *Post*, 79 Ill. 573 (1871).

[21] *Trustees of Schools* v. *People*, 87 Ill. 308 (1877).

[22] *Board of Education* v. *Purse*, 101 Ga. 422, 28 S.E. 899 (1897).

[23] *State* v. *Bailey*, 157 Ind. 324, 61 N.E. 731–732 (1901).

designed to detect and prohibit truancy. Particularly in large urban schools, the current truancy rate is staggering. In New York City, for example, Gordon estimates that 50 percent of the students of ghetto high schools are absent each day.[24] In the school district of Philadelphia, approximately 30 percent of the high school, 20 percent of the junior high school, and 10 percent of the elementary school students were absent each day during the 1970–1971 school year.[25] These figures, moreover, do not include in-school skipping of classes, which is becoming an increasingly taxing problem, particularly at the high school level.

Although increased personnel, such as attendance officers and social workers, and increased utilization of data-processing equipment have provided sophisticated methods for documenting truancy, little progress has been made in preventing willful absenteeism. Unfortunately, even the most ingenious methods for identifying truants are of little value unless the underlying causes of individual truancy are explored, analyzed, and alleviated. Success in this endeavor requires the help of counselors, teachers, social workers, law enforcement officials, and others having an interest in helping the identified truant. They must work in concert to determine means for personalizing the student role within the school, as well as for socializing the student toward the school.

There are many reasons for the development of poor attendance patterns—societal issues, family values, and peer pressures often being responsible. But the principal and the staff should realize also that a number, if not the majority, of the attendance problems are prompted by the school's inability to provide a program that can be tailored to the needs, values, and abilities of each student. In all too many schools, unfortunately, truancy is identified as the problem, rather than as the symptom that it really is.

DISCIPLINE

The disagreements among elementary and secondary educators over student discipline involve both value orientations and role expectations. Elaborate facilities, together with programs characterized by considerable flexibility, have been designed to provide greater freedom of expression and movement for students. In some instances, this freedom has been construed as contributing to a breakdown in student control. Educators committed to a traditional set of values, for example, have maintained that a causal relationship exists between student appearance

[24] David M. Gordon, *Problems in Political Economy: An Urban Perspective*, Lexington, Mass., Heath, 1971, p. 127.

[25] Mark R. Shedd, "Our Stricken Schools: A Proposal to Avert Disaster," *Progressive*, 36 (February 1972), 17.

and student conduct. Such educators view with alarm the abolition of dress and grooming codes. Even so, a visitor to a school of the 1970s notes a much more relaxed atmosphere and casual appearance than was observable in preceding years.

Concerning student discipline, the principal's role conflict is predictable. Usually he is evaluated by the central staff, parents, and teachers partly in terms of his ability to treat discipline problems expeditiously and fairly; but he must be careful not to overreact, thereby risking loss of respect of the student body. Well-defined written policies dealing with discipline problems can be of considerable value, but the principal must be sure of the facts before he decides the severe cases that ultimately reach him for disposition. In large schools, where responsibility for student discipline is often delegated to subordinate administrators, the principal also must be kept apprised of chronic or unusual problems, since these cases will reach him eventually for subsequent recommendations to the superintendent and the board of education.

Recent court decisions, prompted by numerous suspensions and expulsions of students, possess important implications for the principal's role. Students have come to expect treatment consistent with their individual rights under the Constitution, the law, and, lately, the courts. By respecting these individual rights, a principal can avoid many serious confrontations and can counter that apathy and alienation which is a characteristic response of many discontented students.

Failure to respond intelligently and positively to recent court decisions can result in embarrassing and extended legal entanglements for administrators and boards of education. The discretion of building principals arbitrarily to remove a student from school for an extended period of time has been curbed by the courts.[26] To avoid expensive, lengthy litigation for the school system, the principal must keep abreast of prevailing legal opinions regarding suspension and expulsion. The principal also should keep in mind that the court rulings establish minimal, not ultimate, standards of behavior. The principal should not resist or skirt the spirit of the rulings, but should cooperate with both the letter and the intent of the law.

Serving as a constraint to the previously accepted tenet that suspension and expulsion were acceptable means of dealing with students exhibiting undesirable behavior are the Madera and Brown cases, in which the courts reaffirmed the importance of an education for every citizen.[27] In the Brown decision, for example, the court stated: "In these days it is doubtful that any child may reasonably be expected to

[26] *Mills* v. *Board of Education*, 348 F. Supp. 866, Washington, 1972.

[27] *Madera* v. *Board of Education of the City of New York*, 386 F. 2nd 778 (1967); *Brown* v. *Board of Education of Topeka, Kansas*, 347 U.S. 483 (1954).

succeed in life if he is denied the opportunity of an education." Such landmark opinions state conclusively that the right of students to a free public education cannot easily be denied through suspension or expulsion.

FREEDOM OF EXPRESSION

Increased student awareness and societal circumstances have prompted students to attack, sometimes violently, the restrictiveness of the educational setting. At a time when societal and personal secular values center on social responsibility, relevance, authenticity, and commitment, it is understandable that students will question the school's legal jurisdiction to impose restraints on individual freedoms.

Concerning freedom of expression, student disenchantment with dress and grooming codes and administrator reaction to this disenchantment have surfaced repeatedly. Students feel that grooming and clothing styles are a matter of personal taste and self-expression, whereas principals, supported in the main by parents, central office, and teaching staffs, have felt generally that standards designed to restrict individual preference in grooming and attire are necessary to foster a proper learning environment. With consistency, however, the courts have decreed that student grooming and attire should not be regulated unless it directly disrupts the educational setting or is liable to affect the student's health or safety.

One notable court decision concerning personal freedom is exemplary. Addressing itself to the case of a male student who had defied an established dress code by growing his hair longer than the allowable limit, the Supreme Court, in *Breen* v. *Kahl*, stated: "To uphold arbitrary school rules which sharply implicate basic constitutional values for the sake of some nebulous concept of school discipline is contrary to the principle that we are a government of laws which are passed pursuant to the United States Constitution."[28]

As a result of a comprehensive review of court cases involving freedom of expression, Griffiths advised the following:

> School authorities are not permitted to impinge on the freedom of students unless student behavior substantially and materially interferes with the discipline and good order of a school . . . it is not enough that a segment of society—be it teachers, board members, or administrators . . . disapproves of elements of pupil behavior or dress. Nor is it sufficient that school authorities think that the pupil if unrestrained will create some future disorder. Adhering to the standards thus far set by judiciary will

[28] *Breen* v. *Kahl,* 296 F. Supp. 702 (1969).

. . . avoid much needless litigation and . . . will protect the rights of students as American citizens.[29]

The wearing of armbands or buttons by students as an expression of a political point of view also has been challenged by principals. Students maintain that this right is protected under the First Amendment's guarantee of freedom of expression. The courts have concurred with this view, except when school disruptions have resulted. There has been considerable confusion in connection with the student's right to freedom of expression as a result of two decisions handed down by the same circuit court on the same day. In *Burnside* v. *Byars*, the court said, in a ruling that restrained administrator discretion in restricting student expression:

> School officials cannot ignore expressions of feelings with which they do not wish to contend. They cannot infringe on their students' right to free and unrestricted expression as guaranteed to them under the First Amendment to the Constitution, where the exercise of such rights in the school buildings and schoolrooms do not materially and substantially interfere with the requirements of appropriate discipline in the operation of the school.[30]

However, in *Blackwell* v. *Issaquena County Board of Education*, the same court reached a different decision, finding for the defense, on the grounds that the wearing of buttons caused "an unusual degree of commotion, boisterous conduct, a collision with the rights of others, an undermining of authority, and a lack of order, discipline, and decorum."[31]

The case of *Tinker* v. *Des Moines Community School District* clearly confirms the courts' commitment to securing for students the right to freedom of expression. When this case reached the Supreme Court, Mr. Justice Fortas spoke for the majority as follows:

> It can hardly be argued that either students or teachers shed their constitutional rights to freedom of speech or expression at the schoolhouse gate. . . . There is no indication that the work of the schools or any class was disrupted . . . no threats or acts of violence on school premises . . . no disturbances or disorders on the school premises in fact occurred. . . . They caused discussion outside of the classrooms, but no interference with work and no disorder.[32]

[29] William E. Griffiths, "Student Constitutional Rights: The Role of the Principal," *National Association of Secondary School Principals Bulletin*, 52 (September 1968), 30–37.

[30] *Burnside* v. *Byars*, 363 F. 2nd 744 (1966).

[31] *Blackwell* v. *Issaquena County Board of Education*, 363 F. 2nd 749 (1966).

[32] *Tinker* v. *Des Moines Independent School District*, 393 U.S. 503 (1969).

The reference, once again, to the absence of disruption is significant because it implies that had a disruption occurred, the court might have ruled differently.

Freedom from search and seizure

The control of student lockers represents a perplexing problem for building principals. Traditionally, periodic locker inspections and "cleanouts" were regarded as a sound administrative practice that furnished the opportunity to search for such items as cigarettes, drugs, or even overdue library books, while simultaneously affording students the time to eliminate and rearrange items under the guise of maintaining a more orderly and healthful environment. This procedure has prompted considerable antagonism from students who maintain that arbitrary search of lockers and seizure of contents are violations of their Fourth Amendment rights.

There are several significant cases centering on this controversy.[33] Olson, who carefully reviewed this litigation, suggests that a locker search by a responsible school official is lawful if the following four circumstances exist:

1. The search is based on reasonable grounds for believing that something contrary to school rules or significantly detrimental to the school and its students will be found in the locker.

2. The information leading to the search and seizure is independent of the police.

3. The primary purpose of the search is to secure evidence of student misconduct for disciplinary purposes, although it may be contemplated that in appropriate circumstances the evidence would also be made available to the police. If evidence of a crime or grounds for a juvenile proceeding is lawfully obtained by school personnel, it may be turned over to police and used by them.

4. The school has keys or combinations to the lockers and the students are on some form of prior notice that the school reserves the right to search the lockers.[34]

DUE PROCESS

The Fourteenth Amendment forbids the states to deprive any person of life, liberty, or property without due process of law. Concerning sus-

[33] *New York* v. *Overton*, 249 N.E. 2nd, 366 (1969); *Stein* v. *Kansas*, 456, P. 2nd, 1 (1969); *Moore* v. *Student Affairs Committee of Troy State University*, 284, F. Supp. 725; *in re Donaldson*, 269 C.A. 2nd 509.

[34] Eric Olson, "Student Rights—Locker Searches," *National Association of Secondary School Principals Bulletin*, 55 (February 1971), 49–50.

pension or expulsion from school, elementary and secondary students have been successful in curbing the administrator's discretionary powers. Recently it has been maintained that the basic elements of due process— including written charges, hearing notice, preparation time for hearing, opportunity to confront witnesses, and stay pending appeal—must be followed prior to any expulsion, exclusion, dismissal, or lengthy suspension. The following statement by Judge Thornton in the Van Buren case represents prevailing opinion:

> These guidelines include notice containing "a statement of the specific charges and grounds which, if proven, would justify expulsion under the regulations of the Board of Education"; a hearing affording "an opportunity to hear both sides in considerable detail" preserving the rudiments of an adversary proceeding; names of witnesses against the student; and the "opportunity to present to the Board . . . his own defense."[35]

In rendering his opinion, the judge referred to and quoted from the Dixon decision, which had the effect of protecting college students from lengthy dismissals.[36] Increasingly, boards of education, with legal counsel, are adopting policies concerning student suspension and expulsion that will give principals a defensible operational framework in this sensitive area.

Although the courts may disagree in their rulings, a review of the aforementioned cases makes it apparent that the traditional doctrine of *in loco parentis* is being challenged. This creates an understandable role conflict for a principal who must enforce the rules of the organization while respecting the rights of the individual student. However, the Court in *Tinker* clearly stated: "School officials do not possess absolute authority over their students. Students in school as well as out are 'persons' under our Constitution. They are possessed of fundamental rights which the State must respect."[37]

In all cases, the courts have supported the value of a formal education, consistently basing their decisions on this premise. The ruling that a "record of expulsion from high school constitutes a lifetime stigma"[38] has prompted many principals to reconsider past disciplinary, suspension, and expulsion practices. In providing for due process within their schools, principals would do well to remember that "the condition of being a boy does not justify a kangaroo court."[39] Thus the courts have created a new awareness and new concern for student rights that heretofore have been given only tacit acknowledgment.

[35] *Vought v. Van Buren Public Schools,* 306 F. Supp. 1393 (1969).

[36] *Dixon v. Alabama State Board of Education,* 294 F. 2nd 150 (1961).

[37] *Tinker v. Des Moines,* op. cit.

[38] *Vought v. Van Buren,* op. cit.

[39] *In re Gault,* 387 U.S. 1 (1967).

Competencies in improving student personnel services

By way of summary, let us highlight some of the specific competencies required of the principal in improving the school's services to students.

AREA I. STUDENT VALUES

Competency No. 1. The principal analyzes, assesses, and describes the value orientations of the students within the school.

Competency No. 2. The principal reviews and explicates the goals and objectives of the school as an institution.

Competency No. 3. The principal analyzes and understands his own and the value orientations of the school staff.

AREA II. STUDENT INVOLVEMENT

Competency No. 4. The principal makes provisions for involving students meaningfully in the decisions concerning the programs of the school.

Competency No. 5. The principal coordinates the planning, staffing, financing, and evaluation of a viable cocurricular program in the school.

Competency No. 6. The principal supports the development of operational policies and provides the resources for an effective student government within the school.

AREA III. STUDENT GUIDANCE SERVICES

Competency No. 7. The principal stimulates the development of activities directed toward providing information about and to students.

Competency No. 8. The principal places priority on counseling with individual and groups of students, teachers, and parents.

Competency No. 9. The principal participates in setting policies and expediting procedures for in-school and subsequent placement of students.

Competency No. 10. The principal initiates research studies and utilizes research information from present and previous students as a basis for improving the guidance and total educational programs.

Competency No. 11. The principal structures activities that foster understanding and interaction among students, teachers, counselors, and other student personnel specialists.

Competency No. 12. The principal studies and understands recent legislation and court decisions having implications for the administration of the school.

Competency No. 13. The principal utilizes legislative and legal data as a basis for effecting change in the goals, objectives, and procedures of the school and in the values, roles, and behavior of organizational participants.

Summary

The principal's role in providing improved school services both with and for students was discussed in this chapter. First, it was stressed that the principal and other staff members must make serious efforts to appreciate, understand, and accept today's students. To develop such understanding, it was urged that the interactive distance between the staff and the students be decreased.

Next, it was emphasized that as a leader the principal must either change existing structures or develop new mechanisms that will allow students to increase their involvement in making educational decisions. Ways in which the cocurricular program and the student government may be utilized to increase student interest and involvement were delineated.

The principal's leadership role in removing some of the major constraints of or impediments to an effective guidance program was next examined. The five guidance functions viewed as converging on the student were: the individual inventory, information, counseling, placement, and research functions.

Next, the legal relationship of the student to the school was reviewed in terms of current court decisions related to compulsory school attendance, discipline, freedom of expression, freedom from search and seizure, and due process. It also was stressed that the effective principal must keep abreast of recent legislation and court decisions to ensure that the administrative regulations of the school as an organization are in keeping with the basic rights of the student as an individual.

The chapter concluded with the enumeration of 13 basic competencies required of the principal in providing improved student personnel services.

SUGGESTED ACTIVITIES

1. In a school with which you are familiar, analyze student participation in making curricular and cocurricular decisions. How might student involvement be improved?

2. Draw up a list of activities in which a student council is engaged. Have the council members (a) put the activities in rank order according to importance, and (b) analyze the rankings.

3. Conduct an analysis of the actual role of the counselor by determining what percentages of time are spent in fulfilling each of the five guidance services. To what extent are the results consistent with your personal expectations for the counselor's role?

4. Select a contemporary problem faced by principals, and structure the organizational relationships of the teaching and specialized student personnel workers to deal with the problem.

5. Formulate a student expulsion policy that includes provisions for due process. Be specific concerning time limitations and involvement of individuals in the decision-making process.

SELECTED REFERENCES

ANDERSON, LESTER, and LAUREN A. VAN DYKE, *Secondary School Administration,* 2nd ed., Boston, Houghton Mifflin, 1972.

DINKMEYER, DON C., and EDSON CALDWELL, *Developmental Counseling and Guidance: A Comprehensive School Approach,* New York, McGraw-Hill, 1970.

HUMMEL, DEAN, and S. J. BONHAM, *Pupil Personnel Services in Schools,* Skokie, Ill., Rand McNally, 1968.

KNOTT, PAUL D., *Student Activism,* Dubuque, Iowa, Brown, 1971.

MCCLEARY, LLOYD E., and STEPHEN P. HENCLEY, *Secondary School Administration: Theoretical Bases of Professional Practice,* New York, Dodd, Mead, 1965.

MILLER, CARROLL H., and GEORGE D. WEIGEL, eds., *Today's Guidance: A Book of Readings,* Boston, Allyn & Bacon, 1970.

MILLER, FRANKLIN A., et al., *Planning Student Activities,* Englewood Cliffs, N.J., Prentice-Hall, 1956.

MILLER, VAN, GEORGE R. MADDEN, and JAMES B. KINCHELOE, *The Public Administration of American School Systems,* 2nd ed., New York, Macmillan, 1972.

NOLTE, M. CHESTER, *Guide to School Law,* West Nyack, N.Y., Parker, 1969.

PETERS, HERMAN J., and GAIL F. FARWELL, *Guidance: A Developmental Approach,* Skokie, Ill., Rand McNally, 1959.

PETERSON, LEROY J., RICHARD A. ROSSMILLER, and MARLIN M. VOLZ, *The Law and Public School Operation,* New York, Harper & Row, 1968.

VAN HOOSE, WILLIAM H., MILDRED PETERS, and GEORGE E. LEONARD, *The Elementary School Counselor,* 2nd ed., Detroit, Wayne State University Press, 1970.

CHAPTER 12

The principal and financial-physical resources

W hereas the role of the principal concerning material resources was once largely managerial, in an emerging era of account-ability, the leadership required in planning, programming, budgeting, monitoring, and evaluating financial and physical resources represents a dynamic and demanding aspect of the principalship. In fact, it is increasingly recognized that if a resource management system is to become viable in the field of education, it must work at the in-dividual building level. Hence it is the principal who is responsible for orchestrating the material inputs with the human inputs to the school, for monitoring program progress and implementation, and for evaluating educational outcomes in programmatic terms.

In the first half of this chapter we discuss the principal's leadership role in planning, programming, budgeting, purchasing, and evaluating services and supplies. The second half describes the principal's leader-ship role in planning and operating school plant facilities. Systems theory is utilized to highlight the unique decision-making responsibilities of the principal in the two domains.

The principal and fiscal resources

In conceptualizing a system for the management of educational re-sources, the Association of School Business Officials gave as the underly-ing rationale the following basic assumptions:[1]

1. The resources available to the school are less than equal to the demands.

2. The school exists to produce a set of outcomes—to achieve certain objectives expressed as specific changes in the characteristics of the learners.

3. The objectives of the school can be achieved theoretically in a multitude of ways (program plans), some more effective than others.

[1] Adapted from William H. Curtis, Project Director, *Educational Resources Management System*, Chicago, Research Corporation of the Association of School Business Officials, 1971, pp. 37–39.

4. The productivity of the school can be increased by the organization of learning activities and supporting services into programs specifically aimed at the achievement of previously defined goals and objectives.

5. Better decisions regarding the selection of program plans and greater benefits from their operation result when these costs are considered on a long-term (multiyear) basis.

6. Better decisions regarding the selection of program plans and greater benefits from their application result when outcomes are related methodically to objectives.

PLANNING-PROGAMMING-BUDGETING SYSTEMS

Originating at the national level in the U.S. Department of Defense, the concept of planning-programming-budgeting systems (PPBS) has spread quickly and widely to many areas, including education. Although it has been variously defined, Hartley has written that PPBS in the field of education consists of the following:

1. A *mode of thinking* ("common sense by design") in which educators are simply asked to relate scarce resources to clearly defined programs with explicit objectives.

2. A *management tool* for administering complex organizations and studying the desired outcomes, problems, accomplishments and resources of a school district (people, materials, money, facilities, time, environment).

3. A *procedure for establishing priorities* in terms of a school district's total educational program and available resources.

4. An *accountability model* that is a constructive response to the current public demands that the schools should be more directly responsible for the results they produce.

5. An *information system* that generates an interactive flow of relevant data to and from planning, programming, budgeting and evaluating units until the results are either the best possible or at least satisfactory.

6. A *participative planning model* based on the establishment of a professional team or task force to do the detailed work on developing goals, objectives, program descriptions, program structure, program budgets, evaluation, reports and projections.

7. An *analytical tool* for considering alternative ways to resolve school district problems and to improve performance.

8. A *curricular innovation stimulant* that helps to identify obsolete or overlapping programs and to generate new instructional programs and procedures.

9. A *financial tool* that provides for "crosswalk" compatibility with the traditional budget, program budget, latest USOE handbook, or state information system and encourages the use of cost-effectiveness analysis.

10. A *school-community relations model* that can help generate badly needed public support by providing better information about new programs, student accomplishments and budget costs.[2]

The appropriate participation of others is a significant consideration in developing a systematic approach to planning, programming, and budgeting. As a leader, the principal must initiate the appropriate organizational structures to involve teachers, students, and citizens meaningfully in the process. Moreover, the structures for participation at the school building level must relate appropriately to those at the school district level, since any systematic approach to resource management eventually must be consummated at the school district level. Several types of participative structure have been established in the schools. At the earlier stages in the process of assessing needs and defining objectives, for example, either a large committee or several subcommittees may be necessary; at the subsequent stages of formulating alternatives, costing programs, and evaluating outcomes, smaller committees or a representative council may be in order. Obviously, the size of the school conditions the structural leadership decisions to be made by the principal.

The management of educational resources must be an integral aspect of the total administration of the school. Figure 12.1 schematizes the relationship of the stages in resource management to the other stages in the administrative process. The stages in this systems view include the following:

I. Planning
1. Assessing community, school, and student needs, problems, and issues.
2. Identifying and reviewing existing and new goals, developing potential general objectives, and adopting goals and objectives.
3. Translating general objectives into measurable performance terms.
II. Programming
4. Designing a program structure and format consistent with the performance objectives.
5. Formulating alternative approaches and program plans.
III. Budgeting
6. Analyzing alternative approaches in terms of constraints, requirements, and cost effectiveness.
7. Recommending, selecting, and adopting optimal alternatives for attaining objectives.
8. Preparing budgetary documents for the adopted programs.

[2] Henry J. Hartley, *Educational Planning-Programming-Budgeting*, Englewood Cliffs, N.J., Prentice-Hall, 1968, pp. 75–99, as summarized in National School Public Relations Association, *PPBS and the School*, Washington, D.C. 1972, pp. 4–6.

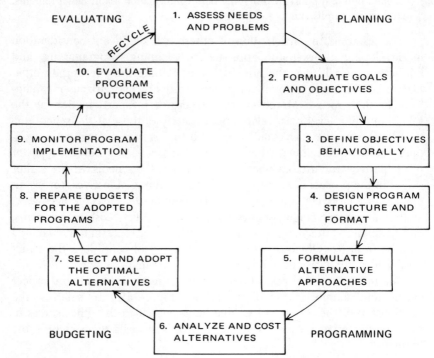

Figure 12.1
Systems approach to the planning, programming, budgeting, and evaluating cycle

IV. Evaluating
   9. Monitoring program implementation in terms of the objectives through the use of process evaluation.
   10. Assessing program outcomes in terms of the objectives through the use of product evaluation.

The above stages clearly merge, one with the other; moreover, the entire process is recycled in subsequent years. Indeed, it is not always necessary to begin with planning, since the process may be entered at any stage.

   In the earlier foundational chapters dealing with systems and decision theory and in the functional chapters covering program and personnel, we discussed fully the planning, programming, and evaluating phases. Additional consideration should be given, however, to the budgeting and purchasing processes.

THE BUDGETING PROCESS

The major concerns in the budgeting process include the reconciliation of program requirements with the available resources; the development, updating, and maintaining of budget documents; and the monitoring, accounting, and progress reporting on the use of resources.[3] In dealing with these concerns, many principals have found it desirable to utilize a representative council of staff members. The council might logically be comprised of department chairmen at the secondary level, whereas unit leaders, team leaders, or grade level chairmen could constitute committee membership at the elementary level. However council membership is formed, and in large schools especially, care must be taken that each instructional group, team, or discipline is represented. Often, for example, members of small departments in secondary schools and specialized staff members in elementary schools in such curricular fields as physical education, art, or music feel deprived of meaningful participation in financial decision making.

Whether a conventional line-item or a systematic PPBS approach to budgeting is utilized, an important first step of the financial council is to analyze alternative instructional approaches in terms of the constraints, requirements, and cost-effectiveness of each component of the school's program. Such assessment, ideally, should be made in terms of the objectives to be achieved rather than in terms of "things" to be bought. At this stage the council's role becomes powerful indeed, for invariably the procedure leads to significant resource allocation decisions. This is why it is imperative that the council be representative.

To accomplish the first stage of work, the council may have to conduct a comprehensive analysis of the existing resources available to each operational unit—department, grade level, or program. In schools without an adequate system of inventory control, this is a necessary step to avoid overbudgeting or duplication in purchasing. It also can serve to acquaint faculty members with equipment or supplies with which they may not be familiar. Many consummable commodities (e.g., those used in laboratory sciences or applied curricula) may be readily identified; however, new instructional methodologies in all fields have led to the utilization of myriad educational devices and supplies—some not so frequently encountered and perhaps relatively unfamiliar to the staff.

Whereas conducting an inventory of equipment and material on hand is a simple process, a realistic assessment of future needs is difficult indeed because of recent advances in educational technology and diversification of curricula. Nevertheless, intelligent determinations must be made concerning which equipment and supplies are on hand, which are mandatory for existing programs, and which would ultimately be desirable. Relative costs per unit of instruction must be assessed if the school is to move from the actual or present program to the ideal or desired program.

[3] Curtis, op. cit., p. 91.

The tendency of staff members to become overly enamored of benefits possible from the utilization of innovative equipment or supplies should be observed and minimized. Each committee member, with the assistance of the professionals he represents, must conscientiously determine which instructional goals are not being realized because of a lack of physical resources, instructional materials, and teaching supplies. Classification of these neglected goals is often an excellent place to begin in projecting minimal resource requirements.

Establishing a rank order of identified needs requires unselfish behavior from all council members. In this sensitive task, the principal's interpersonal skills and knowledge of the total program are of considerable value. Because faculty members are assigned to particular departments or grade levels, their interests can become quite provincial; but the principal, as the leader of the entire school, must remain abreast of the needs and developments in each aspect of the total program. Consequently, it often may fall to the principal either to influence or to adjudicate the final determination of resources.

Just as each department, grade level, or locational unit must compete for a portion of the school's budget, each school must compete for its share of the total district resources available in these categories. Of course the principal should minimize chances that the available funds will be apportioned inequitably by coming prepared with a documented list of needed acquisitions for his building, named in order of priority. As McGivney and Bowles have observed, however, planning-programming-budgeting systems may be of great utility in rational decision-making circumstances, but they have much less usefulness when other modes of political policy formulation are involved, such as persuasion, bargaining, and power play politics.[4]

Recent research has revealed that in some systems of programming, planning, and budgeting the detailed processes utilized have either inadvertently or inappropriately hamstrung the principal's discretionary power to make program, budgetary, or purchasing decisions based on process evaluations of changing needs and priorities. Webster, for example, has cautioned that the building principal who would fulfill the requirements of the two-way street of accountability must have the autonomy to make decisions in implementing learning programs; he needs to decide on day-to-day changes in program design, and he needs enough latitude to make local financial decisions affecting the immediate implementation of program changes.[5] The budget always includes constraints,

[4] Joseph H. McGivney and B. Dean Bowles, "The Political Aspects of PPBS," *Planning and Changing*, 3 (April 1972), 8–12.

[5] Joan M. Webster, "A Cost-Effective Analysis of Selected Reading Programs in the Grand Rapids Public Schools," doctoral dissertation, Michigan State University, 1972.

but corrective procedures for major and minor revisions should be built into the process. This is a particularly critical point, since previously in the field of education so much emphasis has been placed on summative or outcome evaluation rather than on formative or process evaluation.

THE PURCHASING PROCESS

The principal and the council should determine cooperatively the kinds and amounts of acquisitions required for the achievement of objectives. This is not an easy task. As indicated earlier, the selection of proper supplies and equipment to remedy acknowledged program deficiencies or to attain new objectives is complicated by the market availability of a wealth of materials. Again, priorities must be established regarding which acquisitions are best suited for each objective.

In establishing priorities, the principal must remain objective and must identify the financial constraints to the council in terms of the available resources. A principal who reneges on a promise to secure equipment and supplies, blaming "the central office," soon loses the respect of everyone. To ensure orderly budgeting and purchasing processes, the council must be advised of the exact amounts of money needed, and needs must be reconciled with the resources available. Moreover, if subsequent financial difficulties at the district level result in fewer resources for the school, as is often the case, adjustments will be less dysfunctional because priorities already have been established.

Unfortunately, the timing of the professional negotiations process has complicated efforts at approximating the exact amount of money available to school districts for new purchases. Teachers have been adamant in their monetary demands, and boards of education often have granted salary increases much larger than originally anticipated, thus depleting discretionary funds. Despite the most systematic efforts, the budgets of individual schools are sometimes reduced so drastically that only the most critical supplies can be purchased. Many principals have been so frustrated by such circumstances that they have postponed budgetary planning until after the teachers' organization and the board of education have agreed on a financial package for salaries and fringe benefits. This is a poor practice, since it unduly condenses the time frame and reduces the budgetary process to a low level of negative reaction rather than a high level of priority action.

Even after a school's budget for supplies and equipment has been authorized, crises often develop within the district that may prevent expenditure of the entire amounts budgeted. For instance, the number of substitute teachers needed may be greater than anyone could have anticipated, or there may be an equipment breakdown of a magnitude that exhausts all contingency funds. Moreover, levels of state support are always subject to the vagaries of the political process. With most of the money for the year already committed for salaries, transportation, plant operation, and other fixed costs, the only accounts that logically can be tapped for additional funds are teaching supplies, new and replacement equipment, and building maintenance. To compensate for such circumstances, many teachers and principals requisition all budgeted supplies and equipment either a year in advance or as early as possible in the school year. Even this practice is questionable, however, because as the school year progresses there is little room for reestablishing priorities to accommodate program changes revealed as necessary by process evaluation.

Role relationships between the central office and the principal also are important in both budgeting and purchasing. Research has shown that the role of the school district business manager is not clearly understood by principals.[6] For example, the business manager's job is often complicated by principals who, eager to be accepted by the building staff, are reluctant to veto any request. In some schools the principal's approval of a purchase order is perfunctory, and the decision of whether to purchase is left to the central office. A principal is negligent in performing his role if he does not approve or disapprove requests based on their projected capability to fulfill instructional objectives. A forwarded purchase order should assure the business manager that the principal has given careful consideration to the request. Whereas the determination of allotted funds for a building is the joint responsibility of the central office and the principal, the determination of the appropriate distribution of these funds is the joint responsibility of the principal and the teaching staff. The principal's cursory approval of requisitions inappropriately places the responsibility for determination of intrabuilding priorities within the central office and relinquishes priority control within the school.

In addition to concerns with the regular budget, the principal is responsible for the management of student activity funds. To accommodate certain needs of the cocurricular program, it has become standard practice in most secondary schools to maintain a student activities account within the school to safeguard money that flows through the treasury of school organizations. Internal accounting procedures, subject to periodic audit and review, are utilized to facilitate and expedite the numerous transactions necessary to perpetuate a dynamic cocurricular program. Knezevich and Fowlkes have cautioned administrators, however, that student activity funds are derived from public activities,

[6] L. Paul Lansing, "Relationship Between Role Expectations and Performance Effectiveness of the School Business Administrator," doctoral dissertation, University of Wisconsin, 1971.

require the use of public property, and are supervised by public employees; therefore, they must be treated as any other public funds.[7] The courts have ruled that these funds should be administered with the same careful attention given district funds in the planning, programming, budgeting, purchasing, accounting, and evaluating processes.[8]

Prior to recycling the budgetary process for the forthcoming year, the principal and the financial council should evaluate the quality and quantity of equipment and supplies purchased during the preceding year. Moreover, they should carefully review the procedures employed. After thorough evaluation, recycling of the process typically requires a return to the planning and programming processes. Although council members and teachers' organization representatives may be quite well informed about resource allocation, individual teachers may not be as accurately advised. This is unfortunate, because these processes affect each teacher directly. Hence the principal, with consultation and help from central office personnel, must take steps to inform and involve the total staff, permitting a better understanding of planning, programming, budgeting, and evaluating.

The principal and the school plant

"To serve its function well, to meet the educational expectancies of its students and the community, to be truly great, the school building must be more than a container for the educational program," declared the Commission on Buildings of the American Association of School Administrators.[9] The Commission further stressed that the school building should be not only a functional servant of the educational program but also a friendly, attractive, and stimulating place—imparting a feeling of security and a sense of pride to all whom it serves.[10] The principal's role in achieving this ideal includes leadership activities in planning and maintaining the school plant.

SCHOOL PLANT PLANNING

The total process of planning for educational facilities typically is a central office responsibility—particularly when one considers projecting

[7] Stephen J. Knezevich and John Guy Fowlkes, *Business Management of Local School Systems*, New York, Harper & Row, 1960, p. 189.

[8] LeRoy J. Peterson, Richard A. Rossmiller, and Marlin M. Volz, *The Law and Public School Operations*, New York, Harper & Row, 1969, pp. 129–130.

[9] Commission on School Buildings, *Schools for America*, Washington, D.C., American Association of School Administrators, 1967, p. 35.

[10] Ibid., p. 44.

enrollments and needs, financing improvements, and constructing facilities.[11] Yet the principal has significant responsibilities for coordinating the input of teachers, students, and citizens in planning for educational facilities.

Planning for school buildings is a complex, time-consuming process that typically begins with the conduct of a school survey. Castaldi has categorized surveys according to studies of the community and pupil population trends, financial and educational resources, the educational program itself, and the quality of existing school buildings.[12] He has indicated that these studies may be conducted by outside consultants or experts, the local school staff, citizens' committees, or combinations of all three groups.

Having citizens act in an advisory capacity to the central administration and board of education is now an accepted procedure in planning for educational facilities in most school districts. The formation of lay advisory groups can be particularly beneficial in the initial planning stages. Since the citizens will be the beneficiaries of a school construction program, they possess not only a vested financial interest in the new school but also a continuing educational interest. Their inclusion in the planning stage can serve to increase their enthusiasm for and support of the building program. Although the impetus for the formation of an advisory council usually originates with the school board, the principal typically is expected to nominate members, attend meetings, and participate in the deliberations of citizens' advisory councils.

Following the survey, the board of education, acting on recommendations of the superintendent of schools, must assess the feasibility of embarking on a building program to fulfill the expectations of the survey team. This assessment involves consideration of political as well as financial and educational ramifications. After the board has made the decision to expand or alter the number of existing buildings, the principal must formulate a sound program of information dissemination regarding the necessity for new or enlarged facilities. As spokesman for the school, the principal, who is most visible to his attendance community, is the professional to whom the citizens look for advice and information. His understanding, support, and endorsement of a building program are vital if the constituency is expected to react favorably to a bond issue for financing the construction.

The planning for educational facilities is a task of great magnitude,

[11] Grace F. Howell, "The Significance of Educational Planning of the Physical Plant in Adapting to Curricular Innovations," doctoral dissertation, Brigham Young University, 1967.

[12] Basil Castaldi, *Creative Planning of Educational Facilities,* Skokie, Ill., Rand McNally, 1969, pp. 22–38.

and a systematic means for implementing the building program requires the involvement of many people.[13] McIsaac pioneered in the application of program evaluation review technique/critical path method (PERT/CPM) to the multitude of tasks required. He developed PERT programs that specifically delineate the activities, the normal and slack times, the responsibilities, and the costs of more than 1000 tasks called for in moving from the initial assessment of needs to occupying the building. This procedure has great practical utility for school districts.[14] It also possesses significant implications for research on school plant planning. Utilizing PERT, for example, McEnroe discovered that whereas many milestones at the district level are clearly understood, those at the individual school level—which involve the principal and teachers in the school plant planning process—are much less clearly understood and less appropriately implemented.[15]

Thus far, our discussion has dealt with what Leu described as the planning *for* a school building, as contrasted with the planning *of* a school building.[16] Planning of a building includes the development of educational specifications and architectural plans leading to the construction of a new facility. On approval by referendum to finance construction, the principal assumes a more definitive role in the development of educational specifications for the building. His primary responsibility, of course, is to ensure that the learning and auxiliary spaces will accommodate the proposed curricular and cocurricular programs of the school. Attention must be directed to other concerns, as well. For example, the principal is responsible for maintaining a safe and healthy school environment. Any principal can attest that the maintenance program to remedy facility flaws can consume inordinate amounts of time. A well-planned, well-constructed, and easily serviceable building will reduce the number of subsequent building maintenance problems. In short, "contrary to public opinion, a good school is cheaper in the long run than a bad one."[17]

Educational facility planners have stressed that the process of planning the individual school plant involves the following stages: (1) a

[13] Harris A. Taylor and Donald N. McIsaac, "How PERT Works to Speed School Building Programs," *Nation's Schools,* 73 (June 1964), 46–47.

[14] Donald N. McIsaac, "A PERT Program for the Construction of Homestead High School," unpublished report, Board of Education, Dubuque, Iowa, 1969.

[15] Edward J. McEnroe, "The Utility of Critical Path Network in the Analysis of Organizational Stress," doctoral dissertation, University of Wisconsin, 1969.

[16] Donald L. Leu, *Planning Educational Facilities,* New York, Center for Applied Research in Education, 1965, p. 33.

[17] Harold B. Gores, "Schools in the 70's: The Case of the Relevant School House," *National Association of Secondary School Principals Bulletin,* 54 (May 1970), 134.

review of the educational program, including attention to the behavioral objectives to be achieved; (2) an assessment of the learning experiences and the services to be rendered, as well as the determination of quantitative requirements in terms of specific program and space needs; (3) the determination of the qualitative requirements, including the functional details of each space; (4) the preparation of written educational specifications that serve as the educator's guide to the architect; and (5) the review of architectural plans, which may require reinterpretation of the educational specifications to the architect.[18] In each stage of the process, it is important that the principal structure the organization to supply meaningful input by the individuals and groups concerned.

GROUPS INVOLVED IN PLANNING. The intraschool reference groups that must be involved in facility planning include teachers, students, and noncertificated personnel.

TEACHER INVOLVEMENT. Teacher input concerning curricular objectives and the physical requirements for the realization of objectives is essential. The principal's role in coordinating the efforts of the professional staff in developing educational specifications is often complicated because teachers are apt to be quite prescriptive in their requests. Experienced teachers, especially, have preconceived notions regarding the preciseness and exactness of room dimensions and furniture arrangements required for them to function effectively. New teachers also are eager to volunteer their impressions of an ideal room, cluster of rooms, or the total building. The danger, of course, is that the completed facility may become a potpourri reflecting the idiographic or personalistic preferences of each staff member. Consequently, individual preferences are only one factor to be considered in developing specifications expressly suitable to the educational mission of the school. With some justification, teachers have been disenchanted with the educational facilities provided and have been quick to point out deficiencies. Involvement of the faculty can serve both to improve staff morale and to contribute toward their ultimate acceptance of the educational facility.

Since some of the teachers who are involved in the preliminary planning may no longer be employed in the school when the building is completed, it is important to involve all staff members and to reach consensus on the many suggestions. Staff involvement also helps the faculty to understand the nature and severity of the financial constraints in planning for the building. Promoting staff awareness of the actual restraints while simultaneously encouraging people to offer creative

[18] National Council on Schoolhouse Construction, *NCSC Guide for Planning School Plants,* East Lansing, Mich., The Council, 1964, p. 14.

and idealistic suggestions may present conflict for the principal, but it is a responsibility that cannot be ignored.

STUDENT INVOLVEMENT. Of all groups having an interest in the planning of new facilities, none is more directly affected than the students. Just as professionals hold varying expectations regarding the type of physical surroundings in which they could best perform, students differ in their perceptions of an ideal environment. Although students may not have been exposed to a sufficient variety of facilities to make valid comparisons, they are quite adept at recognizing structural and environmental deficiencies in schools they have attended.

To receive student suggestions in the planning of the new structure, the committees engaged in facility planning must include students. Not only will this alert adults directly to student concerns, as with teachers, it will provide student representatives with a better understanding of the financial constraints within which the school must be constructed. An additional benefit from systematic student involvement in planning is that of improved morale resulting from the recognition that programs and facilities are designed both for them and with them.

NONCERTIFICATED PERSONNEL INVOLVEMENT. Custodians, maintenance personnel, secretaries, and food service employees, among others, should be involved in the development of educational specifications for the school. Custodial and maintenance personnel can give valuable insights concerning an important dimension—the ease with which the building can be properly serviced and maintained. Secretarial and kitchen personnel often make valuable suggestions regarding special demands required for effectiveness and efficiency in their domains. The input from employees must be merged with that of other groups, making the recommendations compatible with the overall planning effort.

The recommendations of the various references groups must be synthesized into a set of written educational specifications for the architect.[19] The specifications should include a description of each major space in the building.

THE LEARNING SPACES. Learning spaces include all rooms and laboratories designed to facilitate directly the teaching-learning process. The teaching stations, as they are sometimes labeled, represent the core of the school building, and the design of these spaces is a matter of great concern to the instructional staff. Included should be a detailed quantitative and qualitative analysis of the activities that are to take place

[19] Nickolaus L. Engelhardt, *Complete Guide for Planning New Schools,* West Nyack, N.Y., Parker, 1970.

in each space, the types of equipment and materials needed, structural arrangements of the space, storage requirements, and similar functional considerations. The specifications also must provide for flexibility, so that the learning spaces do not quickly become obsolete. Other considerations include provisions for the utilization of communications media and materials, as well as spaces for individualized learning.

Auxiliary spaces—such as the materials center, cafeteria, multipurpose room, physical education facilities—and school offices, and conference rooms are equally important. Several of these spaces, because of their integral relationship with the entire school program or because of their uniqueness, deserve special mention.

THE INSTRUCTIONAL MATERIALS CENTER. Until a few years ago the school library consisted of a collection of hardbound books housed in a large, austere room, little more than a study hall. In the elementary school, students were ushered to the library once a week to hear a story or to select their books; in the secondary school, students could be seen busily copying from encyclopedia volumes to meet report deadlines. Library staffs were preoccupied with orderliness, and students often perceived library assignments as a disciplinary measure.

Today's library serves a different purpose.[20] Towering book stacks have been rearranged, and the environment has been vitalized. Diversification of activity and excitement about learning characterize the modern instructional materials center—an appropriate name for a resource complex that serves as the learning center of the school. The library is no longer a single, uninviting room; it now includes specially designed spaces for individual and group study, listening, demonstration of materials, and storage of supplies. It is designed to maximize utilization of the collection of books, magazines, pamphlets, pictures, filmstrips, slides, records, tapes, movies, and vertical file materials available to complement instruction in each academic discipline.

With a change in role expectations to that of "directors of learning," teachers are becoming increasingly dependent on library resources to supplement classroom learning experiences. Any curricular program designed to individualize instruction must rely on an extensive, well-organized instructional materials center staffed by dynamic professionals.[21] The traditional image of a library can be altered with careful planning and with a commitment of funds to provide a spatial arrangement that is sufficiently attractive, convenient, and functional. Cheerful,

[20] Eleanore E. Ahlers, "Library Service: A Changing Concept," *Educational Leadership,* 23 (March 1966), 452–453.

[21] Kin Kamanski and David M. Cox, "School for the '70's: The Module Is One," *Nation's Schools,* 85 (March 1970), 67.

inviting surroundings will attract students; a conscientious and well-informed staff will ensure the tapping of every library resource.

Exact spatial and equipment requirements for an instructional materials center vary according to the goals and objectives of the total school program. Probably because of tradition, however, existing library standards continue to provide guidelines depending on the number of students enrolled in a school.[22] For instance, a school of 1500 students is expected to furnish within the instructional materials center more study stations and more materials than a school of 500 students. We hold to the ideal, however, that the scope of the collection of an instructional materials center should be similar in all comparable schools. Students in a high school of 300 students should have access to the same range of materials as students in a high school of 3000 students, just as the length of the football field is the same for smaller schools and for larger schools. Without the necessary materials and a variety of learning stations, an instructional materials center will not serve the purposes for which it is intended. The principal must assume an active role in planning the instructional materials center in ensuring its utility as the learning center of the school.

THE CAFETERIA. Beginning in 1935 with passage of Public Law 320, the federal government has elected to stimulate the establishment of school lunch programs throughout the country. The courts, too, have supported the rights of boards of education to serve food to students.[23] The most significant breakthrough in federal support of food service programs was the 1946 National School Lunch Act, which stated that to safeguard the health and well-being of the nation's children, the states would be assisted in providing an adequate supply of foods for nonprofit lunch programs. The Child Nutrition Act of 1966 and Public Law 91–248 in 1970 have further encouraged the growth of food service programs. In 1968 the number of students served under the National School Lunch Program represented 37 percent of the total school enrollment,[24] and this percentage continues to increase.

Most educators view food service as contributing to several desirable educational outcomes. Roe suggested that food services have the following educational possibilities: helping children learn to select the right

22 Cf. American Association of School Librarians, *Standards for School Media Programs,* Chicago, American Library Association, 1970; "Policies and Criteria for the Approval of Secondary Schools," Chicago, North Central Association of Colleges and Secondary Schools, 1970.

23 *Hailey* v. *Brooks,* 191 S.W. 781 (1916).

24 U.S. Department of Agriculture, Economic Research Service, *Food Service in the Nation's Schools, A Preliminary Report,* Washington, D.C., Government Printing Office, 1969.

foods, stressing the use of correct table manners, encouraging cleanliness and sanitation, and emphasizing working and living together.[25]

The cafeteria should be designed with more than simple efficiency in mind. Nothing is more depressing to students than a cafeteria arrangement that minimizes opportunities to visit with their friends in a cordial atmosphere during meals. Small tables for four to six students organized in a semiprivate setting help to foster good nutritional habits, proper table manners, and a wholesome attitude toward the school lunch program. Students react unfavorably to lunchroom facilities that look like an army mess hall and do not offer a favorable setting for relaxing and socializing. As in the case of the instructional materials center, the facility is only a part of the environment. Lunchroom personnel who are cheerful and friendly can contribute immeasurably toward creating the right atmosphere that is so important if the food service program is to yield positive educational experiences.

MULTIPURPOSE ROOM. No room in the school has more demands placed on it than the multipurpose room, which has become a common feature of many modern schools, particularly at the elementary level.[26] At various times this facility may accommodate physical education classes, community recreation programs, school lunch activities, plays or concerts, large group instruction, and anything else requiring more space than is available in a regular classroom. In most instances the room is used far beyond its capacity to provide a suitable station for each of the aforementioned demands.

Since the school often constitutes the social, educational, and recreational center for the community, expectations of the functions of the multipurpose room should be carefully delineated. Quite possibly, two separate stations or one large station with a movable wall are necessary to accommodate simultaneous student, teacher, and community demands. Many multipurpose rooms are too small and too poorly equipped to provide necessary services to the school and community. Shower rooms, for instance, are usually considered a luxury, although for the strenuous activities in physical education showers are an integral part of the health education program. In addition, use of the facility for adult recreational activities would be enhanced if proper locker room and shower facilities were available.

PHYSICAL EDUCATION FACILITIES. Along with concern over instructional utility, those who design physical education spaces must give attention

[25] William Roe, *School Business Management*, New York, McGraw-Hill, 1961, pp. 281–282.

[26] Emery Stoops and Russell E. Johnson, *Elementary School Administration*, New York, McGraw-Hill, 1967, p. 103.

to storage, locker room, and shower facilities. At the secondary level, interscholastic athletics and community usage often tax these areas to their maximum. Locker rooms should be healthful and sanitary. If projected traffic and usage patterns are not carefully considered, custodial personnel will be frustrated in their attempts to comply with prevailing sanitation standards. Wise planning of the physical education components will relieve many subsequent traffic, health, and maintenance problems.

Swimming pools, once a luxury within a school plant, are now gaining widespread acceptance. Swimming is one of the most popular and least expensive of all leisure-time activities, and the school program is the logical vehicle through which the principles of water safety can be taught. Extensive community use of a pool causes several problems, but it should be encouraged, for the entire community, including pre- and post-school-age students, are beneficiaries of a well-designed natatorium.

SCHOOL OFFICES. Historically, the offices of the administrative staff have been located near the front entrance of the school to serve the public expeditiously. Although some portion of the principal's time must go to public relations efforts, his proximity to the main entrance frequently necessitates lengthy involvement in activities that could be performed by others. Certainly some type of greeting station for visitors is desirable, but this service can easily be performed by an attendance clerk-receptionist, especially in larger schools. A more suitable place for the principal's office is near the center of the learning activities of the school, where his role as instructional leader can be reinforced. The physical seclusion of the principal's office from the instructional program has hindered the provision of instructional leadership when it is needed. The principal's office should serve as the nerve center for the school—for coordination, for leadership, and for influencing the climate of the organization.

Offices for other personnel—guidance counselors, health officers, and other specialists—should be easy to find, easy to enter, and pleasant to be in; they should be designed to facilitate movement of people and arranged to provide privacy when necessary.[27] Likewise, teachers need office spaces for planning, preparation of materials, and conducting individual conferences. All the office spaces should be equipped with telephones and files and should be inviting and attractive.

PLANNING FOR THE FUTURE. In today's school construction, with innovation and individualization the norm, it is difficult to project future space requirements and designs. Science laboratories, performing arts facilities,

[27] Commission on School Buildings, op. cit., p. 31.

indoor and outdoor physical education and recreation stations, and classroom clusters are being planned to maximize the positive impact of the physical environment. Neither the principal nor the faculty can possibly keep abreast of all the research on school construction. In planning a new school, therefore, it is important to consult with experts to help ensure a forward-looking design.

Rather than designing the curriculum to fit a particular building, the facilities should be designed to serve the educational program. Specialists in environmental design who are skilled in controlling the thermal, sonic, visual, and aesthetic environments are helpful in shaping school facilities that provide the utmost in comfort, convenience, beauty, and utility.[28] Perhaps the most important criterion for the building, however, is flexibility. Curricular and cocurricular programs of today may be irrelevant in the future. Prohibitive construction costs preclude the erection of new facilities to accommodate major program changes. Consequently, school plants must be constructed such that substantial revisions can be made with minimum effort and expense; thus the facility does not dictate the program. In coordinating facility planning, the principal must assume leadership in forecasting future societal demands on the schools and must offer constructive advice regarding the appropriateness of planned facilities in terms of their flexibility for meeting future expectations and program demands.

SCHOOL PLANT MAINTENANCE

The maintenance program for buildings and grounds must accomplish the following objectives: (1) promoting a physical environment conducive to enhancing the teaching-learning process, and (2) protecting the financial investment of the community. Visitors to the school are quick to form impressions about how the building and grounds are maintained—some even view a well-kept physical plant as "the hallmark of a good principal." Although this point may be overstated, to gain community support and respect, as well as to fulfill his role as the guardian of a substantial investment, the principal must emphasize school maintenance.

Complicating the efforts of administrative, maintenance, and custodial staffs to plan a conscientious maintenance program are the many demands placed on the building. No longer are schools occupied only during the daylight hours. The requests of student and community groups for building utilization, both before and after school, are so numerous that

[28] Ross L. Neagley et al., *The School Administrator and Learning Resources,* Englewood Cliffs, N.J., Prentice-Hall, 1969, p. 86.

custodial staffs become frustrated in their attempts to perform even daily housekeeping chores. Nor is the opportunity to compensate for "time lost" during the school year found in the summer. Recreational, enrichment, remedial, athletic, and adult educational programs housed in the school during the summer months hamper the efforts of the most dedicated maintenance workers. Moreover, since these personnel are also entitled to summer vacations, maintenance routines may be further complicated.

Although the principal is the immediate supervisor of all custodial and maintenance workers within the building, he ordinarily (except in small school districts) is assisted by a system-wide supervisor who will help to establish work schedules, to identify and procure needed supplies, and to inspect the building periodically. The existence of a plant manager, however, does not relieve the principal of direct responsibility for maintenance supervision. Instead, it provides him with technical and supportive assistance. If during his regular inspection of custodial services the principal determines that certain areas need increased attention, he and the custodial supervisor should plan cooperatively to remedy the observed deficiencies.

Increasing demands of the instructional program also require increased numbers of maintenance personnel. Schools no longer resemble egg crates with all classrooms of identical shape and size, nor are students usually confined to a single learning station for an extended period of time. Modern schools encourage diversification of activities and freedom of movement, thus compounding and extending daily housekeeping routines because of the multiple use of space. Hallways, entrances, lavatories, and locker rooms also demand continual attention. The principal must help school boards to recognize that the demands on custodial time are growing and that sufficient maintenance personnel must be employed to accommodate programs of individualized instruction.

In facilitating the individualized learning process, teachers also make continuous demands on the time of custodial personnel, who often must help with rearrangements of furniture and equipment (e.g., from large group lectures to small group discussions). They assist with movement and placement of television, demonstration, and film projecting equipment, as well as a host of printed materials and instructional aids, since these must often be shared throughout the school. As an experienced custodian remarked recently, "It's move this, move that! Nothing is nailed down around here anymore—especially the kids." The instructional and maintenance staffs must work harmoniously to prevent the loss of instructional time from setting up and moving equipment and supplies.

THE PRINCIPAL AND THE CUSTODIAL STAFF. Hill and Colmey maintain that a "clear statement of school board policies should be the starting point in determining a plan for assigning custodial personnel."[29] Such a policy should state that no custodian will be assigned to a building without approval of the principal, who uses a personal interview to assess the prospective employee's potential to function effectively in that particular building. As in the employment of teachers, the interview with prospective custodians is the time for exploring the congruence between the demands of the institutional role and the personal values, needs, and dispositions of the applicant.

Organizational level should be considered in examining the role demands and in making assignments. Some custodians enjoy working with elementary students; others work best around older students. The demands at each organizational level are quite different, and it is incorrect to assume that custodians can experience equal success at either level. For example, in small elementary schools the demands on the position usually are quite varied. Typically, one custodian is employed during the day, and he must be able to perform multitudinous chores effectively, cooperatively, and efficiently. He has great visibility both to students and to staff, who often call on him for assistance within classrooms and on the playground. By contrast, custodians in large secondary schools may have more routinized roles and a relatively formal, if not remote, relationship with students and teachers—of the order, "They don't hassle me; I don't hassle them."

The identification of excellent prospective custodians is no less difficult than the identification of excellent prospective teachers. Of course, custodians must exhibit a wholesome attitude toward their work, possess a cooperative disposition, and display a relatively high degree of resourcefulness. Equally important is their understanding and internalization of the vital role they perform and the significant contribution they make toward realization of the school's objectives. Most custodians enjoy the opportunity to be of assistance to maturing youth, and the principal should capitalize on this feeling. Efforts at establishing good rapport with the custodial staff, moreover, are well worth the principal's time.

As in the case of teachers, unless custodians have an understanding of and a love for young people of school age, they will experience frustration. They must realize that schools of today provide opportunities for increased student expression and movement, thereby complicating the custodian's job. Student behavior deviating from traditional value orientations and norms is rather commonplace in many schools, but

[29] Frederick W. Hill and James W. Colmey, *School Custodial Services*, Minneapolis, Denison, 1968, p. 31.

it must be realized that such behavior reflects many societal, situational, and personal factors. Students occasionally vent their emotions through mischievous behavior that usually results in additional work for the custodian but seldom is directed toward him personally.

Custodians, as well as other staff personnel, appreciate a close working relationship with the principal. Often they are intensely proud, if not possessive, of their schools. They enjoy praise for a job well done and are receptive to objective, constructive suggestions for improvement. Moreover, they can provide the principal with input and suggestions that reflect a substantial segment of community opinion. In this regard it is well to remember the preachment, "It is impossible to fool two reference groups in the school—kids and custodians." A principal who wants to increase the productivity of the maintenance and custodial staff will make every effort to acknowledge both formally and informally the positive impact of each individual on the total school program.

Competencies in improving finances and facilities

Some specific competencies required to improve the principal's leadership in providing adequate financial and physical resources for the school are as follows:

AREA 1. FINANCIAL RESOURCES

Competency No. 1. The principal ascertains the needs, goals, and objectives of the school and translates them into instructional and support outcomes that are measurable in performance terms.

Competency No. 2. The principal leads the staff in the development of a program structure and format consistent with the measurable objectives.

Competency No. 3. The principal identifies, analyzes, and costs alternatives for achieving each objective.

Competency No. 4. The principal recommends the selection and adoption of optimal instructional alternatives.

Competency No. 5. The principal conducts or maintains an adequate inventory of equipment, supplies, and materials for achieving objectives.

Competency No. 6. The principal prepares a budget that establishes a priority of needs for each program within the school.

Competency No. 7. The principal evaluates and approves requisitions for equipment, supplies, and materials to be purchased for the school.

Competency No. 8.   The principal forecasts multiyear resource needs of the school.

AREA II. SCHOOL PLANT RESOURCES

Competency No. 9.   The principal coordinates the input of teachers, students, and citizens in long-range district planning for educational facilities.

Competency No. 10.   The principal leads the staff in the determination of the quantitative and qualitative requirements of new instructional spaces.

Competency No. 11.   The principal determines and describes the nature and arrangement of specialized service areas and facilities when the school is being designed.

Competency No. 12.   The principal develops and transmits a complete set of educational specifications for the architect to use in planning new or remodeled facilities.

Competency No. 13.   The principal assesses the progress of planning and construction in terms of any subsequent changes needed to provide for instructional utility and flexibility.

Competency No. 14.   The principal interviews, assigns, and supervises custodial and maintenance personnel to provide a physical environment that will enhance instruction.

Summary

In the first part of this chapter the principal's decision-making role in planning, programming, budgeting, and evaluating the instructional program was described, and a cyclical model of the process was presented. Particular attention was given to leadership in the budgeting process, as well as in purchasing equipment, supplies, and materials required for the instructional program.

In the second half of the chapter the principal's leadership roles in planning educational facilities and in maintaining the school plant were discussed. Techniques for obtaining the inputs of staff members, students, and citizens in facility planning were described. The planning of the instructional and auxiliary spaces in school facilities was considered in terms of the criteria of utility and flexibility. Finally, the custodian's role was treated and some guidelines presented for maintaining an environment that will enhance the teaching-learning process.

The chapter concluded with an enumeration of 14 competencies required of the principal in providing adequate financial and physical resources for the school.

SUGGESTED ACTIVITIES

1. Devise a program format for achieving a particular instructional objective stated in measurable terms; project alternatives for achieving the objective, and cost each alternative.

2. Utilizing a flow chart, depict and compare the steps necessary for the purchase of a piece of classroom equipment in school systems of varying size.

3. Sample a faculty and a student body to determine their concerns about the appropriateness of their school facility, as well as their suggestions for improvement. To what extent are the concerns and suggestions of the two groups congruent?

4. Utilizing PERT/CPM, depict the major activities, relationships, and time constraints in district-wide planning *for* an educational facility and in school-wide planning *of* an educational facility.

5. Obtain, compare, and evaluate the quality of the educational specifications presented to the architect for schools of various levels and sizes.

6. Inspect a school to evaluate the quality of maintenance and custodial services. Suggest ways in which the services could be improved without an increase in staff.

SELECTED REFERENCES

ANDERSON, LESTER, and LAUREN VAN DYKE, *Secondary School Administration,* 2nd ed., Boston, Houghton Mifflin, 1972, pp. 443–514.

CASTALDI, BASIL, *Creative Planning of Educational Facilities,* Skokie, Ill., Rand McNally, 1969.

COMMISSION ON SCHOOL BUILDINGS, *Schools for America,* Washington, D.C., American Association of School Administrators, 1967.

CURTIS, WILLIAM H., *Educational Resources Management System,* Chicago, Research Corporation of the Association of School Business Officials, 1971.

ENGELHARDT, NICKOLAUS L., *Complete Guide for Planning New Schools,* West Nyack, N.Y., Parker, 1970.

HARTLEY, HARRY J., *Educational Planning-Programming-Budgeting,* Englewood Cliffs, N.J., Prentice-Hall, 1968.

IMMEGART, GLENN L., and FRANCIS J. PILECKI, *An Introduction to Systems for the Educational Administrator,* Reading, Mass., Addison-Wesley, 1973, pp. 157–173.

JARVIS, OSCAR T., et al., *Public School Business Administration and Finance,* West Nyack, N.Y., Parker, 1967.

JORDAN, K. FORBIS, *School Business Administration,* New York, Ronald, 1969, pp. 213–260.

KNEZEVICH, STEPHEN, *Program Budgeting (PPBS),* Berkeley, Calif., McCutchan, 1973.

OVARD, GLEN F., *Administration of the Changing Secondary School,* New York, Macmillan, 1966, pp. 357–445.

STOOPS, EMERY, and RUSSELL E. JOHNSON, *Elementary School Administration,* New York, McGraw-Hill, 1967, pp. 153–253.

CHAPTER 13
The principal
and the community

itizens typically cannot or do not relate well to large school districts; they can and do relate meaningfully to their schools. Thus we see increased emphasis on school district decentralization and on local control of schools. Today citizens are becoming active and involved in many educational functions that heretofore have been considered to be the province of professional educators—instructional programming, use of facilities, and selection of staff (including the principal), to name but a few. Citizens' advisory groups for each school, once optional, are now mandatory for participation in several federal and state educational programs. Hence it may be observed that the role of the principal in the future will not be unlike that of the superintendent today, particularly in the area of school-community relations.

In fostering a sound program of school-community relations, the principal must become intimately acquainted with the values, expectations, needs, and aspirations of the local community. General systems theory and social systems theory provide the basis for developing such understanding. The principal also must become skilled in communicating and interacting with diverse reference groups and in shaping their understanding of school purposes, programs, operations, costs, and outcomes. Leadership and decision theory are the basis for developing and exercising these skills.

Whereas the literature is replete with suggestions about the roles of the school superintendent or the central office personnel in establishing and maintaining a viable program of school-community relations, relatively little attention has been paid to the role of the principal vis-à-vis the community. In fact, Carr discovered that the principal's role and responsibilities in this functional area traditionally have been "assumed rather than defined."[1] Hence the need for a careful examination of the school-community relations function at the building level.

We begin by focusing on some recent societal issues that give rise to increased citizen concern about participation in educational decision

---

[1] David S. Carr, "An Analysis of the Principal's Perceptions of Public Relations Programs in Selected Suburban Elementary Schools," doctoral dissertation, Northwestern University, 1969.

making; some techniques are suggested for documenting the concerns and needs. Next the "why," "who," "what," "when," and "how" of communications are discussed, and guidelines are presented for establishing an effective community relations program in terms of the many reference groups with whom the principal must interact. Consideration is then given to some emerging educational programs having great potential for enhancing the school-community relationship. The chapter concludes with an enumeration of the competencies required of the principal in providing leadership to the community.

Causes for community concern

Several reasons for the increased concern of citizens about the schools may be cited; the foremost relate to the cost of the schools, the educational program, and citizen involvement in decision making.

Undoubtedly, the price tag for financing the nation's schools has risen dramatically during the past decade, and there is every indication that expenditures will continue to skyrocket.[2] For example, spending for capital outlay jumped 43 percent, from $2.8 billion in 1960–1961 to $4.1 billion in 1970–1971, while the average salary for the public school instructional staff increased 77 percent, from $5449 to $9689 during the same time span.[3] These increases have burdened local taxpayers so heavily that they are critically analyzing all school expenditures—stubbornly refusing to grant money even for "necessary" improvements.[4] This skeptical outlook is partly reflected in the frequency of school bond issue rejections. In 1969, for example, voters disapproved nearly $2.2 billion for new school construction, approving only 56 percent of the proposed bond issues. By comparison, in 1960, only $368 million for new construction was rejected, reflecting an approval rate of 79 percent of all bond issues.[5] Concerning operational levies, moreover, taxpayer revolts are commonplace. At all levels of government, citizens and educators are searching not only for revenue sharing and other means for financing the schools, but also for more equitable formulas for bearing the costs of education.

Concomitant with the concern over the rising costs of education is

[2] Charles S. Benson, *The Economics of Public Education,* 2nd ed., Boston, Houghton Mifflin, 1968, pp. 12–13.

[3] Committee on Educational Finance, *Financial Status of the Public Schools,* Washington, D.C., National Education Association, 1971.

[4] Andrew M. Greeley, "The Public and Non-Public Schools—Losers Both," *School Review,* 81 (February 1973), 196.

[5] Mark R. Shedd, "Our Stricken Schools: A Proposal to Avert Disaster," *The Progressive,* 36 (February 1972), 16.

the demand for financial accountability—that the quality of the curricular and cocurricular programs of the school merit the associated costs. Parents of today have received considerable formal schooling; they tend to hold even higher educational expectations for their children. To this end, they expect the school to prepare students adequately for varied career aspirations—whatever they may be—and parents are quick to indict the educational system if their children experience failure in school or college, are unable to secure employment, or display problems adapting to societal norms.

Neither the costs nor the benefits of a formal education were as obvious once as they are in today's technological society. Traditionally, students experiencing difficulty in school were able to terminate their formal education and locate fairly lucrative employment with comparative ease. To enter most attractive positions now, however, at least a high school diploma is required as evidence of achievement.[6] In addition, the avid pursuit of academic training beyond high school has intensified the competition for entrance into technical schools and colleges. Once accepted by a post-high school institution, the student faces even stiffer competition for academic survival. The demand for quality educational programs is increasing, since the knowledge acquired and attitudes developed by students in elementary and secondary school are instrumental in assuring eventual success.

Each of the foregoing phenomena—increased taxpayer concern over burgeoning tax increases and parental demands for quality programs—creates continuing problems in school-community relationships. At the building level, the financial concerns of the local community typically are translated into at least two basically conflicting types of expression: a "bare bones" orientation and a "fair share" orientation. Citizens committed to the "bare bones" position, which probably derives from a traditional set of values, are primarily interested in reducing expenditures, hence the overall tax burden. They suggest to the principal myriad ways to "hold the line" on all expenditures—that school carpeting is not needed, that food services are unnecessary, that specialized staff can be reduced, that the pupil-teacher ratio should be increased, that the principalship should be abolished, *ad infinitum*. Conversely, those committed to a "fair share" orientation, which probably derives from an emergent set of values, are primarily concerned with the quality of the instructional program. They keep abreast of changes in neighboring schools and frequently make comparisons, sometimes invidious, pointing out to the principal specific ways in which they feel that their youngsters are being shortchanged.

[6] Ivar Berg, "Rich Man's Qualifications for Poor Man's Jobs," *Trans-Action,* 6 (March 1969), 45–50.

Regardless of the orientations, citizens today demand extensive involvement in educational decision making. This movement has prompted a reexamination of existing power relationships in the school organization, resulting in a definite trend toward school district decentralization. In large cities particularly, the efforts of citizens to participate in educational decision making are systematically being channeled to the building, hence the principalship, level.[7] Through daily contact with citizens who insist on being heard, the principal immediately becomes the representative of the school system in his attendance community. Thus the movement toward decentralization has numerous implications for the role of the principal in community relations.

Increased citizen involvement and local control necessitate increased local responsibility. The principal, therefore, must conceptualize, understand, and analyze the needs of the community served by the school to plan and implement appropriate curricular and cocurricular programs.

Identifying community needs

The necessity of identifying community needs prior to establishing, evaluating, or revising the school's instructional program was stressed in Chapter 9. Although the procedures delineated are primarily for reconciling differences in values and expectations among groups of citizens and between citizens and educators regarding the purposes and programs of the school, they also can serve as a basis for an effective community relations program.

Each individual community—herein considered as the attendance area for a given school—has specific needs to which the school must address itself; these needs depend on the school's location, population characteristics, values, and other factors. Nor should the needs of youth be explored in a vacuum. Adults, also, have academic, cultural, social, and recreational needs that deserve attention.[8]

The relationship of the school as an institution to the community that it serves is schematized in Figure 13.1. Based on social systems theory, it may be observed that the culture, ethos, and values of a community have systematic and continuing interaction with the expectations for the school as an institution.[9] Instead of viewing the community as an entity, the principal should recognize that the formal and

[7] Sylvester M. King, Robert D. Sullivan, and David I. Glick, "Viewpoints: Community Participation in Education," *Urban Review,* 5 (January 1972), 46–47.

[8] Cf. William F. Totten and Frank J. Manley, *The Community School,* Galien, Mich., Allied Education Council, 1969.

[9] J. W. Getzels, James M. Lipham, and Roald F. Campbell, *Educational Administration as a Social Process,* New York, Harper & Row, 1968, pp. 157–181.

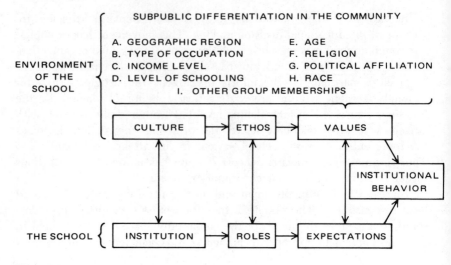

Figure 13.1
The school-community relationship

informal subpublic cleavages within the community often have a powerful and direct influence on the nature and frequency of citizen interaction with the school.[10] Research has confirmed that these cleavages
typically exist along such lines as geographic region, type of occupation,
income level, amount of schooling, age, religion, political party affiliation, race, and other individual characteristics and group memberships.
To take only one example, the importance of where in the attendance
area of the school a citizen lives may become evident not only in terms
of major program and curricular issues, but also in terms of such minor
issues as control by a particular neighborhood of the PTA or a neighborhood furor over where the school bus should stop. The major meaningful relationships between the subpublic cleavages and expectations for
the task of the public schools were delineated in Chapter 4, which dealt
with educational values.

One of the most useful techniques for documenting and understanding the expectations held by subpublics and for synthesizing the expectations meaningfully is the assessment of educational needs through a
comprehensive community survey. As may be seen from an examination
of Table 13.1, the principal who conducts such a survey must assume

[10] Cf. Laurence W. Downey, Roger C. Seager, and Allen T. Slagle, *The Task of
Public Education*, Chicago, Midwest Administration Center, University of Chicago,
1958; Marvin J. Fruth, Dennis W. Spuck, and Howard E. Wakefield, *Opening the
Door*, Madison, Cooperative Educational Research and Services, University of Wisconsin, 1972.

Table 13.1
ACTIVITIES IN CONDUCTING A COMMUNITY SURVEY

PRECEDING EVENT	SUCCEEDING EVENT	ACTIVITY NAME	ACTIVITY DURATION (DAYS)	RESPONSIBILITY
10	20	Specify study objectives	4	Principal, teachers, and citizens
20	30	Identify survey consultant	6	Principal
20	50	Obtain district approval	8	Principal
20	60	Identify community representatives	3	Principal
20	70	Appoint faculty committee	2	Principal
30	40	Meet with survey consultant	5	Principal
40	80	Dummy activity[a]	–	–
40	90	Develop survey design		
40	100	Define survey population	3	Consultant
			6	Consultant
50	80	Dummy activity[a]	–	–
60	80	Meet with community	5	Principal
70	80	Meet with faculty committee	4	Principal
80	120	Develop questionnaire	10	Consultant and citizens
90	110	Specify data analysis	4	Consultant
100	110	Obtain address lists	2	Secretary
110	120	Select sample	2	Consultant
120	130	Print questionnaire	6	Secretary
120	140	Address envelopes	4	Secretary
130	140	Dummy activity[a]	–	–
140	150	Mail questionnaire	2	Secretary
150	160	Analyze survey results	15	Consultant
160	170	Prepare survey report	15	Consultant and principal

[a] A dummy activity takes neither time nor resources but is required to preserve the continuity of the network.

primary responsibility for many of the major activities, such as identifying consultant help, obtaining district approval, appointing faculty members, and appointing community representatives to the study. But at many junctures—even during the initial activity of specifying the objectives of the survey—the principal should involve citizens. Later in the process, at the point of developing the specific survey questions to be asked, the involvement of community representatives is absolutely essential. Typically, citizens will join willingly and enthusiastically in the work of conducting a community survey when their roles and responsibilities, as well as those of other participants, are clearly delineated. Moreover, such participation greatly enhances both the quality and the acceptance of the survey findings.

In conducting a community survey, some principals have found the application of the program evaluation review technique (PERT/CPM) to be particularly useful. A simple PERT/CPM network for conducting a community survey appears in Figure 13.2. The network is composed of activities and events. The activities, identical with those in Table 13.1, are symbolized by arrows in the network, whereas events are symbolized by circles. Activities consume time and/or resources, and associated with each activity is an individual or group that is responsible for carrying it out. Events are points in time that mark both the beginning and the end of each activity. The critical path of the network for conducting the community survey (double line in Figure 13.2) is the path of longest duration through the network. Each activity on this path is critical in that failure to complete it on schedule will delay completion of the community survey.

In addition to conducting a comprehensive survey, the principal frequently will find it advantageous to explore community needs through individual contacts and conferences with community leaders and citizens. Moreover, such open forums as community or parent meetings are often functional. Citizens' advisory councils, which have increased from an estimated 150 in 1960 to more than 18,000 in 1970,[11] are an excellent mechanism for concerned community members to use in identifying needs and expectations held for the schools. Since citizens' advisory councils ordinarily function with the official sanction of the board of education and central administration, council concerns must be accorded prompt attention. It should be noted, however, that the mere creation of a citizens' council is not a sufficient response to legitimate community demands. Any school dedicated to the needs of the community will be sensitive to public approval or disapproval of existing programs and will seek a variety of means to encourage candid communication with the community.

The accurate assessment of community needs is only the initial step toward establishing a school program that is relevant to those needs. Moreover, the citizens constitute only one reference group, albeit an important one, from which information must be sought. Frequently the needs as identified by citizens are not congruent with those needs as identified by other important reference groups—administrators, teachers,

[11] Calvin Greider, "How Big Cities Can Revive Real 'Community Schools,'" *Nation's Schools*, 85 (January 1970), 6.

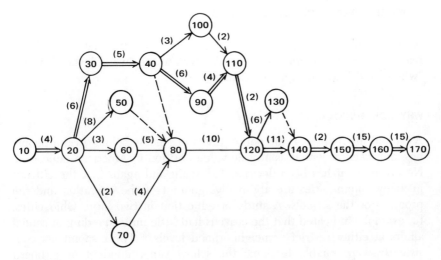

Figure 13.2
Network for conducting a community survey

and students. Moreover, a community may be so limited that citizens experience difficulty in pinpointing the needs of their youth. For example, if cultural activities are lacking in a community, the necessity for creating such interests may be overlooked by citizens. Whereas educators cannot rely entirely on citizens' perceptions of educational needs as the ultimate basis for curriculum development, neither are they empowered to fashion a program of their own choosing.

In assessing community educational needs, the principal must see to it that the expectations of all important reference groups are sought. As a leader, the principal must establish the organizational mechanisms and structures for reducing the communicative distance within and among the reference groups. Such communication is particularly important because the misperception of basic values and viewpoints does more to thwart the achievement of organizational and individual goals than disagreement in basic values and viewpoints.[12] Opening the channels of communication, or reducing the communicative distance, can be instrumental in assuring mutual identification of needs and identifying appropriate programs and processes to meet those needs.

[12] Cf. Max G. Abbott, "Values and Value Perceptions of School Superintendents and School Board Members," doctoral dissertation, University of Chicago, 1960; Roderick F. McPhee, "The Relationship Between Individual Values, Educational Viewpoint, and Local School Approval," doctoral dissertation, University of Chicago, 1959; Kenneth C. DeGood, "The Perceptions of School Superintendents," doctoral dissertation, Ohio State University, 1958.

Communicating with the community

A successfully implemented program of community relations will be realized only after careful attention is given to the "why," "who," "what," "when," and "how" of communicating.

WHY COMMUNICATE

As stated in Chapter 4, the notion that the schools belong to the people has long been accepted as a basic value position in American education. Nevertheless, it has been documented again and again that the citizens in many communities are abysmally ignorant of the operation and the program of the schools. A study of education in two large Ohio cities, for example, indicated that the citizens had little understanding of school affairs at either district or neighborhood levels.[13] The respondents consistently were unable to name the school superintendent or a board member and often were uncertain whether the board was elected or appointed. On the school level, citizens could not support their opinions about the school with any facts relating to its operation. Jennings' findings were similar, leading him to suggest that the lack of understanding of school issues is constant for all socioeconomic strata.[14]

The findings just cited confirm the results of our earlier studies of citizens' expectations for the schools in 31 Wisconsin communities.[15] It appeared from our data that the typical citizen has only a minimal knowledge of the roles of the board of education and the administration, financial and business operations, staff and pupil personnel policies and procedures, and curricular and cocurricular programs of the schools— either at the district level or at the individual school level.[16] It also was discovered that citizens who had no children in school or whose children attended non-public schools knew even less about the schools than the parents of public school youngsters. Lack of knowledge, however, did not deter any of the respondents from holding definite opinions about what the schools should be doing or how they should be doing it. Citizens

[13] Paul F. Kleine, Raphael O. Nystrand, and Edwin Bridges, "Citizen Views of Big City Schools," *Theory into Practice,* 8 (October 1969), 223–228.

[14] Kent M. Jennings, "The Non-Involved Public," *School and Society,* 97 (November 1969), 406.

[15] James M. Lipham, Russell T. Gregg, and Richard A. Rossmiller, *The School Board as an Agency for Resolving Conflict,* USOE Project No. 5-0338-2-12-1, Madison, University of Wisconsin, 1967.

[16] James M. Lipham, Russell T. Gregg, and Richard A. Rossmiller, *Expectations for the School Board Role,* Madison, Department of Educational Administration and Wisconsin Survey Research Laboratory, University of Wisconsin, 1967, pp. 12–17.

quite willingly, often emphatically, stated their expectations. One answer to the question "Why communicate?" is so that the opinions held at least might be enlightened.

Bringing to life the premise that the schools belong to the people probably will require a change in attitudes and behavior of citizens and educators alike. In some communities, citizens are apathetic concerning the schools and all other public institutions. In still others, citizens have been reluctant to question or challenge school policies and operations for a variety of reasons—lack of technical pedagogical knowledge, previous failures in their efforts to affect change, and even fear of overt or covert reprisals against their children. In still other communities educators have assumed a defensively arrogant stance: Keep out. In one school with which we are fmiliar—we hope it is not a typical one—the new principal graciously extended an invitation at PTA for the parents to visit the school at any time, only to discover the next day that a mere two teachers out of twenty would support and help to implement his invitation. In still other communities, contact occurs between the school and the community only when there is trouble—ranging from such minor problems as "Johnny cut school" to such major problems as "We need approval of another building referendum."

Basically, we communicate because the schools are dependent on the community for financial and program support. Even though education is a state function, the current structure for school operation grants considerable discretionary power to local communities. It is necessary, therefore, that all the intraorganizational reference groups intimately concerned with the success of the schools know and fulfill adequately their roles in extraorganizational relationships.

WHO COMMUNICATES

Whereas the principal must assume direct responsibility for planning, coordinating, and implementing the public relations program within the community, the success of the program depends on the efforts of each person connected with the operation of the schools—principal, teachers, students, and school employees.

THE PRINCIPAL AND COMMUNICATION. The priority attached by the principal to communicating with the community undoubtedly serves as a model by which others will gauge their efforts. The principal's encouragement of school-community contacts and his participation in diverse community groups is essential. Citizen expectations of the principal as a community leader are high. The demands on his time for attendance at and participation in school-sponsored and non-school-sponsored activities often are great,[17] and only educators who can tolerate the interrole conflict precipitated thereby should consider the principalship as a profession.

The principal's involvement in community organizations and activities contains both quantitative and qualitative dimensions. Frequently it is urged that the principal maintain a high profile—that he be a "joiner" and assume an active leadership role in many community organizations and activities. Our research has revealed, however, that there are desirable upper and lower limits to such participation if the principal would be effective.[18] Undoubtedly one can belong to too few organizations, yet it also is possible to belong to so many groups that considerable interrole conflict is generated between and among incompatible roles and the primary role of principal. In some communities, in fact, membership in certain organizations tends automatically to alienate substantial other subpublics. We urge widespread participation, but we suggest limited affiliation, even though societal restrictions on all educator roles appear to be less prohibitive than was once the case.

Concerning the quality of one's participation, our research also indicates that the principal, in working with the various community groups, frequently is called on to represent the viewpoint of the schools concerning a multitude of issues and problems.[19] The effective principal must clearly and accurately communicate such values, views, and expectations, since openness of communication is a significant element in the development of mutual understanding. A principal who openly defends the school but who nevertheless respects and encourages the community's right to question will foster a climate in which the school and community can work cooperatively toward developing a quality educational program.

Participation in community affairs represents only one means whereby the principal displays leadership in establishing sound community relationships. His numerous spontaneous contacts with staff, students, parents, and concerned citizens are under constant surveillance—particularly insofar as they relate to the major functions of his role. In one sense it is not necessary to "work at" public relations, since it is easy for all to spot the pseudo-principal engaged in such inauthentic, image-building charades as effusively greeting others or otherwise behaving like a "mother hen, principalizing all over the place." Such a stereotypic "PR" syndrome is inappropriate in the schools. The principal who is perform-

[17] *Report of the Junior High School Principalship*, Washington, D.C., The National Association of Secondary School Principals, 1966, p. 65; *The Elementary School Principalship*, Washington, D.C., Department of Elementary School Principals, National Education Association, 1968, pp. 94–97.

[18] James M. Lipham, "Personal Variables Related to Administrative Effectiveness," doctoral dissertation, University of Chicago, 1960.

[19] Ibid.

ing well the major functions of his role, particularly the program and personnel functions, will automatically become visible as a vital educational leader.

THE TEACHERS AND COMMUNICATION. Teachers must be impressed with the importance of positive school-community relations and must be encouraged to exert effort in this highly sensitive domain. The recent struggles between teachers' organizations and boards of education to determine adequate financial compensation for teachers have modified the public's former image of teachers. Whereas most citizens have sympathized with the financial plight of the teaching profession, many do not endorse such tactics as strikes and sanctions to improve teachers' salaries. The numerous strikes and sanctions,[20] although successful for raising salaries and improving working conditions, are still unlawful in many states and are considered to be unethical by some citizens. Teachers must be reminded, therefore, to redouble their efforts to keep the public's attitude toward them positive and supportive.

As with the principal, the most obvious way to mitigate the negative consequences of public disenchantment with the schools is for the teachers to improve their role performance. Because of an awareness of the importance of quality education, parental expectations for the school continue to increase. Outstanding teaching is still the foundation of any school-community relations program. Now more than ever, superior teaching can serve to reduce latent or manifest citizen dissatisfaction with the schools. Whereas taxpayers are willing to reward outstanding teaching with appropriate financial compensation, they will not tolerate mediocre teaching performance—particularly with equal pay for all. As additional salary demands are made, teachers must become more competent in teaching and more sensitive to the necessity of attention to school-community relations.

THE STUDENTS AND COMMUNICATION. No emissary group has more extensive contact with the community than the student body. For example, parents receive substantially more information about schools from their children than from any other source.[21] Parents of successful students who speak favorably about the school are usually quite supportive. Consequently, the ideal is not only educationally sound but also politically advantageous that each student should experience some success during every school day. In this way the student's sense of satisfaction and be-

[20] Melvin L. Hayes, "Teacher Strikes Reach Record Heights," *School and Society*, 98 (November 1970), 433–434.

[21] Cf. Kleine, Nystrand, and Bridges, op. cit., 225; Harold Van Winkle, "A Study of School-Community Information Programs in Northwest Ohio," doctoral dissertation, Indiana University, 1956.

longingness will be enhanced, and as a result he will identify with and become a positive ambassador for the school. Conversely, it is indeed difficult for parents to support the school enthusiastically when their children continually report, "It's really a bummer."

Perhaps no group is as impressionable and sensitive to student opinion regarding the school as the students themselves. Lippitt and Lippitt maintain that younger children naturally look to older peers for accepted norms and examples of what they themselves can become.[22] This potential for positive influence between older and younger students is the basis for tutorial programs operating in many schools, and it can serve to minimize student transition problems. The younger student, impressed by his older siblings, is quick to form opinions of the next organizational level of which he will become a part. Students who speak openly of their positive experiences can assist in easing the psychological transition from home to the elementary school, and subsequently to the middle or senior high school. On the other hand, student negativism quickly diffuses to younger children, heightening their anxiety and apprehension about vertical movement through the schools.

Various cocurricular activities, particularly those that provide a public service, can be another positive mechanism for improving school-community relations. Special student groups, such as ecology clubs, have unselfishly given their time to be of service in many communities. This type of activity is easily recognizable as a positive force within the entire community. Many students are eager to engage in such service activities, not only for the personal satisfactions derived from participation, but also to establish the image that the students of today are dedicated and responsible citizens, despite mass media reports or adult suspicions to the contrary.

In addition to specific cocurricular activities, student behavior in the community and at school-sponsored events is often watched as a barometer of school effectiveness. Therefore, students must be made aware of their responsibilities in shaping public opinion.

THE NONCERTIFICATED STAFF AND COMMUNICATION. "Principals come and teachers go," a parent commented recently, "but thank God for the school secretary. She's probably the only one there who really knows what's going on." To the secretary could well be added custodians, clerks, cooks, bus drivers, teacher aides, and paraprofessionals. These men and women often have long tenure in the school and usually are established members of the community; often their opinions regarding the school are eagerly sought and sometimes readily shared. Whereas

[22] Ronald Lippitt and Peggy Lippitt, "The Peer Culture as a Learning Environment," *Childhood Education*, 47 (December 1970), 135–138.

a credibility gap may exist between educators and citizens and even between students and parents, the communicative distance between the noncertificated employees and many reference groups in the community may be small indeed. Certainly these employees should be encouraged to share objective, accurate, and timely information about the schools with interested citizens. Moreover, all school employees must realize the importance of the public relations aspects of their positions.

In the performance of their roles in the school, the noncertificated employees often have a great deal of formal and informal contact with the community. Their discretion in dealing with the public is an important facet of the school-community relations program. The treatment that one receives from any school employee reflects upon the entire school. Parents often express annoyance, for instance, with the aloof or officious attitudes of school secretaries who "really turn them off." Neither is it uncommon for citizens to judge the effectiveness or morale of the school by observing whether the lawns are shaggy. Although principals may be very concerned with the relationship of effectiveness, satisfaction, and efficiency to the morale of the professional staff, they often err by failing to recognize that the same dynamics exist for the noncertificated staff. Employees who identify with the goals of the organization and exhibit pride in their work will maintain and foster a positive relationship between the school and many of the significant subpublics that are beyond the reach of the principal, the teachers, or even the students.

WHAT SHOULD BE COMMUNICATED

One of the major weaknesses in programs of school-community relations has been a failure by school personnel to differentiate adequately the contents of communications for the various subpublics of the school. The informational needs of primary reference groups intimately concerned with the educational enterprise (e.g., parents, central administration, and fiscal control boards) are much greater in terms of scope and detail of communication than the needs of such secondary reference groups as civic, religious, and special interest groups, or the man in the street. Unfortunately, however, failure to ascertain what the various subpublics want to know has resulted in programs that give some groups less information than they need, whereas others feel inundated with detail—"more about the hippopotamus than they care to know." The principal must view the community in terms of its differentiated subpublics, and he must ascertain or estimate the informational needs of the different groups. In differentiating the content of communications in terms of proximity to the school, communication with parents and communication with other community groups may be considered.

COMMUNICATION WITH PARENTS. Parents form the most concerned and interested reference group with which the school must communicate intelligently. In an extensive study in ten states, Stout and Langdon found that parents were extremely interested in their children's schools and wanted a variety of information grouped around curriculum, methods of teaching, school services, the details of school operation, the teacher, and other relationships in the school.[23] Unfortunately, however, the communications effort in most schools, is still confined to report cards, plus the informal communications from students mentioned earlier. Most schools should communicate to parents more information, and more detailed information about the purposes, programs, processes, and products of the schools. Hence the important criterion in determining what to communicate with parents is *comprehensiveness.*

The basic motivations for parental concern with communicative detail should not be overlooked. Although specific motivations may vary greatly, the underlying theme is ensuring that one's child is receiving the best education possible—however variously "best" is defined by parents. There often is a direct relationship between the degree of parental acceptance of the school program and the amount of success the children are realizing. Similarly, parents who were successful in school themselves usually are supportive, whereas those who experienced difficulty or whose children are having trouble often tend to be quite critical of and skeptical about the school. Even so, the staff must do all that is possible to provide parents with a wealth of information, not only about the performance of their children but also about the total program of the school. If those parents who have so much at stake in the success of the school cannot be reached, it is hardly logical to expect that other, less vitally concerned groups will support the school.

The formal mechanisms for communicating with parents vary somewhat by grade level. Ordinarily the first formal contact between the elementary principal and parents is during a "kindergarten roundup" in the spring, when pre-schoolers and parents are invited to participate in orientation sessions designed to reduce the child's anxieties about attending school in the fall. The principal's involvement in the planning of such activities is important. Too frequently, the word "principal" generates a negative response from parents, who perceive him as the chief disciplinarian. Parental comments to children such as "That's the principal; be sure he doesn't catch you doing something wrong" or "Don't get sent to the principal's office" are commonplace and merely reinforce student misconceptions of the principal's role. No principal can hope to win the esteem of students or parents until he convinces

---

[23] Irving W. Stout and Grace Langdon, "What Parents Want to Know About Their Schools," *Nation's Schools,* 60 (August 1957), 45–48.

them through his daily behavior that his primary responsibility is not to discipline students but to assist them.

While their children are in the elementary grades, parents tend to follow the school program through fairly close personal contact. In many communities the school is in close geographic proximity to the home, and visits to and from the school can be made with comparative ease. Also, since early childhood activities tend to revolve around school-related activities, family discussions may center on school experiences.

When students reach the secondary level, however, the school is usually a greater distance from the home, students become more independent and guarded in discussions of their activities, and parents become reluctant to initiate personal contact with the school. During these years, parental understanding of the school program may become hazy. In addition, some parents feel that secondary schools are somewhat impersonal and not receptive to individual parental contact. For these reasons, many middle schools and high schools have intensified their communication networks through special programs, printed materials, and periodic parent-teacher conferences during which parents and teachers discuss in depth the students' progress. These programs, materials, and conferences tend to increase the level of mutual understanding between the home and the school.

Regardless of organizational level (elementary or secondary), parents should be invited to participate frequently in school activities. Contacts with teachers, counselors, and administrators must be encouraged so that parents will feel comfortable about initiating communication with the school whenever they have questions. Only in an environment of openness and trust can parents fully comprehend the school's mission and the means by which the school is attempting to fulfill that mission.

School-related groups, such as the Parent-Teacher Association or Organization, have as their primary objective the improvement of communication and understanding between the school and the home. Many principals, however, have become disenchanted with the efforts of these groups and are reluctant to offer the support necessary to promote a viable organization. The relative ineffectiveness of parent-teacher groups, despite their worthy intentions, might be blamed on the following causes: (1) negative attitudes, (2) lack of objectives, (3) poor leadership, (4) unbalanced programs, and (5) conflict situations. Other possible causes have been mentioned by Kindred.[24] In the hope of overcoming such weaknesses, those listed are discussed briefly.

1. NEGATIVE ATTITUDES. Principals and teachers are not always eager to participate in formal association with parents, and the feeling may be

[24] Leslie W. Kindred, *School Public Relations*, Englewood Cliffs, N.J., Prentice-Hall, 1957, p. 185.

mutual. Further resentment may be precipitated if attendance of educators at meetings is obligatory. Some teachers not only begrudge the imposition on their time, they also view with apprehension a close relationship with parents. In fairness, it must be mentioned that too often the responsibility for direction and leadership in parent-teacher groups has reverted to the professional staff for lack of parent enthusiasm. Teachers rightfully become discouraged when the activities of the organization are not enthusiastically supported by parents. Likewise, even the most dedicated parents become disheartened when by their verbal and nonverbal behavior the teachers say, "Let's get it over with!"

2. LACK OF OBJECTIVES. Many parent-teacher groups have difficulty in defining objectives for the particular school, relying instead on general lists of goals formulated by national councils, the school district, or other groups. The mutual identification of local needs and the deployment of resources to focus on them is necessary to give direction to parent-teacher groups. As parents typically comment, "Baking and selling cookies to buy something that the school should have bought in the first place is not my idea of fun."

3. POOR LEADERSHIP. Some parent-teacher groups falter for lack of leadership. Even interested, well-intentioned parents who have not had the opportunity to develop basic leadership skills can hamper group functioning. In such situations interest wanes quickly, membership drops, and the professional staff feels compelled to dominate the meetings and activities. In still other schools a clique of parents representing one neighborhood, social class, or value orientation unfortunately is allowed to dominate the group—particularly in organizations whose membership is not truly representative in the first place.

4. UNBALANCED PROGRAMS. The quality of programs of parent-teacher groups is often uneven. Meetings with long and boring agendas of committee reports provide little opportunity for teacher-parent interaction. Sometimes there is excessive dependence on utilizing the talents of students, perhaps to entice parent attendance. It is unfortunate that in many schools the assets of the group are often squandered by concern with trivial *things*, rather than being invested in meaningful *processes*.

5. CONFLICT SITUATIONS. Although a sharing of authority between parents and professionals is the ideal, in reality the two groups sometimes side against each other. Elsewhere, ideological, procedural, or interpersonal conflicts rage within a school, and the intrafaculty cliques may appeal to the total organization for endorsement and active political support at either the school or the district level. Differing expectations regarding which activities and responsibilities fall within the province of the organization may prompt conflict that can be reduced only through an early agreement on the limits of authority within which the organization may function.

For reasons such as these, parent-teacher organizations have become much less popular in recent years—especially in secondary schools. Some parents who have become disenchanted with the value of such endeavors have formed special interest groups, such as athletic clubs or band boosters, that have been considerably valuable in promoting specific programs. Unfortunately, such well-intentioned groups usually champion the cause of only one phase of the cocurricular program that may have been threatened because of budgetary cuts or other problems. To reiterate a point made earlier, it is the responsibility of the board of education to provide financial support for all the programs of the school.

Other special interest groups of parents derive from ideological, racial, and other subpublic cleavages in the larger society. For example, in their zeal to preserve and strengthen awareness of the American heritage, some groups have championed student rights. In urban areas particularly, organizations of black parents or other ethnic groups have been vehement in their demands for equality and quality education. Regardless of the legitimacy of the demands, it is the responsibility of the principal to appreciate, understand, and work cooperatively with parents of all persuasions. This, indeed, is a tall order. Yet each parent group represents a potentially powerful force for changing and improving the school.

COMMUNICATION WITH COMMUNITY ORGANIZATIONS. Whereas the main criterion to be considered in deciding what to communicate to parents is *comprehensiveness*, the criterion for communicating with most community organizations is *selectivity*. Many community organizations are quite supportive of the schools. In return, they expect support for their programs. In this regard the principal may be exposed to sensitive role conflicts. To satisfy their enthusiasm to be of service to young people of the community, some community groups impose on the school with requests to involve students in contests, projects, or other activities. Many of the projects are worthwhile and of educational value, but the principal must not sanction student participation merely because students are always available in a normative yet coercive institution.

Community groups often expect active participation from professional educators. Involvement in civic organizations that meet during the noon hour is of course impossible for teachers and difficult for administrators; but participation in cultural, fraternal, patriotic, political, and religious groups can enhance an educator's value to the community and provide him with numerous opportunities to disseminate information about the schools. Again, however, it should be cautioned that an individual should keep the scope of his participation down to a reasonable level.

Many community groups, such as the YMCA, YWCA, Junior Achievement, 4-H Club, and Scout organizations, provide outlets for students to pursue a variety of interests. The principal must be familiar with the goals and activities of each of these organizations and should initiate personal contact with the adult and student leaders whose purposes are identical to his own—to provide meaningful learning experiences for young people. In meeting the informational needs of these groups, the principal not only should respond to their requests for specific data but should indicate ways in which the programs, facilities, and activities of the schools are congruent with and reinforcing of the activities of each community organization. Being sensitive to community interests, and subsequently accommodating those interests, represents only one facet of the public relations program. An effective program also includes the dissemination of information intended to prompt favorable response from the community toward the school.

WHEN TO COMMUNICATE

Communication should be continuous, not spasmodic. In this regard, the periodic preparation of printed materials or press releases to increase the community's knowledge of the school is a necessary but not sufficient community relations technique. If all of the reference groups within the school—administrators, teachers, employees, and students—are engaged in promoting sound school-community relations, the usual formal releases of information are a minor part of the program.

The school cannot isolate itself from the community it serves; therefore, a two-way flow of communications between the two is important. All citizens have impressions of the degree of excellence characterizing their schools. A continuous community relations program will serve not only to alter negative opinions but to reinforce positive views as well.

Citizens use a variety of criteria in formulating and continually modifying their opinions of the school. These standards may be classified according to three kinds of criteria—quantitative, physical, and product.

QUANTITATIVE CRITERIA. Quantitative criteria include factors measurable through simple tabulation, such as level of professional staff salaries, number of special programs, student-teacher ratios, number of books in the library, and physical plant descriptions. Each criterion represents a measure of the community input to the school and is a potential indicator of excellence—at least in comparison with other schools.

A word of caution is in order concerning the use and interpretation of quantitative criteria. Usually they are expressed in terms of minimum standards—number of students per teacher, amount of square footage per student, and the like. Unfortunately, however, these standards are often viewed by citizens not as absolutely minimal but as maximally desirable.

The principal will find it necessary, therefore, not only to keep abreast of changing professional standards but also to inform others of the minimal-maximal ranges in standards and the theoretical and practical bases from which the quantitative criteria are derived.

PHYSICAL CRITERIA. Physical criteria include the standards of perfection in safety, maintenance, and housekeeping that are expected by a community for the provision of a positive teaching-learning atmosphere and the protection of the community's investments. School facilities are daily visible to many citizens. If a casual glance in passing assures a taxpayer that the buildings and grounds are well maintained, he often assumes that all is well inside the school. On the other hand, if the building and grounds have deteriorated through lack of care, observers often conclude that standards have declined in the school program as well. Good community relations, therefore, are yet another reason for close attention to buildings and grounds.

PRODUCT CRITERIA. The third group of criteria considered by parents in evaluating the school focuses on outcomes. Whereas quantitative and physical criteria are readily discernible, product criteria are more judgmental. For example, regardless of how objectively the progress of each child has been evaluated, a report card that parents do not understand is a communication that can prompt considerable antagonism toward the school.

Placing children in less advanced, homogeneously grouped sections, continually calling the home regarding discipline problems, and retaining students in the same grade for two years are other forms of communication that greatly affect parental attitudes toward the school. Although these measures may sometimes be necessary, parents who have experienced a number of negative school contacts of this type will tend to retain their conviction that the school has betrayed their child. To guard against negative information's becoming the dominant method of communicating with the home, the principal and staff must provide positive information, as well. At the elementary level, music and drama programs, open house, parents' night, and other formal and informal contacts should be utilized to draw the community closer to the school and to provide positive feedback—especially to parents whose children experience limited success.

At the secondary level, the tendency to evaluate the school through product criteria is even more pronounced. Interscholastic athletic contests, competition for a plethora of awards and scholarships, performance on College Board examinations, student acceptances at prestigious colleges, and other competitive measures are used. Unfortunately, because of vast differences between communities in our stratified society, some fine schools have difficulty competing favorably with other schools athletically, scholastically, musically, or artistically, and the community support they receive may be unduly influenced by such output measures.

Possibly no other phase of the school program receives as much unfavorable and favorable attention as the interscholastic athletic program. Especially vocal are the taxpayers who criticize interscholastic sports for being too expensive and potentially harmful. During fiscal crises this and other cocurricular progams may be threatened with severe cutbacks. Many communities, however, exhibit great pride in the athletic accomplishments of their school, and the athletic program represents a constant source of school spirit, pride, and morale.

The athletic program is merely one illustration of the type of cocurricular activity that serves as a continuous communicator to the community. Vocal groups, marching bands, drama clubs, and vocational organizations represent other school-related groups whose output is scrutinized by the public unceasingly. Such programs are a very effective means for improving school-community relations.

HOW TO COMMUNICATE

The principal must develop greater skills in communicating accurately and intelligibly with the subpublics of the school. Concerning the complexity of communications, for example, Pinnie suggested that to ensure proper reception "any school message should be written at least two levels below the reading audience."[25] This may be an overstatement, but the reading level of the intended audience should first be determined. Quite probably, some misunderstood communications between the school and the community involve no more than dispensing with esoteric style or pedagogical terminology.

Typically educators have relied heavily on unilateral or one-way communication in transmitting messages. Bulletins are sent to parents, or speeches are made to large groups, with little or no opportunity for feedback that would permit the message to be further explained or interpreted. Bilateral communication, which provides for a free exchange between sender and receiver to increase the comprehension level of the message, is preferable but of course difficult because of the distance and dispersion of the people involved. To minimize the misunderstanding of messages, however, communications not only must be phrased clearly and succinctly, they must permit response and reaction. The practice

[25] Anthony F. Pinnie, "Reported Research Studies Dealing with Printed Mass Media of Communication, and the Implications of the Findings for School-Community Relations Programs," doctoral dissertation, Temple University, 1965.

of attaching a simple reaction form is all too frequently ignored in printed communications; talking rather than listening is all too typical of meetings.

An additional issue with which the communicator must be concerned is the distortion that frequently alters the message being transmitted. A visual presentation of this phenomenon appears in Figure 13.3, which also calls attention to the following causes of distortion: The message may be unclear, the receiver may have little interest in the message, the receiver may be biased about the sender of the message, or the receiver may reject the nature and content of the communication. Since the validity of a sender's expectation that his message will be received accurately depends on the intensity of distortion, every effort must be made to minimize the causes. The same dynamics exist in the feedback of communication; therefore, bilateral communication is necessary. The

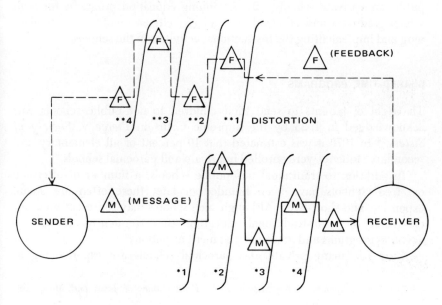

*1. Clarity of the message
*2. Receiver's interest in the message
*3. Receiver's perception of the sender
*4. Receiver's bias regarding the message

**1. Clarity of the feedback
**2. Sender's interest in the feedback
**3. Sender's perception of the receiver
**4. Sender's bias regarding the feedback

Figure 13.3
The bilateral communications process

proper transmission of an important message requires considerable preparation and time. The core of an effective school-community relations program depends on the principal's ability (1) to determine the most appropriate medium for transmission of a particular message, (2) to prepare the message carefully, and (3) to provide opportunity for feedback. Attention to these three ingredients should reduce distortion and improve communication with the community and its subpublics.

Emerging programs in school-community relations

During recent years several educational programs have emerged possessing powerful implications for the improvement of school-community relations. These include (1) shared-time educational programs between public and private schools, (2) continuing education programs for high school graduates and other adults, and (3) citizen involvement in planning and implementing the instructional activities in the schools.

SHARED-TIME PROGRAMS

The right of parents to send their children to non-public schools was acknowledged in 1925 by the Supreme Court in *Pierce* v. *Society of Sisters*.[26] In 1970 it was estimated that 10 percent of all elementary and secondary students were enrolled in private and parochial schools.[27]

In addition to traditional non-public schools, a number of alternate or "free" schools have been founded of late; these often are small, expensive, and short-lived. Although such schools may represent vigorous dissatisfaction with traditional education, they frequently attempt innovative programs and practices that merit attention.[28]

Currently many private and parochial schools are experiencing fi-

[26] *Pierce* v. *Society of the Sisters of the Holy Names of Jesus and Mary*, 268 U.S. 510, 45 Sup. Ct. 571 (1925).

[27] *Financial Status of Public Schools,* Washington, D.C., National Education Association, 1971.

[28] Joshua L. Smith, "Free Schools: Pandora's Box," *Educational Leadership*, 28 (February 1971), 464–468; Bonnie B. Stretch, "Rise of the Free School," *Saturday Review*, 53 (June 1970), 76–79; Nathaniel Blackman, "Experimental High School Without Walls: Chicago," *National Association of Secondary School Principals Bulletin*, 55 (May 1971), 147–159; William C. Nelson, "Storefront School: Vehicle for Change," *Journal of Negro Education*, 40 (Summer 1971), 248–254; Judith C. Areen, "Alternative Schools: Better Guardians Than Family or State?" *School Review*, 81 (February 1973), 175–193.

nancial difficulty, and the closing of numerous non-public schools has caused consternation among public school educators whose buildings are already filled to capacity. Under theories of "child benefit," some states allow local school districts to transport parochial students to and from school. In addition, specialized services by nurses or school psychologists, educational materials, and resource centers have been extended to non-public school students.

By far the most significant cooperative undertaking between public and non-public schools has been that of shared-time programs. Under such plans, private or parochial schools have been able to enrich their curricula by directly sharing resources of the public school. Often the demand for specialized courses in the non-public school is so small that the expenditure of funds to establish these courses is inadvisable. In some communities agreements have been negotiated allowing non-public students to enroll in certain classes offered in the public schools. The community relations impact of this arrangement is obvious. In such communities the parents of non-public school children are typically more supportive of the public schools, and this support is reflected in subsequent building and operational referenda.

Other consequences of shared-time programs are apparent. The specialized courses most in demand usually are those requiring expensive equipment and facilities, thereby disproportionately increasing costs per pupil. Moreover, the danger exists that the non-public school may become increasingly dependent on the comprehensive offerings of the public school and will not be able to offer a quality program. Even so, shared-time programs are worthy of exploration in many communities.

CONTINUING EDUCATION PROGRAMS

Until recently principals of schools located in communities that also housed a post-high school educational institution considered themselves fortunate because quality education is often accorded top priority by the citizens. Recently, however, some concern has been expressed by public school educators because of such proximity. The expressed emergent values of post-secondary students that have filtered down to high school students have been at variance with the values of the school as an institution. Nevertheless, the promotion of good relations between schools and colleges is of considerable importance.

A primary reason for the formation of regional accrediting associations was to improve communication, understanding, and articulation between the two levels, and some of the associations have been successful in achieving that purpose. High schools in particular can benefit from close working relations with post-secondary schools. College or career nights during the school year provide an opportunity for post-secondary representatives to converse with seniors. School-sponsored trips to nearby colleges, universities, and vocational schools; visits and interviews on campus; and attendance at college cultural events all directly benefit students. Other indirect relationships with colleges enhance the school-community relationship, including the conduct of research, the training of student teachers, and the sharing of library and other resources.

INVOLVING THE COMMUNITY IN INSTRUCTION

Within each community there exists a wide variety of human and physical resources that should be tapped for the enrichment of the instructional program. Speakers with specific competencies should be asked to address student groups; school-sponsored field trips should be held to provide reality-centered learning experiences. Such activities also give the community a better understanding of the school program. Elementary students in particular enjoy contact with policemen, firemen, merchants, professional people, and other citizens who can help to develop in children a greater degree of career awareness and community understanding. Students at the secondary level should be encouraged to observe local governments and boards of education in action and to participate actively in civic affairs, thereby utilizing the entire community as a learning laboratory.

Perhaps the most successful programs for involving the school in the community have been at the high school level in the development of career and vocational skills. On-the-job training stations in work-study programs, part-time employment, and volunteer work related to cocurricular activities all help to ensure for many students a smooth transition between school and the world of work. Thus the boundaries of the community truly become the boundaries of the school.

Competencies in improving school-community relations

The competency-based approach highlights several processes for enhancing the principal's leadership in the improvement of school-community relations. They are as follows:

AREA I. COMMUNITY ANALYSIS

Competency No. 1.   The principal coordinates the work of local lay advisory councils or other representative citizens' groups in analyzing the goals, objectives, programs, and procedures of the school.

Competency No. 2.   The principal conducts a systematic assessment of citizens' perceptions of the needs of and expectations for the school.

AREA II. COMMUNICATING WITH THE COMMUNITY

Competency No. 3.   The principal participates widely in the activities of community groups and affiliates selectively with community organizations.

Competency No. 4.   The principal stresses to teachers, students, and school employees the public relations implications of their roles.

Competency No. 5.   The principal consults with leaders and members of the parent-teacher organization to improve its effectiveness.

Competency No. 6.   The principal analyzes the informational needs of the school's subpublics and prepares and presents communications to meet those needs.

Competency No. 7.   The principal elicits and analyzes systematically the feedback from communications.

Competency No. 8.   The principal clarifies the quantitative and qualitative criteria used by citizens for assessing the processes and products of the school.

AREA III. UTILIZING COMMUNITY RESOURCES

Competency No. 9.   The principal explores innovative programs and plans for the cooperative utilization of the total resources of the community.

Competency No. 10.   The principal encourages educational practices that utilize the community as a learning laboratory.

Summary

In this chapter several reasons for increased citizen interest and involvement in the schools initially were described—including the issues of financing the schools, improving the instructional program, and involvement in decision making. We observed that the concerns of citizens typically receive meaningful expression at the level of the individual school.

As a basis for an effective program of school-community relations, it was first suggested that the principal know and understand the perceived educational needs and expectations of the various subpublics within the community. A model for developing such understanding was presented, based on social systems theory. The conduct of a systematic needs assessment was suggested as a viable procedure for analyzing community perceptions of educational needs and objectives.

In stating "Why communicate," the need was stressed for the enlightenment of public opinion. Specific responsibilities of the principal, teachers, students, and school employees were delineated to the end of enhancing continuous school-community communication. Moreover, it was indicated that the content of communications should be differentiated in terms of the proximity of the subpublics to the school. Concerning the process of communication, a model was presented that highlights the causes of message distortion and stresses the importance of feedback in improving the communication process.

Emerging instructional programs possessing potential for enhancing the school-community relationship were described, including shared-time, continuing education, and cooperative educational programs. It was urged that increased utilization be made of instructional practices that use the total community as a learning laboratory.

The chapter concluded with an enumeration of 10 specific competencies required of the principal who would provide leadership in the improvement of school-community relations.

SUGGESTED ACTIVITIES

1. Utilizing a sociometric-type analysis, plot all the organizations and groups in a community that have a significant and continuing relationship with the school; indicate also the interorganizational relationships. Compare the results according to type or location of school.

2. Select a random sample of citizens from the attendance area of a school and conduct a systematic educational needs assessment. Compare and contrast the results according to meaningful subpublics.

3. Interview the officers of a parent-teacher organization either to ascertain the extent of agreement on the goals of the organization or to obtain specific suggestions for improving the program of the parent-teacher organization.

4. Survey a group of parents concerning the type, nature, content, source, and adequacy information they receive about the school. Synthesize suggestions for improving communication methods and media.

5. Evaluate the extent of direct utilization of community resources in the teaching-learning process. Propose a plan for increasing school-community interaction in instructional activities.

SELECTED REFERENCES

ANDERSON, LESTER, and LAUREN VAN DYKE, *Secondary School Administration,* 2nd ed., Boston, Houghton Mifflin, 1972, pp. 417–442.

CAMPBELL, ROALD F., et al., *The Organization and Control of American Schools,* 2nd ed., Columbus, Ohio, Merrill, 1970.

CUNNINGHAM, LUVERN L., *Governing Schools: New Approaches to Old Issues,* Columbus, Ohio, Merrill, 1971.

DAPPER, GLORIA, *Public Relations for Educators,* New York, Macmillan, 1964.

GETZELS, J. W., JAMES M. LIPHAM, and ROALD F. CAMPBELL, *Educational Administration as a Social Process,* New York, Harper & Row, 1968, pp. 376–396.

GORTON, RICHARD A., *Conflict, Controversy, and Crisis in School Administration and Supervision: Issues, Cases, and Concepts for the '70s,* Dubuque, Iowa, Brown, 1972, pp. 21–64.

HAVIGHURST, ROBERT, and DANIEL U. LEVINE, *Education in Metropolitan Areas,* 2nd ed., Boston, Allyn & Bacon, 1971.

KINDRED, LESLIE, *School Public Relations,* Englewood Cliffs, N.J., Prentice-Hall, 1957.

OLSEN, EDWARD G., ed., *The School and Community Reader: Education in Perspective,* New York, Macmillan, 1963.

SCHMUCK, RICHARD A., et al., *Handbook of Organization Development in Schools,* Palo Alto, Calif., National, 1972, pp. 31–97.

SUMPTION, MERLE R., and YVONNE ENGSTROM, *School-Community Relations— A New Approach,* New York, McGraw-Hill, 1966.

TOTTEN, WILLIAM F., and FRANK J. MANLEY, *The Community School,* Galien, Mich., Allied Education Council, 1969.

PART IV

The principalship:
a future perspective

THE CHAPTER IN THIS FINAL SECTION INCLUDES AN EXAMINATION OF THE CONCEPTUAL, HUMAN, AND TECHNICAL COMPETENCIES REQUIRED OF THE PRINCIPAL. BASED ON THE THEORETICAL FOUNDATIONS OF THE PRINCIPAL-SHIP, ILLUSTRATIVE INDICATORS ARE DESCRIBED FOR INCREASING THE SKILLS OF THE PRINCIPAL IN THE MAJOR FUNCTIONS OF HIS ROLE. THE COMPETENCY-BASED APPROACH IS DISCUSSED IN TERMS OF ITS POTEN-TIAL FOR IMPROVEMENT OF THE PRINCIPALSHIP TODAY AND TOMORROW.

CHAPTER 14
The principalship: a competency-based approach

he competency-based approach to the principalship provides a systematic means for analyzing and synthesizing the conceptual, human, and technical skills required for effective and efficient performance in the principal's role. Several years ago, Katz called attention to the need for a competency-based view, indicating that when we concentrate on performance or "what a man can accomplish," we must become concerned with the kinds of skills that administrators exhibit in performing their jobs.[1]

In this chapter attention is first directed to the conceptual skills required of the principal. Suggestions are made whereby the principal may continue to expand his understanding and to test in action the theoretical foundations of administration described in the first half of this book. Next attention is given to the human skills the principal should possess. The personal qualities as well as the training required of the principal are considered. The final section of the chapter is concerned with technical skills in the principalship. Exemplary competencies are selected from the lists given in each of the foregoing functional chapters, and procedures for operationalizing the competency-based approach are described. Such assessment should result in improved performance in the principalship now and in the future.

Conceptual skills of the principal

Of the three types of skills required of the principal, conceptual skills are most directly associated with knowledge. We indicated at the outset that to conceptualize, an individual must possess or have access to a wealth of cognitively organized information. In organizing information, a set of theories and taxonomies or constructs and concepts is absolutely essential. In a sense, these represent the "tools" of the principal. And "if concepts are tools, his tool-kit should be full." To the principal facing a specific problem the conceptual approach says, "Look at it this way.

---

[1] Robert L. Katz, "Skills of an Effective Administrator," *Harvard Business Review,* 33 (February 1955), 33–42.

Maybe you will see something which has escaped you. Maybe things will make sense. No? . . . Well, try looking at it from this angle, or from this perspective."[2]

For many reasons a persistent and pervasive antitheoretical bias continues to permeate the practice of educational administration. At the same time, it generally is acknowledged that appreciation and understanding of theory are positively and meaningfully related to career success. Even so, many administrators continue to attempt to cognize the complex variables they face by utilizing such global and non-descriptive concepts as power, line-staff relationship, democratic administration, human relations, and educational needs. It is not that such global concepts are not useful; however, they have been reexamined and refined, and these refinements enhance the utility of theory for the principal. We have reported the refinements concerning theories of general systems, social systems, values, organization, role, decision making, and leadership. Undoubtedly, additional clarifications will be made of these and other bodies of conceptual knowledge. As a minimal prerequisite for developing conceptual skills, therefore, the principal must continue to be a scholar in his own field, educational administration. Moreover, as a leader, the principal should motivate others with whom he works, such as teachers, to remain current in their fields of specialization so that their conceptual skills may also continue to be enhanced.

We have shown that the principalship places inordinate time demands on an individual in terms of the frequency, nature, number, and scope of problems and people he deals with. We also acknowledge that it is impossible to "read and run" at the same time. Even so, the principal must continue to update his conceptual knowledge through utilizing the existing theory-practice linkage structures. These include graduate courses, seminars, and professional meetings, as well as the professional literature.

Although conceptualizing permeates everything that the principal does, conceptual knowledge is not equivalent with conceptual skills. As Abbott has indicated recently, conceptual skills represent more than the mere acquisition of knowledge about concepts. He stated:

> If an individual possesses conceptual skills, that individual has developed the ability to apply information and concepts to practice. This involves the ability to see the organization as a whole and to understand how various parts of the organization relate to and affect each other. Conceptualization thus involves diagnosis and analysis; conceptual skills

[2] Roald F. Campbell, W. W. Charters, Jr., and William L. Gragg, "Improving Administrative Theory and Practice: Three Essential Roles," in Roald F. Campbell and James M. Lipham, eds., *Administrative Theory as a Guide to Action*, Chicago, Midwest Administration Center, University of Chicago, 1960, p. 180.

refer to the ability to discern meaning in and to establish relationships among events and bits of information that at first glance would appear to be discrete and unrelated.[3]

Gaynor also concisely summarized the relationship of conceptual knowledge to conceptual skills in the principal's role functions as follows:

A. *Knowing*
   The effective principal knows:
   1. Himself, and he articulates clearly what he hopes to achieve in both the short and the long term.
   2. Significant others around him, and he articulates accurately how their expectations, goals, and priorities (as individuals and groups) compare with his own.
   3. And can describe accurately how significant others see them.

B. *Doing*
   The effective principal behaves in a way which is:
   1. Consistent with the expectations, goals, and priorities of significant others, or
   2. Calculated to alter (with some reasonable probability of success) the expectations, goals, and priorities of significant others in directions which are consistent with his own.[4]

In moving between theory and practice or knowing and doing, the principal is well advised to remember that the issues and problems with which he is faced must be viewed "in the round."[5] Theories are usually quite limited, whereas problems are quite diffuse. A recent Ph.D. recipient who returned to the principalship described this dilemma thus: "In working on my dissertation at the university, I had to narrow and narrow the focus of my attention to examine in scientific detail only a minute segment of reality. Now, on the job, I have to broaden my attention and examine everything at once." To deal with the complex, sometimes baffling, world of the here-and-now, it is essential that the administrator know and understand the refinements of many theories so that alternative views may be called on and instantaneously applied. The development of such understanding requires concentrated attention in training programs, not only on individual research but also on a variety of learning experiences.

Although the correspondence between knowledge and its immediate

[3] Max G. Abbott, "Administrative Performance in the School Principalship: A Synthesis," in Jack A. Culbertson, Curtis Henson, and Ruel Morrison, eds., *Performance Objectives for School Principals*, Berkeley, Calif., McCutchan, 1974.

[4] Alan K. Gaynor, "Developing Criteria and Measures of Performance for School Principals," in Culbertson, Henson, and Morrison, eds., op. cit.

[5] Andrew W. Halpin, "Ways of Knowing," in Campbell and Lipham, eds., op. cit., pp. 3–20.

application typically is not direct, we have found that it is possible to improve specifically both the conceptual knowledge and the conceptual skills of the principal. Since this approach utilizing several theories has been described in detail elsewhere,[6] only an illustrative example is needed here. Let us consider the conceptual skills required in decision making, since this function constitutes the heart of the administrative process. How is it possible to improve one's decision-making skills?

For many years, lectures and discussions designed to provide "knowledge about" decision making have been standard fare in most college and university programs in educational administration. Analysis of administrative issues and cases also has been utilized in an effort to move from "knowledge about" to "use of" decision theory. During recent years, however, simulation has emerged as a powerful tool for the exercise and development of conceptual skills—particularly in making decisions.[7]

Under the sponsorship of the University Council for Educational Administration urban simulation project, teams of professors have developed the requisite background materials and decision problems for serving as principal of Wilson Senior High School, Janus Junior High School, or Abraham Lincoln Elementary School in "Monroe City."[8] Utilizing these or similar materials, an individual can assume the role of principal in the simulated school and his decision-making behavior can be analyzed along relevant content, style, and involvement dimensions. In the Simulation Laboratory in the Department of Educational Administration at the University of Wisconsin-Madison, for example, research and training are being conducted concerning the conceptual skills required in searching for information prior to making decisions. Through the use of computer-controlled problem stimuli and computer-monitored responses, it is possible to score instantaneously and to feed back to the trainee performance data concerning such variables as information type, source, cost, time, and search patterns in decision making. Because of such rapid advances being made in computer technology and linkages, it may be envisioned that in the years ahead such programs can be utilized nationwide to provide training and practice in decision making and other conceptual skills required of the principal.

Simulation, of course, is only one means for practicing the exercise of conceptual skills. If a skill is to be developed, it must continue to be exercised and evaluated. Therefore, apprenticeship, externship, and in-

---

[6] James M. Lipham, "Content Selection in Organizational Theory and Behavior in Education," in Jack A. Culbertson et al., eds., *Social Science Content for Preparing Educational Leaders,* Columbus, Ohio, Merrill, 1973, pp. 306–326.

[7] Dale L. Bolton, ed., *The Use of Simulation in Educational Administration,* Columbus, Ohio, Merrill, 1971.

[8] University Council for Educational Administration, *Instructional Materials Catalog,* Columbus, Ohio, The Council, 1972–1973, pp. 43–74.

ternship programs also may serve to provide situations permitting the refinement in the exercise of decision-making skills. Concerning these programs, however, it should be cautioned that if a skill is to be improved, its exercise must be systematically observed, analyzed, evaluated, and the results fed back meaningfully to the individual. Simulation— particularly when laboratory controlled and instantaneously analyzed— holds considerable promise for improving conceptual skills in decision making and in other theoretical domains, as well.

In analyzing decision-making skills we also have found it essential to examine the personalistic characteristics of the trainee that have a meaningful and direct relationship to the quality of decision behavior. This calls attention to the human skills required of the principal.

Human skills of the principal

As indicated earlier in our discussions of social systems and leadership theory, the values, abilities, interests, needs, and dispositions of the principal as a person are basic determinants of behavior. As research has revealed time and again, however, there is no universally accepted pattern of personality "traits" that is predictive of effective performance in a particular principalship.[9] The *person-in-situation* must be taken into account.

To the extent that general similarities exist in principalship position situations, however, studies of the role-personality relationships of principals are instructive. From a close examination of the principal's role, for example, Lipham observed that the effective principal may be expected to exert himself energetically; to achieve and improve his performance; to strive for higher status in the profession and in society in general; to relate himself successfully to other people; to view the future with confidence, the present with understanding, and the past with satisfaction; and to adjust well to frustrations, irritations, confusions, and criticisms in pressure situations.[10] It was hypothesized, therefore, that effective principals would rank higher than ineffective ones on the following measurable personality variables:[11]

1. ACTIVITY DRIVE: To move forward purposefully; to direct strong mental or physical effort toward the solution of problems.

[9] John K. Hemphill, Daniel E. Griffiths, and Norman Frederiksen, *Administrative Performance and Personality,* New York, Bureau of Publications, Teachers College, Columbia University, 1962, p. 332.
[10] James M. Lipham, "Personal Variables of Effective Administrators," *Administrator's Notebook,* 9 (September 1960), 1–4.
[11] Adapted from ibid.

2. ACHIEVEMENT DRIVE: To do one's best; to improve one's competencies through general and specialized study.

3. MOBILITY DRIVE: To become a leader of groups; to operate in a position of prestige, power, and authority.

4. SOCIAL ABILITY: To associate successfully with others in the solution of problems; to participate in friendly groups.

5. FEELINGS OF SECURITY: To view family relationships with pride poses.

6. EMOTIONAL CONTROL: To assess environmental conditions objectively and realistically; to adjust well to irritations, frustrations, confusion, and criticism.

From the administration of quasi-projective personality measures and from an analysis of the verbal and nonverbal behaviors of a sample of elementary and secondary school principals in a large midwestern school district, data were obtained to test the basic hypotheses. The criterion of effectiveness was the combined rankings by school district personnel of all the subjects, in terms of the promotability or effectiveness of the principals.

Concerning activity drive, it was found that the effective principal is inclined to engage in strong and purposeful activity. While on the job he is particularly sensitive to the pressing responsibilities of the principalship. He evidences a high degree of concern for the appropriate use of time and finds curbs to activity, such as physical illness, most unpleasant. At retirement he looks forward to continuing a high level of activity. During leisure hours he participates in the activities of community organizations and holds a number of leadership positions in these groups. The ineffective principal, on the other hand, is inclined to be deliberate and slow to act. At work he engages in numerous random behaviors—serving as an errand boy, report maker, substitute teacher, and "baby sitter" with disciplinary cases. At retirement he looks forward to a reduction in activity. During leisure hours the ineffective individual participates in a limited number and range of activities.

Keen achievement and mobility drives also were found to be characteristic of the effective principal. He may be portrayed as holding specific goals for further graduate study, as well as stressing better job performance as a goal in life. In contrast, the ineffective principal evidences little concern for undertaking a planned program of further study or attaining any position higher than his present job assignment.

The effective principal is also high in social ability. He is able to relate effectively to others in solving problems. He feels that he obtained his initial principalship because of his ability to relate well to others and that his present relationships with teachers, students, central office personnel, and parents are satisfactory. Helping teachers with problems of instruction is his greatest source of job satisfaction. By contrast, the ineffective principal experiences frequent conflict with teachers, parents, and central office personnel. He derives his greatest job satisfaction from helping children.

The effective principal is secure in his home and work environments. He views family relationships with pride and satisfaction, and he perceives authority figures as friendly and serving constructive purposes. The ineffective individual tends to have difficulties at home and at work, such as feeling that groups of teachers or members of the central administration may be "down" on him. He also feels that his own mental, emotional, or physical weaknesses may prevent the attainment of his life goals.

In reacting to frustrating, confusing, and irritating situations, the effective principal possesses greater emotional control than the ineffective principal. The ineffective individual tends to "fly off the handle," to clash frequently with others, to feel that actions by other people are most likely to drive him to distraction, and to engage in self-sympathy or similar strong emotional reactions in conflict situations.

The composite results of the analysis portrayed the effective principal as follows: inclined to engage in strong and purposeful activity, concerned with achieving success and positions of higher status, and stable in the face of highly affective stimuli. The ineffective principal was described as inclined to be deliberate, accepting with a meek attitude his present level of achievement and status, lacking the skills essential for working with adults but anxious to give assistance to children, highly dependent on others for support, and likely to exhibit strong emotional reactions in upsetting situations.

The foregoing contrasts between effective and ineffective individuals are only illustrative of systematic differences in the personal qualities of principals. Other studies should be conducted in different situations, such as rural and suburban schools, to determine how much generalization can be applied to the stereotypic personalistic syndromes described. Moreover, a multifaceted approach to effectiveness, including such organizational outcome variables as adaptiveness, production, efficiency, and job satisfaction, would strengthen the conclusions. To some extent, however, the existing findings correspond with those of other studies.

In a recent survey professors of educational administration were asked to indicate the importance of certain admissions criteria for entry into university training programs for principals.[12] In general, the following criteria were rated as very important: "displays social sensitivity," "shows commitment to educational and social reform," "exhibits per-

[12] Neal C. Nickerson, "Status of Programs for Principals," *National Association of Secondary School Principals Bulletin,* 56 (March 1972), 10–20.

sistence in task completion," and "communicates a sense of social mission." Such studies are of particular value, since apparently these are the overt or covert criteria utilized by university personnel for admitting applicants to preparation programs for principals. It well may be that in the development of human skills, selection for the principalship is more important than preparation, since it is doubtful that one can perform effectively in the principalship unless he possesses the requisite personality characteristics. We hope that future research will be directed toward improving the selection and admission criteria in preparation programs for the principalship.

Regarding graduate programs for preparing administrators, McCleary and McIntyre have enumerated 17 methodologies utilized to prepare administrators and have classified these according to required levels of learning—whether the prospective principal should be familiar with, understand, or be able to apply the learnings (see Figure 14.1).[13] They also have classified the methods according to their utility in developing technical, conceptual, or human skills. For example, they have indicated that simulation is high in developing understanding and application of skills; it is likewise high in developing technical and conceptual skills, but medium in developing human skills. The classifications and ratings in Figure 14.1 are useful not only to professors but also to present and prospective practitioners in deciding which activities will contribute meaningfully to their continued education.

In recent years training in human relations has captured a great deal of interest and attention for developing human skills. With considerable justification, proponents of this approach maintain that the fostering of skills in interpersonal interaction is a necessary ingredient of successful administrative behavior. A substantial portion of the principal's time is consumed in interacting with individuals and groups. Thus the principal must understand himself, others, and small and large group dynamics, and he must sharpen his skills while functioning in interpersonal situations. Yet human relations training, though essential, is not sufficient. In a few colleges and school districts with which we are familiar, for example, an inordinate emphasis has been placed on encounter group, T-group, and sensitivity group experiences, almost to the exclusion of other approaches and methodologies. In the hands of novices, moreover, such procedures can be exceedingly dysfunctional for both the individual and the organization. We concur with McCleary and McIntyre that laboratory approaches, gaming, simulation, clinical study, and the internship all should be utilized, since they also possess

---

[13] Lloyd E. McCleary and Kenneth E. McIntyre, "Competency Development and University Methodology," *National Association of Secondary School Principals Bulletin,* 56 (March 1972), 53–68.

	LEVELS OF LEARNING			COMPETENCIES TO BE LEARNED		
	Familiarity	Understanding	Application	Technical	Conceptual	Human
Reading	High	Medium	Low	Low	Medium	Low
Lecture	Medium	Medium	Low	Low	Medium	Low
Discussion	Medium	Medium	Low	Low	Medium	Low
Field trip	Medium	Low	Low	Low	Medium	Low
Case	Low	High	Low	Low	High	Low
Scenario	Low	High	Low	Low	High	Low
Individualized instructional package	Low	High	Low	Low	High	Low
Computer-assisted instruction	Low	High	Low	Low	High	Low
Tutorial	Low	Medium	Low	Low	Medium	Low
Student research	Low	Medium	Low	Low	Medium	Low
Laboratory approach	Low	High	Medium	Medium	High	Medium
Gaming	Low	High	Medium	Medium	High	Medium
Simulation	Low	High	High	High	High	Medium
Human relations training	Low	High	High	High	High	High
Clinical study	Low	High	High	High	High	Medium
Team research	Low	High	High	High	Medium	Low
Internship	Low	Medium	High	High	Medium	Medium

High, Medium, Low = Extent to which the method, when competently employed, tends to be practical and effective in learning the designated skills at the levels desired.

Figure 14.1

Instructional methodologies, levels of learning, and competencies to be learned in the principalship
SOURCE: Lloyd E. McCleary and Kenneth E. McIntyre, "Competency Development and University Methodology," *National Association of Secondary School Principals Bulletin,* 56 (March 1972), 58.

potential for enhancing the human as well as the conceptual and technical skills of the principal.

Technical skills of the principal

The competencies delineated in each of the preceding functional chapters provide a viable starting point for refinement and utilization of the competency-based approach. We recognize that the various competencies listed are only a beginning and that they suffer some limitations. First, it should be understood that the enumerated competencies are not discrete—they shade one into the other and they overlap somewhat both within and across the role functions. For example, the following competency is related to the instructional program: "The principal directs a study of the assessment of the needs of learners that are unique to the school and community." It is very similar, in terms of the technical skills required, to the following competency, which is related to school-community relationships: "The principal conducts a systematic assessment of citizens' perceptions of the needs of and expectations for the school." In demonstrating either of the macroscopic competencies, a similar subset of microscopic competencies would be required, such as initiating the study, designing the study, developing survey instruments, obtaining the data, analyzing the data, and reporting the results. Thus the user of the competency-based approach must be aware that some overlap between and among competencies probably is inevitable.

The competencies as listed here are also limited in that they vary greatly in generality. Whereas some of the competencies subsume many specific activities, others are more limited in scope. Hence one should not be disturbed to find that in some cases several indicators may be utilized as evidence of the competency, whereas in others only one or two indicators are sufficient.

Another variable that some will consider to be a limitation is the choice of the competencies themselves. The competencies we have listed derive from our own value orientations and observations concerning the functions of the principal. Some will decry our emphases; others will note what appear to them to be glaring omissions. It should be reiterated, therefore, that the lists of competencies are exemplary rather than exhaustive; hence clarifications, restatements, refinements, and additions are needed to improve the competencies in the future.

A final limitation of the present list of competencies is that they are stated in process terms. As we indicated earlier, existing assessment procedures for process evaluation are much less fully developed than existing instruments and procedures for product or outcome evaluation.

Hence in using the competency-based approach a desirable first step is to consider the competency as an educational objective, convert it into measurable components, and analyze the behavioral products or indicators illustrating that the principal has developed the competency.

As examples only, some competencies are selected from each of the functional chapters, and some illustrative indicators of the competency are cited.

I. IMPROVEMENT OF THE EDUCATIONAL PROGRAM (CHAPTER 9)

Competency No. 3. The principal directs the assessment of the needs of learners that are unique to the school and com-community.

Indicators: 1. Report of an educational needs assessment study.
2. Summary reports of student attitudes, interests, and/or achievement test data.
3. Recommended modifications in school goals or programs to meet unique local needs.

II. IMPROVEMENT OF STAFF PERSONNEL SERVICES (CHAPTER 10)

Competency No. 1. The principal defines the specific role requirements for each position vacancy.

Indicators: 1. Position requests and role descriptions for each position vacancy.
2. A long-range staffing plan for the school.

III. IMPROVING STUDENT PERSONNEL SERVICES (CHAPTER 11)

Competency No. 12. The principal studies and understands recent legislation and court decisions having implications for the administration of the school.

Indicators: 1. Attendance by the principal in a course or seminar on student rights.
2. Requests for change in school district policies and regulations to conform to recent legal decisions.

IV. IMPROVING FINANCIAL-PHYSICAL RESOURCES (CHAPTER 12)

Competency No. 6. The principal develops and transmits a complete set of educational specifications for the architect to use in planning new or remodeled educational facilities.

Indicators: 1. Committee reports of educational objectives and space requirements.
2. A set of educational specifications for the architect.

V. IMPROVING SCHOOL-COMMUNITY RELATIONSHIPS (CHAPTER 13)

Competency No. 7.   The principal elicits and analyzes systematically the feedback from communications.

Indicators: 1. Feedback forms accompany school publications.
2. Presentations feature discussion and reaction time.
3. Reactions and suggestions by school patrons are summarized in reports.

The competency-based approach, of course, does not alter the responsibility of the principal himself, as well as significant others, to make value judgments concerning the adequacy of his role performance. In fact, it pinpoints 'and highlights the necessity for such judgments as a prerequisite for improved performance. The illustrative indicators still must be assessed in terms of their quality and quantity. Wide differences may exist, for example, in the scope and specificity of such illustrative indicators as a completed educational needs assessment or a set of educational specifications for the architect.

We concur with Lamb that both personal and professional dimensions must be considered if the performance of the principal is to be enhanced.[14] Thus the competency-based approach is most valuable to the principal in conducting a quantitative and qualitative assessment of his role performance. Undoubtedly, however, this approach will be of considerable utility in school district efforts to improve the performance of all principals. In doing so, it may be desirable (1) to reach agreement on the competencies to be assessed, (2) to determine what indicators that will be accepted as evidence of the competence, and (3) to establish procedures for evaluating the evidence. Several approaches to implementing such programs have recently been suggested by the National Association of Secondary School Principals.[15] Undoubtedly additional refinements will be made as individual principals, school districts, professional associations, and colleges and universities continue to experiment with the competency-based approach.

Some will view the competency-based approach to the development of the requisite conceptual, human, and technical skills required of the principal as anathema, for all the reasons mustered against the systems approach to the administration of the school. To those who decry our present state of knowledge, however, we issue the following simple

[14] Gene Lamb, "Programmed Self-Renewal," in Committee of Professors of Secondary School Administration and Supervision (PSSAS), *Where Will They Find It?* Washington, D.C., National Association of Secondary School Principals, 1972, pp. 84–87.

[15] PSSAS, op. cit., pp. 1–87.

request: Help improve our understanding of the foundations and the functions of the principalship.

Summary

In this chapter it was stressed that the competency-based approach to the principalship involves activities designed to enhance the conceptual, human, and technical skills of the principal.

Concerning conceptual skills, it was emphasized that the principal should know about and should be able to apply in practice the foundational theories and constructs of administration. Laboratory-based, computer-controlled simulation was viewed as a viable means for the development and refinement of conceptual skills.

Regarding the requisite human skills, research findings were presented that describe the personalistic stereotypic syndrome required for effective performance in the principalship. Several criteria for the selection of principals and numerous procedures for the training of principals were rated and discussed.

Concerning the technical skills required of the principal, it was suggested that the competencies delineated in each of the functional chapters be refined, permitting us to assess them in terms of quantitative and qualitative exemplary indicators. Such assessment was seen as a prerequisite for improvement of performance in the principalship both now and in the years ahead.

SUGGESTED ACTIVITIES

1. Utilizing the UCEA urban or other simulation materials, obtain measures of decision-making and other conceptual skills along relevant scoring dimensions. Critique and suggest ways in which the skills might be improved.

2. Compare and contrast the selection procedures utilized by various school districts for making appointments to the principalship. How might the specificity and quality of the procedures be improved?

3. Compare and contrast the admissions criteria utilized by several colleges and universities for accepting applicants in graduate principalship programs. How might the nature and relevance of the criteria be enhanced?

4. Interview different reference groups (e.g., teachers, students, and parents) concerning the personal qualities they feel that the principal should possess. Compare and contrast the results by reference groups or by size, level, and location of schools.

5. Devise an instrument for utilization by self or others in assessing evidence of technical competency in the principalship. Compare the amount and quality of the evidence available for different principals.

SELECTED REFERENCES

BOLTON, DALE L., *The Use of Simulation in Educational Administration,* Columbus, Ohio, Merrill, 1971.

COMMITTEE OF PROFESSORS OF SECONDARY SCHOOL ADMINISTRATION AND SUPERVISION (PSSAS), *Where Will They Find It?* Washington, D.C., National Association of Secondary School Principals, 1972.

CULBERTSON, JACK A., CURTIS HENSON, and RUEL MORRISON, eds., *Performance Objectives for School Principals,* Berkeley, Calif., McCutchan, 1974.

CULBERTSON, JACK A., et al., eds., *Social Science Content for Preparing Educational Leaders,* Columbus, Ohio, Merrill, 1973.

EURICH, ALVIN C., *High School 1980,* New York, Pitman, 1970.

FABER, CHARLES F., and GILBERT F. SHEARRON, *Elementary School Administration,* New York, Holt, Rinehart and Winston, 1970, pp. 357–382.

HACK, WALTER G., et al., *Educational Futurism 1985,* Berkeley, Calif., McCutchan, 1971.

Author Index

Subject Index